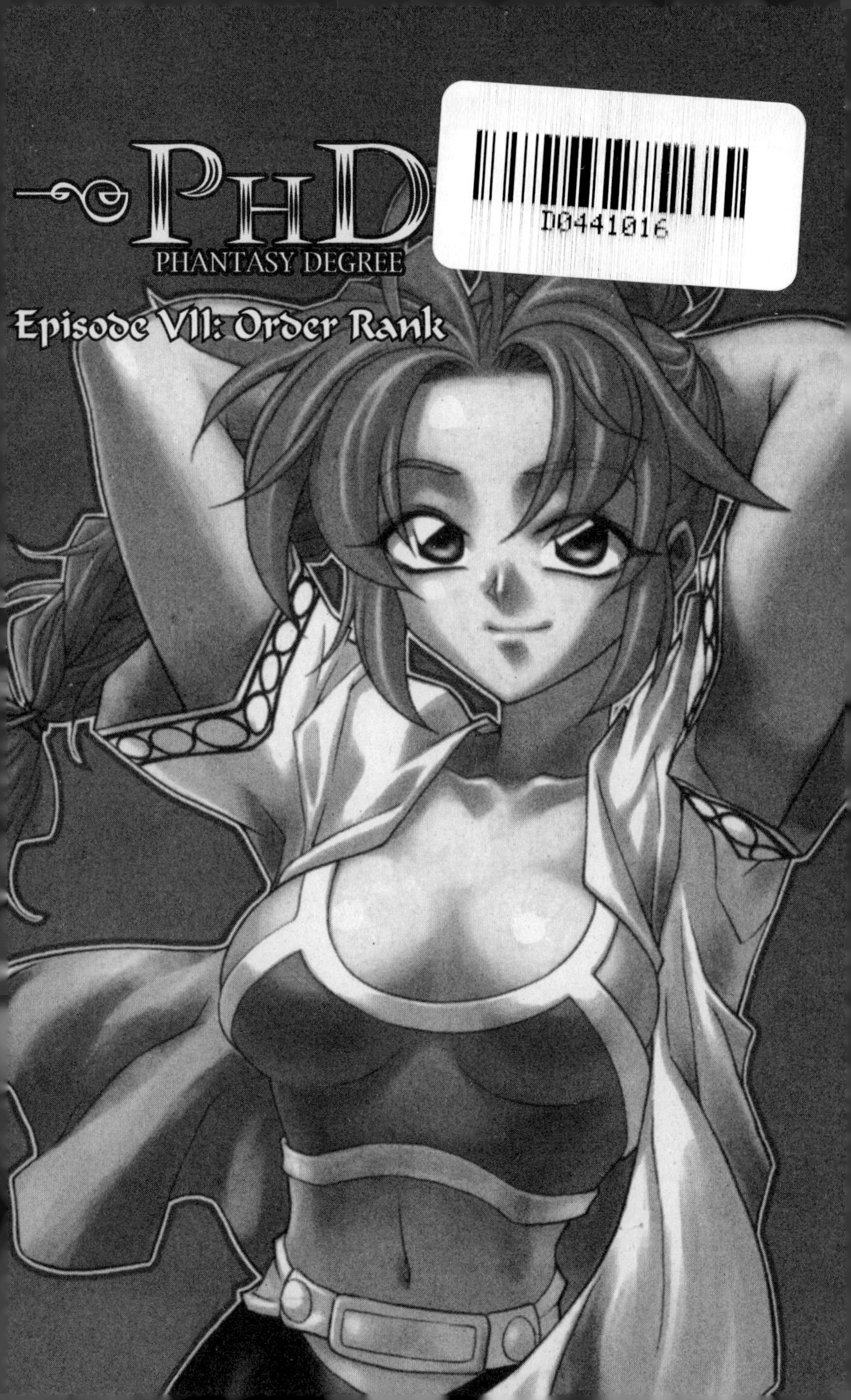
PhD
PHANTASY DEGREE
Episode VII: Order Rank

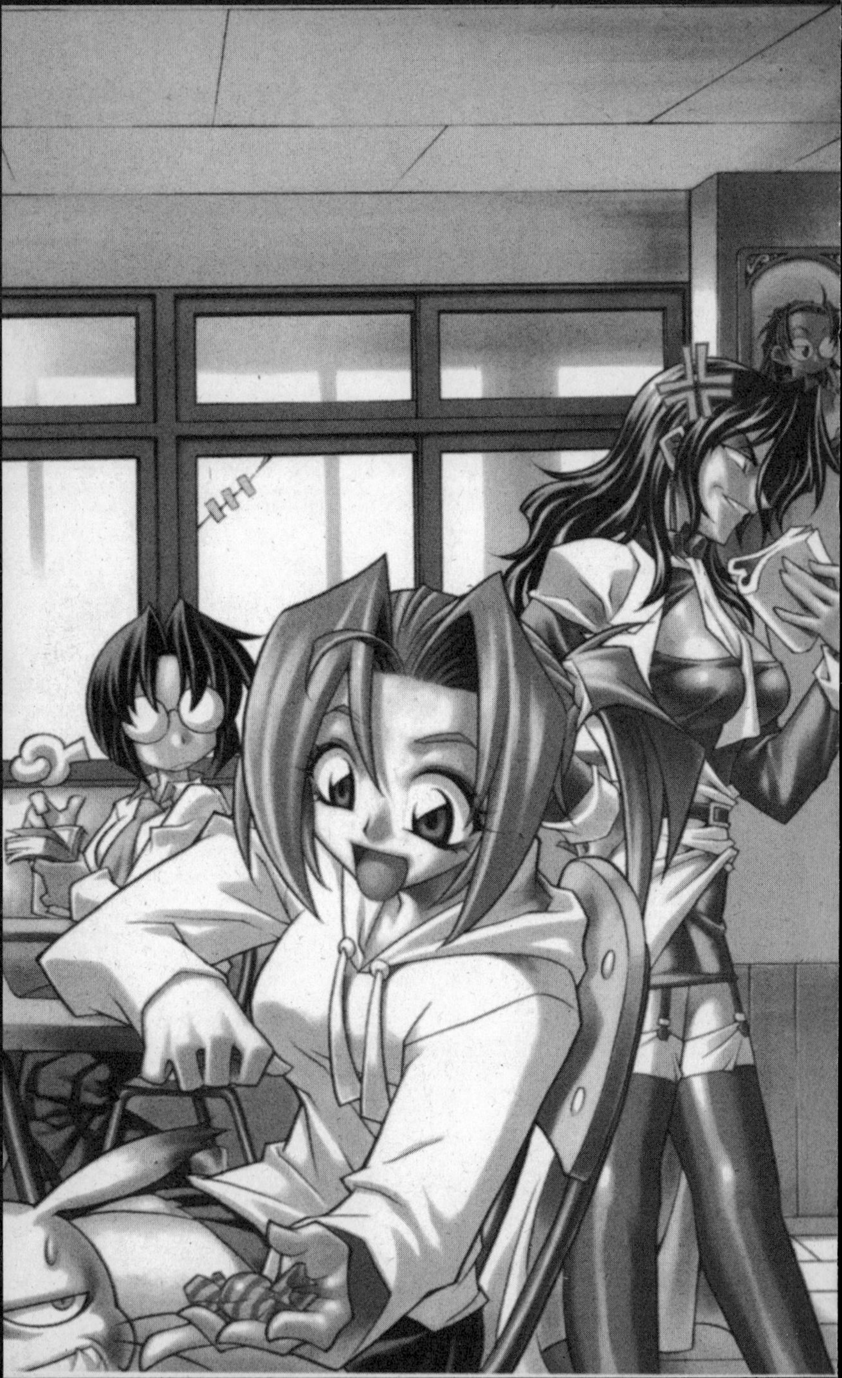

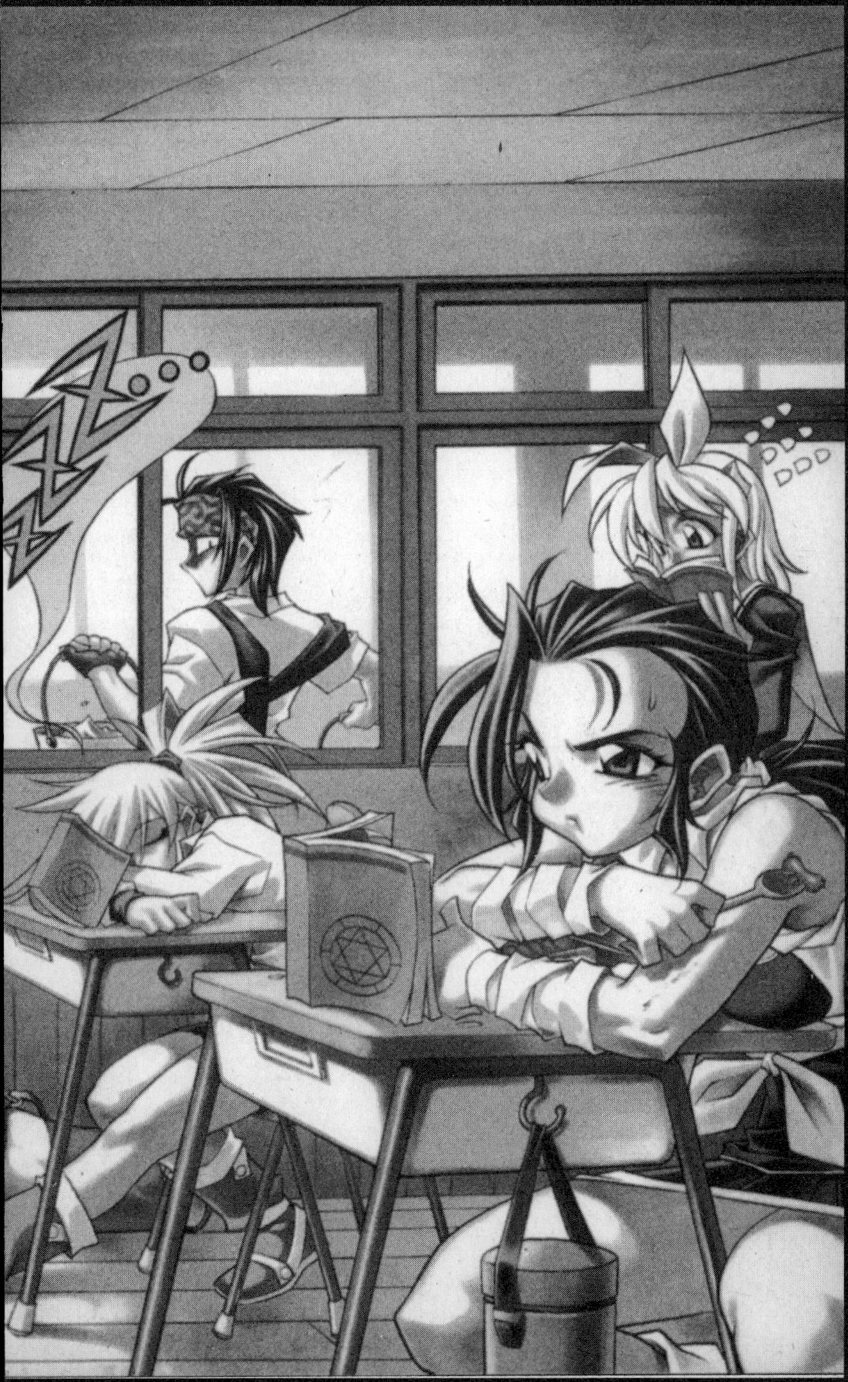

PhD: Phantasy Degree Vol. 7
Created by Son Hee-Joon

Translation - Grace Min
Copy Editor - Sarah Tangney
English Adaptation - Aaron Sparrow
Retouch and Lettering - Lucas Rivera
Production Artist - Jihye "Sophia" Hong
Cover Design - Christopher Tjalsma

Editor - Paul Morrissey
Digital Imaging Manager - Chris Buford
Pre-Production Supervisor - Erika Terriquez
Art Director - Anne Marie Horne
Production Manager - Liz Brizzi
Managing Editor - Vy Nguyen
VP of Production - Ron Klamert
Editor-In-Chief - Rob Tokar
Publisher - Mike Kiley
President and C.O.O. - John Parker
C.E.O. and Chief Creative Officer - Stuart Levy

A  Manga

TOKYOPOP Inc.
5900 Wilshire Blvd. Suite 2000
Los Angeles, CA 90036

E-mail: info@TOKYOPOP.com
Come visit us online at www.TOKYOPOP.com

ISBN: 1-59532-325-2

First TOKYOPOP printing: October 2006
10 9 8 7 6 5 4 3 2 1
Printed in the USA

PhD
PHANTASY DEGREE

Volume 7

By
SON HEE-JOON

WITHDRAWN

HAMBURG // LONDON // LOS ANGELES // TOKYO

Previously in...

PhD

PHANTASY DEGREE

A spunky, ring-wearing girl named Sang searches for the Demon School Hades...and a legendary ring contained within its walls. When she encounters a group of misfit monsters that are playing hooky from school, her hunt is over. They reluctantly take her to Hades, where Sang meets Notra, a female monster who's wearing a very special ring! But before Sang can snatch Notra's ring, a group of humans from the Madosa Guild attack the school! A deadly battle ensues, and Sang fights alongside her new beastly buddies...

The body count rises as the Madosa Guild continues its ruthless attack on the Demon School Hades. During the conflict, the power of Sang's rings is revealed: Not only does her jewelry make her stronger, but they can change the gender of their wearer. In Sang's case, when she takes off her rings, she becomes a muscular and powerful man! Holy gender-bender defender!

Despite a valiant effort by the denizens of the Demon School, the Madosa Guild emerges victorious. In the aftermath of all the fighting, the Demon School students bury their dead and search for a faraway land rumored to be inhabited by creatures like them. Sang, meanwhile, begins another adventure.

In a dark forest, Sang meets a girl swordmaster named Chun-Lang. A ring on Chun-Lang's finger piques Sang's curiosity. Lost, the two try to make their way out of the woods and come across Alcan, a villainous warlock from the Madosa Guild, who has unleashed a behemoth named Gigantes. With the aid of forest elves Shumiro and Hexion, Sang foils Alcan's plan...but not without a price: Sang awakens after an epic battle to shockingly discover that she has a bad case of amnesia!

Now nicknamed "Limbo," Sang recuperates in Hexion's village. As Sang struggles to remember her identity, she joins Hexion in search of a young girl named Iris who has gone missing in the troll-infested Forest of the Ants! Along the way, they encounter trolls, students from the Magic Academy Athena...and old friends Dev and Notra! Will they be able to help Sang recover her lost memories?

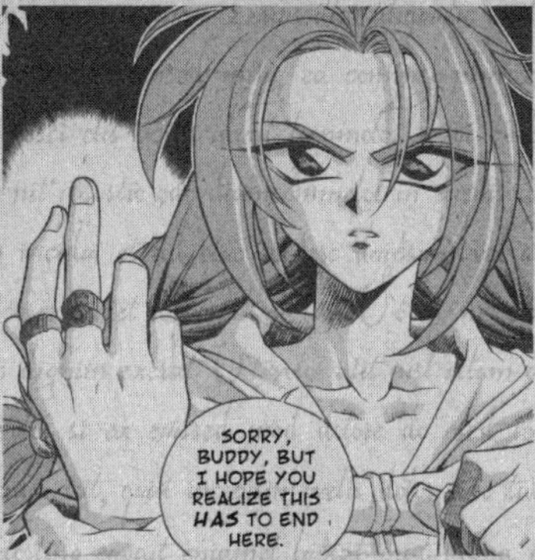
SORRY, BUDDY, BUT I HOPE YOU REALIZE THIS HAS TO END HERE.

Sang as a woman

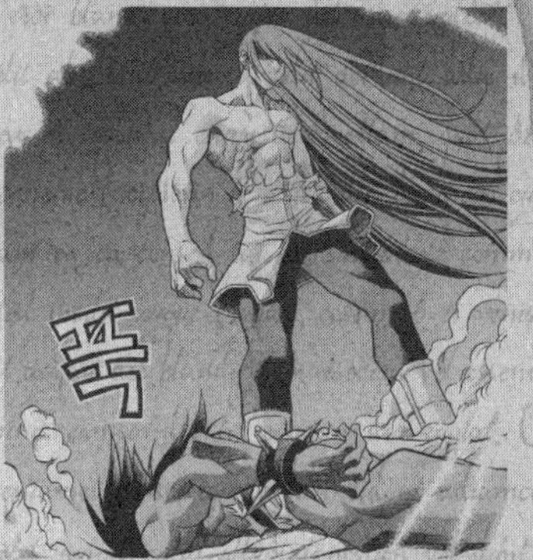

Sang as a man

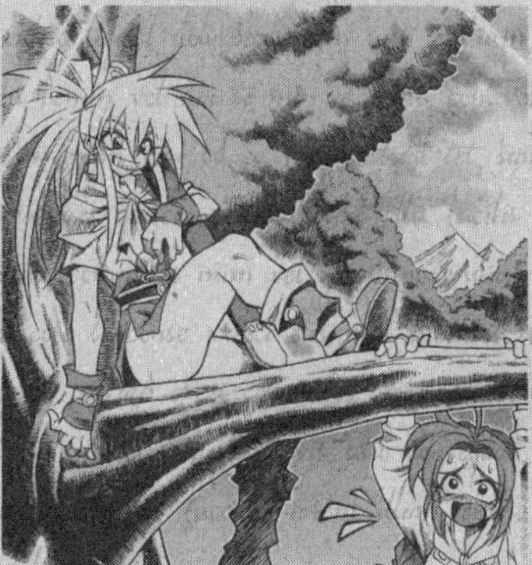

Chun-Lang & Sang

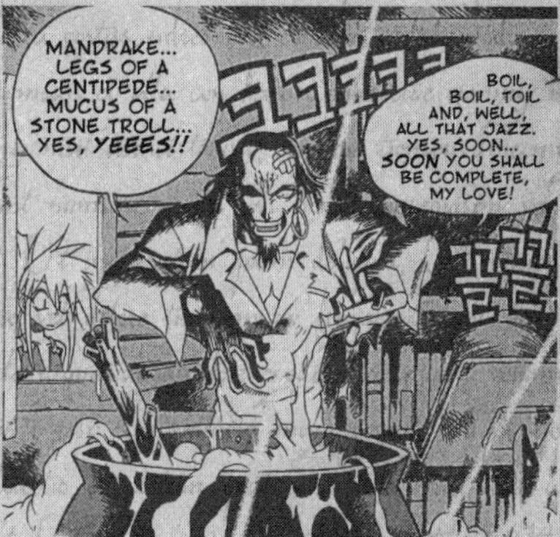
MANDRAKE... LEGS OF A CENTIPEDE... MUCUS OF A STONE TROLL... YES, YEEES!!
BOIL, BOIL, TOIL AND, WELL, ALL THAT JAZZ. YES, SOON... SOON YOU SHALL BE COMPLETE, MY LOVE!

Alcan

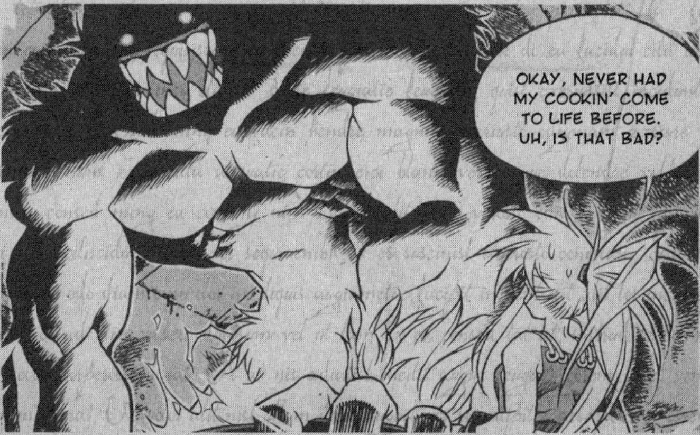
OKAY, NEVER HAD MY COOKIN' COME TO LIFE BEFORE. UH, IS THAT BAD?

Gigantes

Table of Contents

Order Rank

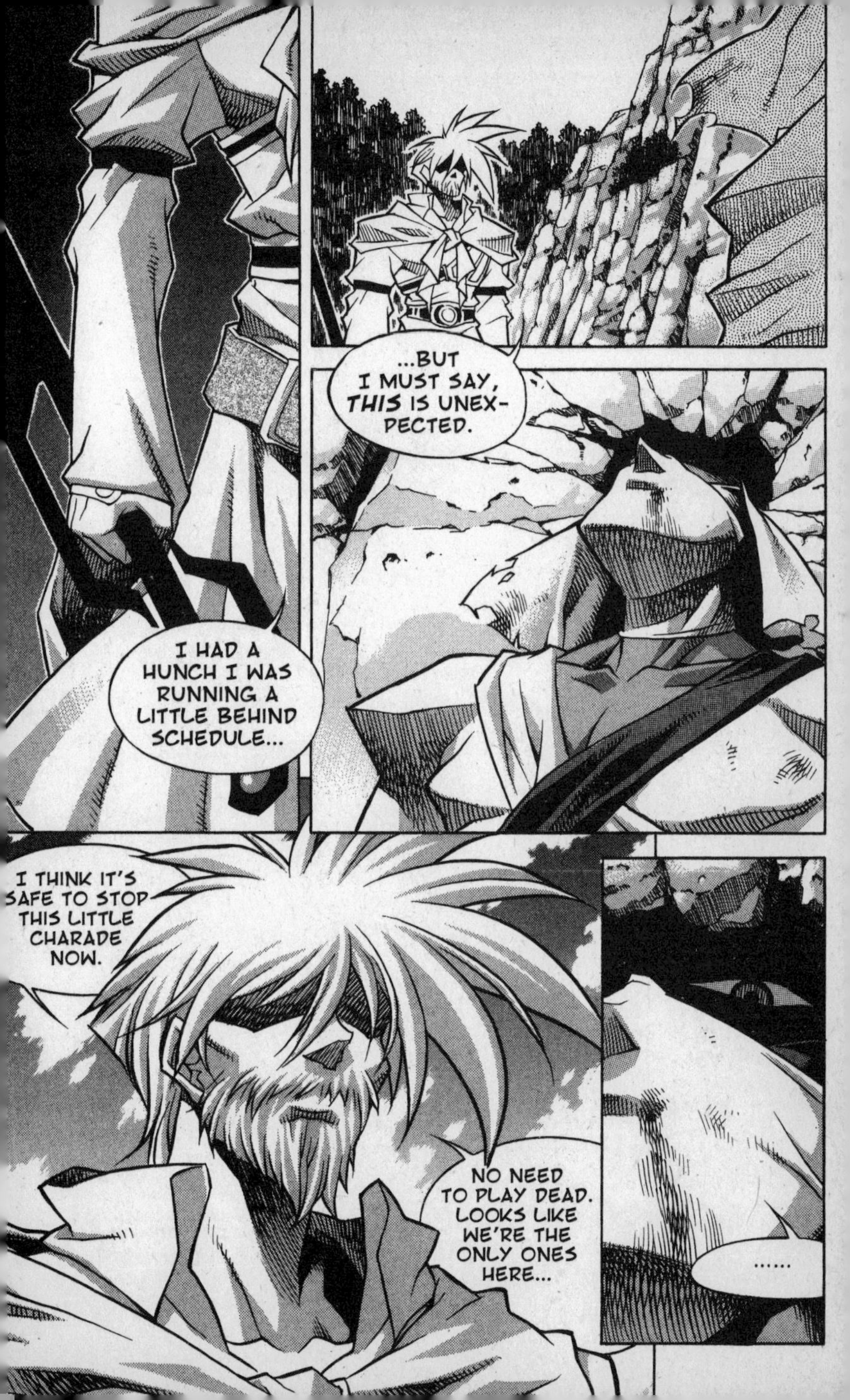
...BUT I MUST SAY, *THIS* IS UNEXPECTED.
I HAD A HUNCH I WAS RUNNING A LITTLE BEHIND SCHEDULE...
I THINK IT'S SAFE TO STOP THIS LITTLE CHARADE NOW.
NO NEED TO PLAY DEAD. LOOKS LIKE WE'RE THE ONLY ONES HERE...
......

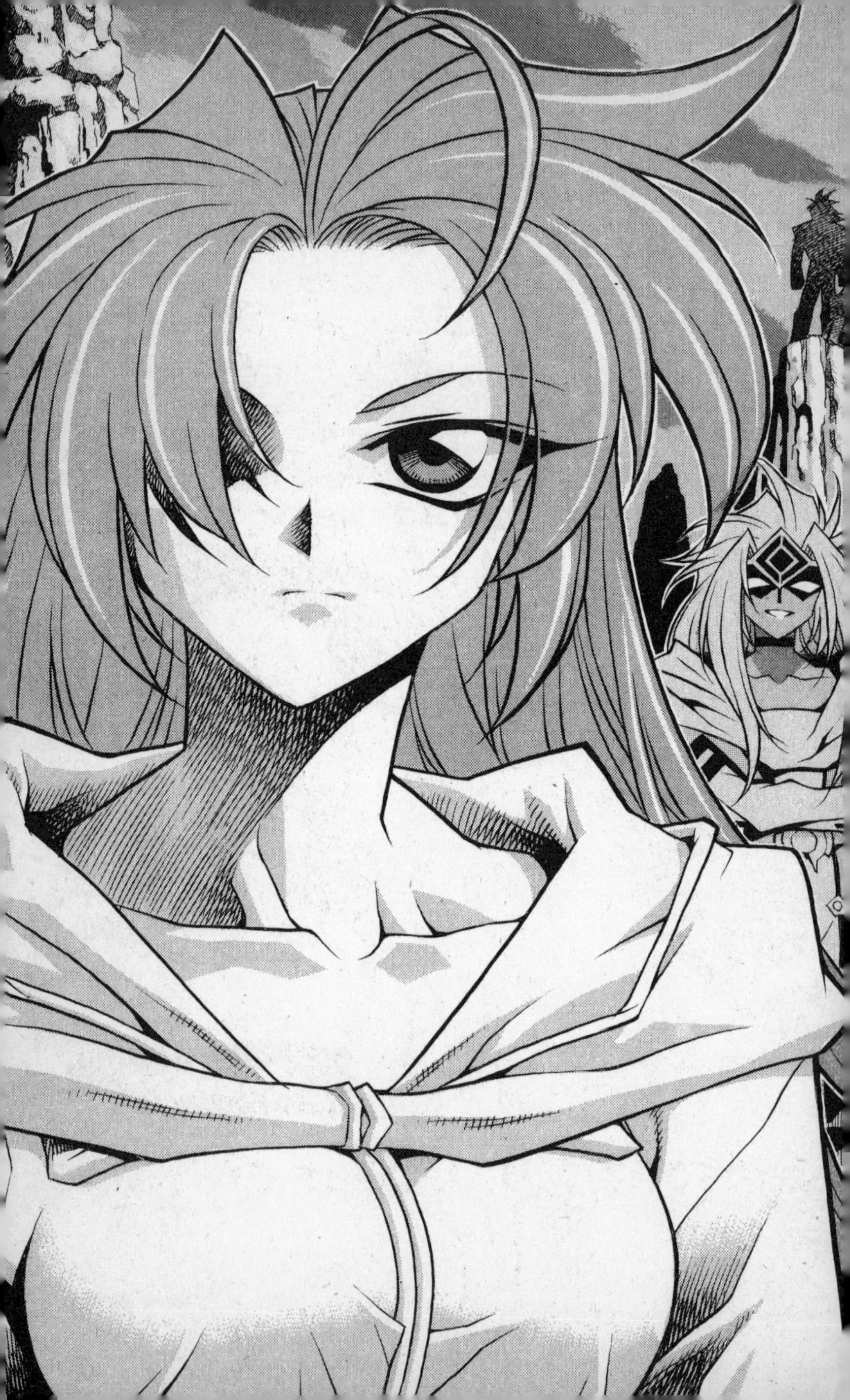

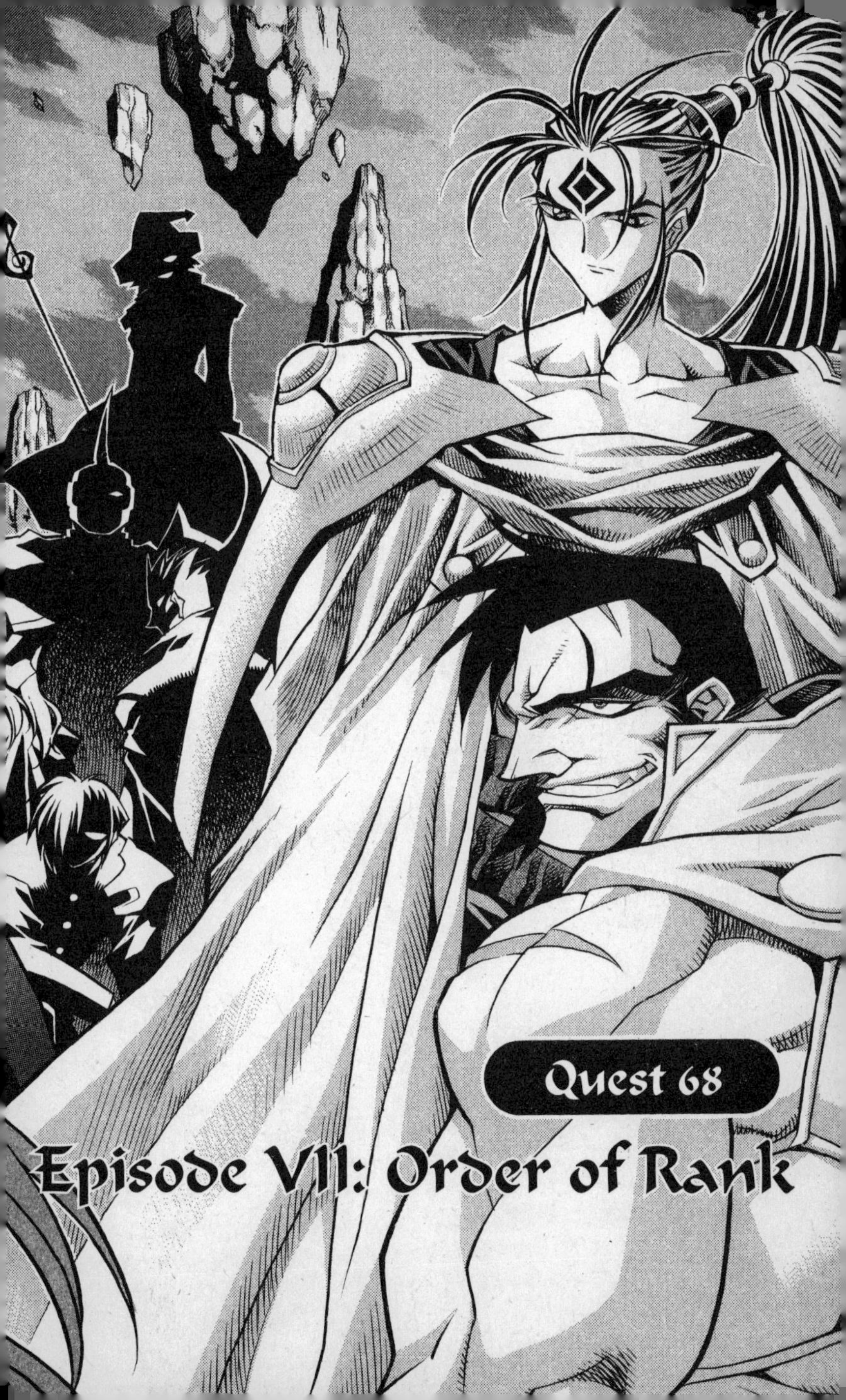
Quest 68
Episode VII: Order of Rank

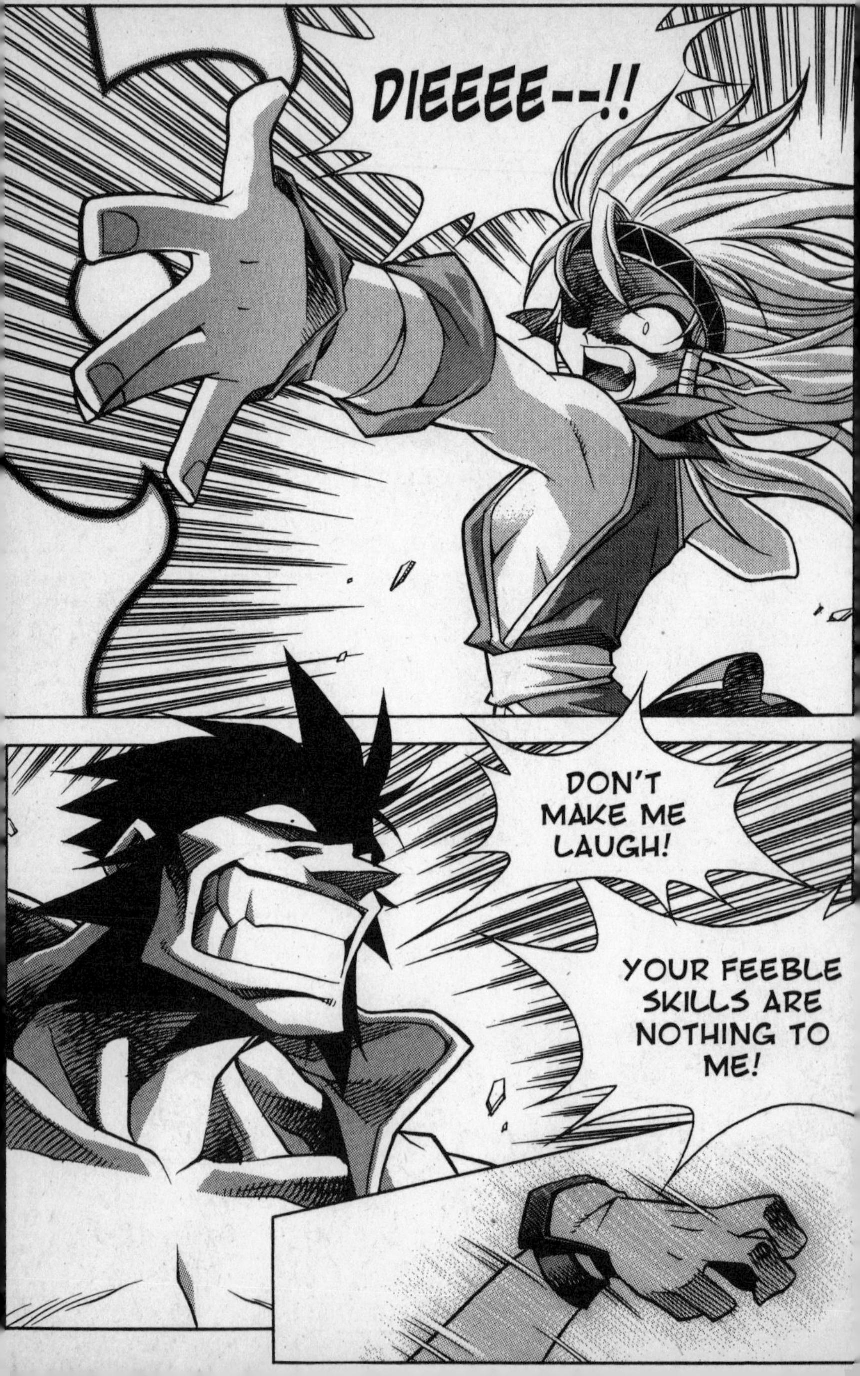
DIEEEE--!!
DON'T MAKE ME LAUGH!
YOUR FEEBLE SKILLS ARE NOTHING TO ME!

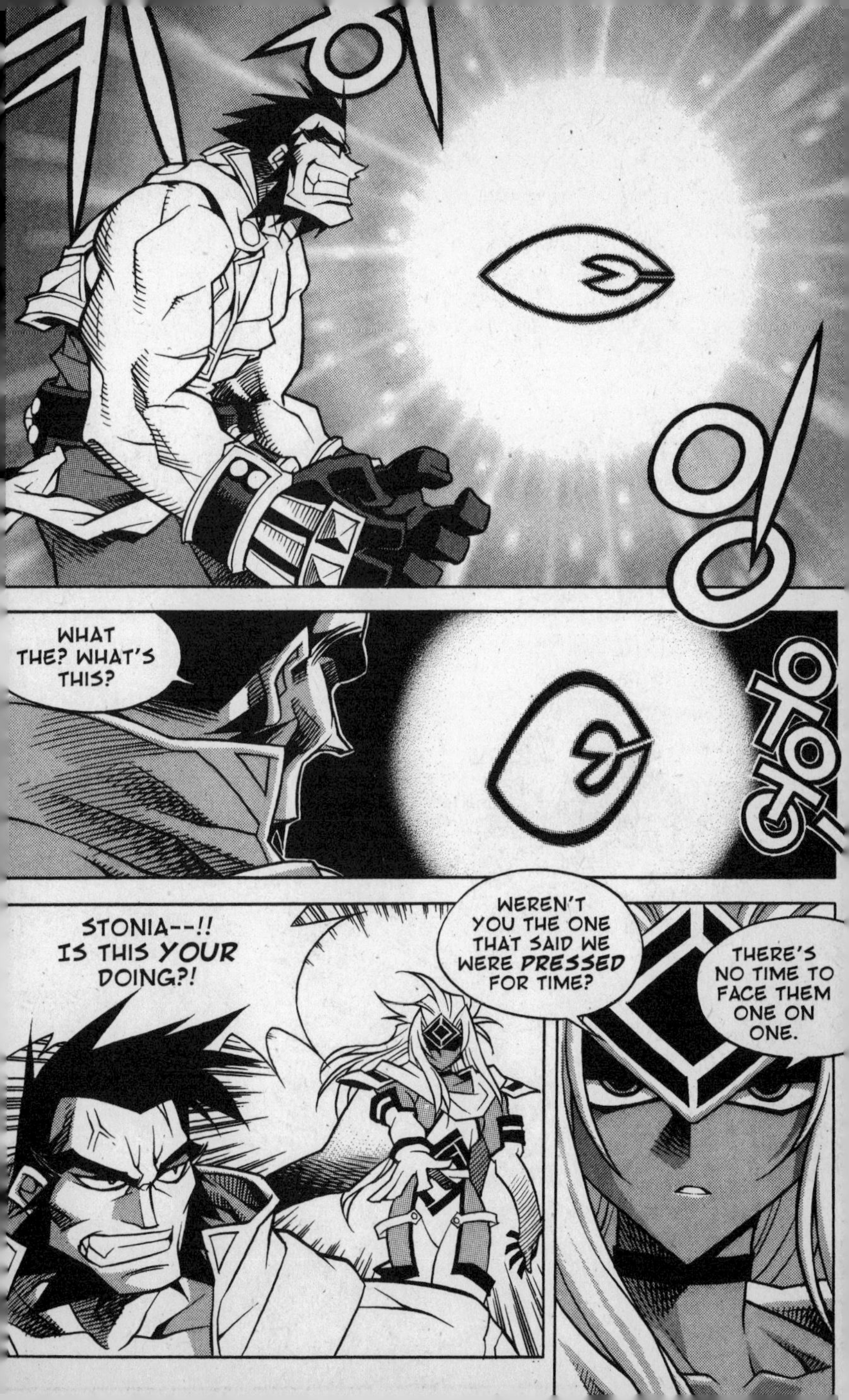
WHAT THE? WHAT'S THIS?
STONIA--!! IS THIS *YOUR* DOING?!
WEREN'T YOU THE ONE THAT SAID WE WERE *PRESSED* FOR TIME?
THERE'S NO TIME TO FACE THEM ONE ON ONE.

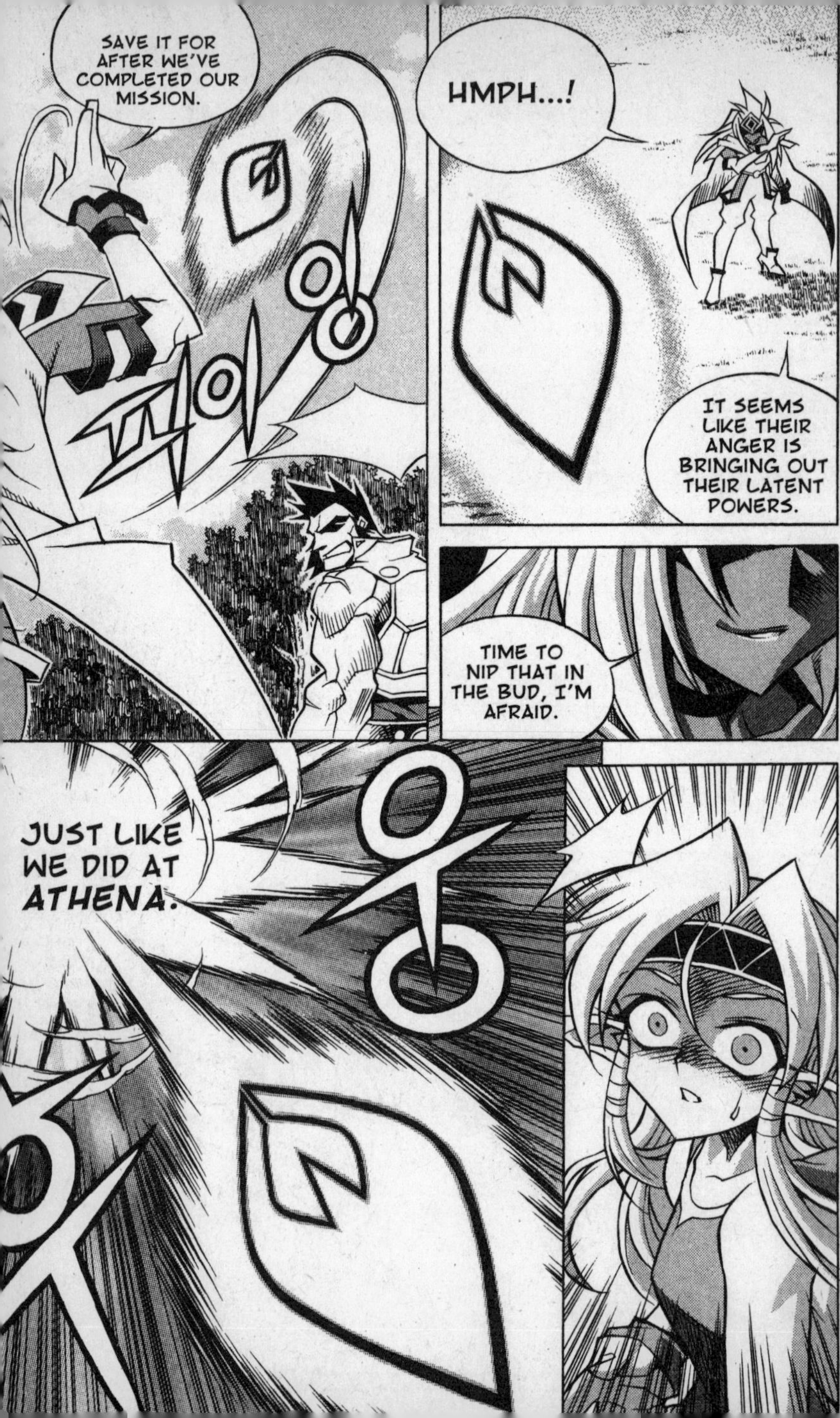

SAVE IT FOR AFTER WE'VE COMPLETED OUR MISSION.
HMPH...!
IT SEEMS LIKE THEIR ANGER IS BRINGING OUT THEIR LATENT POWERS.
TIME TO NIP THAT IN THE BUD, I'M AFRAID.
JUST LIKE WE DID AT ATHENA.

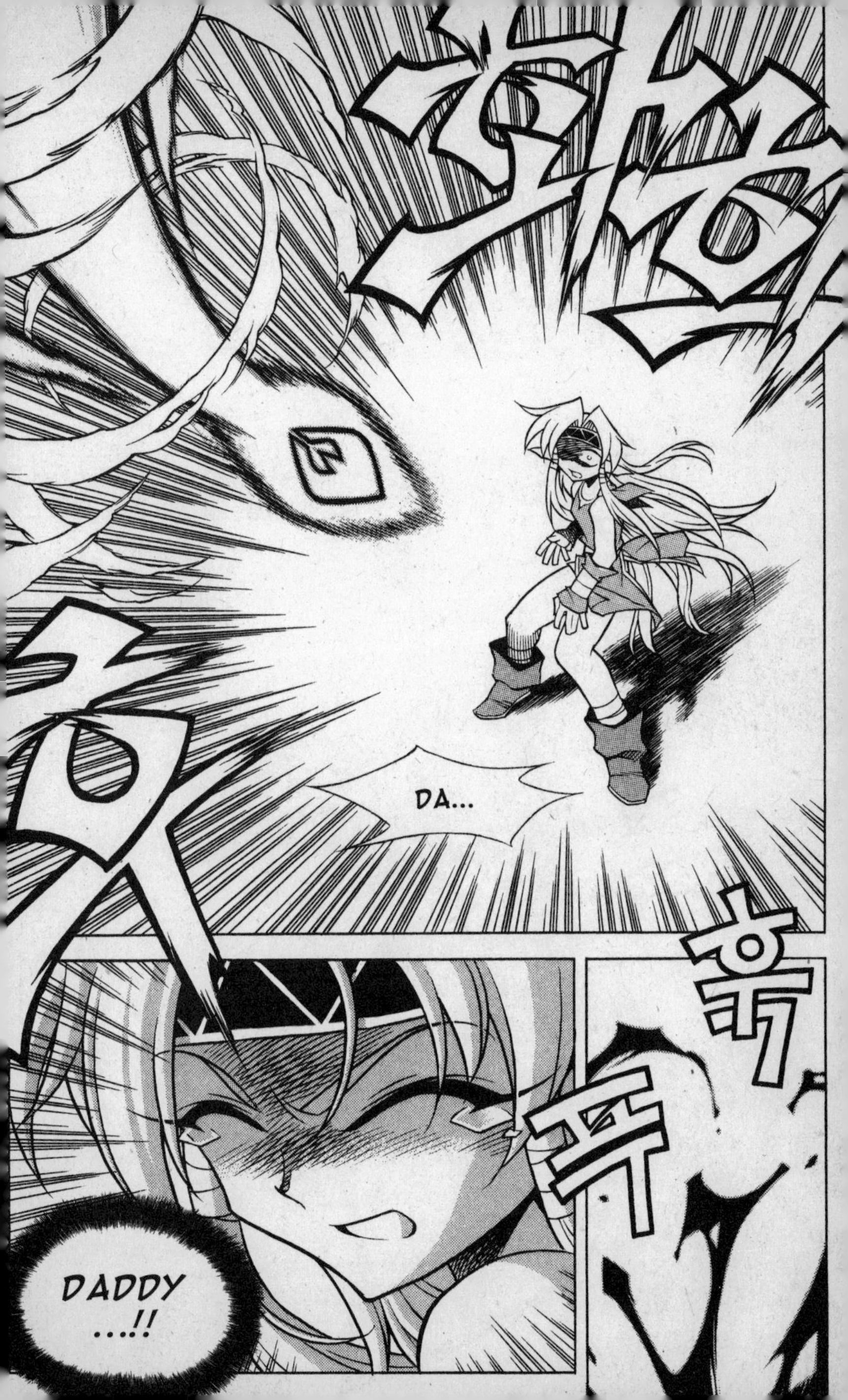
DA...
DADDY ....!!

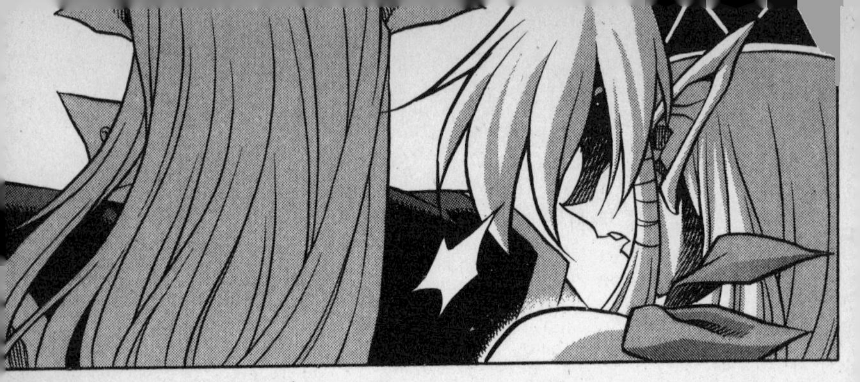

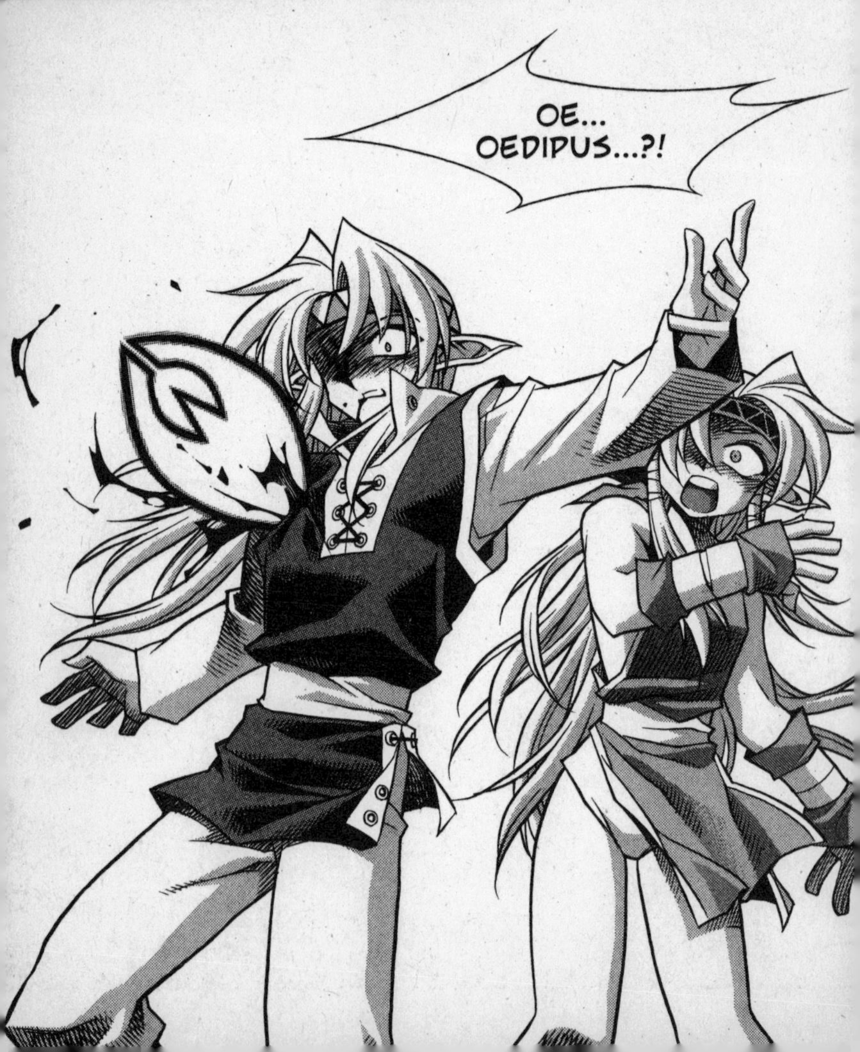
OE... OEDIPUS...?!

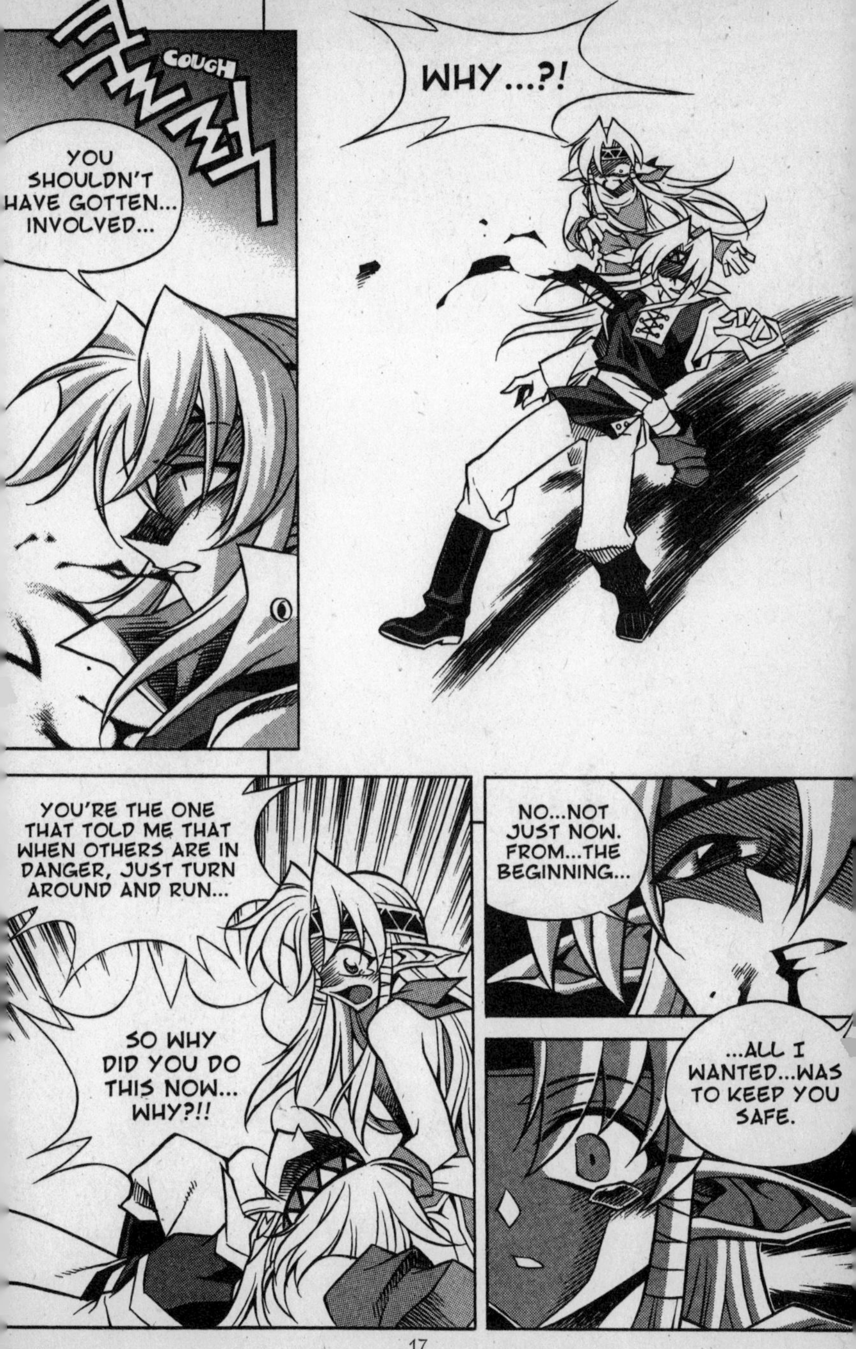
COUGH
YOU SHOULDN'T HAVE GOTTEN... INVOLVED...
WHY...?!
YOU'RE THE ONE THAT TOLD ME THAT WHEN OTHERS ARE IN DANGER, JUST TURN AROUND AND RUN...
SO WHY DID YOU DO THIS NOW... WHY?!!
NO...NOT JUST NOW. FROM...THE BEGINNING...
...ALL I WANTED...WAS TO KEEP YOU SAFE.

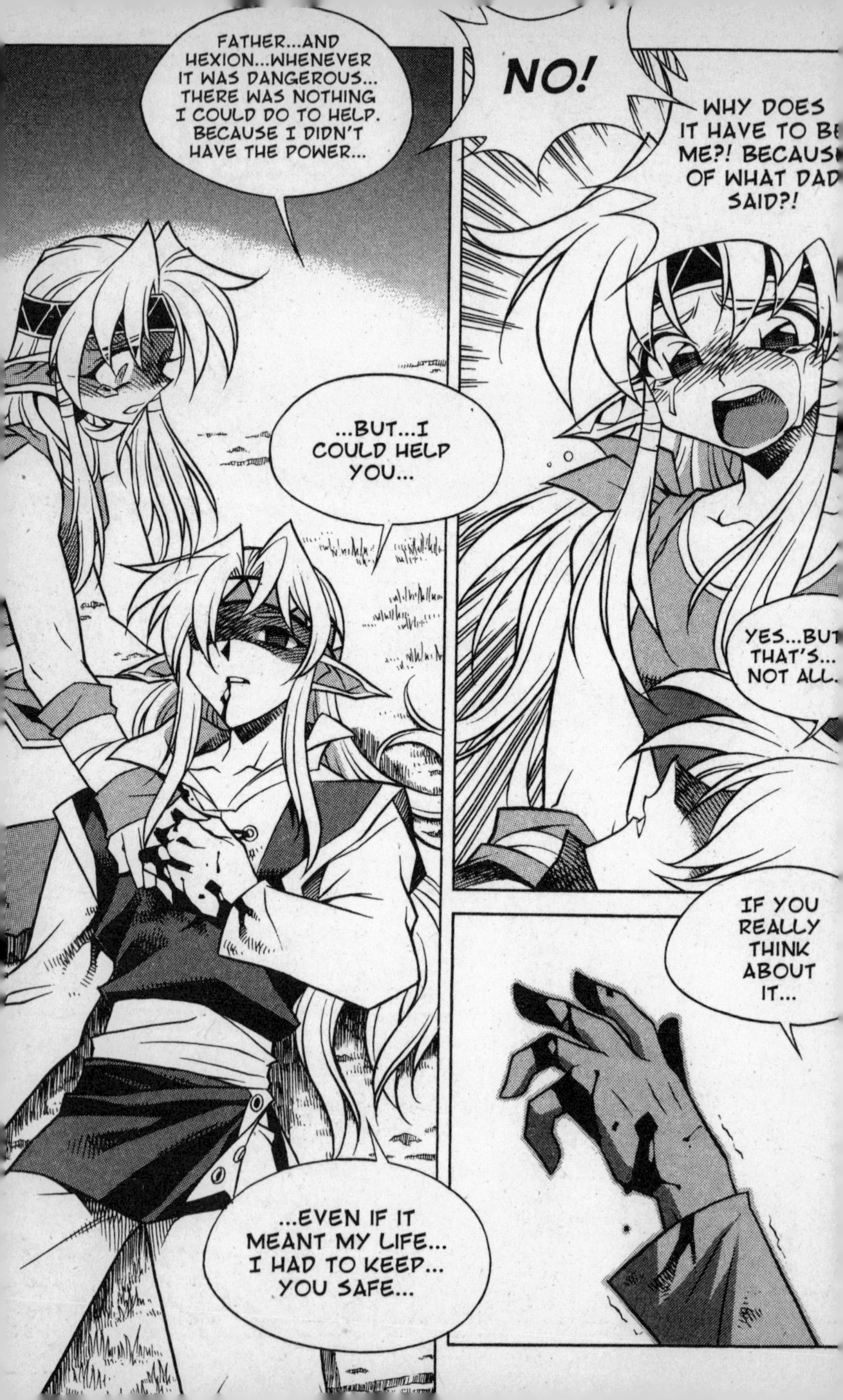
FATHER...AND HEXION...WHENEVER IT WAS DANGEROUS... THERE WAS NOTHING I COULD DO TO HELP. BECAUSE I DIDN'T HAVE THE POWER...
...BUT...I COULD HELP YOU...
...EVEN IF IT MEANT MY LIFE... I HAD TO KEEP... YOU SAFE...
NO!
WHY DOES IT HAVE TO BE ME?! BECAUSE OF WHAT DAD SAID?!
YES...BUT THAT'S... NOT ALL.
IF YOU REALLY THINK ABOUT IT...

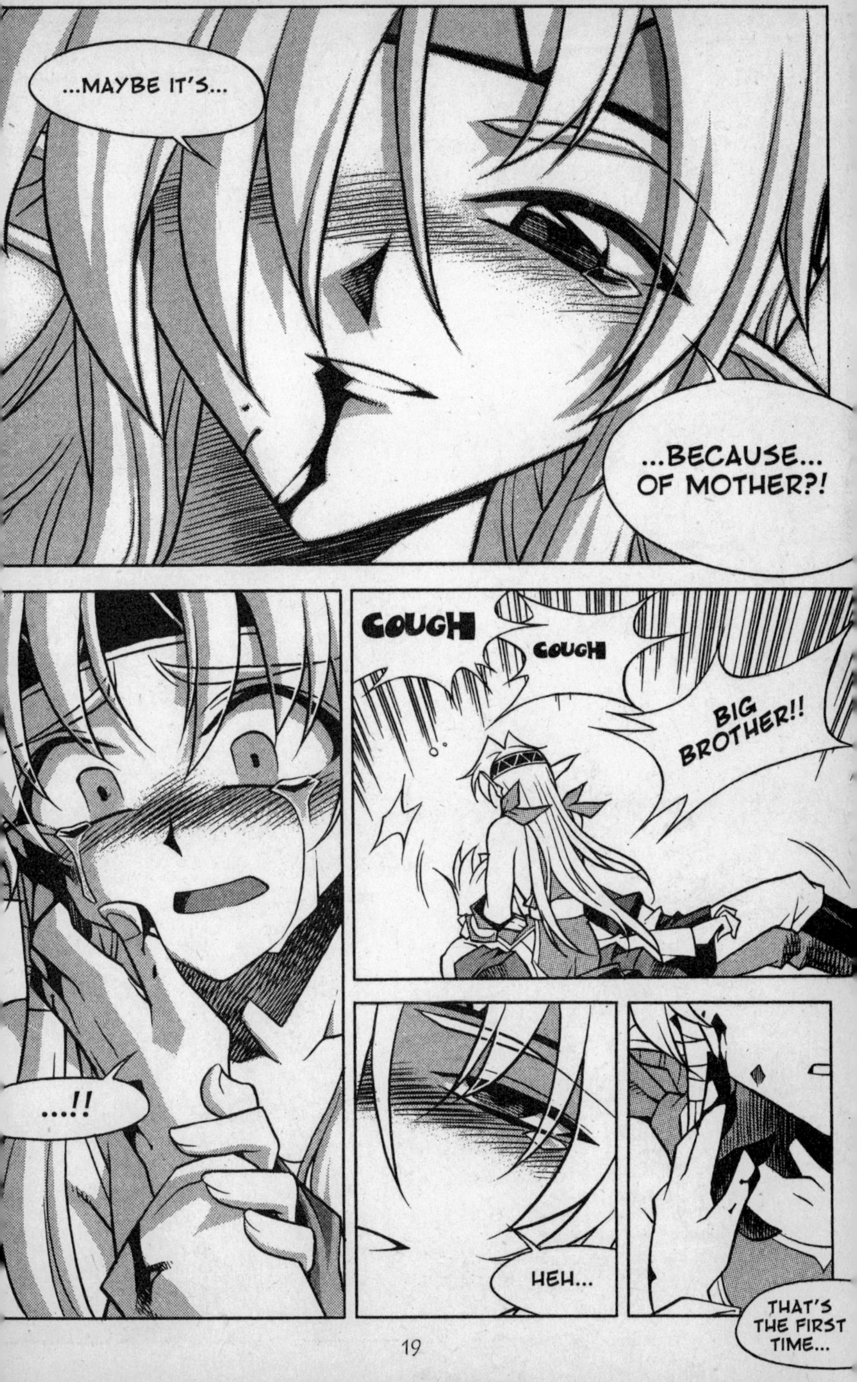
...MAYBE IT'S...
...BECAUSE... OF MOTHER?!
...!!
COUGH
COUGH
BIG BROTHER!!
HEH...
THAT'S THE FIRST TIME...

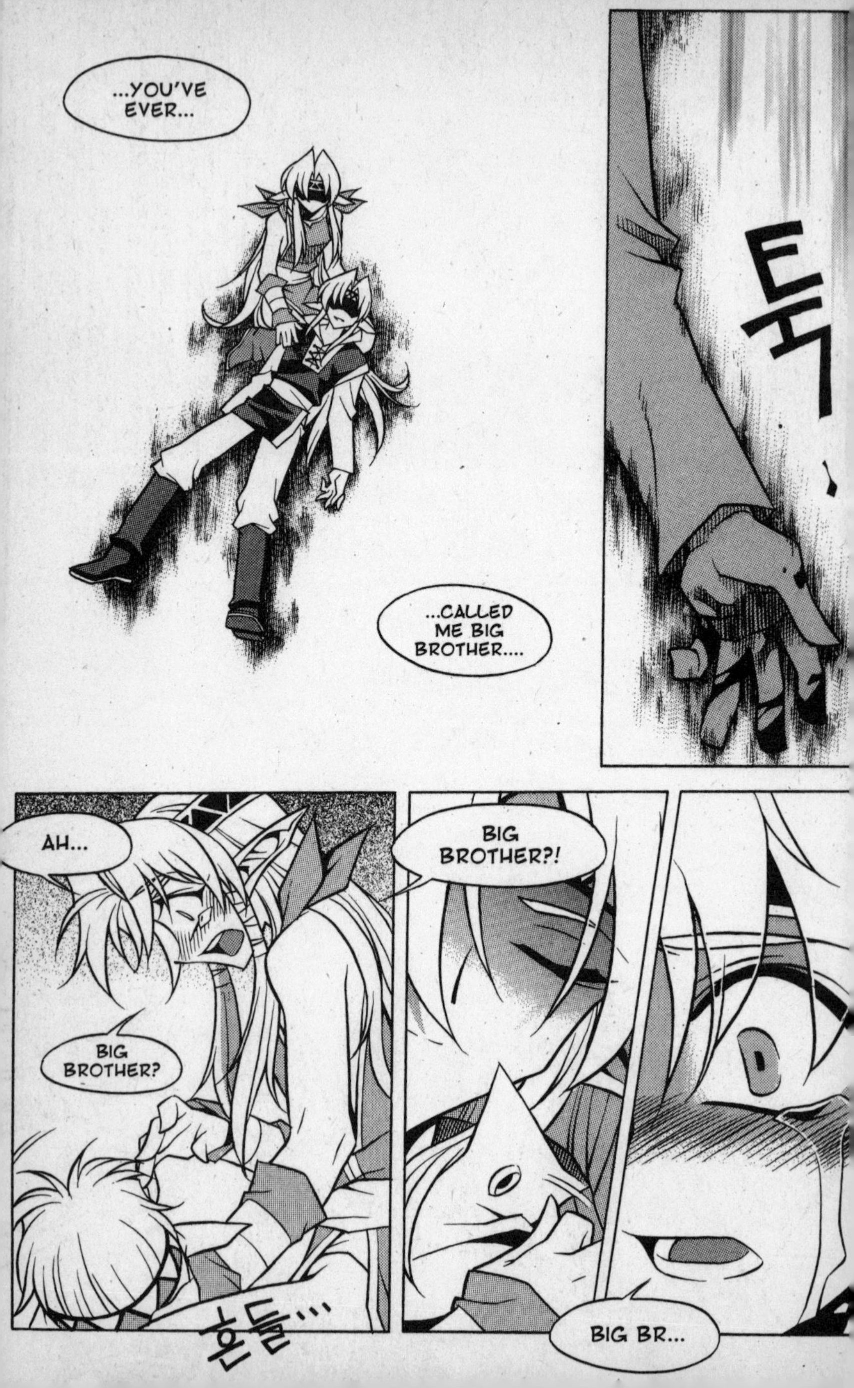
...YOU'VE EVER...
...CALLED ME BIG BROTHER....
AH...
BIG BROTHER?
흔들...
BIG BROTHER?!
BIG BR...

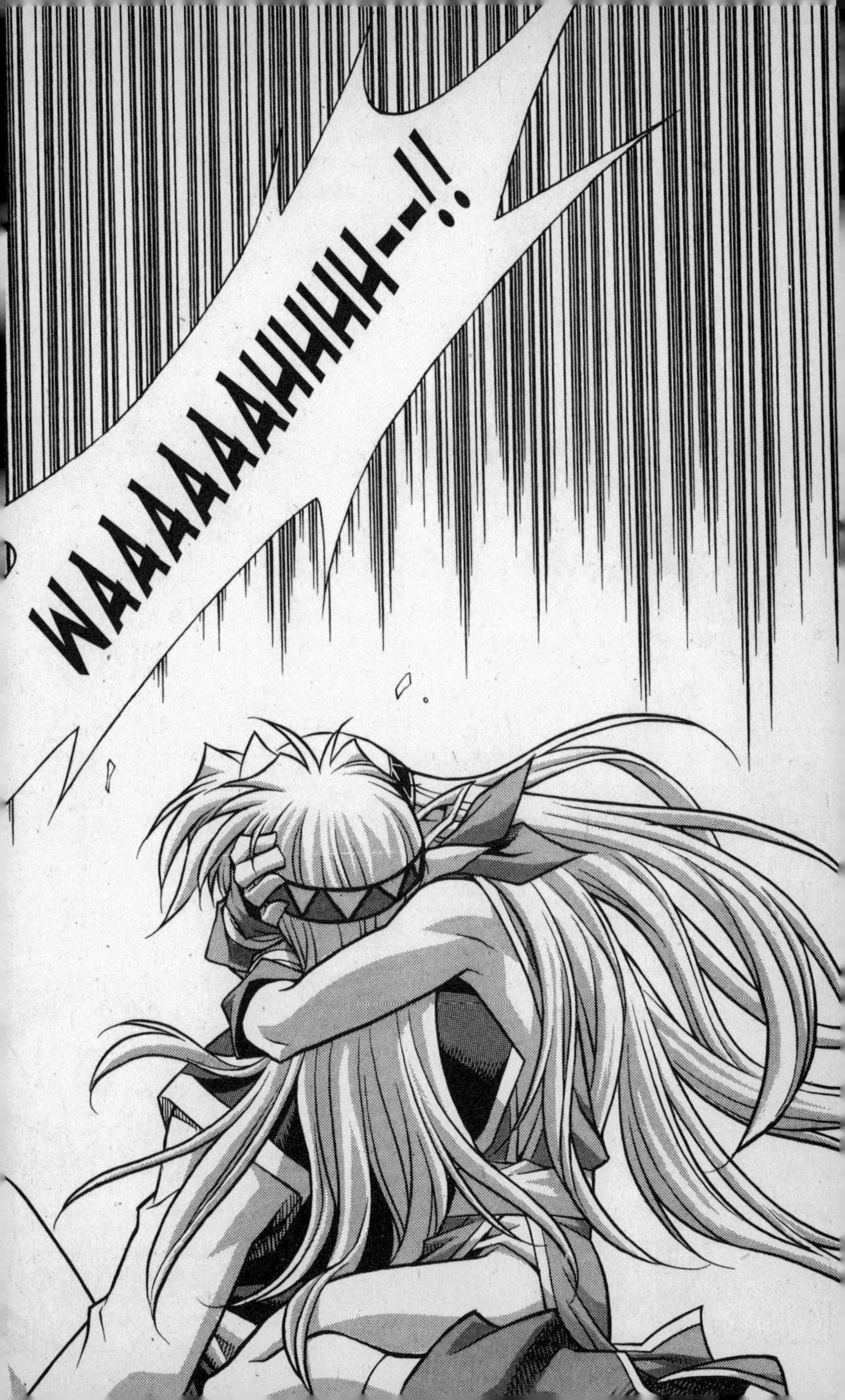
WAAAAAAHHH--!!

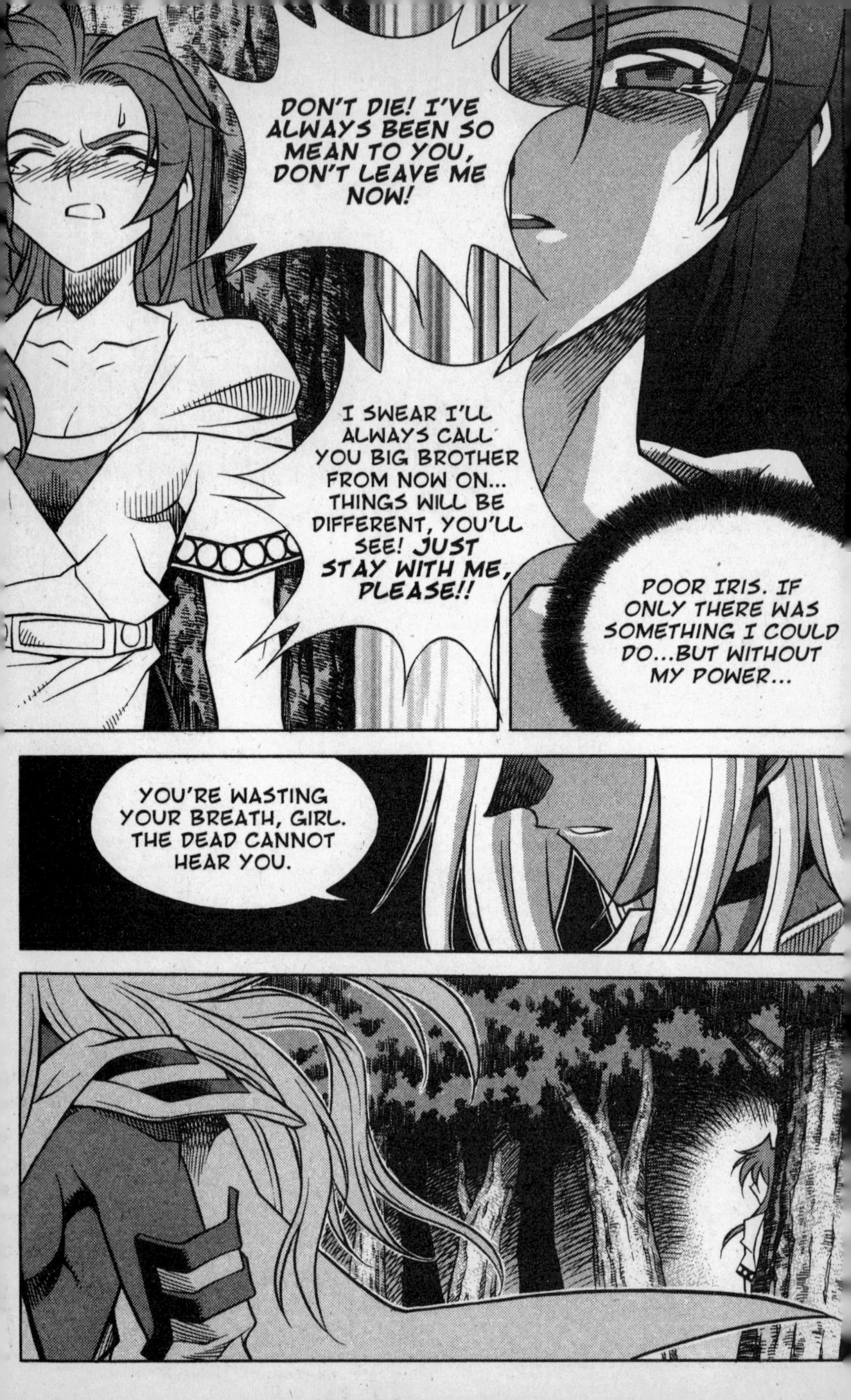
DON'T DIE! I'VE ALWAYS BEEN SO MEAN TO YOU, DON'T LEAVE ME NOW!
I SWEAR I'LL ALWAYS CALL YOU BIG BROTHER FROM NOW ON... THINGS WILL BE DIFFERENT, YOU'LL SEE! JUST STAY WITH ME, PLEASE!!
POOR IRIS. IF ONLY THERE WAS SOMETHING I COULD DO...BUT WITHOUT MY POWER...
YOU'RE WASTING YOUR BREATH, GIRL. THE DEAD CANNOT HEAR YOU.

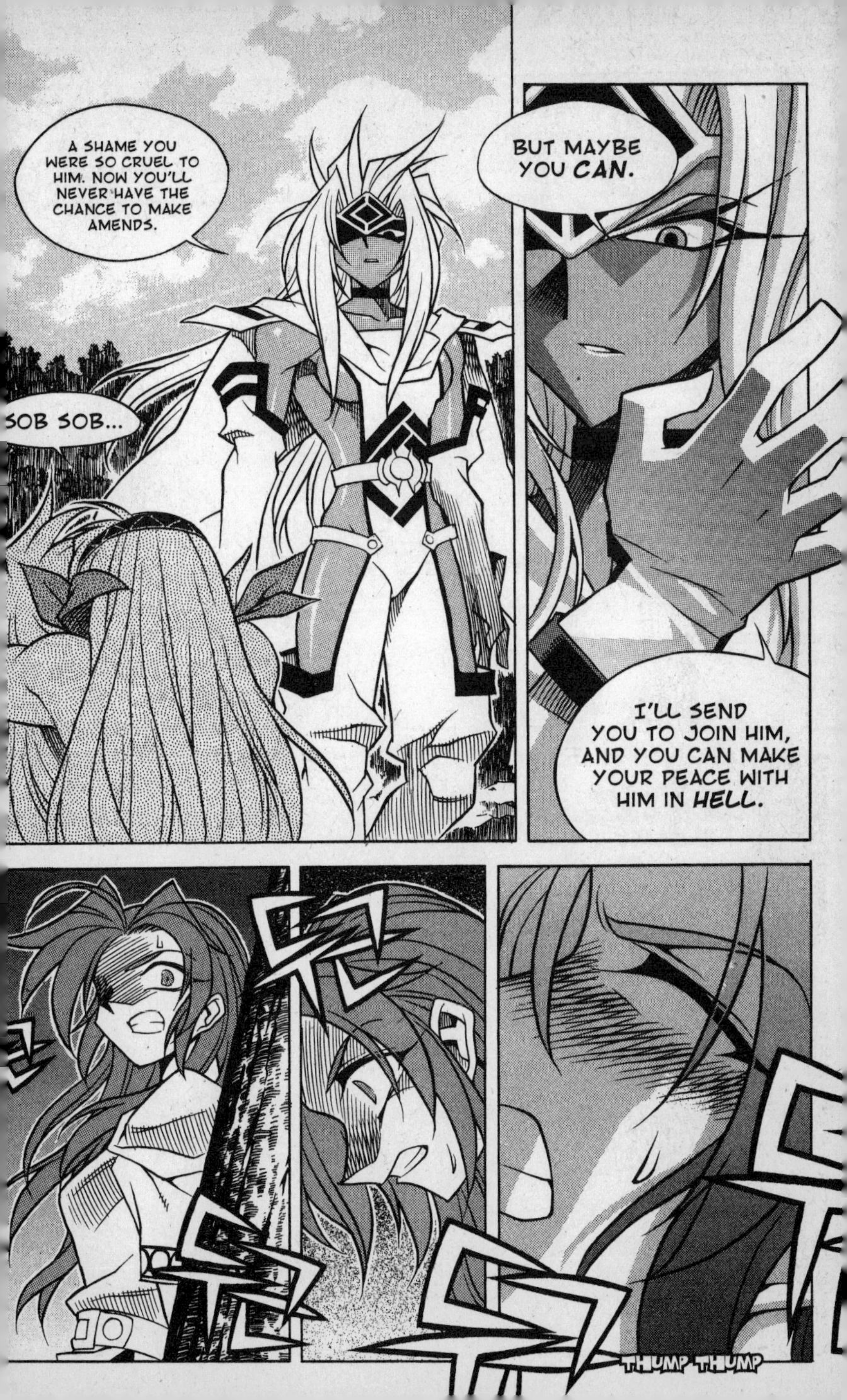
A SHAME YOU WERE SO CRUEL TO HIM. NOW YOU'LL NEVER HAVE THE CHANCE TO MAKE AMENDS.
SOB SOB...
BUT MAYBE YOU CAN.
I'LL SEND YOU TO JOIN HIM, AND YOU CAN MAKE YOUR PEACE WITH HIM IN HELL.
THUMP THUMP

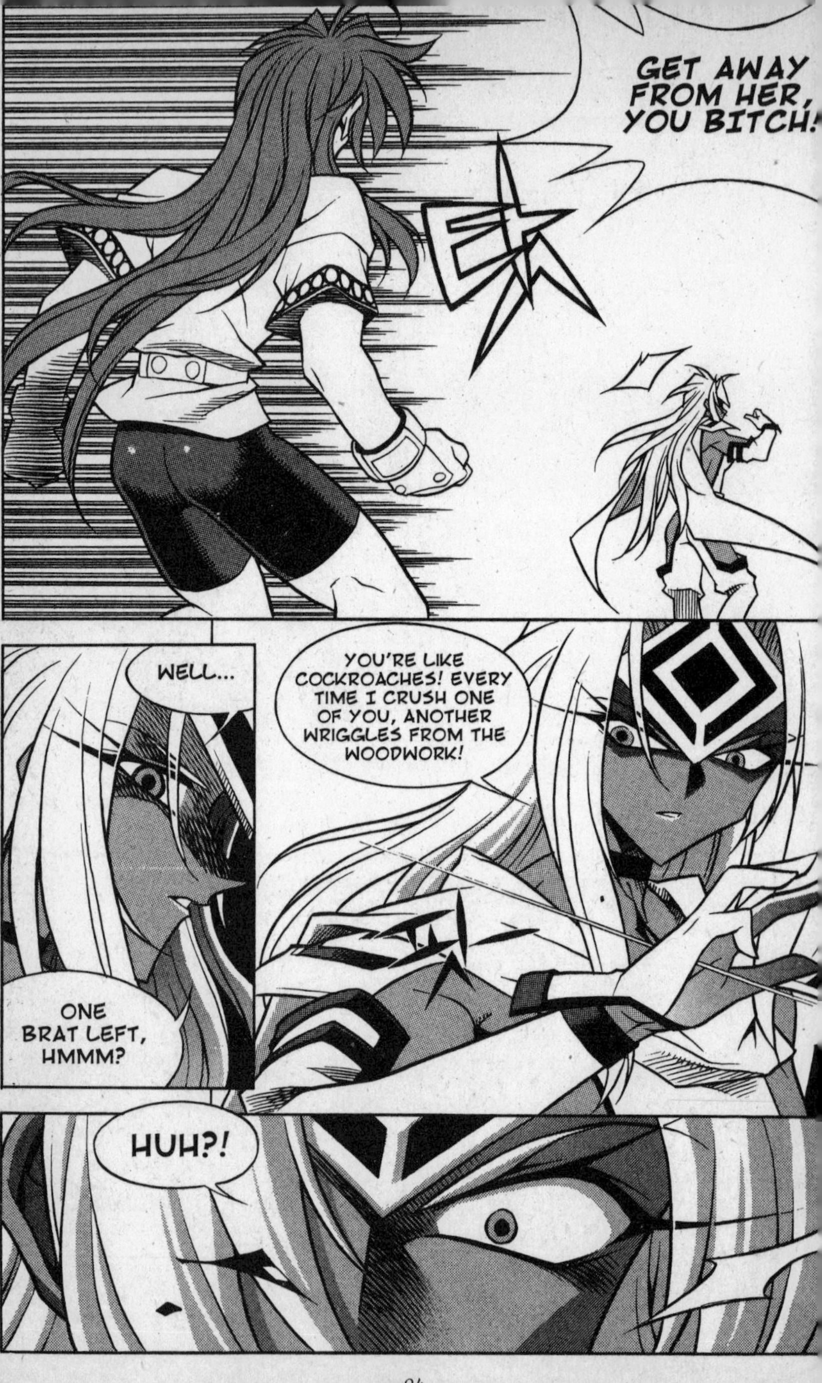
GET AWAY FROM HER, YOU BITCH!
WELL...
ONE BRAT LEFT, HMMM?
YOU'RE LIKE COCKROACHES! EVERY TIME I CRUSH ONE OF YOU, ANOTHER WRIGGLES FROM THE WOODWORK!
HUH?!

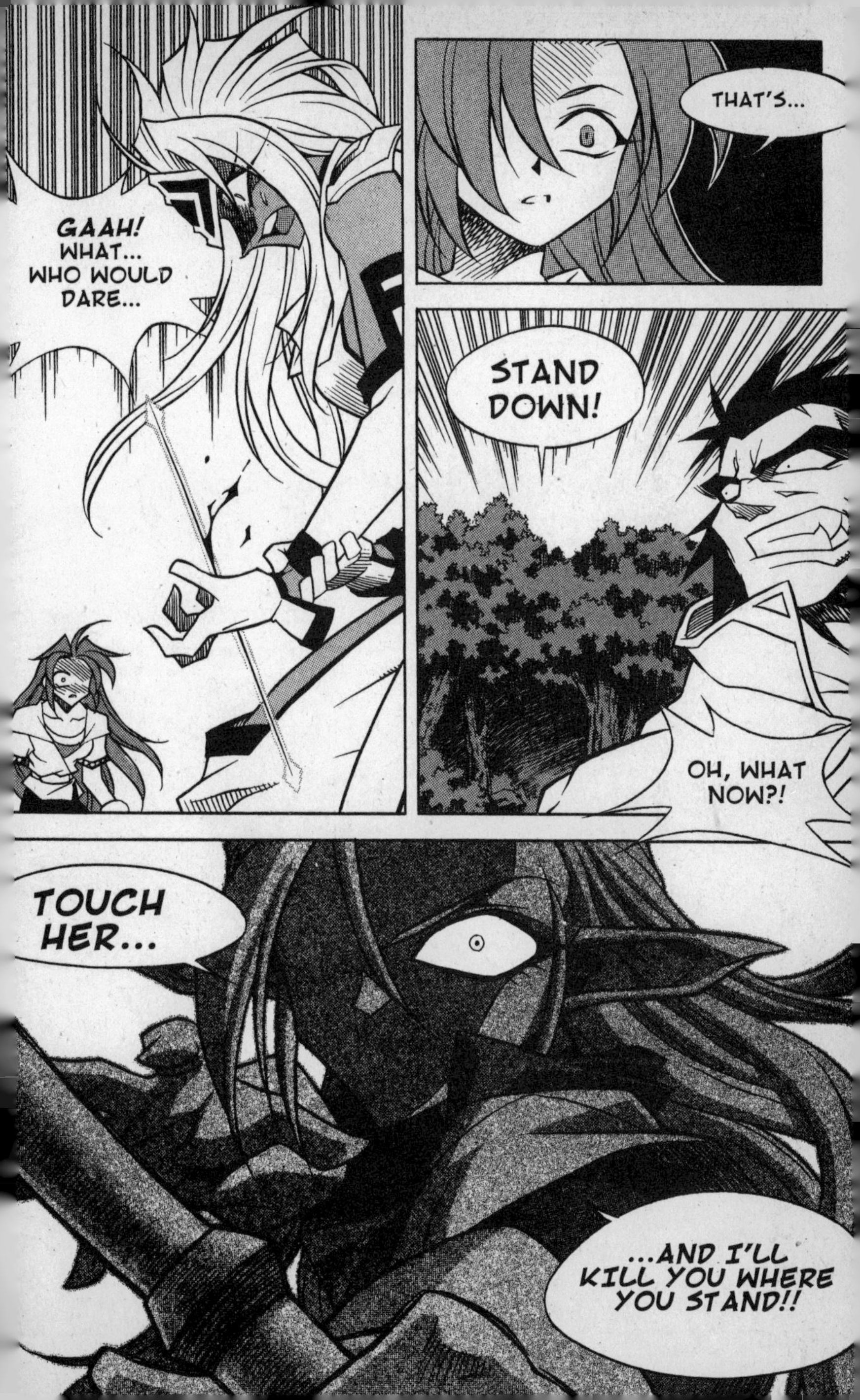
GAAH! WHAT... WHO WOULD DARE...
THAT'S...
STAND DOWN!
OH, WHAT NOW?!
TOUCH HER...
...AND I'LL KILL YOU WHERE YOU STAND!!

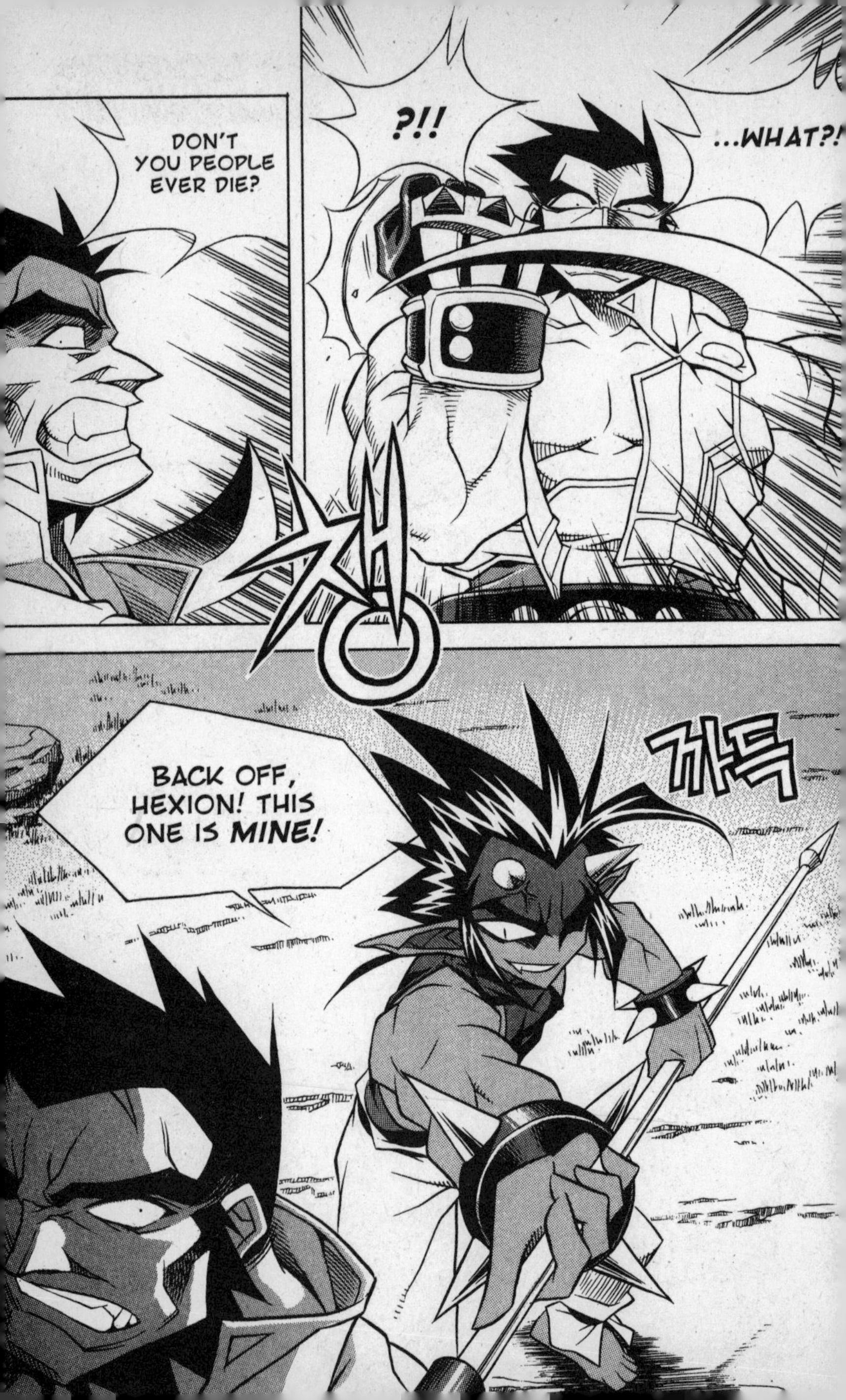
DON'T YOU PEOPLE EVER DIE?
?!!
...WHAT?!
BACK OFF, HEXION! THIS ONE IS MINE!

Quest 69

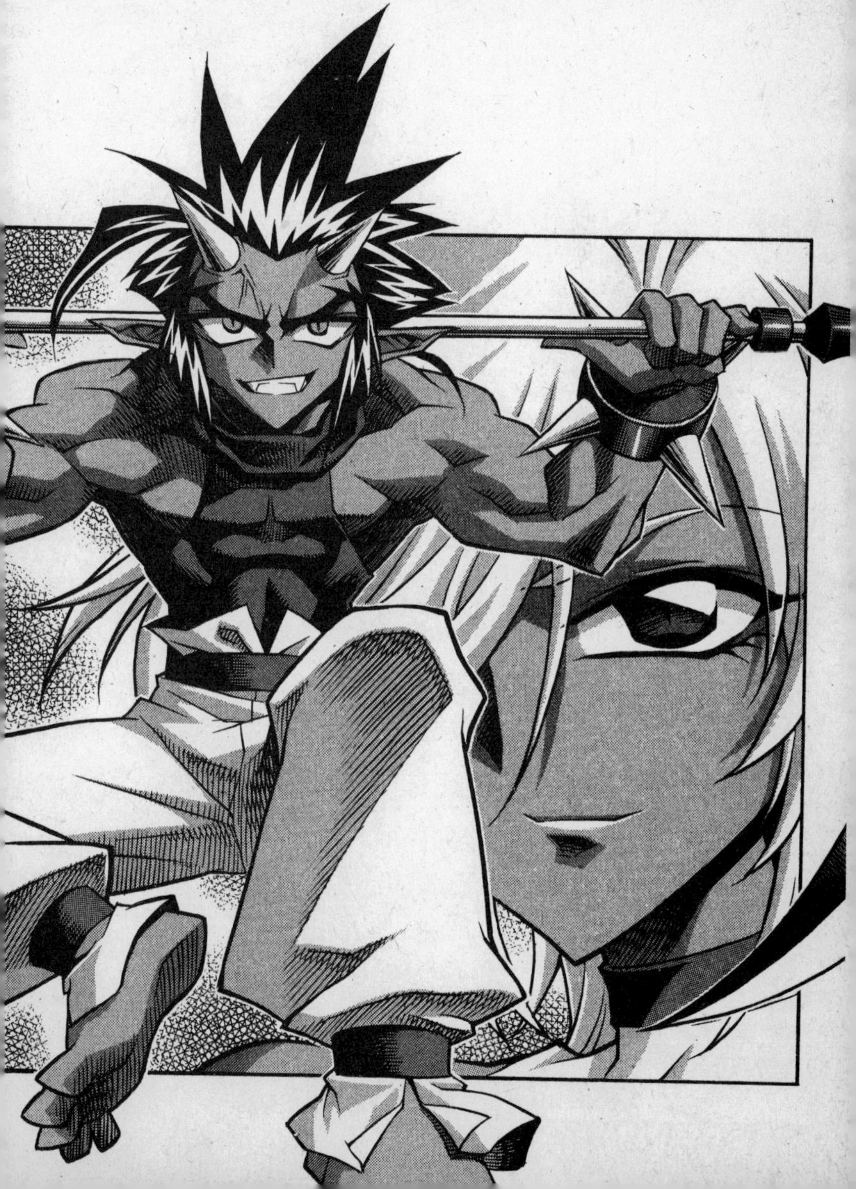

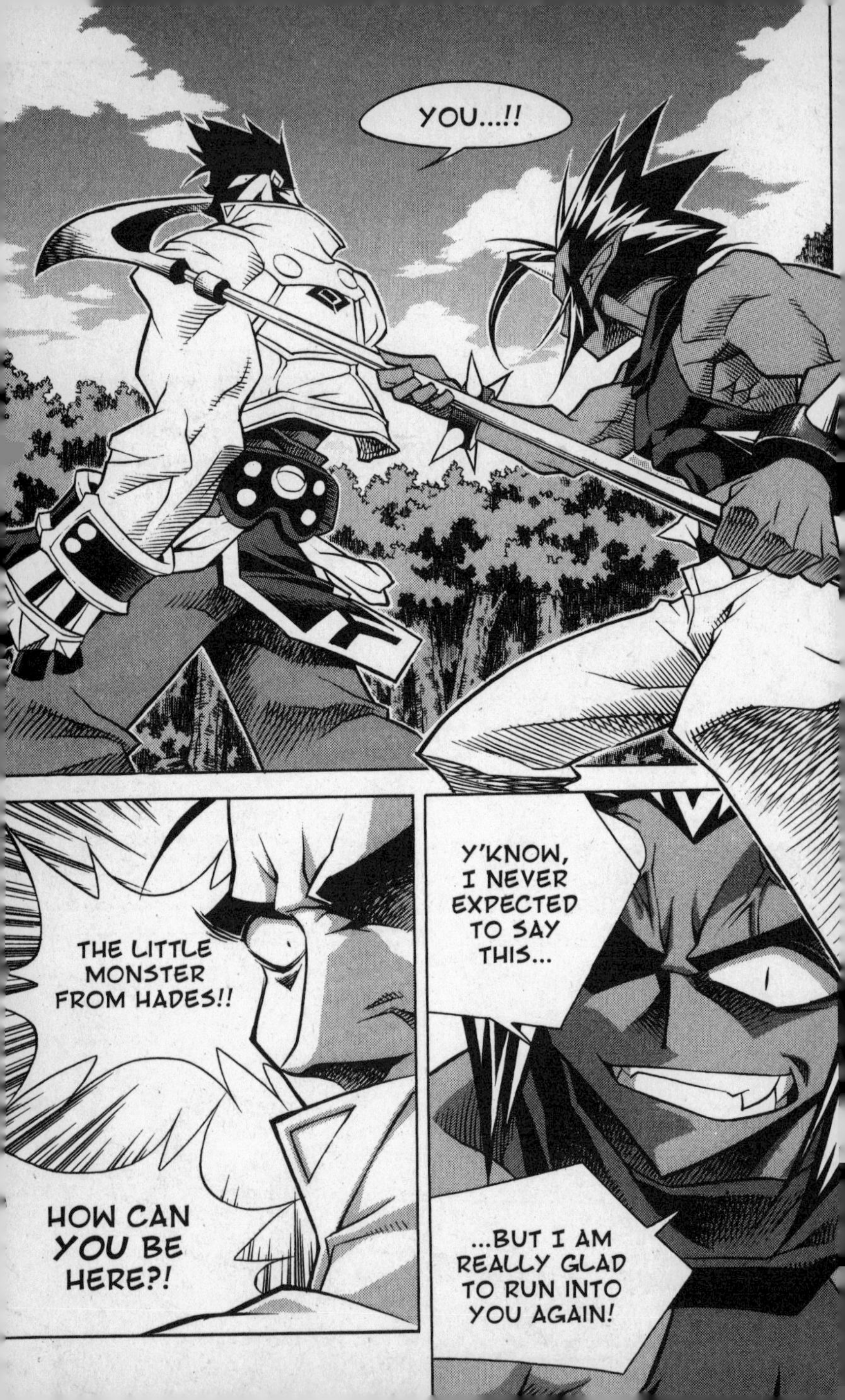
YOU...!!
THE LITTLE MONSTER FROM HADES!!
HOW CAN YOU BE HERE?!
Y'KNOW, I NEVER EXPECTED TO SAY THIS...
...BUT I AM REALLY GLAD TO RUN INTO YOU AGAIN!

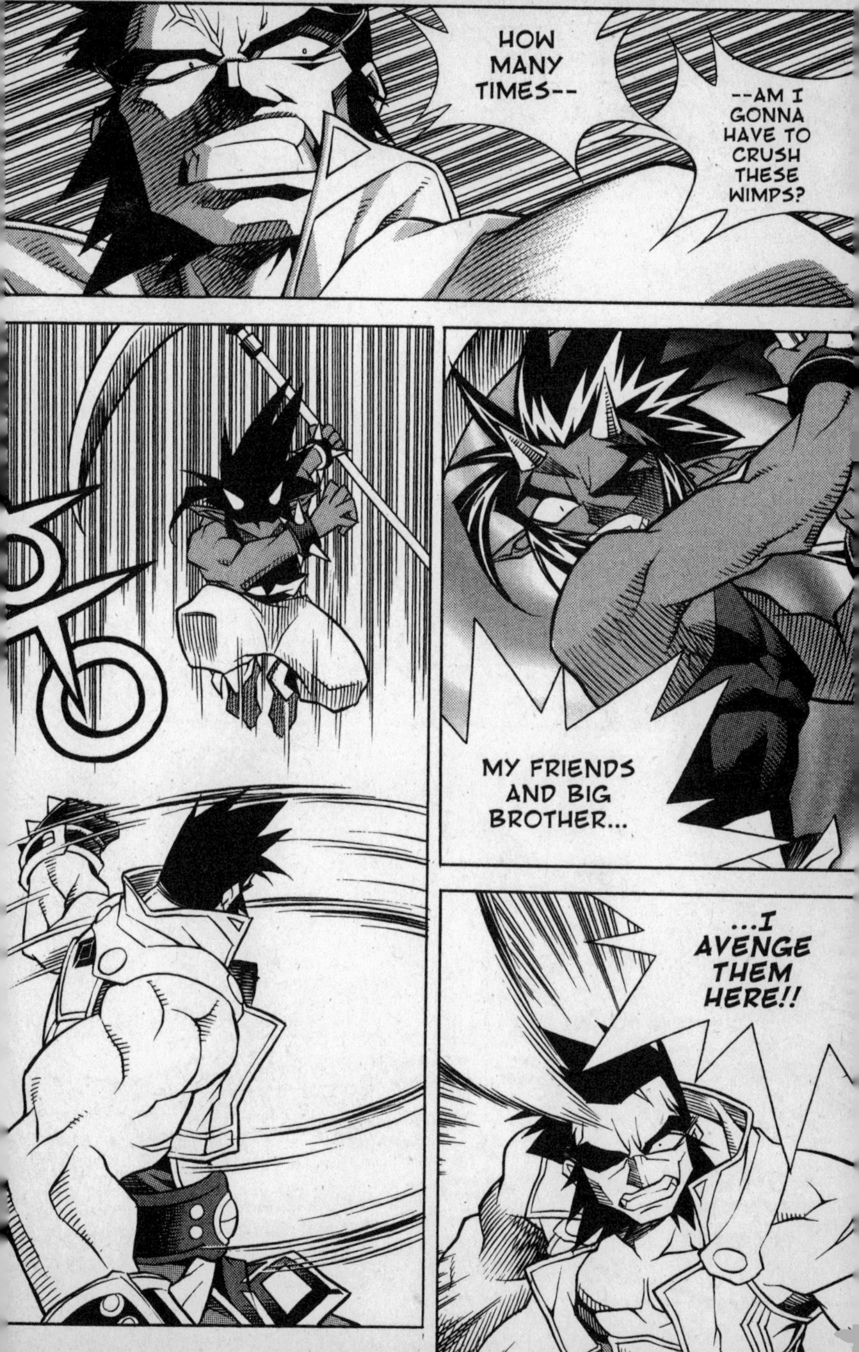
HOW MANY TIMES--
--AM I GONNA HAVE TO CRUSH THESE WIMPS?
MY FRIENDS AND BIG BROTHER...
...I AVENGE THEM HERE!!

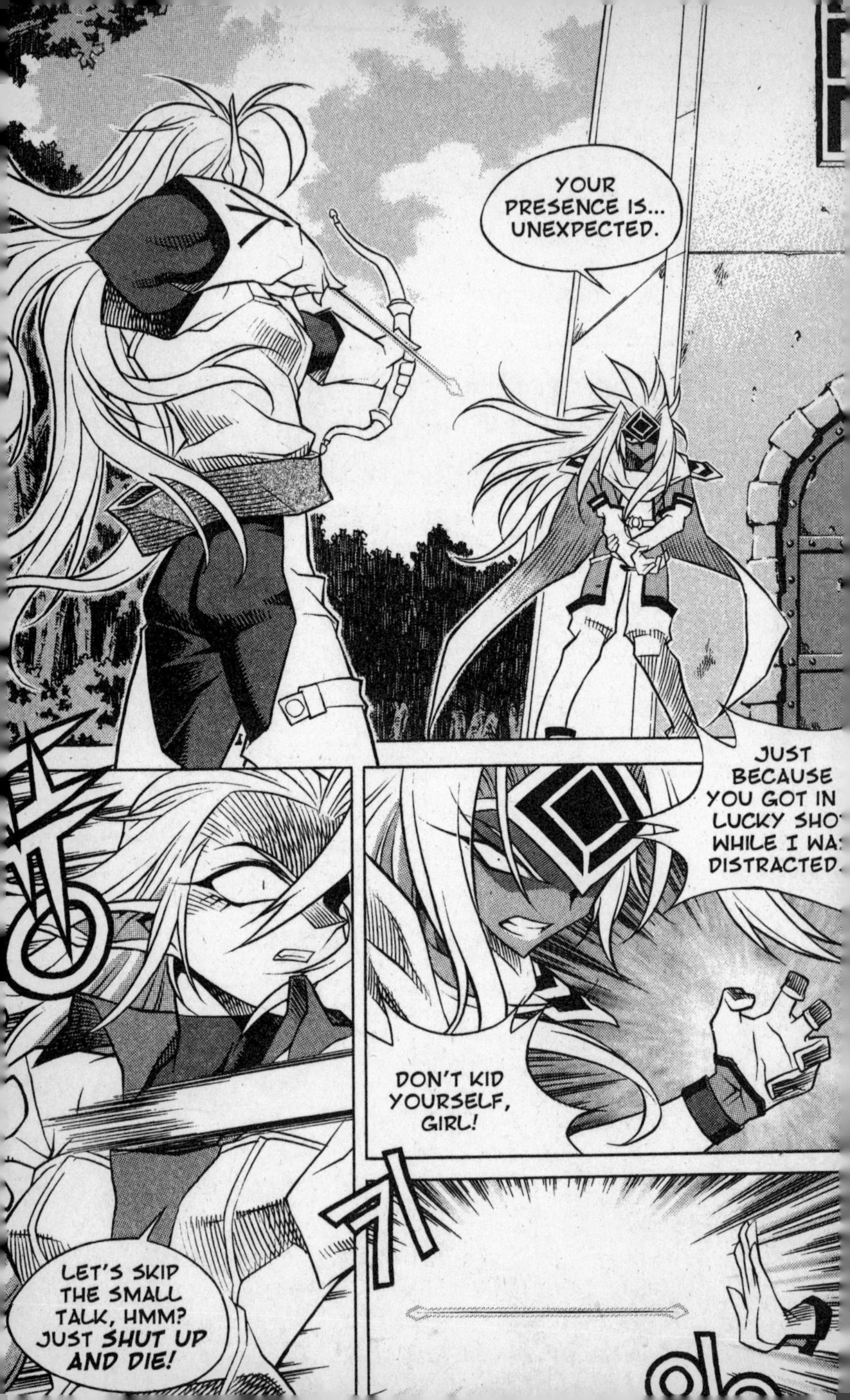
YOUR PRESENCE IS... UNEXPECTED.
LET'S SKIP THE SMALL TALK, HMM? JUST SHUT UP AND DIE!
JUST BECAUSE YOU GOT IN LUCKY SHO WHILE I WA DISTRACTED.
DON'T KID YOURSELF, GIRL!

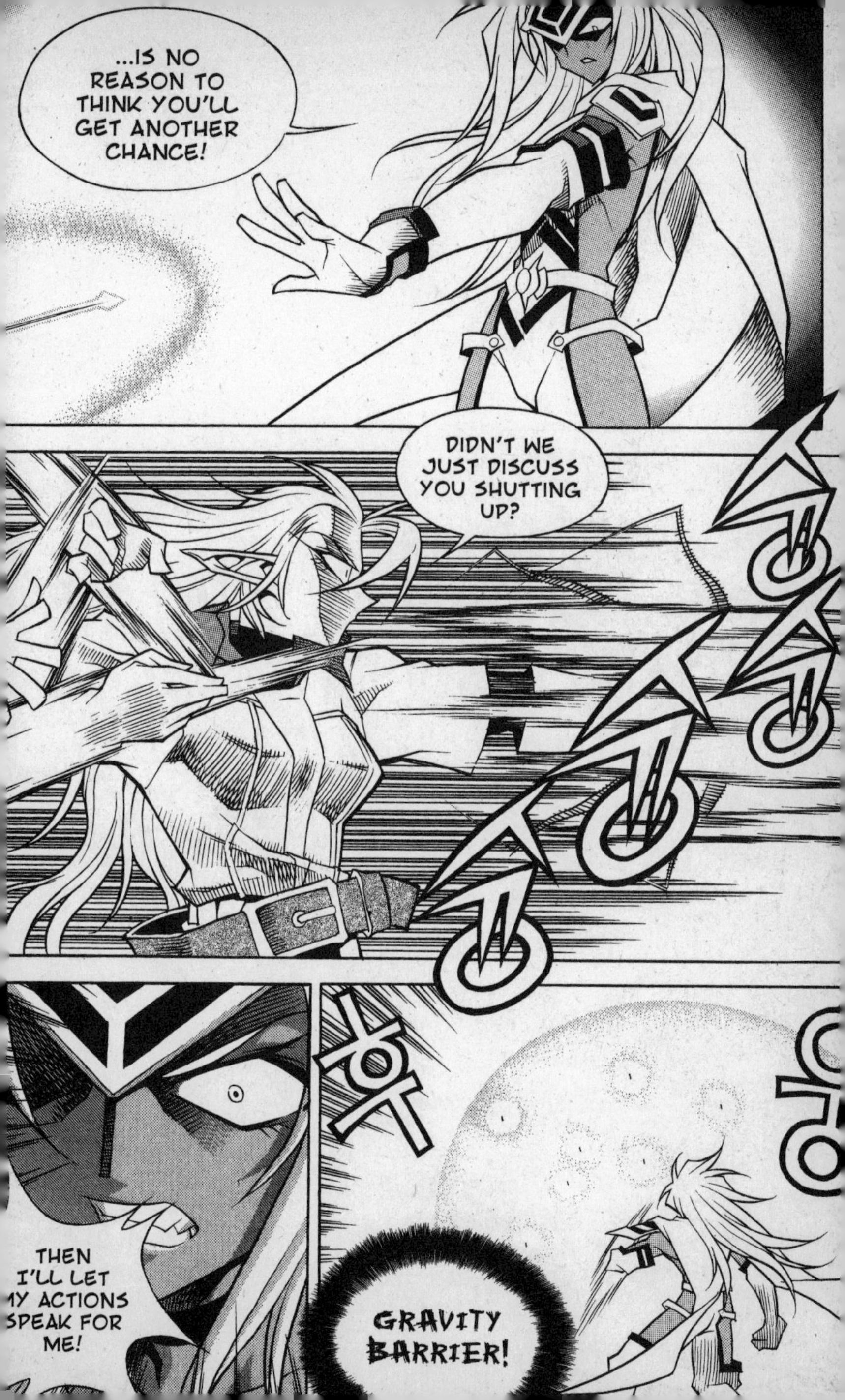
...IS NO REASON TO THINK YOU'LL GET ANOTHER CHANCE!
DIDN'T WE JUST DISCUSS YOU SHUTTING UP?
THEN I'LL LET MY ACTIONS SPEAK FOR ME!
GRAVITY BARRIER!

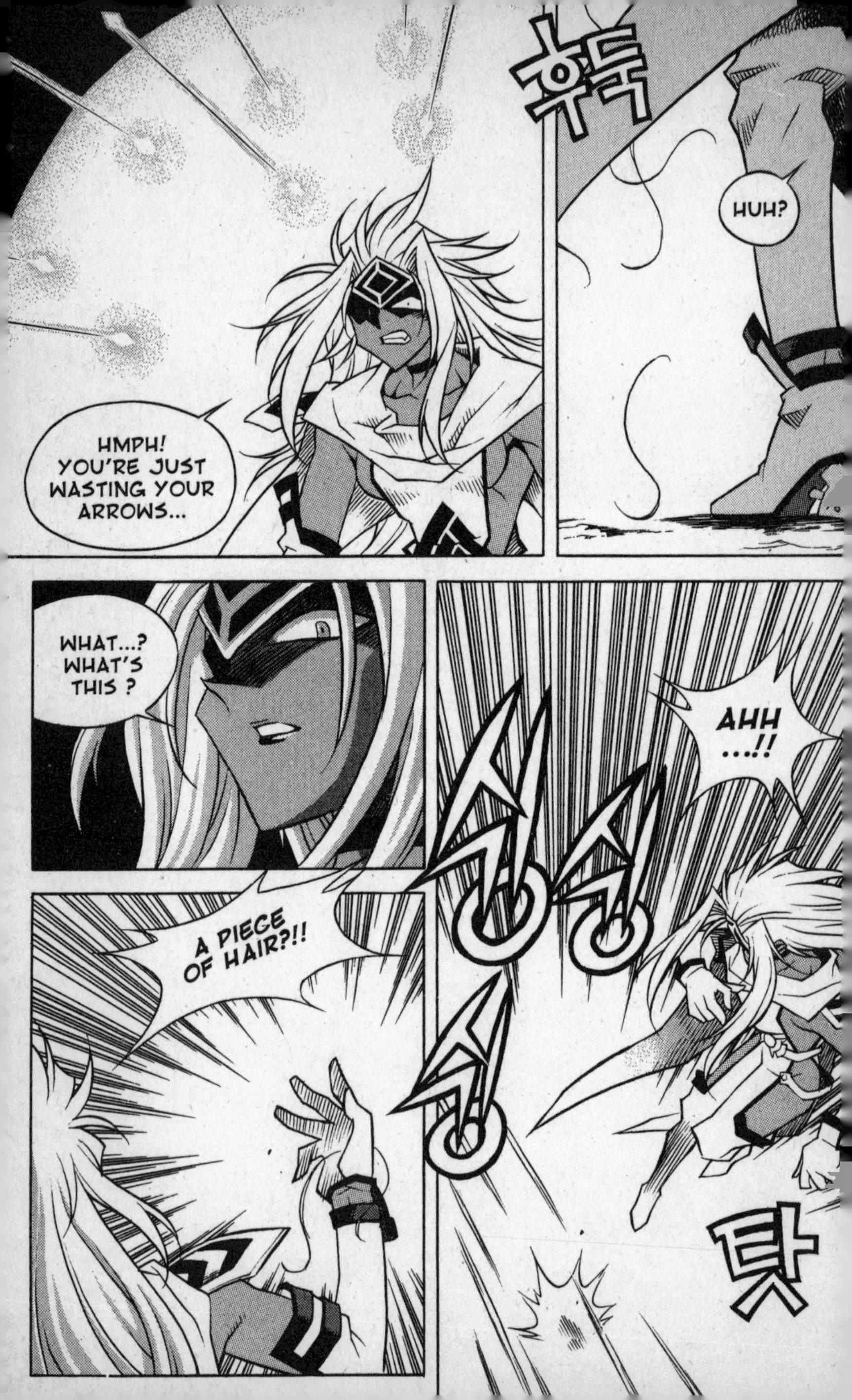
HMPH! YOU'RE JUST WASTING YOUR ARROWS...
후둑
HUH?
WHAT...? WHAT'S THIS ?
A PIECE OF HAIR?!!
AHH ...!!
탓

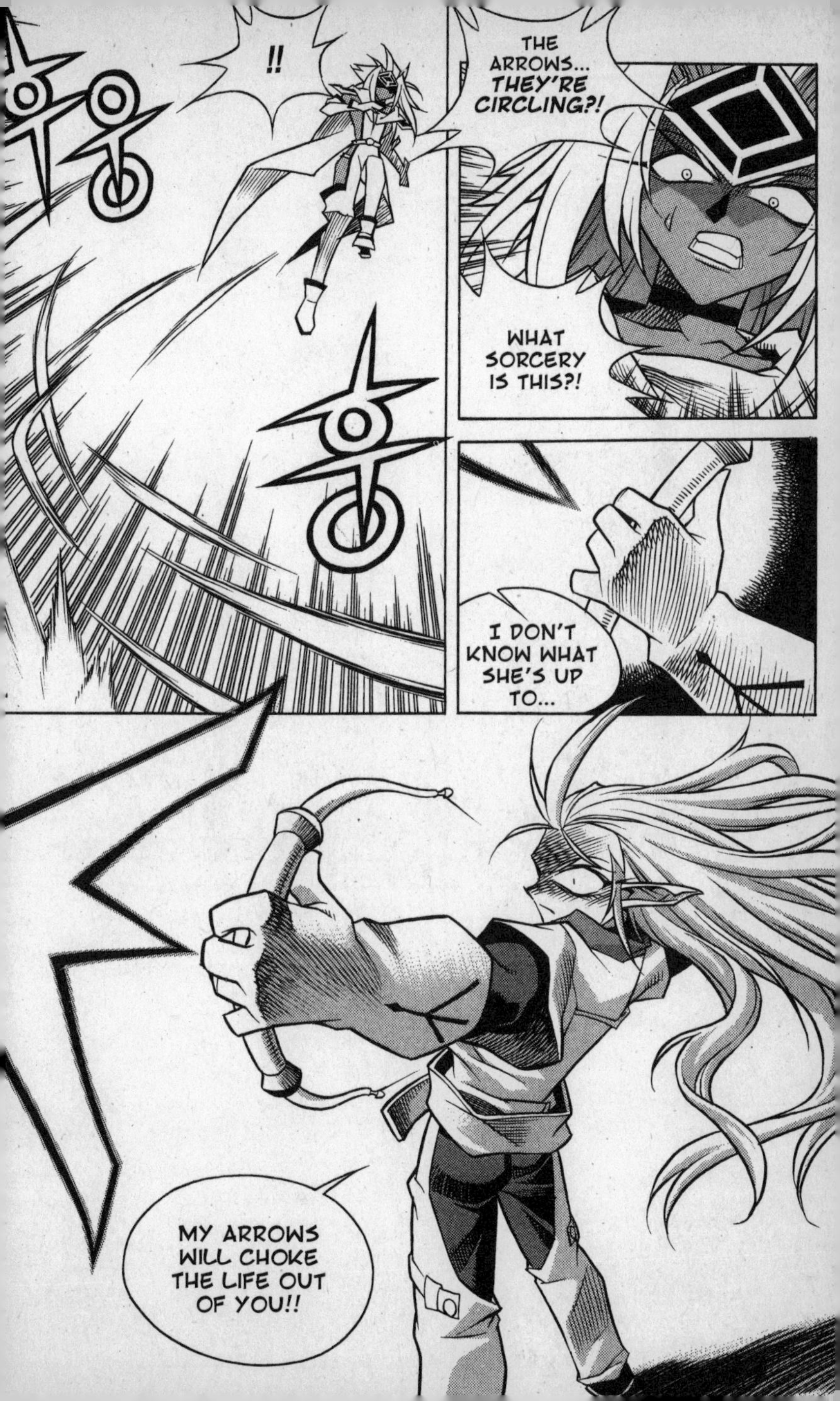
!!
THE ARROWS... THEY'RE CIRCLING?!
WHAT SORCERY IS THIS?!
I DON'T KNOW WHAT SHE'S UP TO...
MY ARROWS WILL CHOKE THE LIFE OUT OF YOU!!

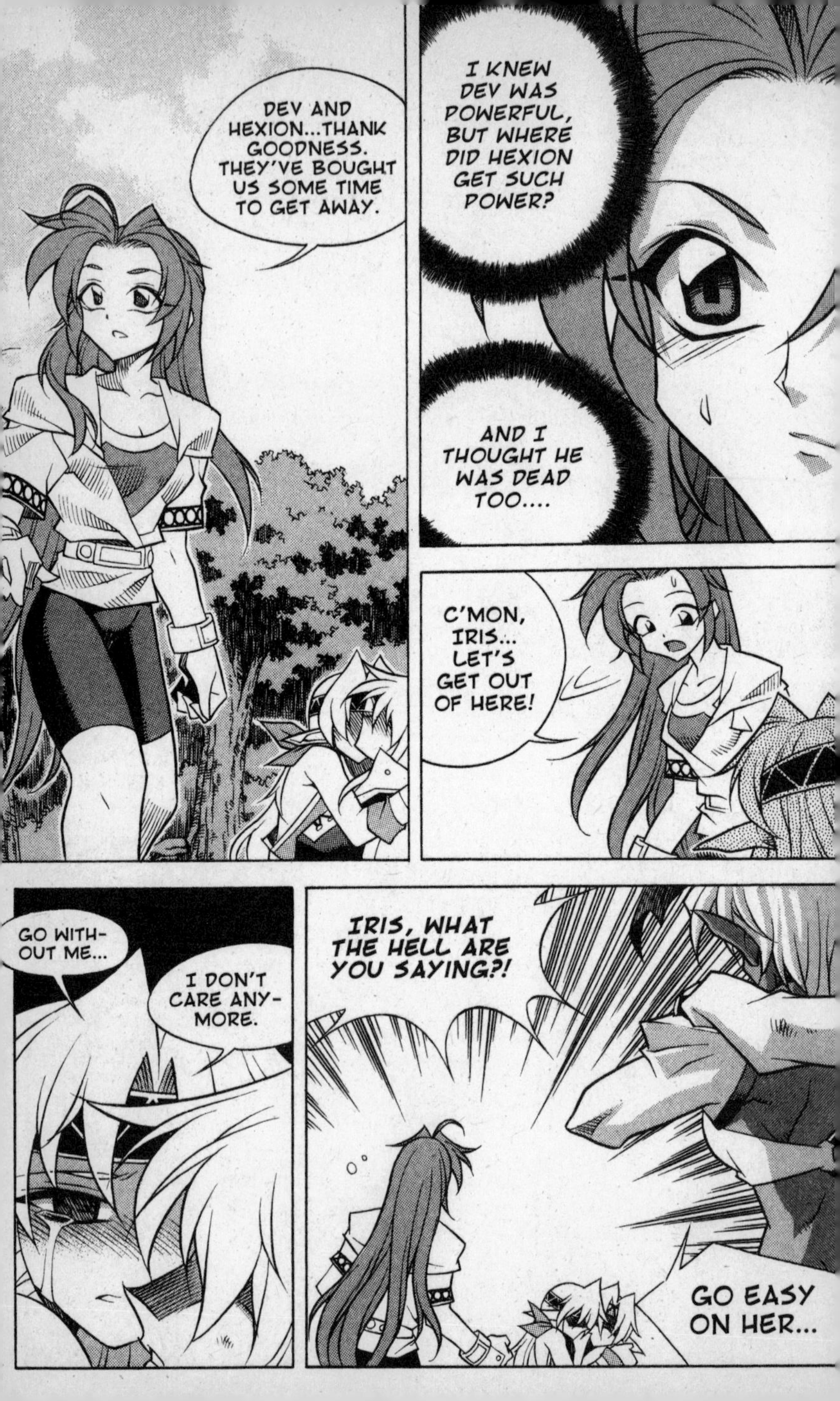
DEV AND HEXION...THANK GOODNESS. THEY'VE BOUGHT US SOME TIME TO GET AWAY.
I KNEW DEV WAS POWERFUL, BUT WHERE DID HEXION GET SUCH POWER?
AND I THOUGHT HE WAS DEAD TOO....
C'MON, IRIS... LET'S GET OUT OF HERE!
GO WITH-OUT ME...
I DON'T CARE ANY-MORE.
IRIS, WHAT THE HELL ARE YOU SAYING?!
GO EASY ON HER...

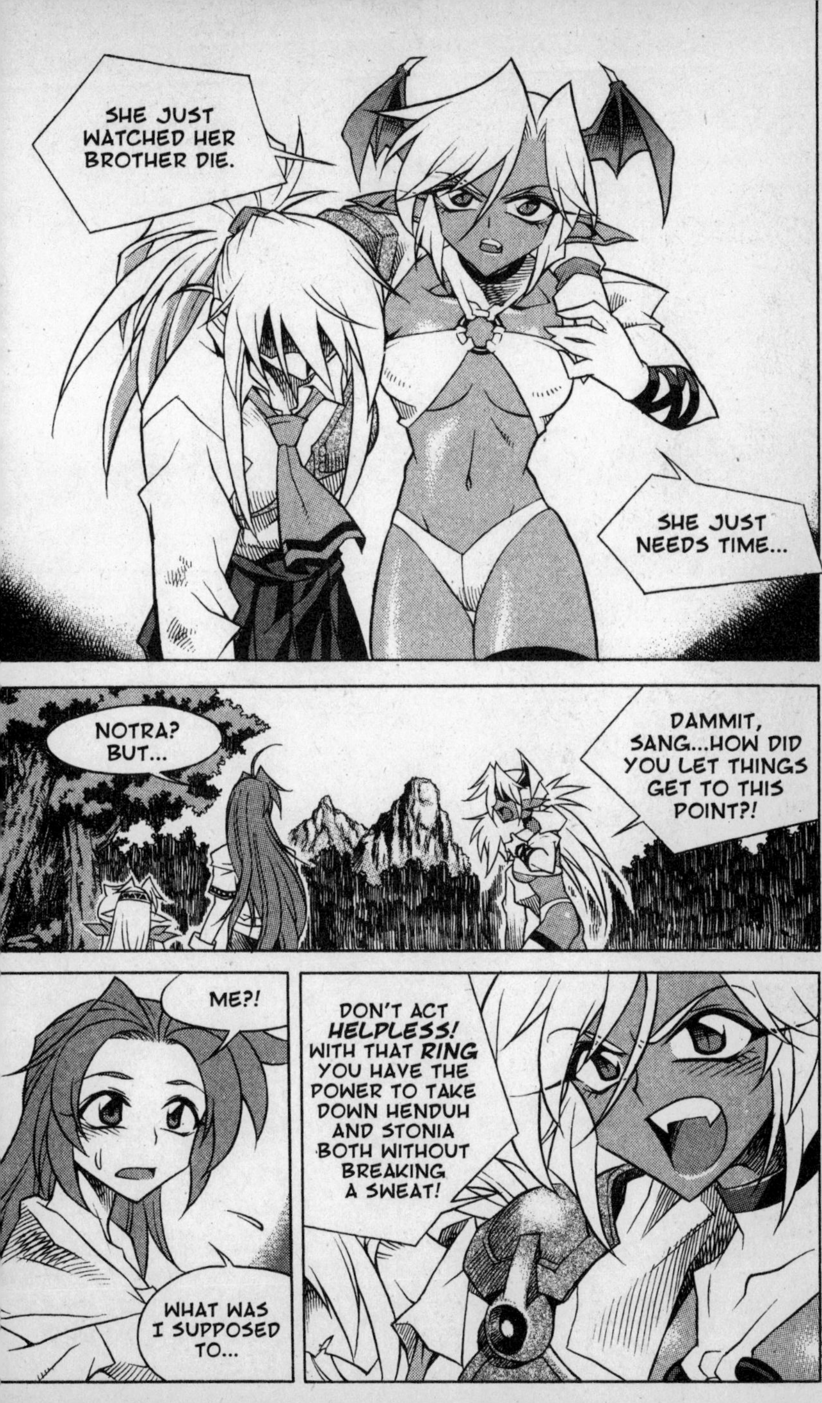
SHE JUST WATCHED HER BROTHER DIE.
SHE JUST NEEDS TIME...
NOTRA? BUT...
DAMMIT, SANG...HOW DID YOU LET THINGS GET TO THIS POINT?!
ME?!
WHAT WAS I SUPPOSED TO...
DON'T ACT *HELPLESS!* WITH THAT *RING* YOU HAVE THE POWER TO TAKE DOWN HENDUH AND STONIA BOTH WITHOUT BREAKING A SWEAT!

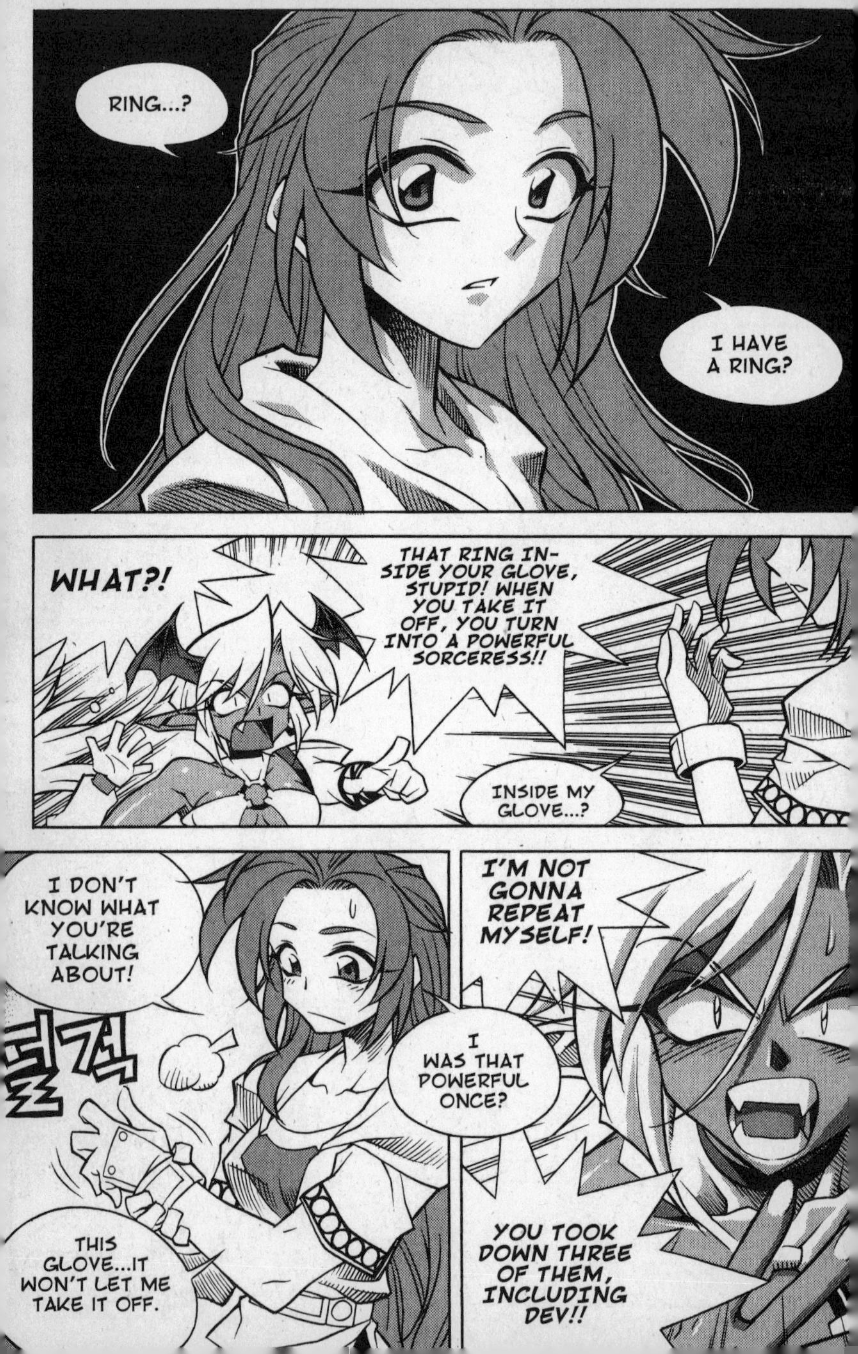
RING...?
I HAVE A RING?
WHAT?!
THAT RING IN-SIDE YOUR GLOVE, STUPID! WHEN YOU TAKE IT OFF, YOU TURN INTO A POWERFUL SORCERESS!!
INSIDE MY GLOVE...?
I DON'T KNOW WHAT YOU'RE TALKING ABOUT!
THIS GLOVE...IT WON'T LET ME TAKE IT OFF.
I'M NOT GONNA REPEAT MYSELF!
I WAS THAT POWERFUL ONCE?
YOU TOOK DOWN THREE OF THEM, INCLUDING DEV!!

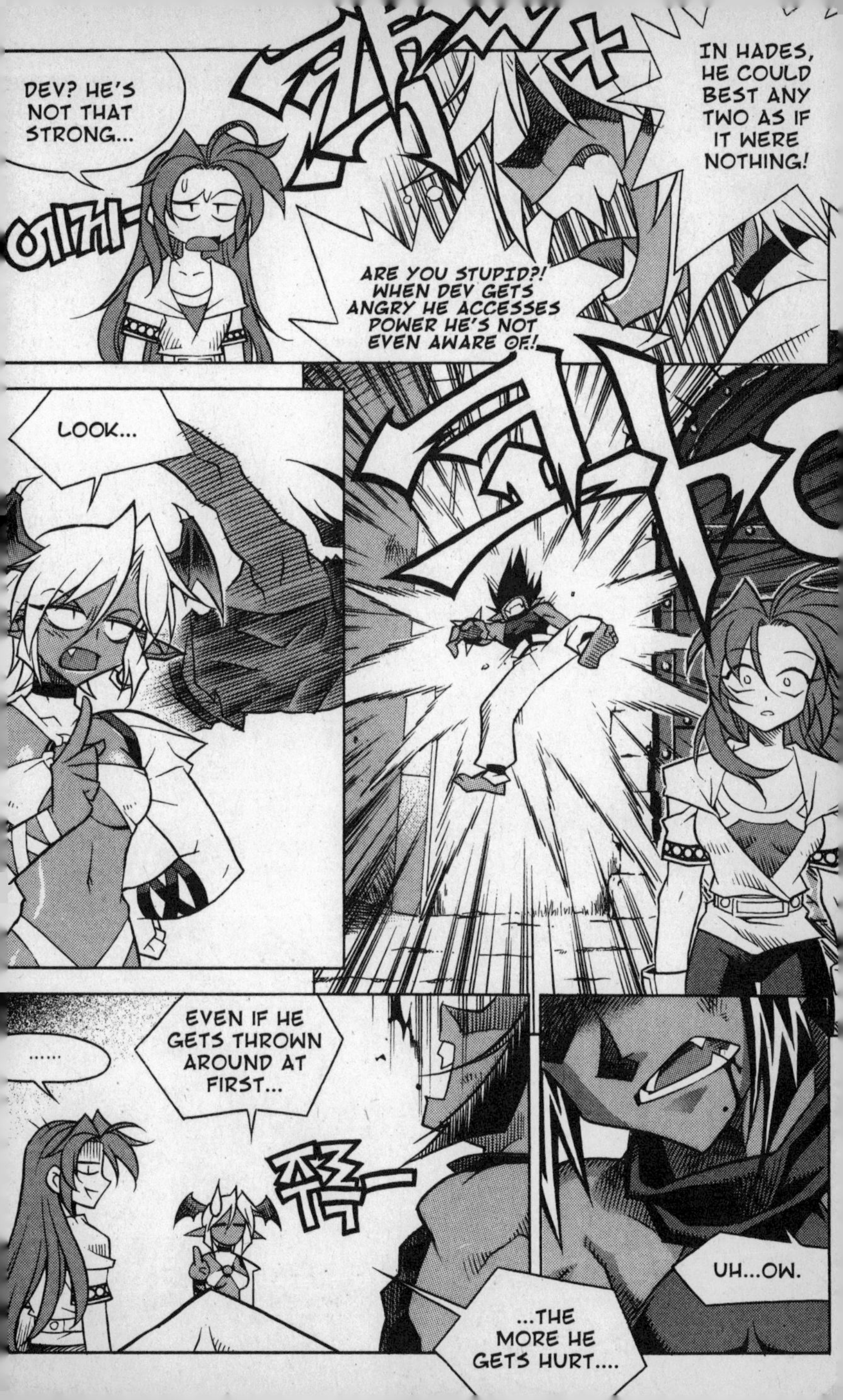
DEV? HE'S NOT THAT STRONG...
IN HADES, HE COULD BEST ANY TWO AS IF IT WERE NOTHING!
ARE YOU STUPID?! WHEN DEV GETS ANGRY HE ACCESSES POWER HE'S NOT EVEN AWARE OF!
LOOK...
......
EVEN IF HE GETS THROWN AROUND AT FIRST...
...THE MORE HE GETS HURT....
UH...OW.

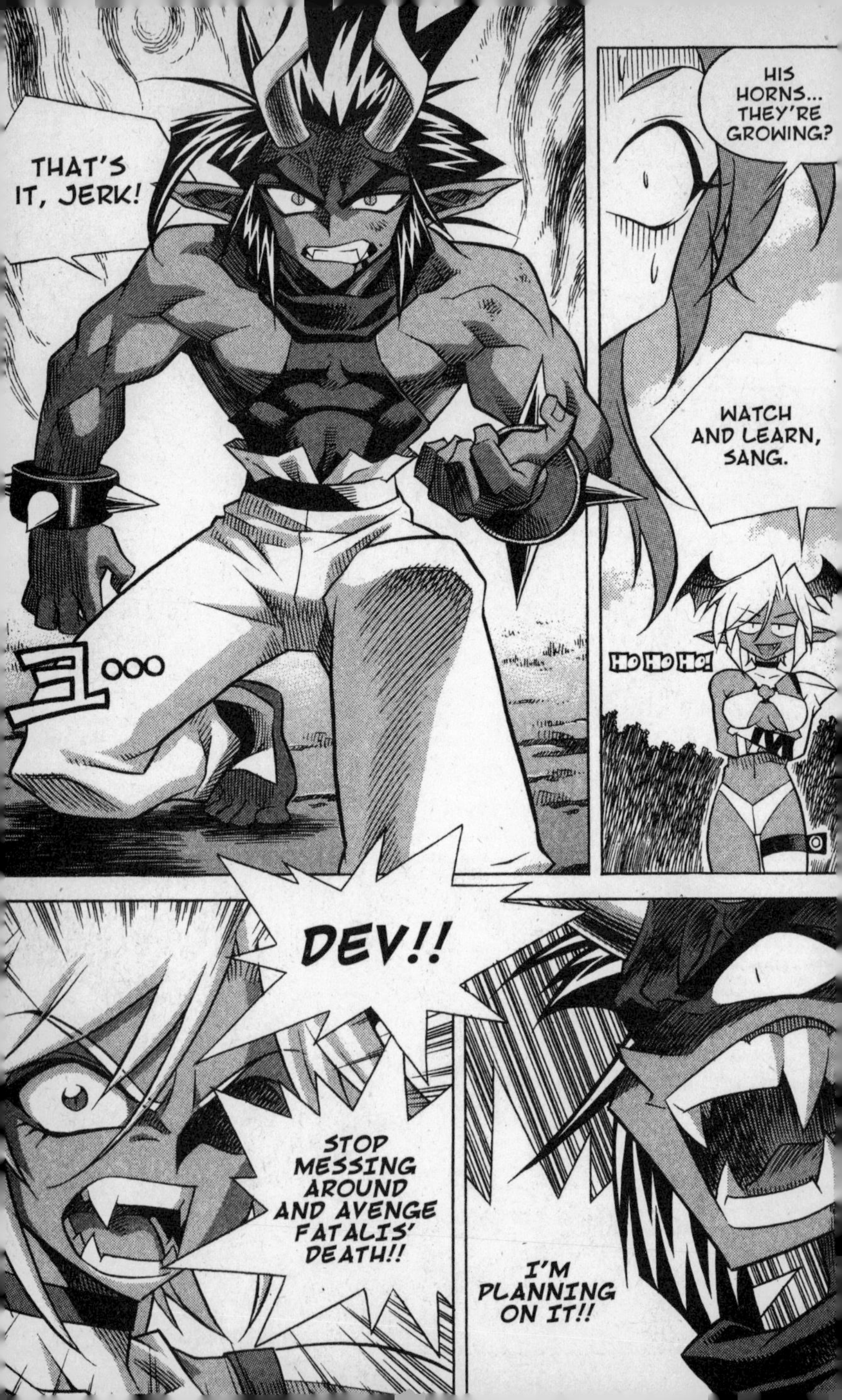
THAT'S IT, JERK!
ƎƎ...
HIS HORNS... THEY'RE GROWING?
WATCH AND LEARN, SANG.
HO HO HO!
DEV!!
STOP MESSING AROUND AND AVENGE FATALIS' DEATH!!
I'M PLANNING ON IT!!

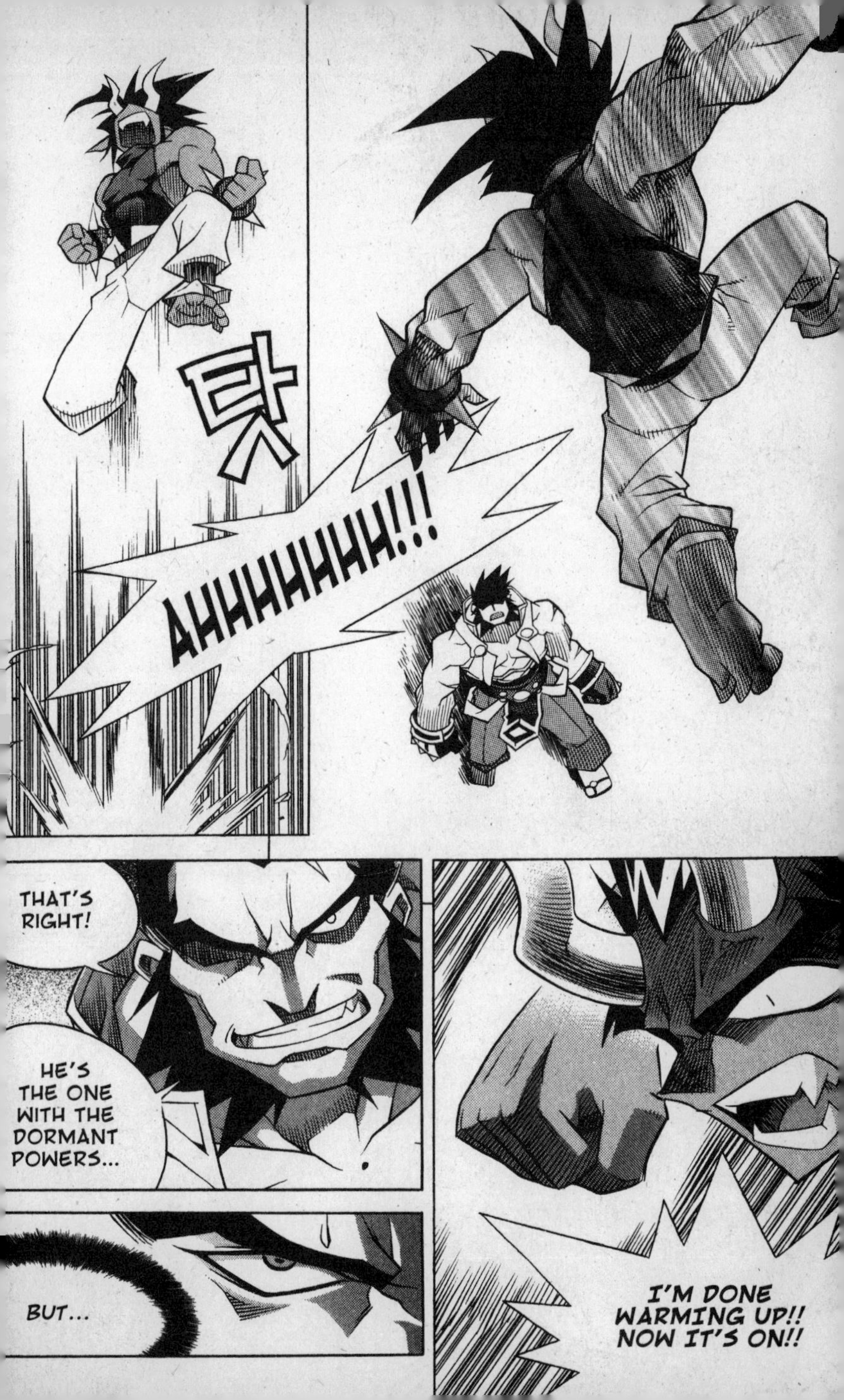
탓
AHHHHHHH!!!
THAT'S RIGHT!
HE'S THE ONE WITH THE DORMANT POWERS...
BUT...
I'M DONE WARMING UP!! NOW IT'S ON!!

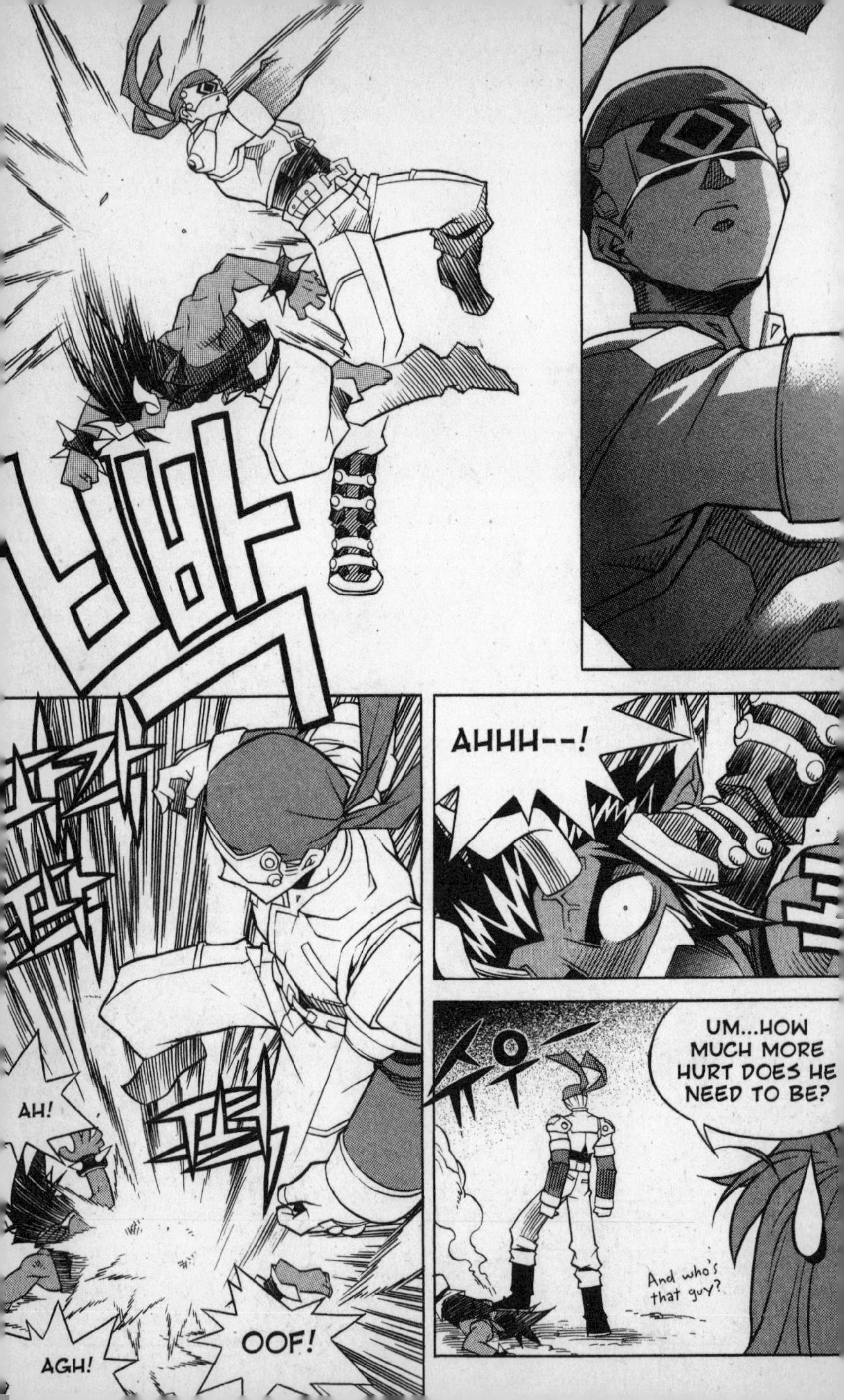
AHHH--!
AH!
AGH!
OOF!
UM...HOW MUCH MORE HURT DOES HE NEED TO BE?
And who's that guy?

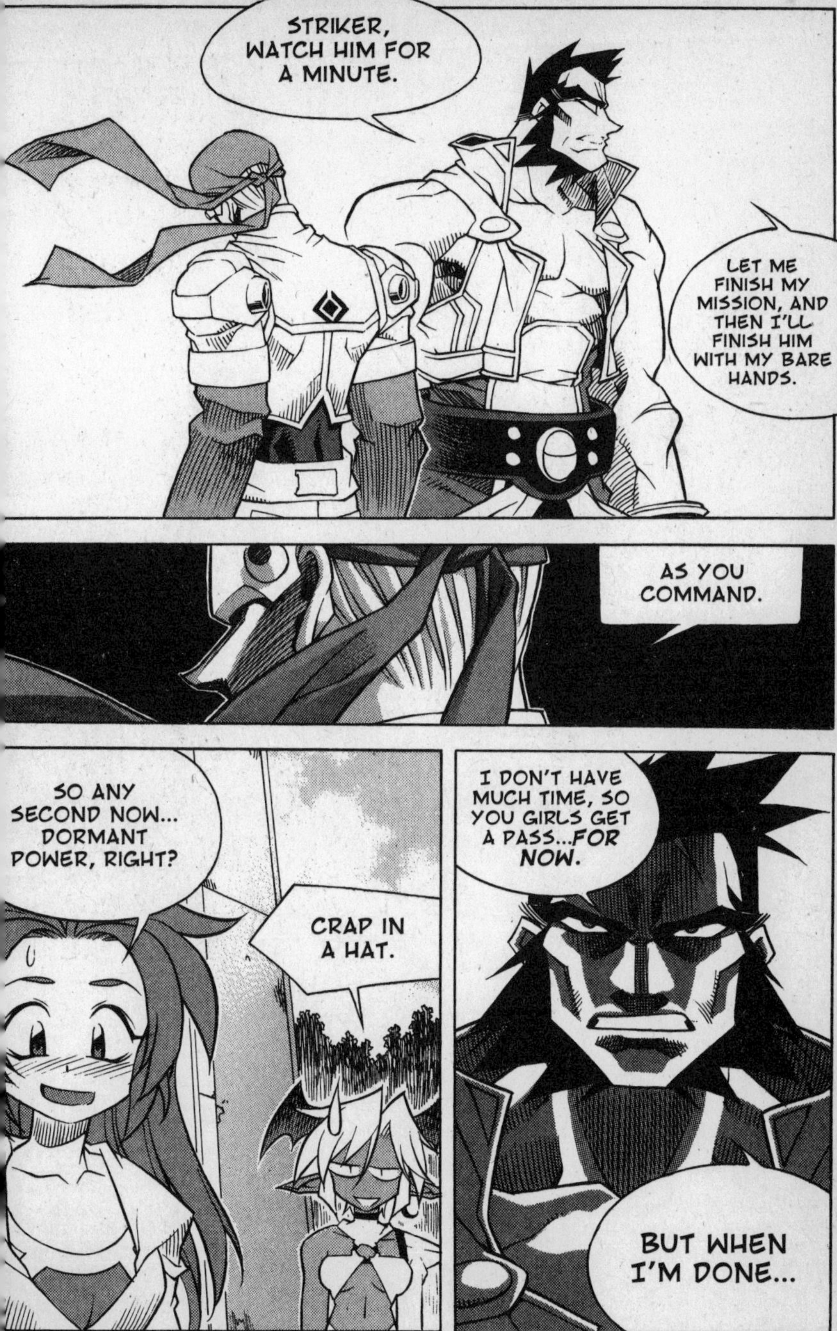
STRIKER, WATCH HIM FOR A MINUTE.
LET ME FINISH MY MISSION, AND THEN I'LL FINISH HIM WITH MY BARE HANDS.
AS YOU COMMAND.
SO ANY SECOND NOW... DORMANT POWER, RIGHT?
CRAP IN A HAT.
I DON'T HAVE MUCH TIME, SO YOU GIRLS GET A PASS...FOR NOW.
BUT WHEN I'M DONE...

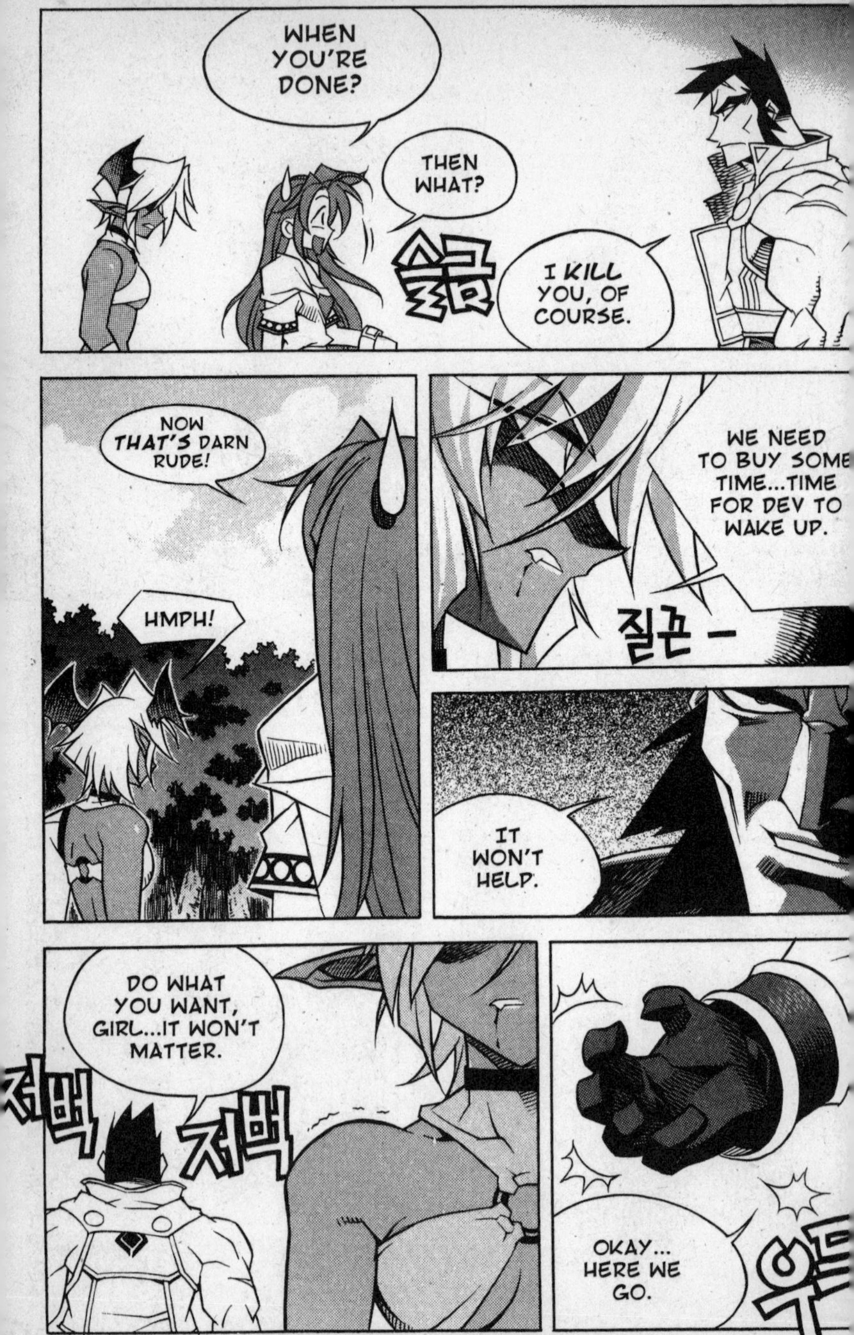
WHEN YOU'RE DONE?
THEN WHAT?
I KILL YOU, OF COURSE.
NOW THAT'S DARN RUDE!
HMPH!
WE NEED TO BUY SOME TIME...TIME FOR DEV TO WAKE UP.
질근 –
IT WON'T HELP.
DO WHAT YOU WANT, GIRL...IT WON'T MATTER.
저벅 저벅
OKAY... HERE WE GO.

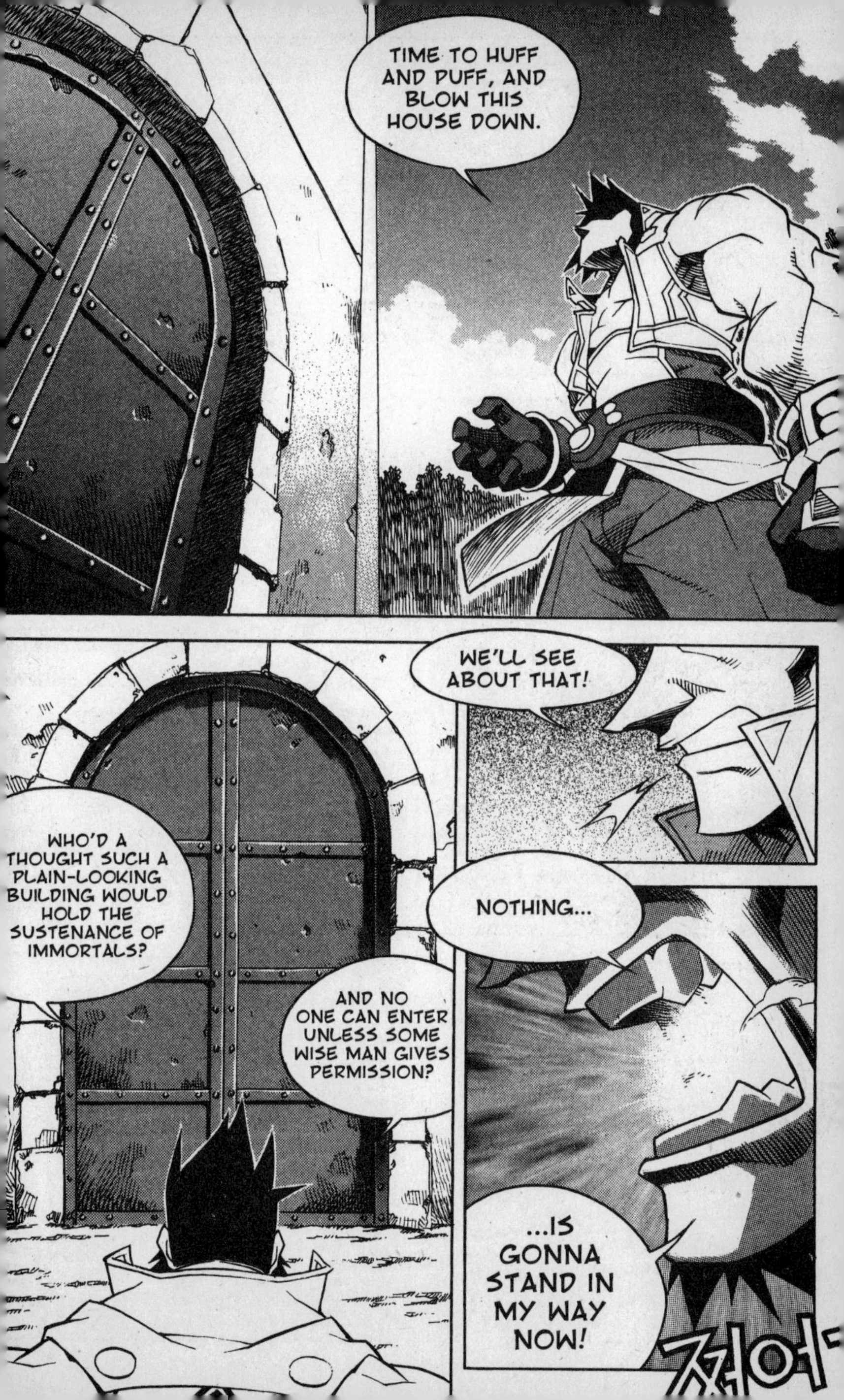
TIME TO HUFF AND PUFF, AND BLOW THIS HOUSE DOWN.
WHO'D A THOUGHT SUCH A PLAIN-LOOKING BUILDING WOULD HOLD THE SUSTENANCE OF IMMORTALS?
AND NO ONE CAN ENTER UNLESS SOME WISE MAN GIVES PERMISSION?
WE'LL SEE ABOUT THAT!
NOTHING...
...IS GONNA STAND IN MY WAY NOW!

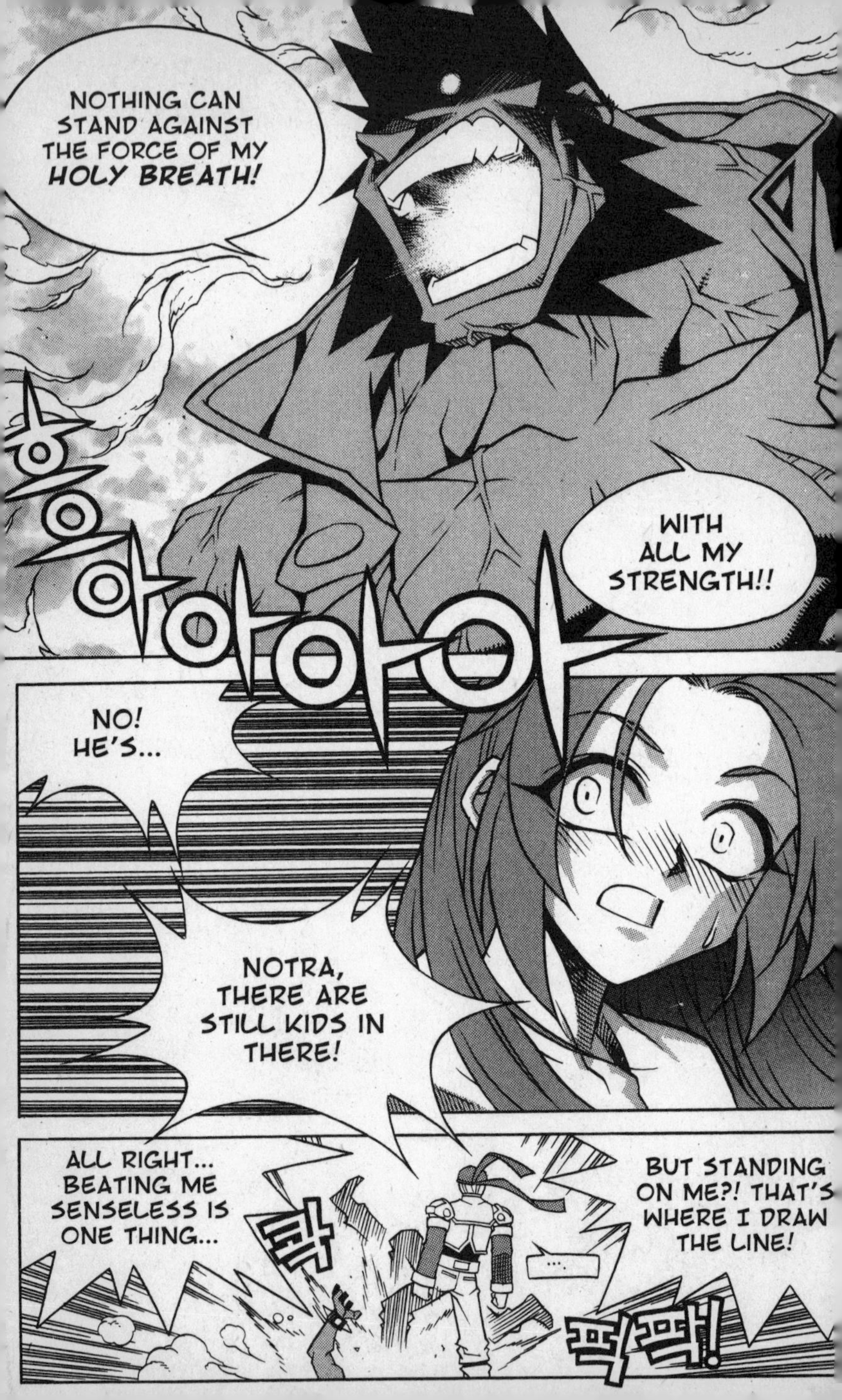
NOTHING CAN STAND AGAINST THE FORCE OF MY HOLY BREATH!
WITH ALL MY STRENGTH!!
NO! HE'S...
NOTRA, THERE ARE STILL KIDS IN THERE!
ALL RIGHT... BEATING ME SENSELESS IS ONE THING...
BUT STANDING ON ME?! THAT'S WHERE I DRAW THE LINE!
....

Quest 70

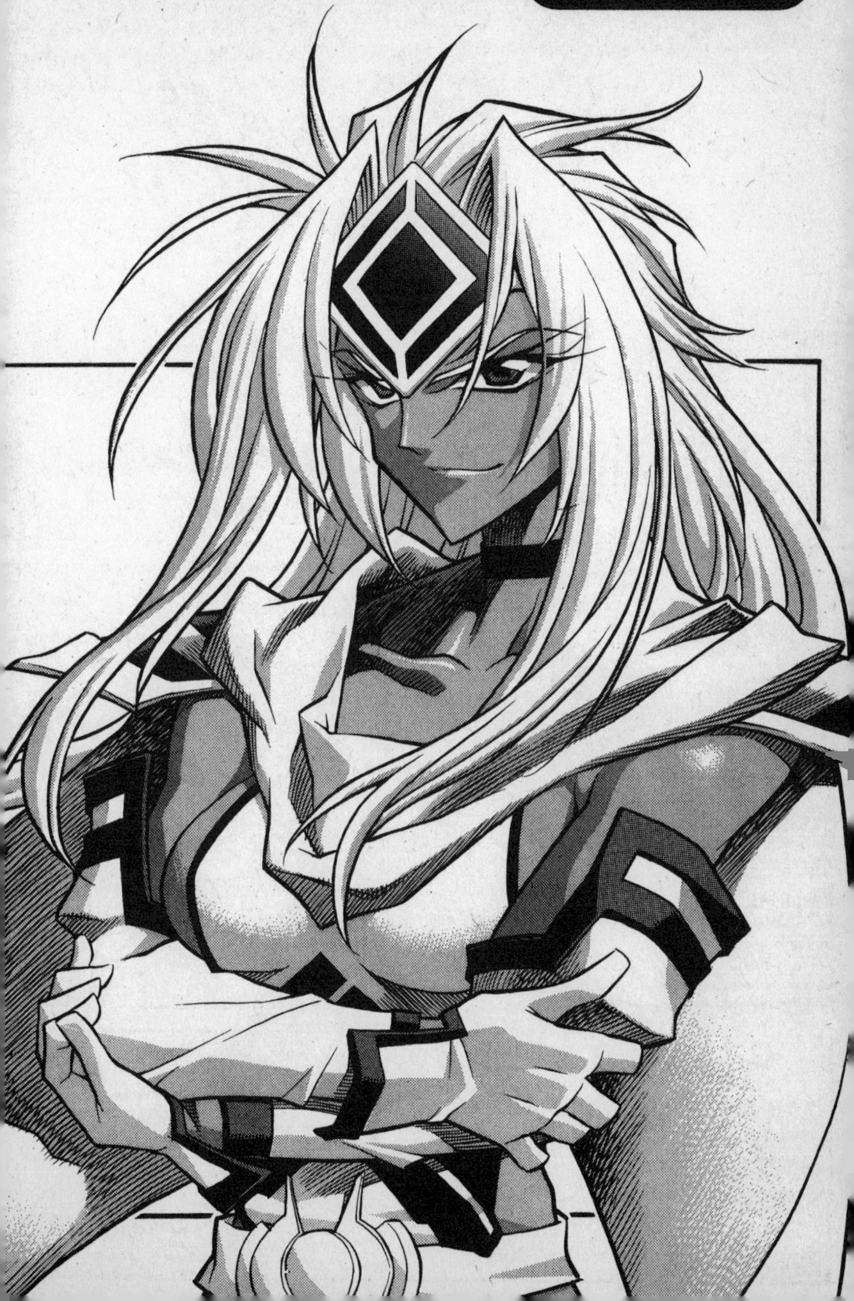

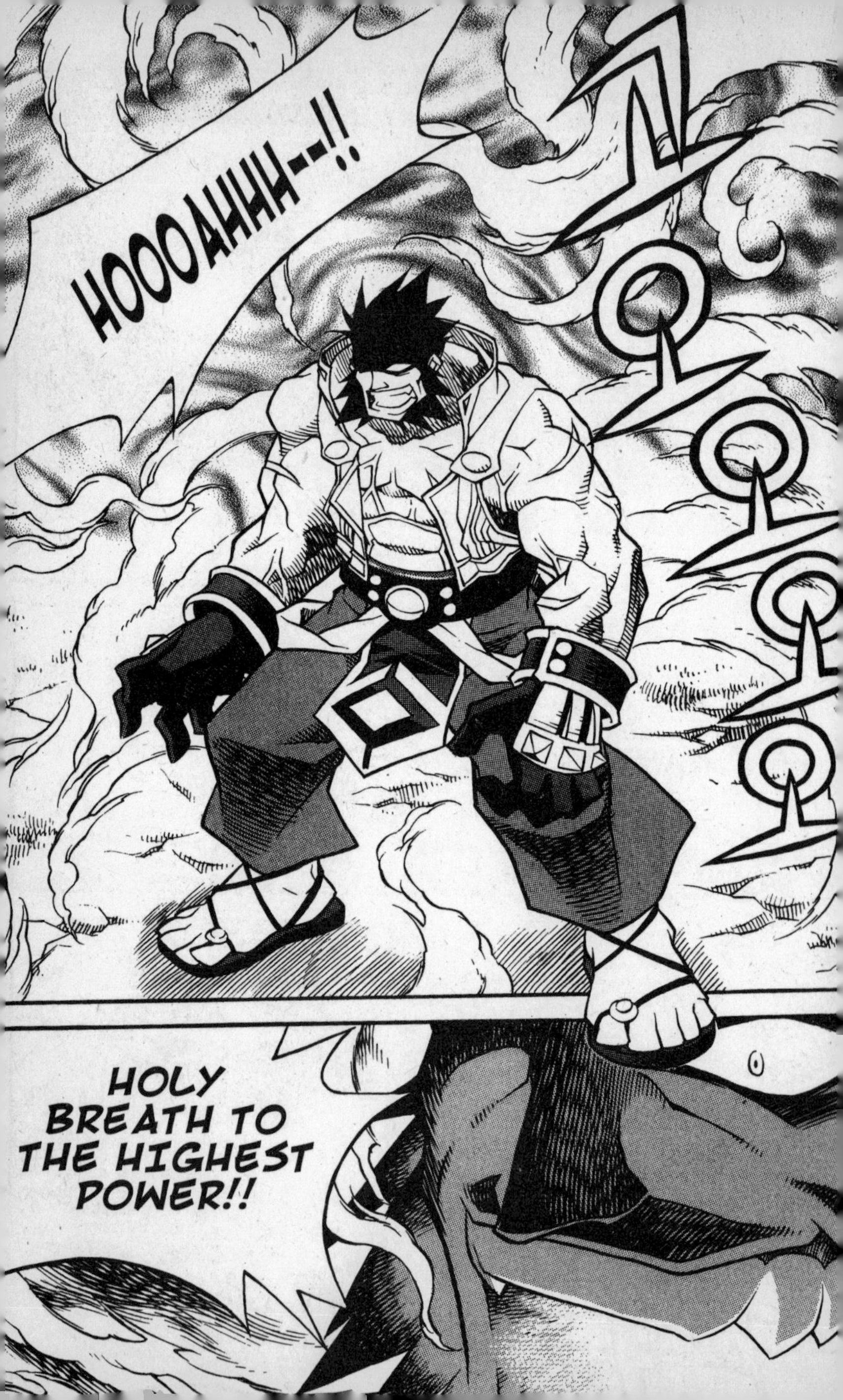
HOOOAHHH--!!
HOLY BREATH TO THE HIGHEST POWER!!

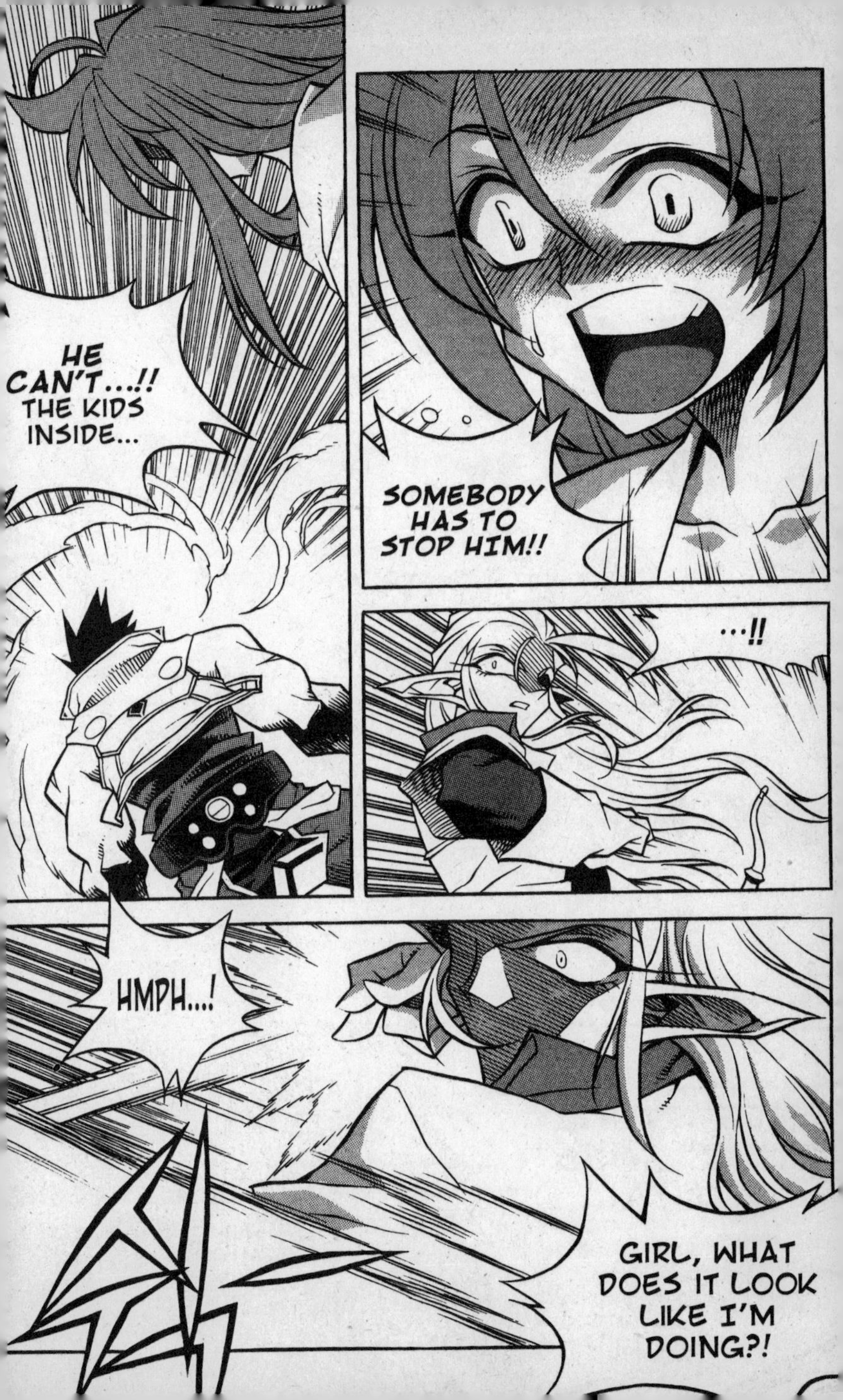
HE CAN'T...!! THE KIDS INSIDE...
SOMEBODY HAS TO STOP HIM!!
...!!
HMPH...!
GIRL, WHAT DOES IT LOOK LIKE I'M DOING?!

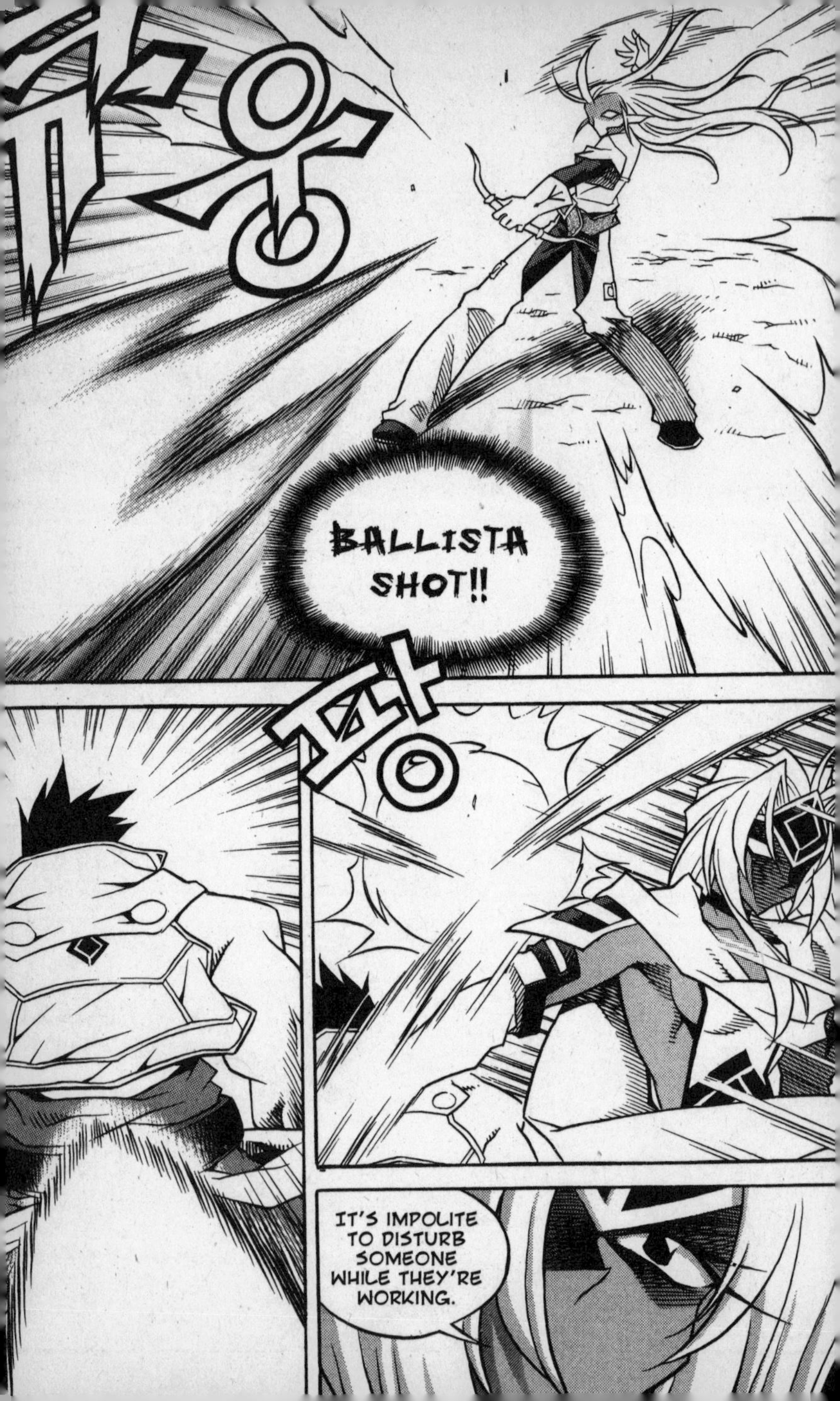
BALLISTA SHOT!!
IT'S IMPOLITE TO DISTURB SOMEONE WHILE THEY'RE WORKING.

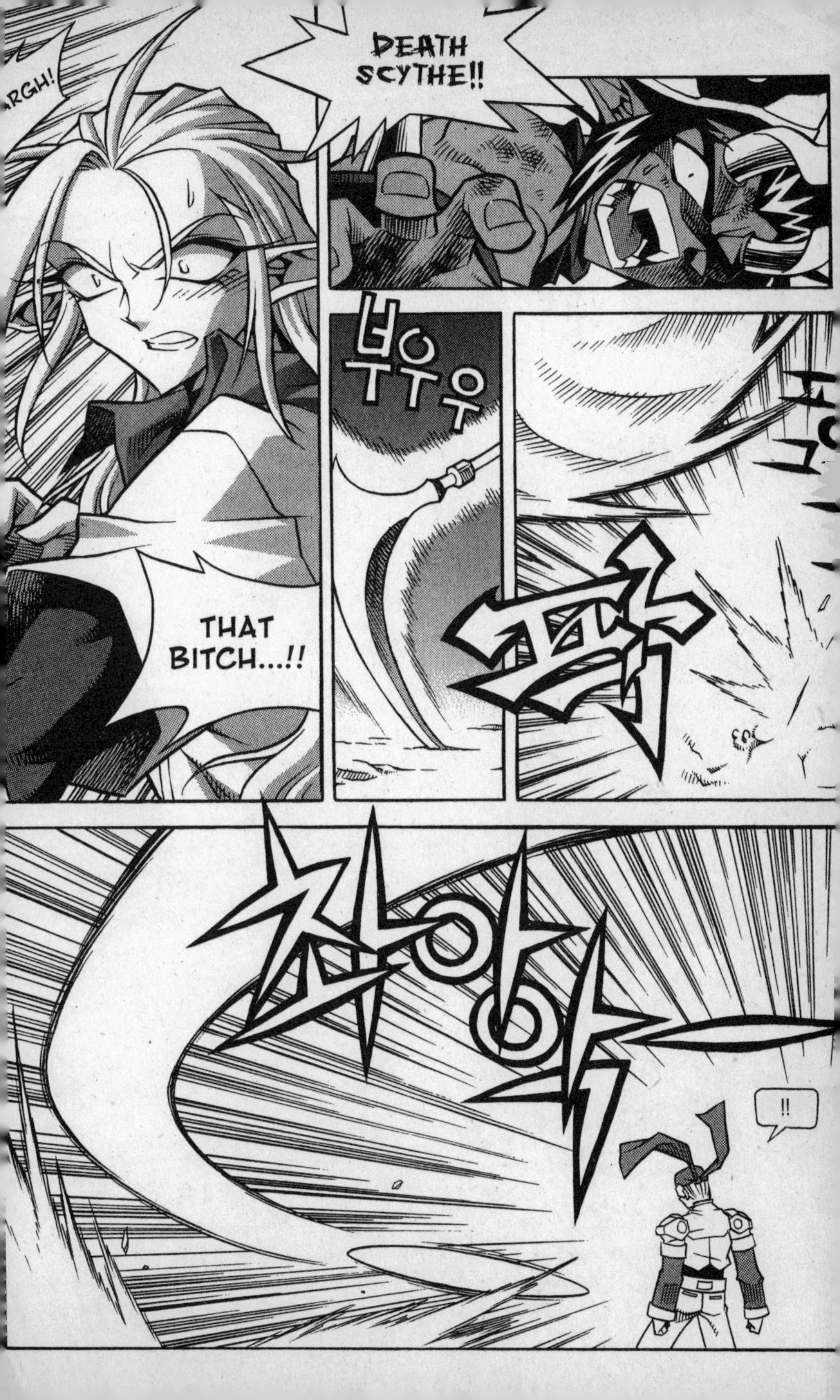
ARGH!
THAT BITCH...!!
DEATH SCYTHE!!
!!

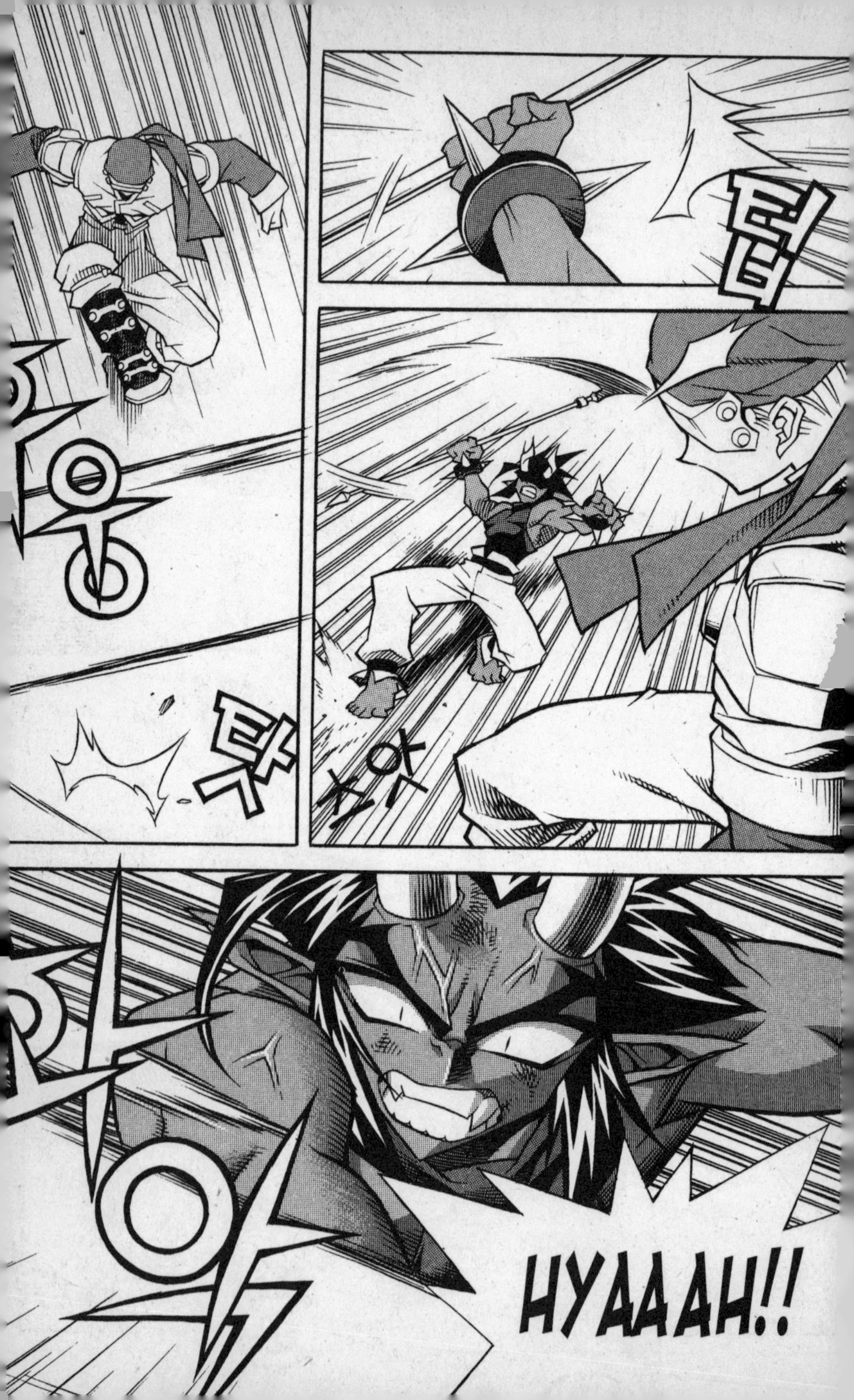
텁
탁
HYAAAH!!

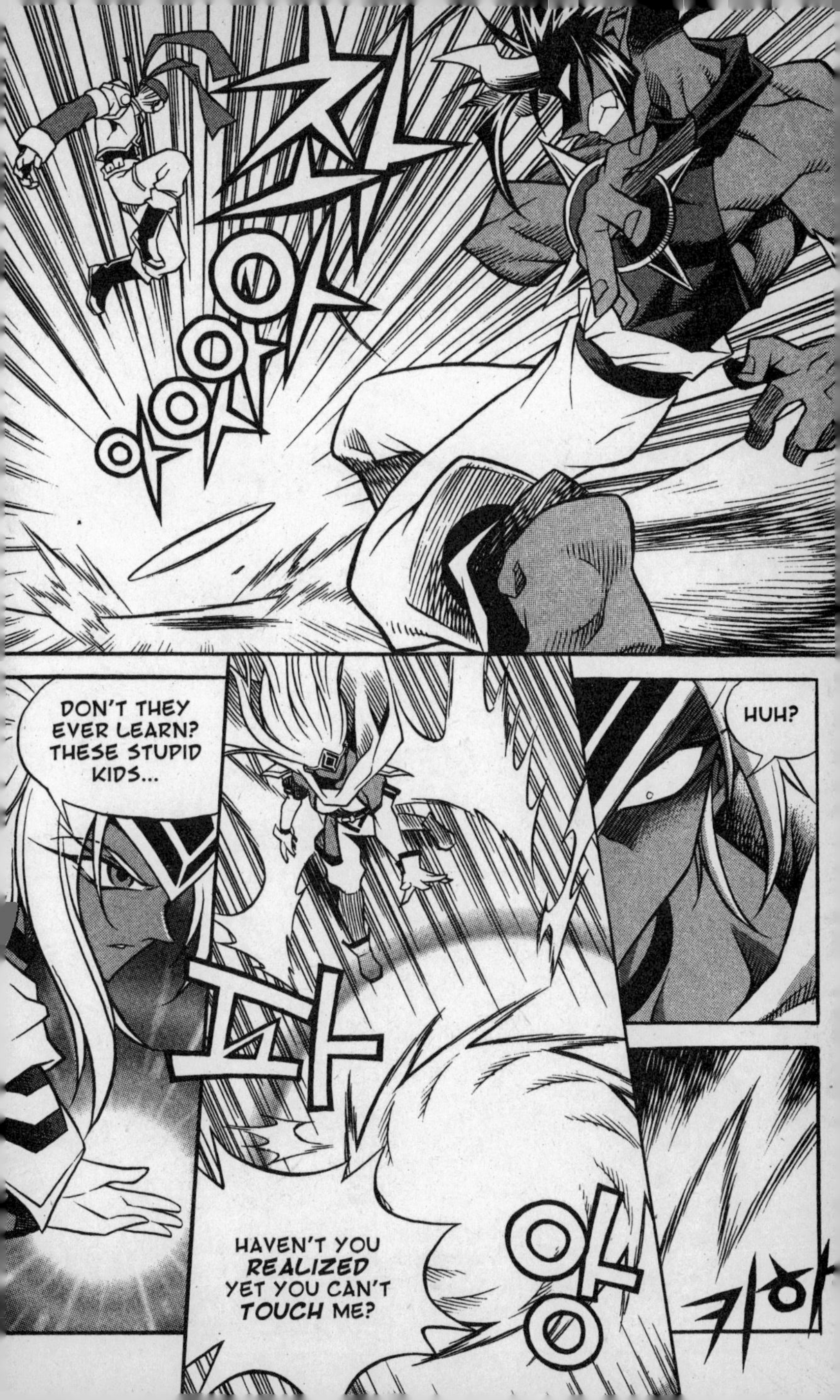
DON'T THEY EVER LEARN? THESE STUPID KIDS...
HAVEN'T YOU *REALIZED* YET YOU CAN'T *TOUCH* ME?
HUH?

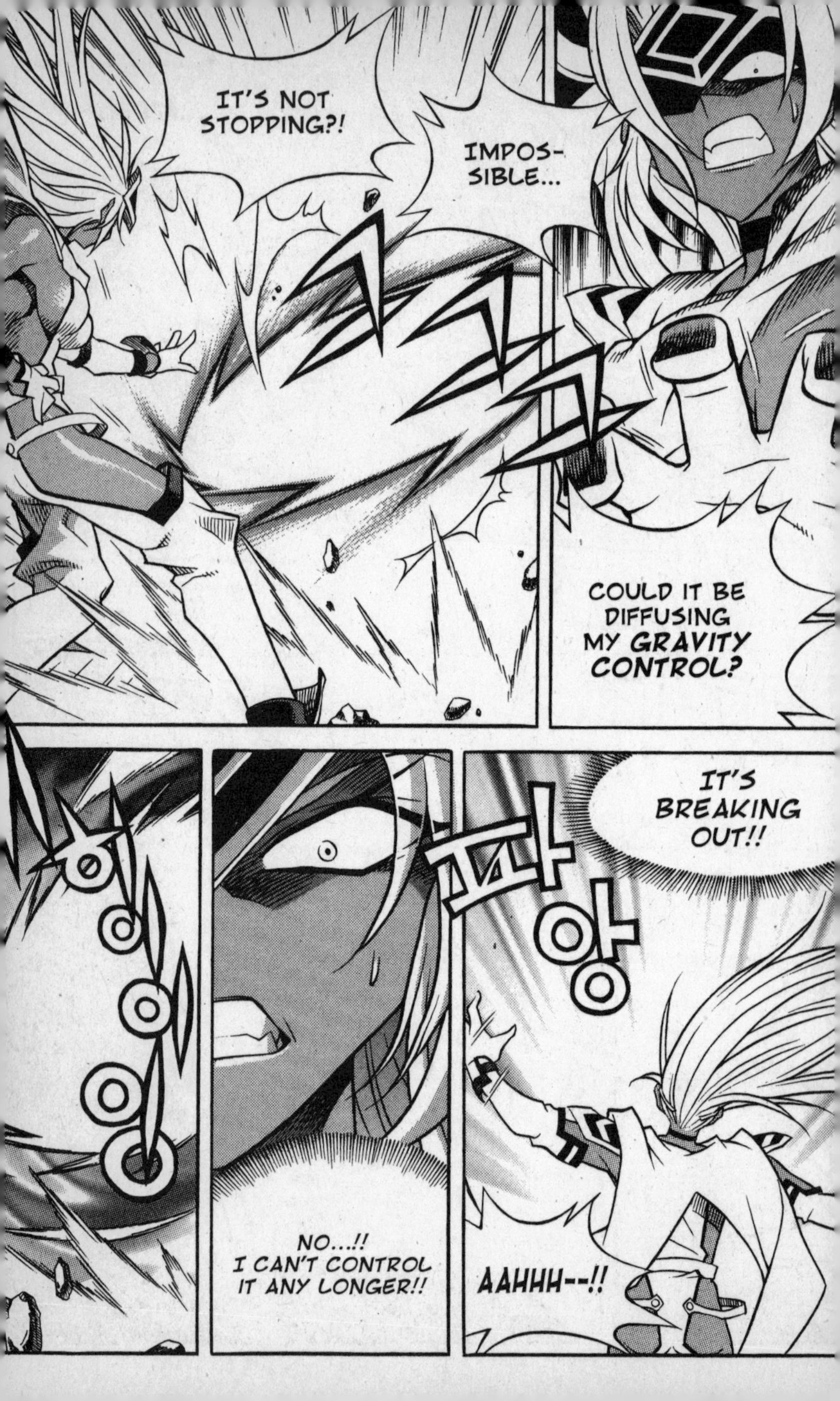
IT'S NOT STOPPING?!
IMPOS-SIBLE...
COULD IT BE DIFFUSING MY GRAVITY CONTROL?
NO...!! I CAN'T CONTROL IT ANY LONGER!!
IT'S BREAKING OUT!!
파앙
AAHHH--!!

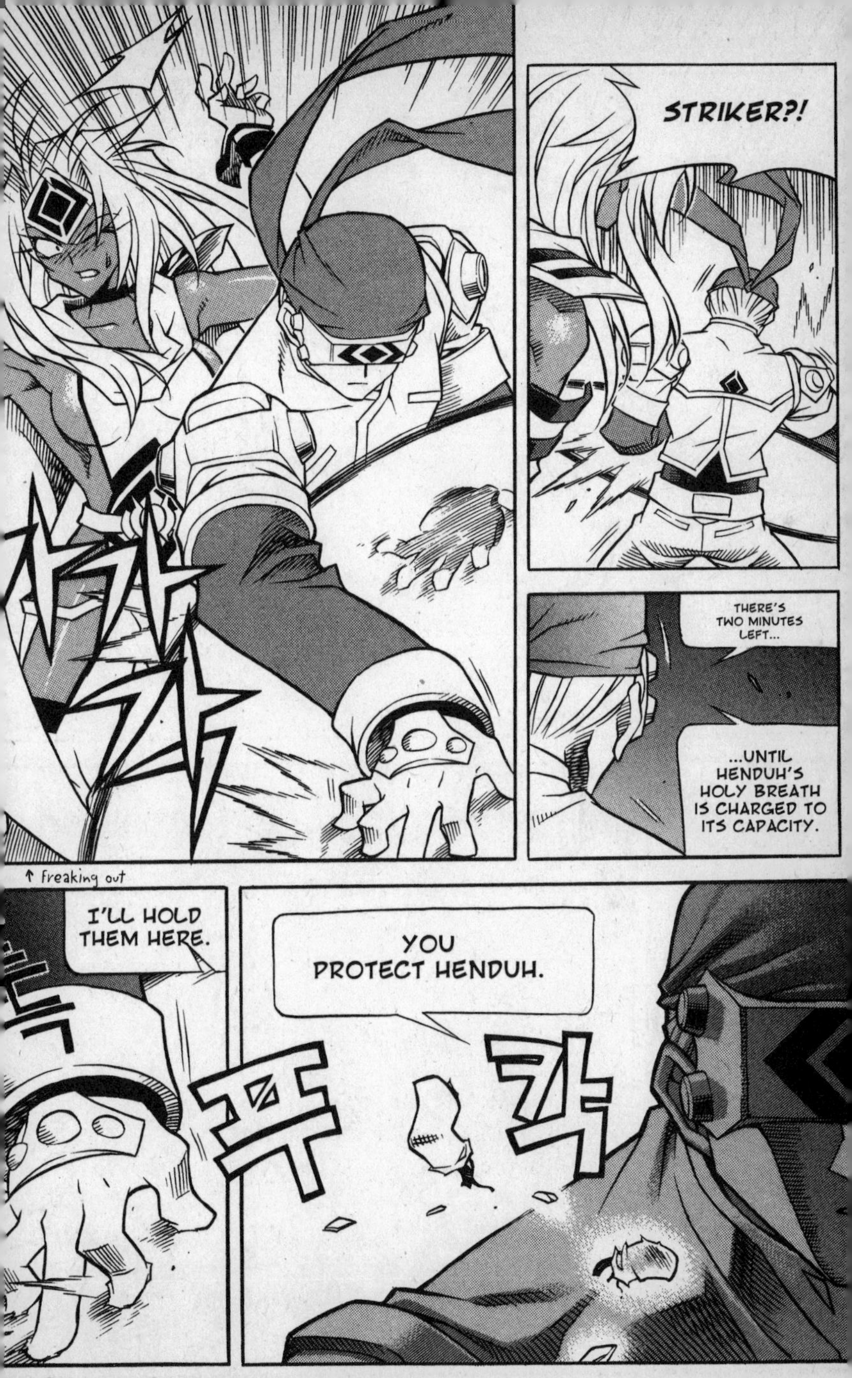
STRIKER?!
THERE'S TWO MINUTES LEFT...
...UNTIL HENDUH'S HOLY BREATH IS CHARGED TO ITS CAPACITY.
↑ freaking out
I'LL HOLD THEM HERE.
YOU PROTECT HENDUH.
푸칵

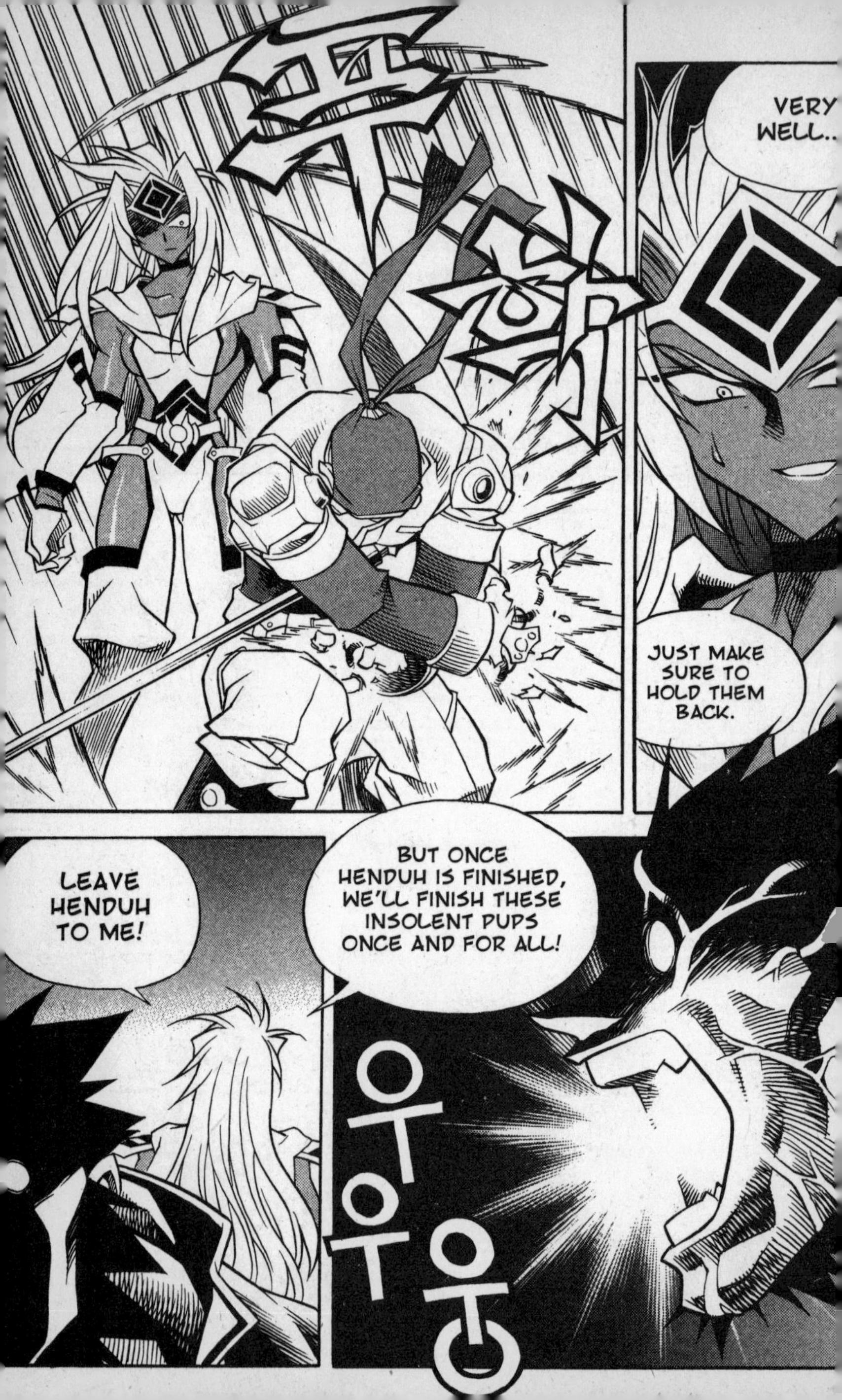
VERY WELL..
JUST MAKE SURE TO HOLD THEM BACK.
LEAVE HENDUH TO ME!
BUT ONCE HENDUH IS FINISHED, WE'LL FINISH THESE INSOLENT PUPS ONCE AND FOR ALL!

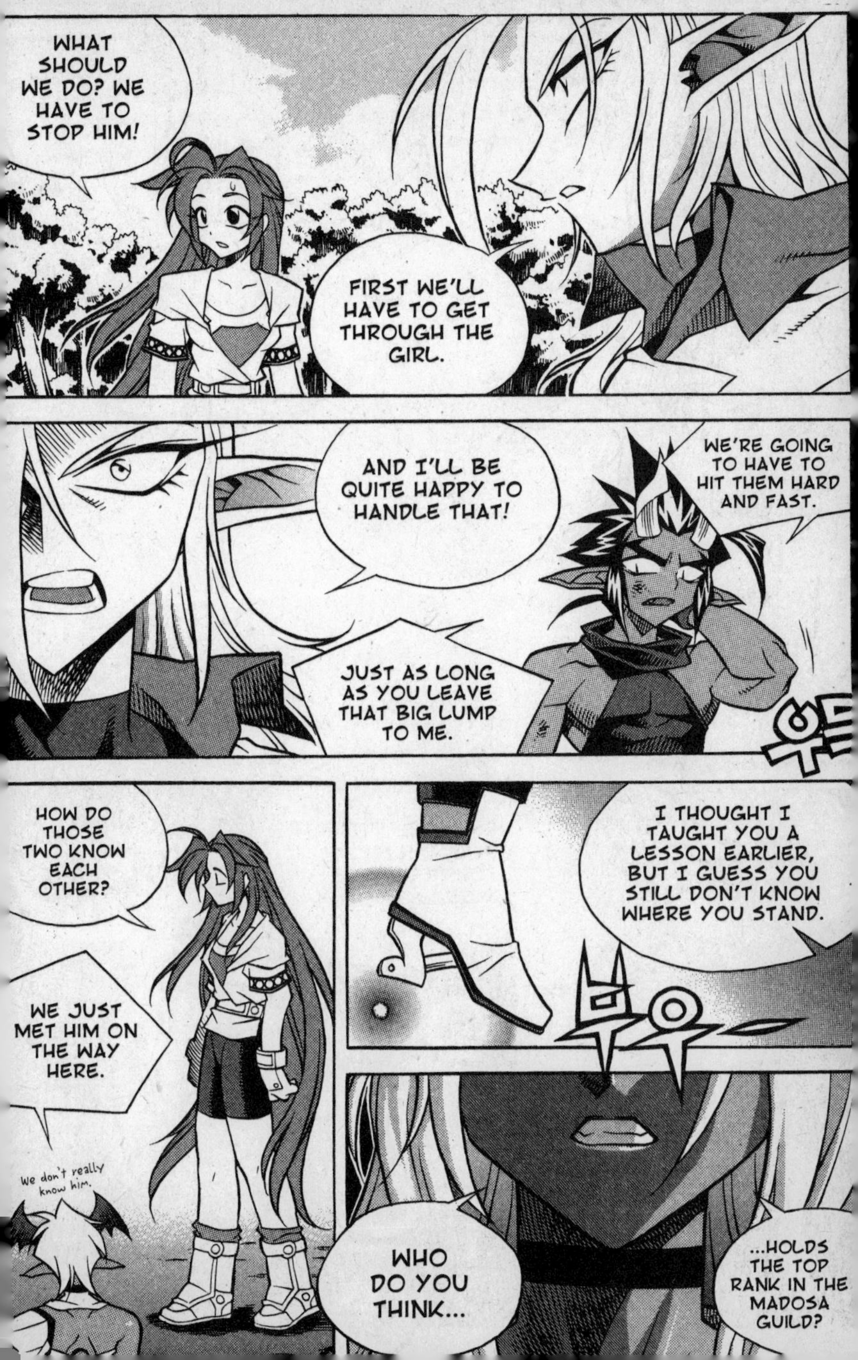
WHAT SHOULD WE DO? WE HAVE TO STOP HIM!
FIRST WE'LL HAVE TO GET THROUGH THE GIRL.
AND I'LL BE QUITE HAPPY TO HANDLE THAT!
WE'RE GOING TO HAVE TO HIT THEM HARD AND FAST.
JUST AS LONG AS YOU LEAVE THAT BIG LUMP TO ME.
HOW DO THOSE TWO KNOW EACH OTHER?
WE JUST MET HIM ON THE WAY HERE.
We don't really know him.
I THOUGHT I TAUGHT YOU A LESSON EARLIER, BUT I GUESS YOU STILL DON'T KNOW WHERE YOU STAND.
WHO DO YOU THINK...
...HOLDS THE TOP RANK IN THE MADOSA GUILD?

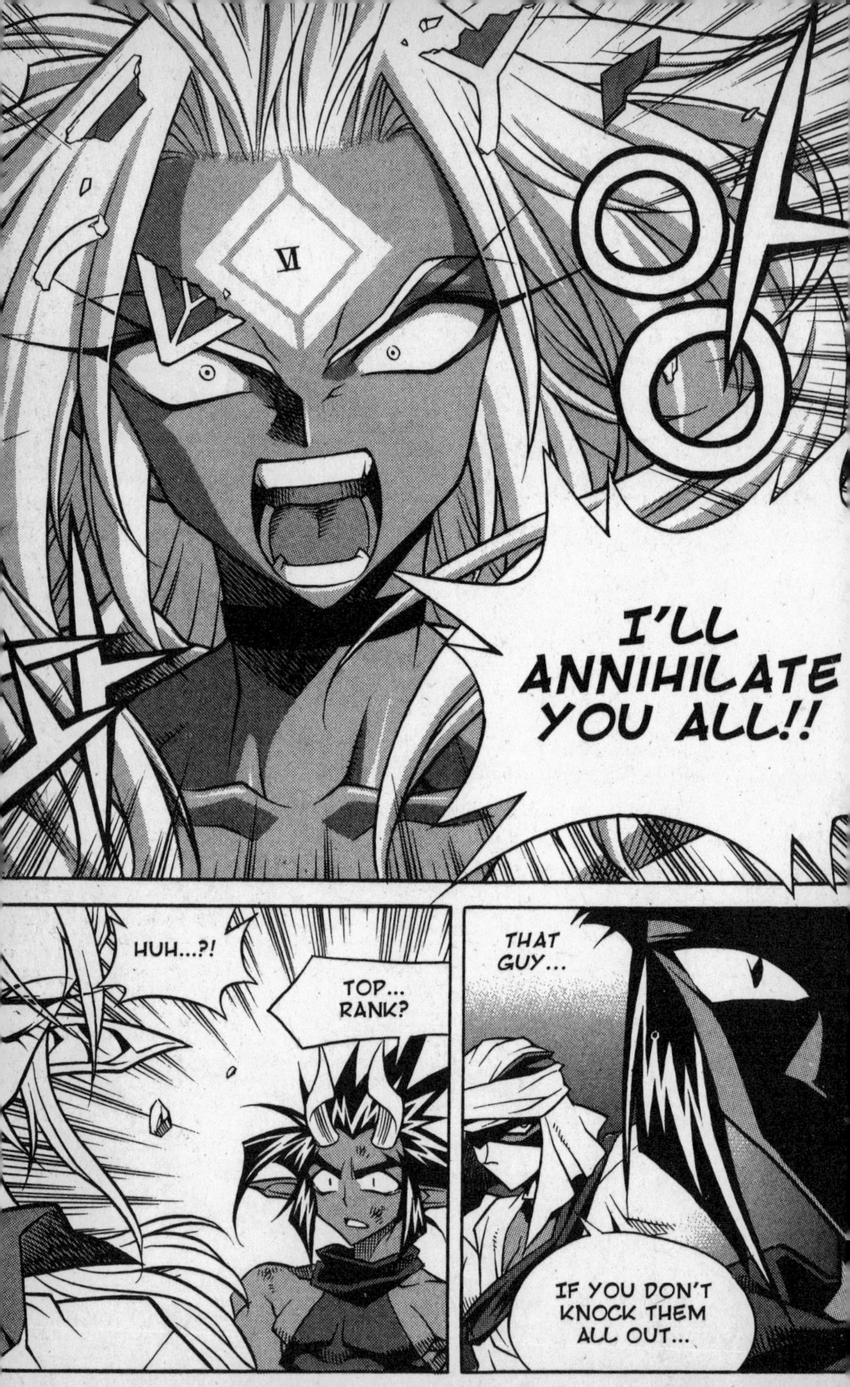
I'LL ANNIHILATE YOU ALL!!
HUH...?!
TOP... RANK?
THAT GUY...
IF YOU DON'T KNOCK THEM ALL OUT...

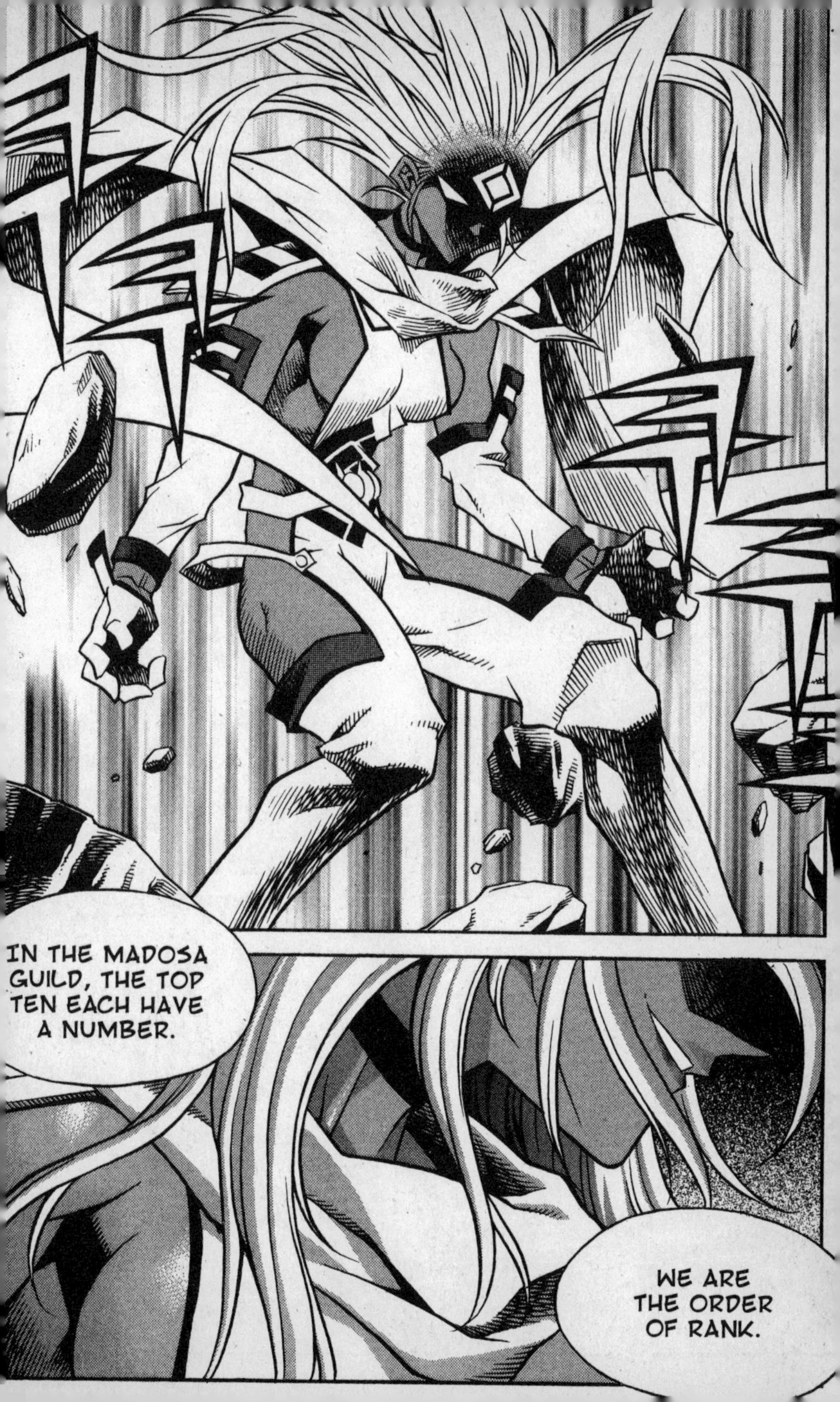
IN THE MADOSA GUILD, THE TOP TEN EACH HAVE A NUMBER.
WE ARE THE ORDER OF RANK.

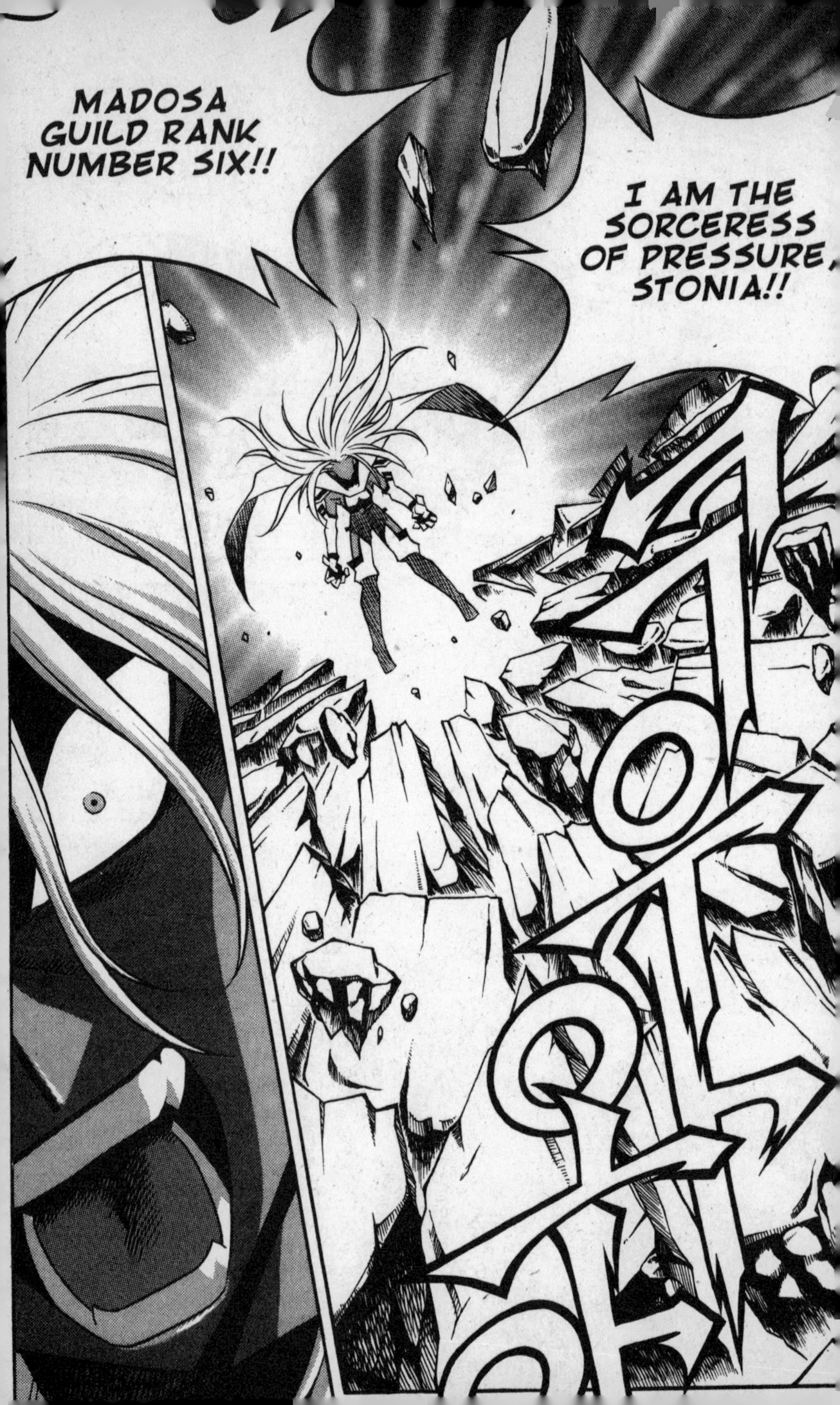
MADOSA GUILD RANK NUMBER SIX!!
I AM THE SORCERESS OF PRESSURE, STONIA!!

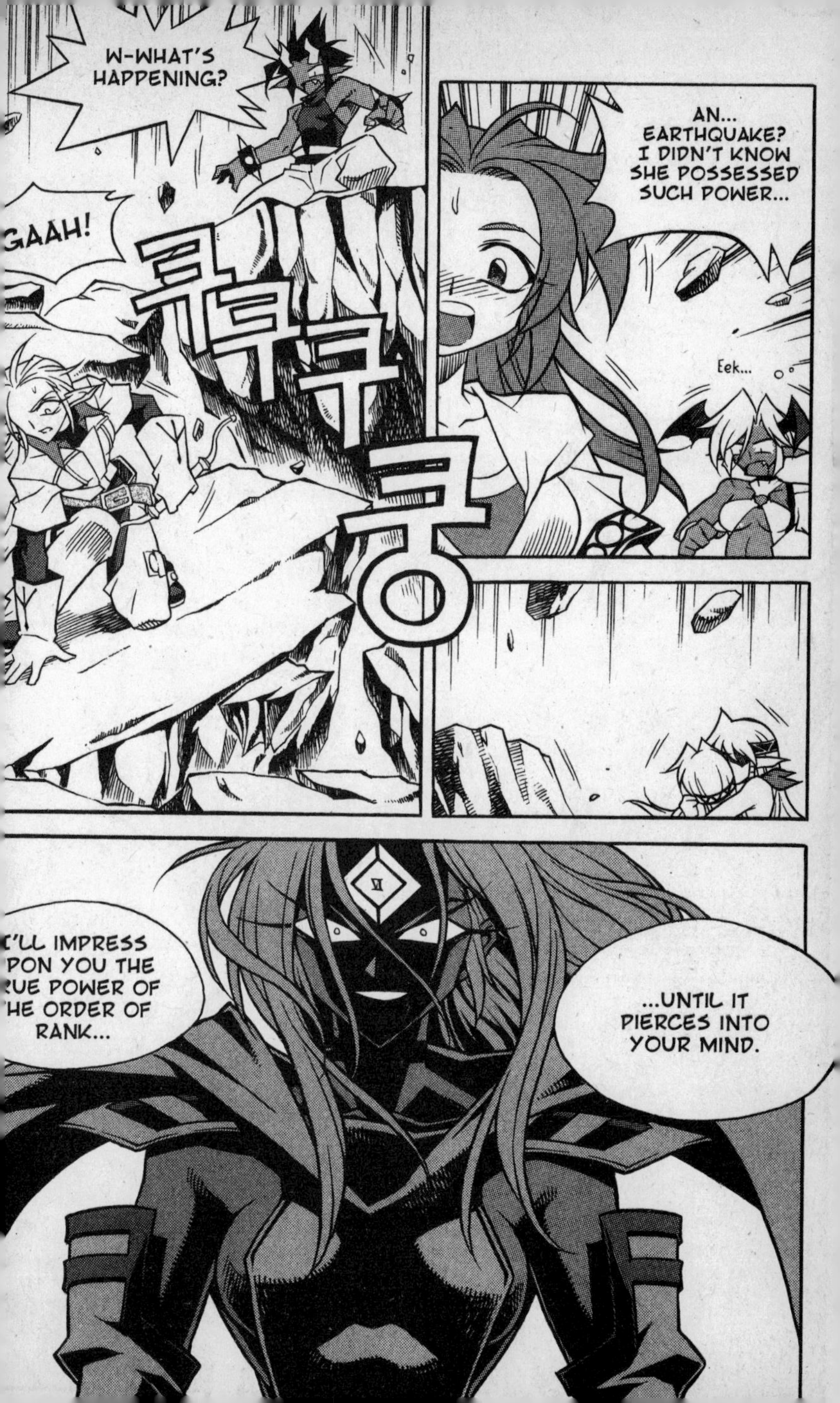
W-WHAT'S HAPPENING?
GAAH!
AN... EARTHQUAKE? I DIDN'T KNOW SHE POSSESSED SUCH POWER...
Eek...
I'LL IMPRESS UPON YOU THE TRUE POWER OF THE ORDER OF RANK...
...UNTIL IT PIERCES INTO YOUR MIND.

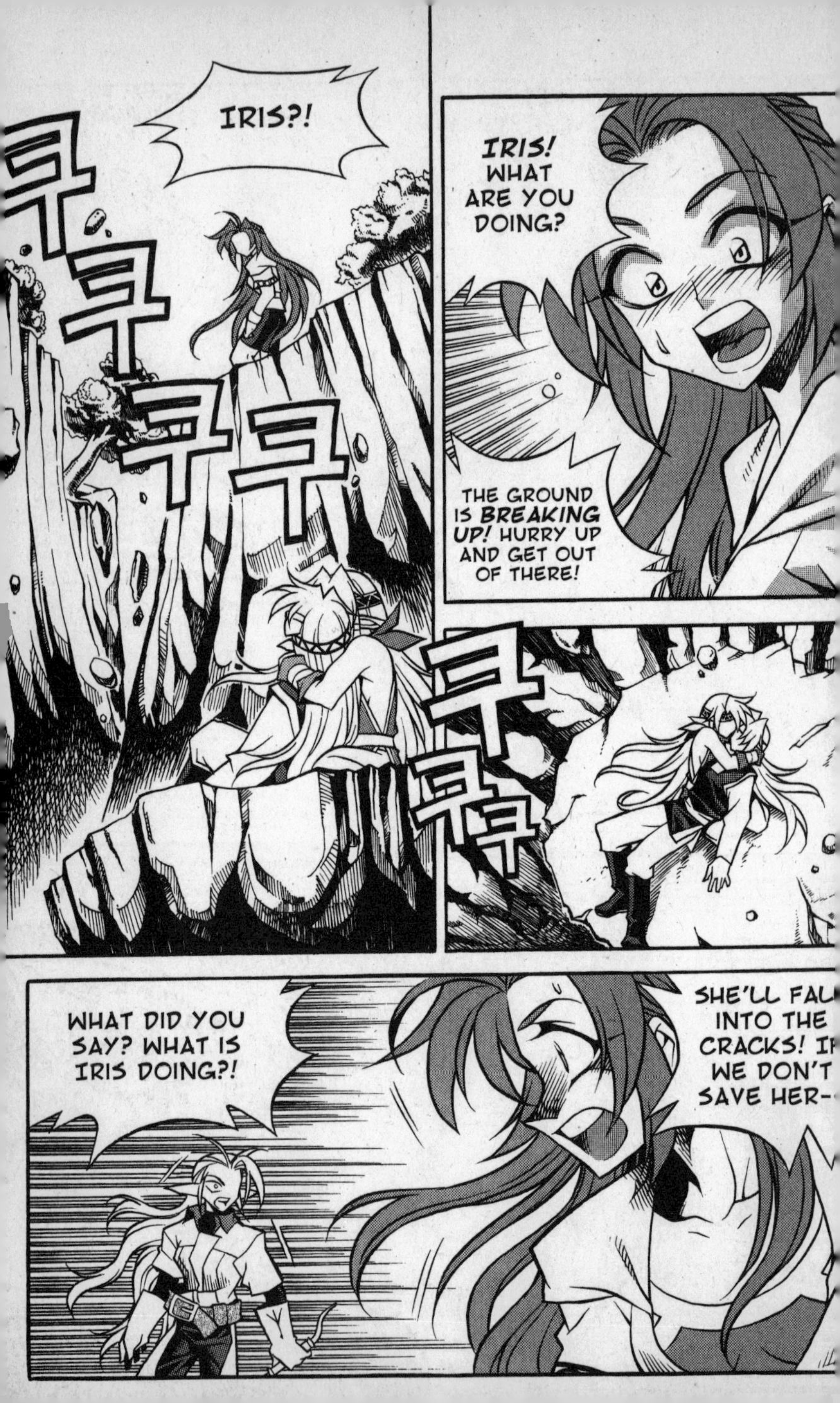
IRIS?!
IRIS! WHAT ARE YOU DOING?
THE GROUND IS BREAKING UP! HURRY UP AND GET OUT OF THERE!
WHAT DID YOU SAY? WHAT IS IRIS DOING?!
SHE'LL FALL INTO THE CRACKS! IF WE DON'T SAVE HER--

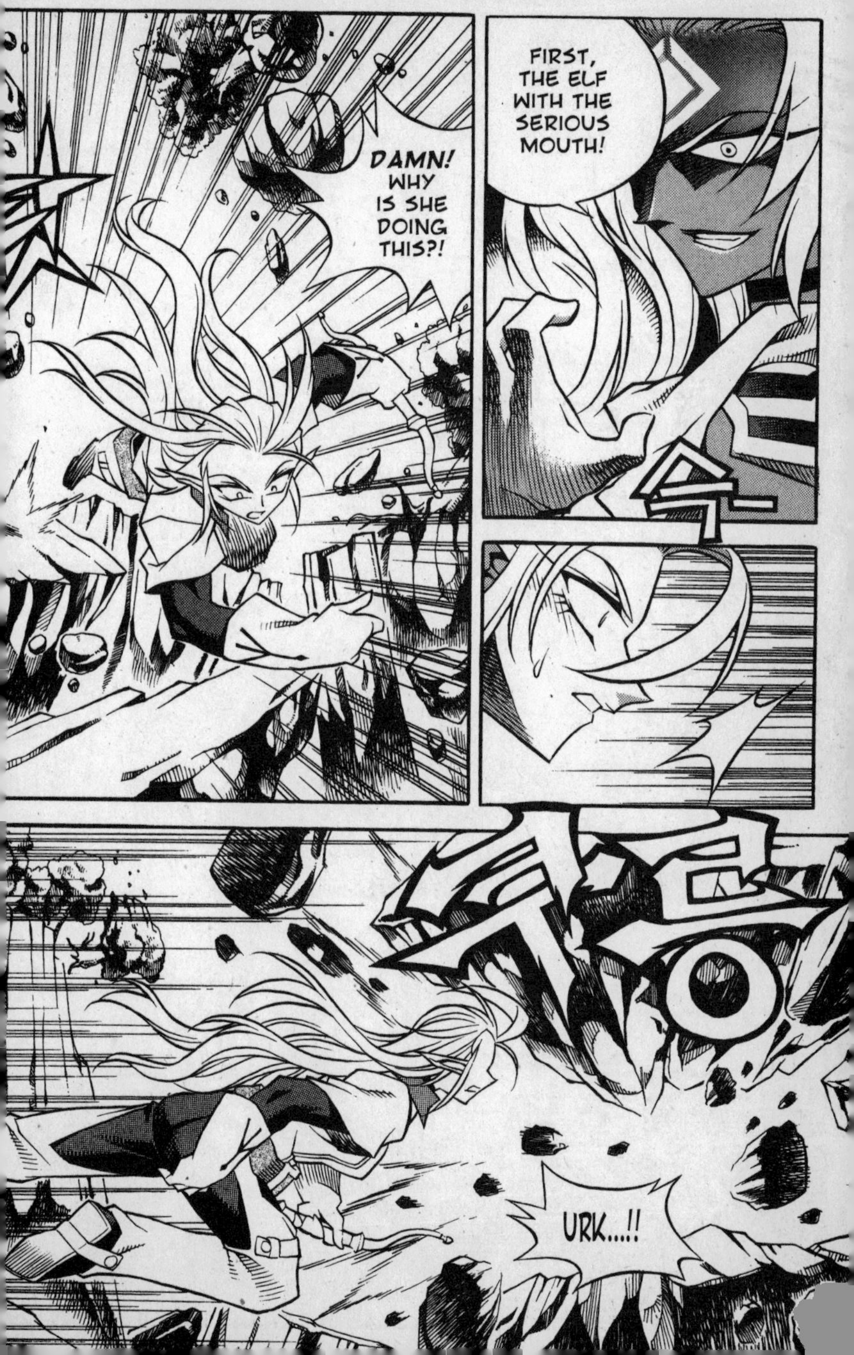
DAMN! WHY IS SHE DOING THIS?!
FIRST, THE ELF WITH THE SERIOUS MOUTH!
URK...!!

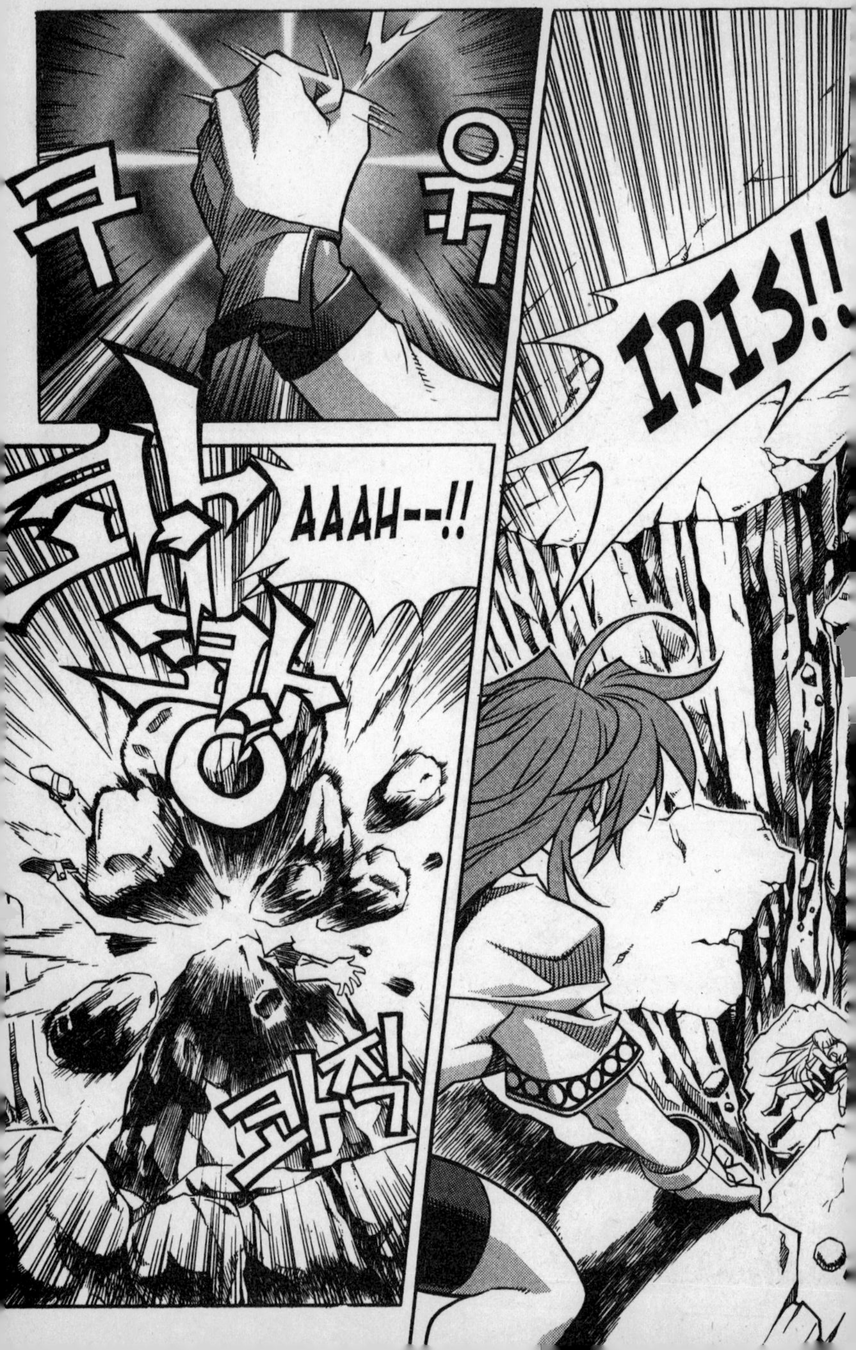
쿠웅
AAAH--!!
콰직
IRIS!!

Quest 71

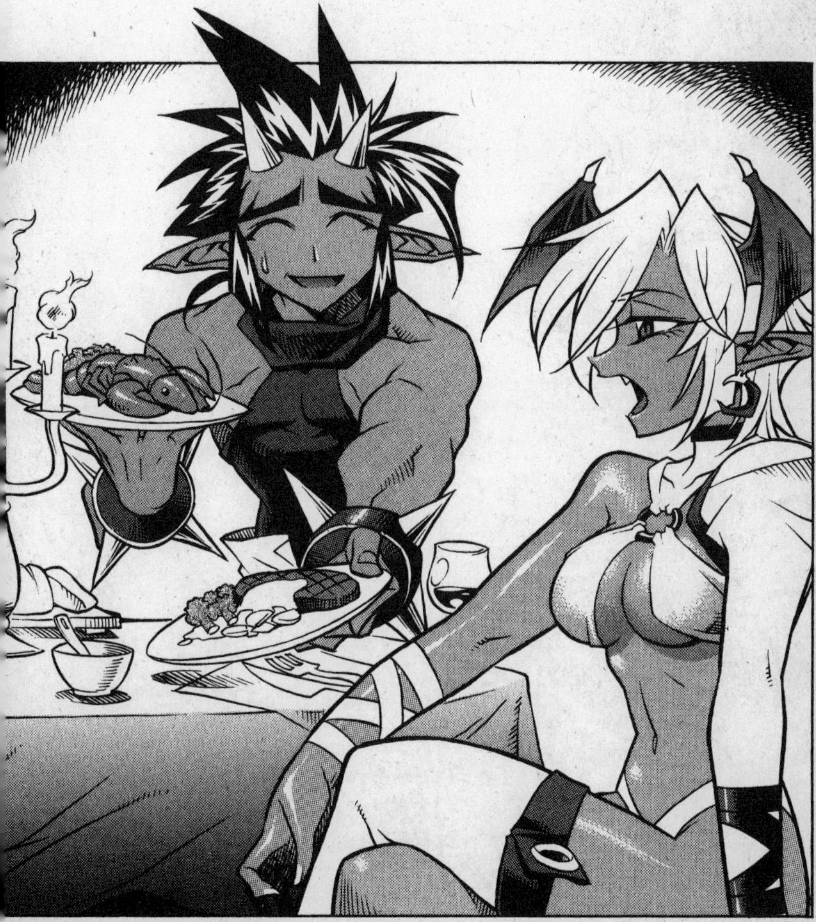

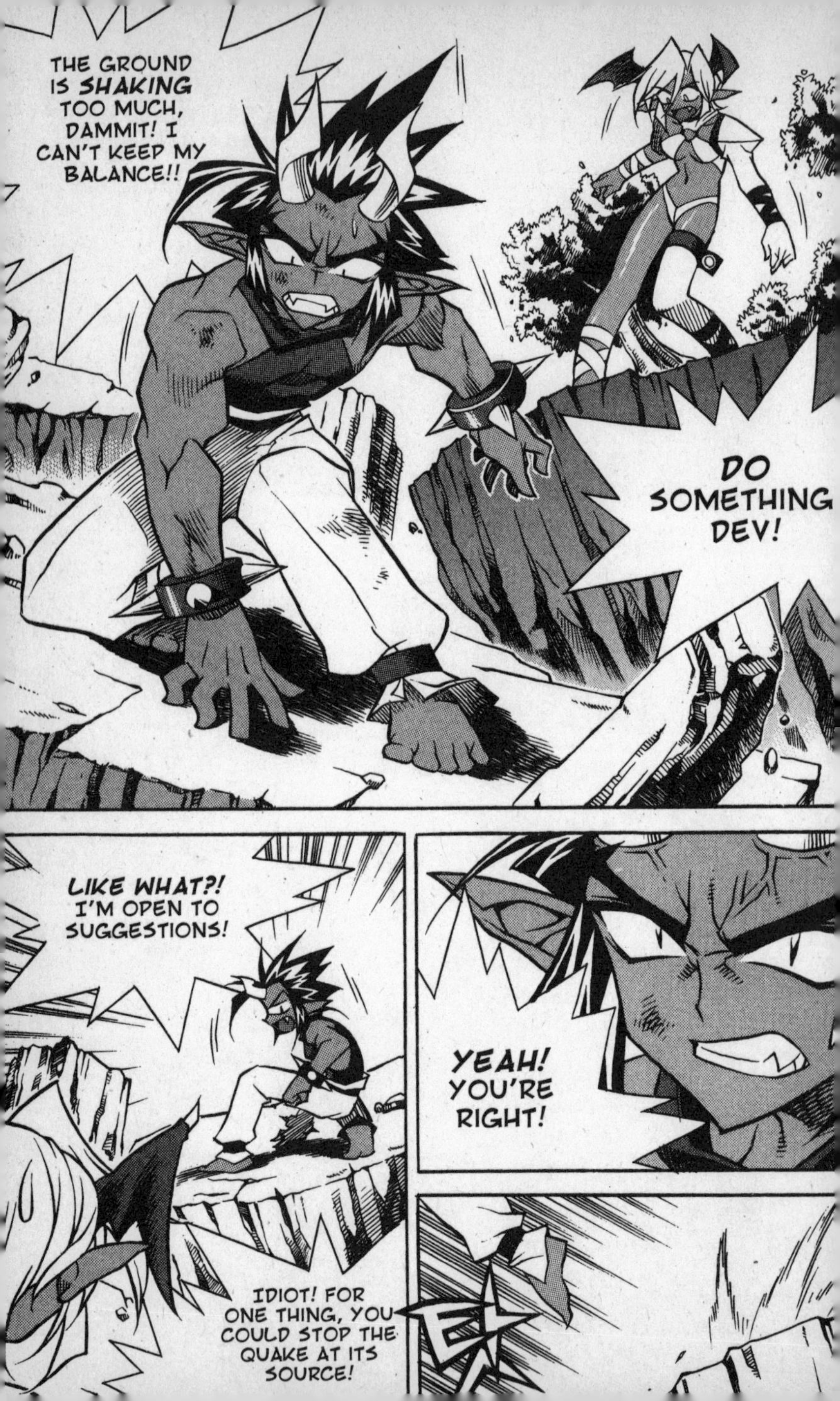
THE GROUND IS SHAKING TOO MUCH, DAMMIT! I CAN'T KEEP MY BALANCE!!
DO SOMETHING DEV!
LIKE WHAT?! I'M OPEN TO SUGGESTIONS!
YEAH! YOU'RE RIGHT!
IDIOT! FOR ONE THING, YOU COULD STOP THE QUAKE AT ITS SOURCE!

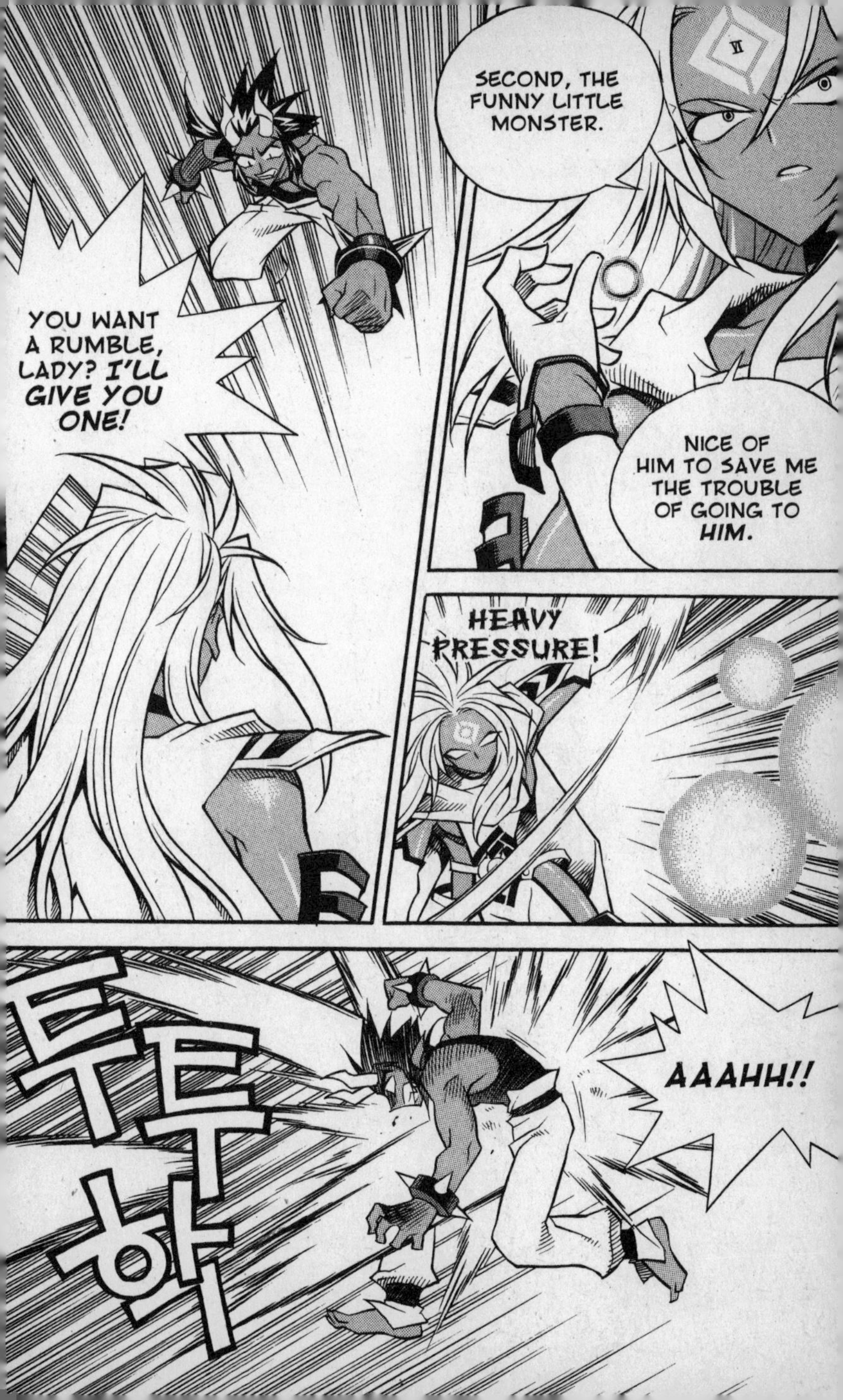
YOU WANT A RUMBLE, LADY? I'LL GIVE YOU ONE!
SECOND, THE FUNNY LITTLE MONSTER.
NICE OF HIM TO SAVE ME THE TROUBLE OF GOING TO HIM.
HEAVY PRESSURE!
AAAHH!!

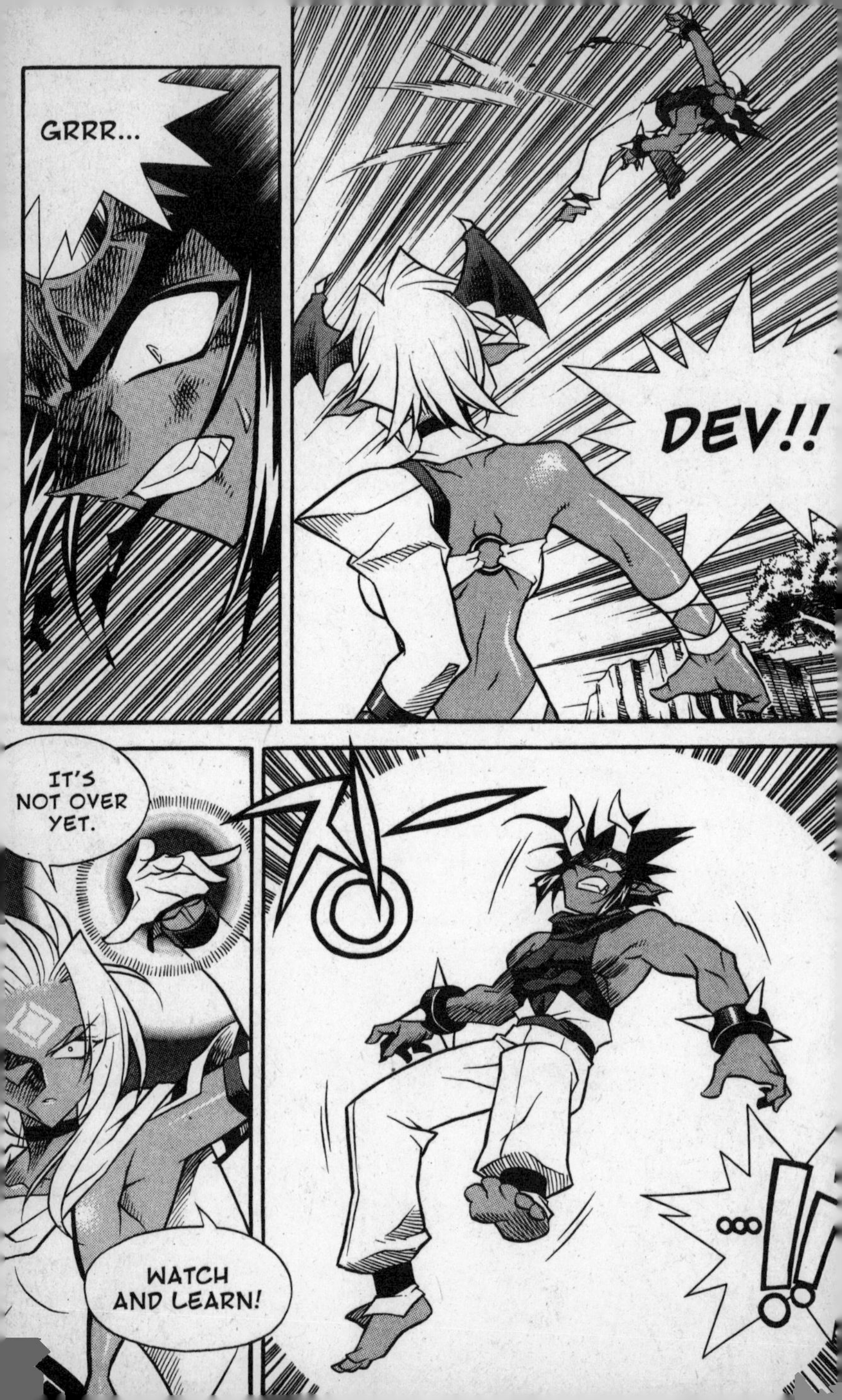
GRRR...
DEV!!
IT'S NOT OVER YET.
WATCH AND LEARN!
!!

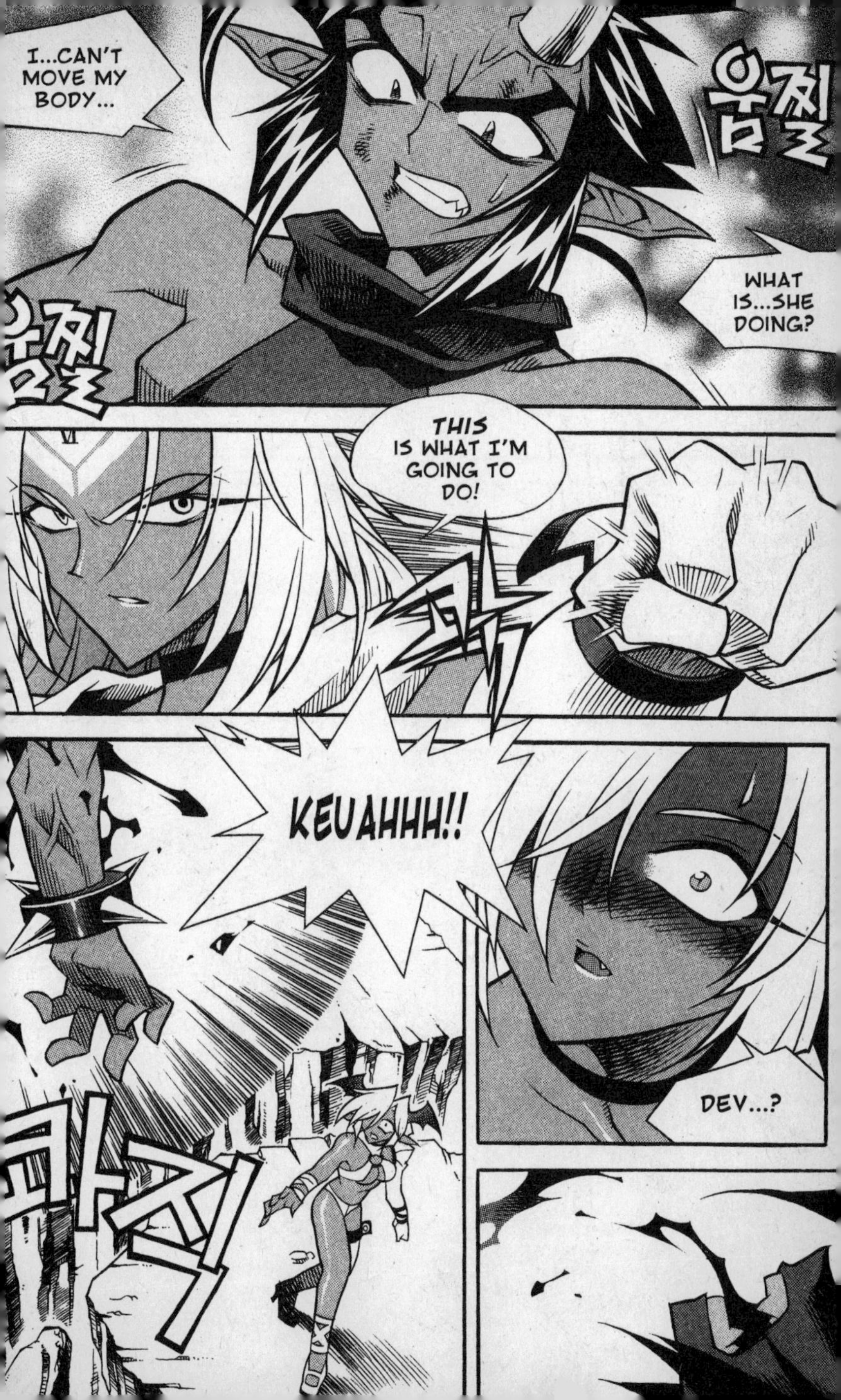

I...CAN'T MOVE MY BODY...
움찔
WHAT IS...SHE DOING?
움찔
THIS IS WHAT I'M GOING TO DO!
KEUAHHH!!
DEV...?

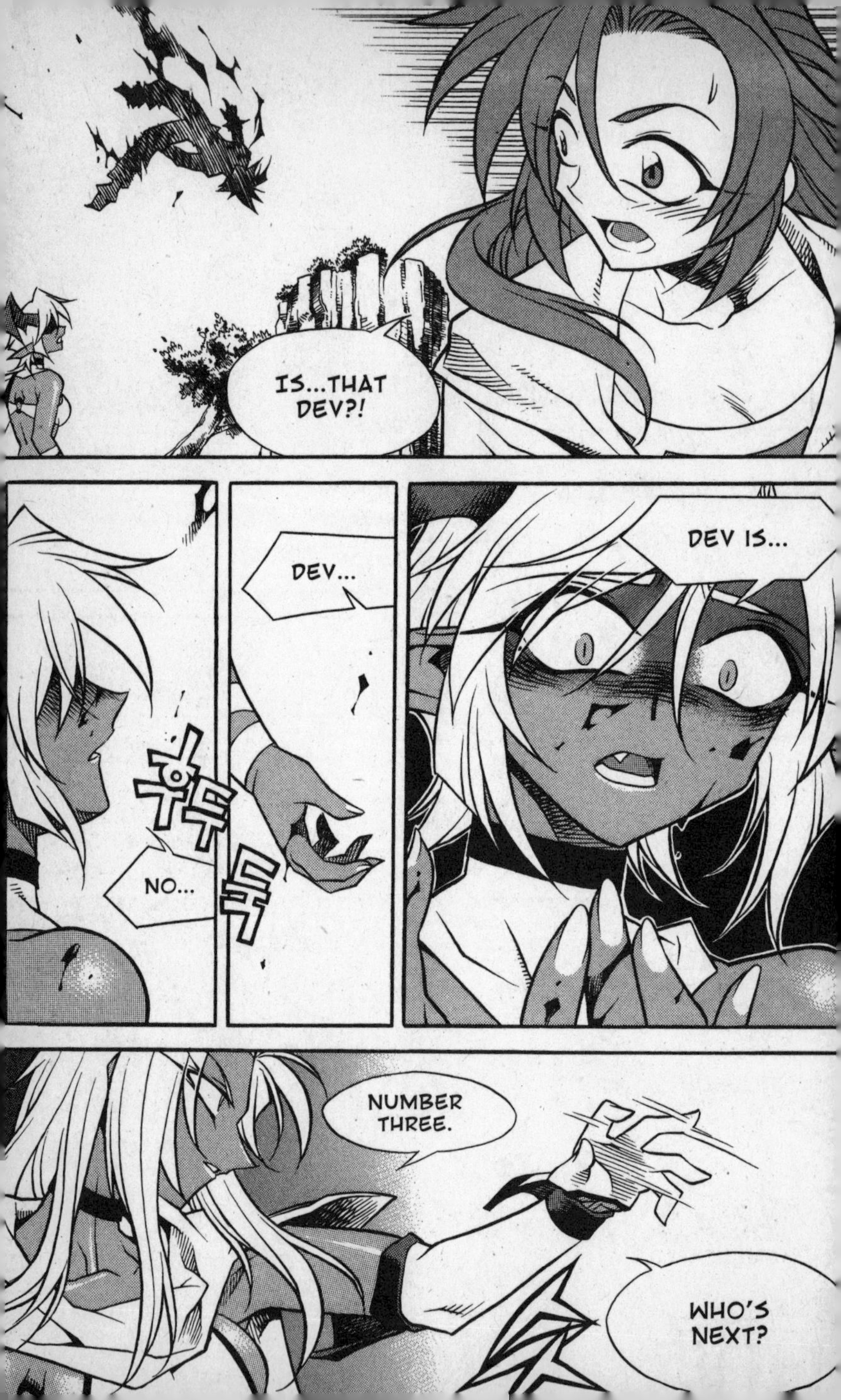
IS...THAT DEV?!
NO...
DEV...
DEV IS...
NUMBER THREE.
WHO'S NEXT?

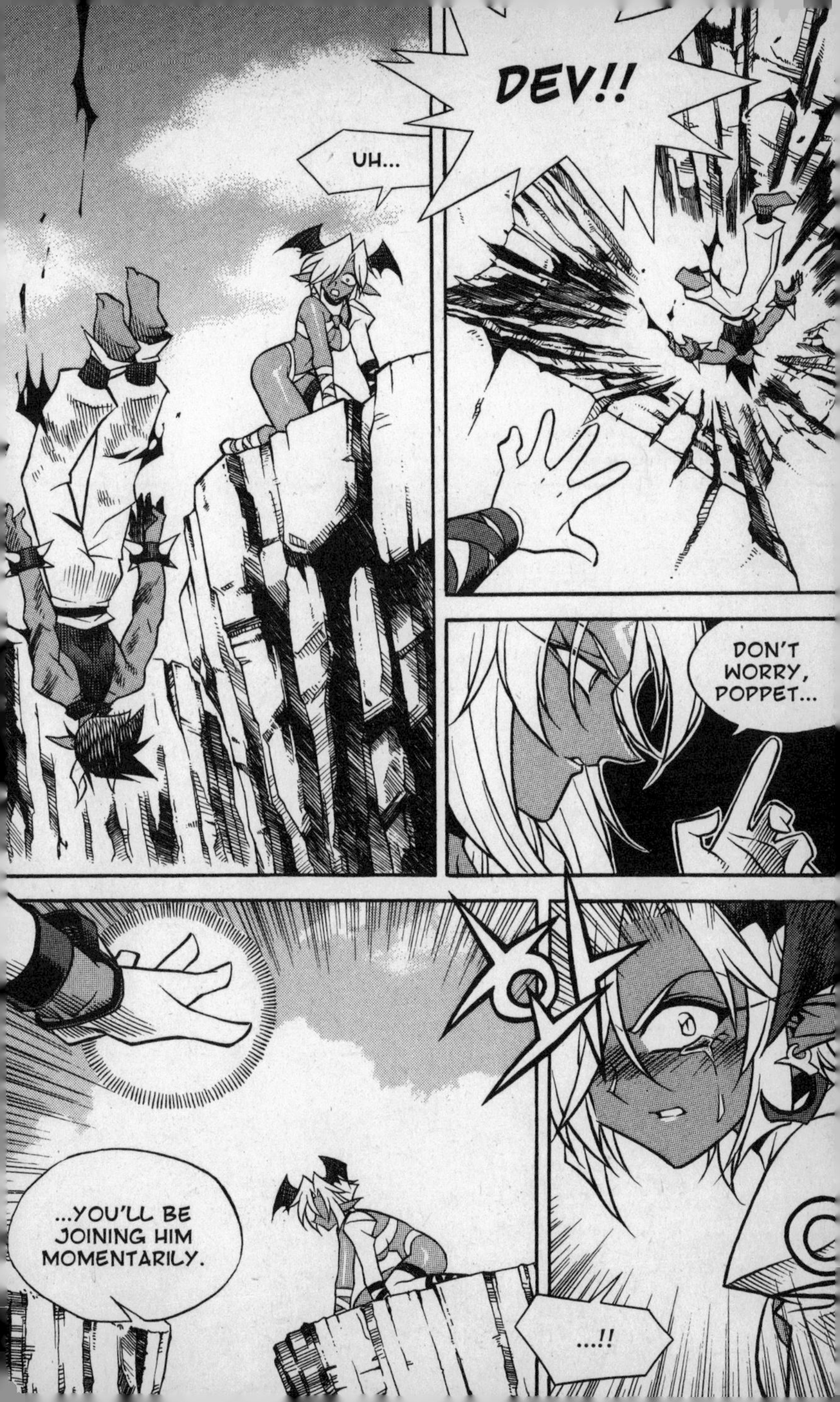
UH...
DEV!!
DON'T WORRY, POPPET...
...YOU'LL BE JOINING HIM MOMENTARILY.
...!!

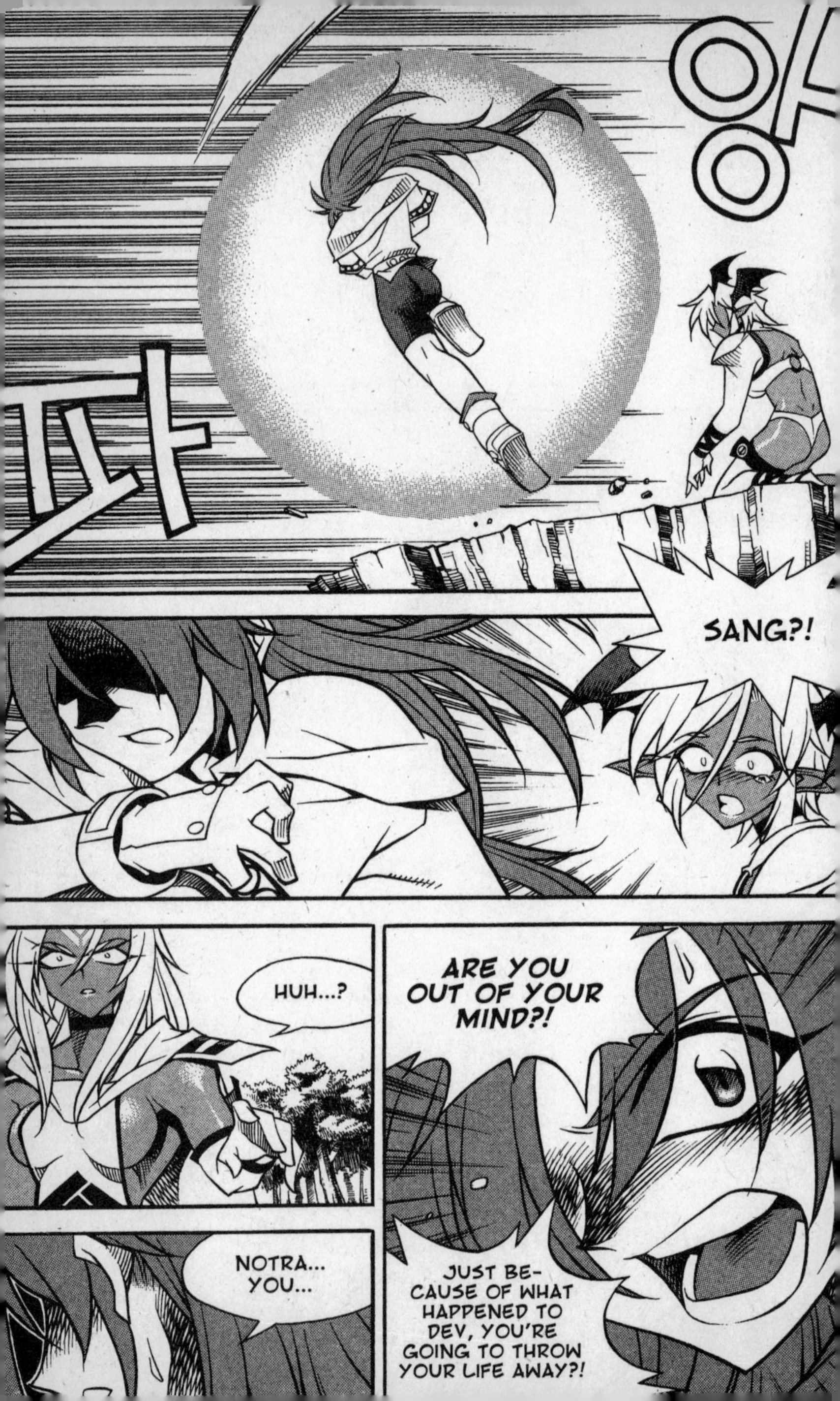
SANG?!
HUH...?
NOTRA... YOU...
ARE YOU OUT OF YOUR MIND?!
JUST BE- CAUSE OF WHAT HAPPENED TO DEV, YOU'RE GOING TO THROW YOUR LIFE AWAY?!

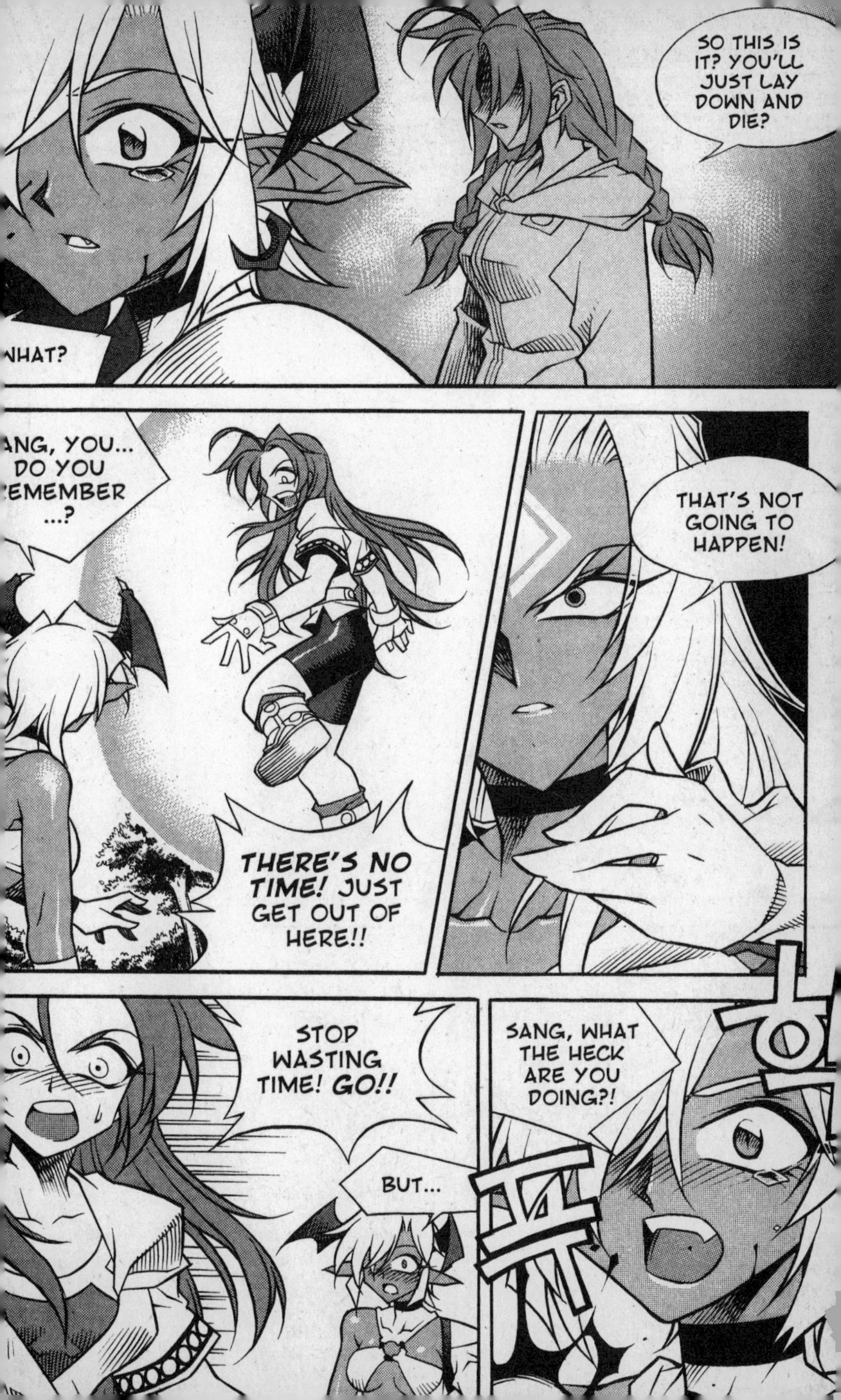

SO THIS IS IT? YOU'LL JUST LAY DOWN AND DIE?
WHAT?
SANG, YOU... DO YOU REMEMBER ...?
THERE'S NO TIME! JUST GET OUT OF HERE!!
THAT'S NOT GOING TO HAPPEN!
STOP WASTING TIME! GO!!
BUT...
SANG, WHAT THE HECK ARE YOU DOING?!

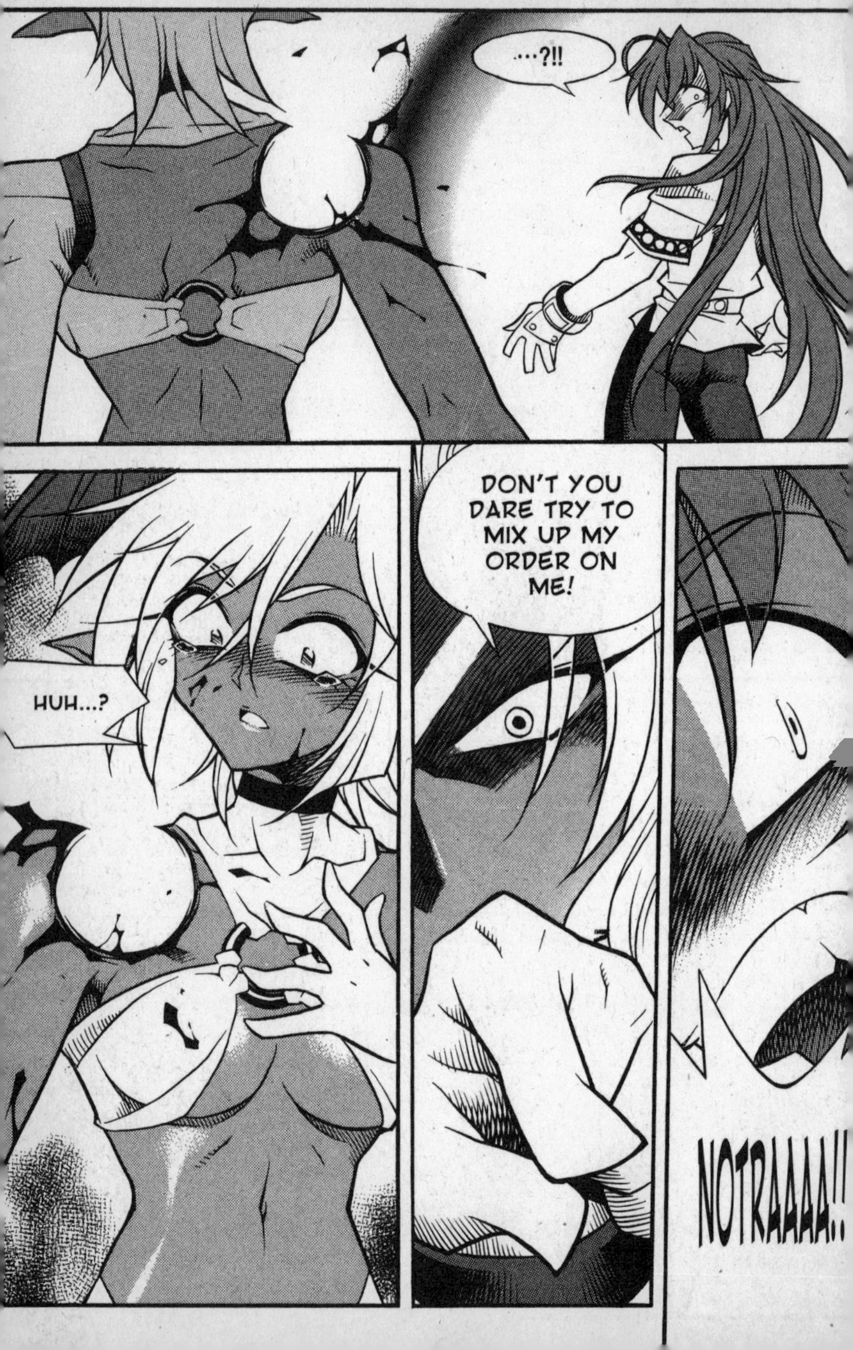
...?!!
NOTRAAAA!!
DON'T YOU DARE TRY TO MIX UP MY ORDER ON ME!
HUH...?

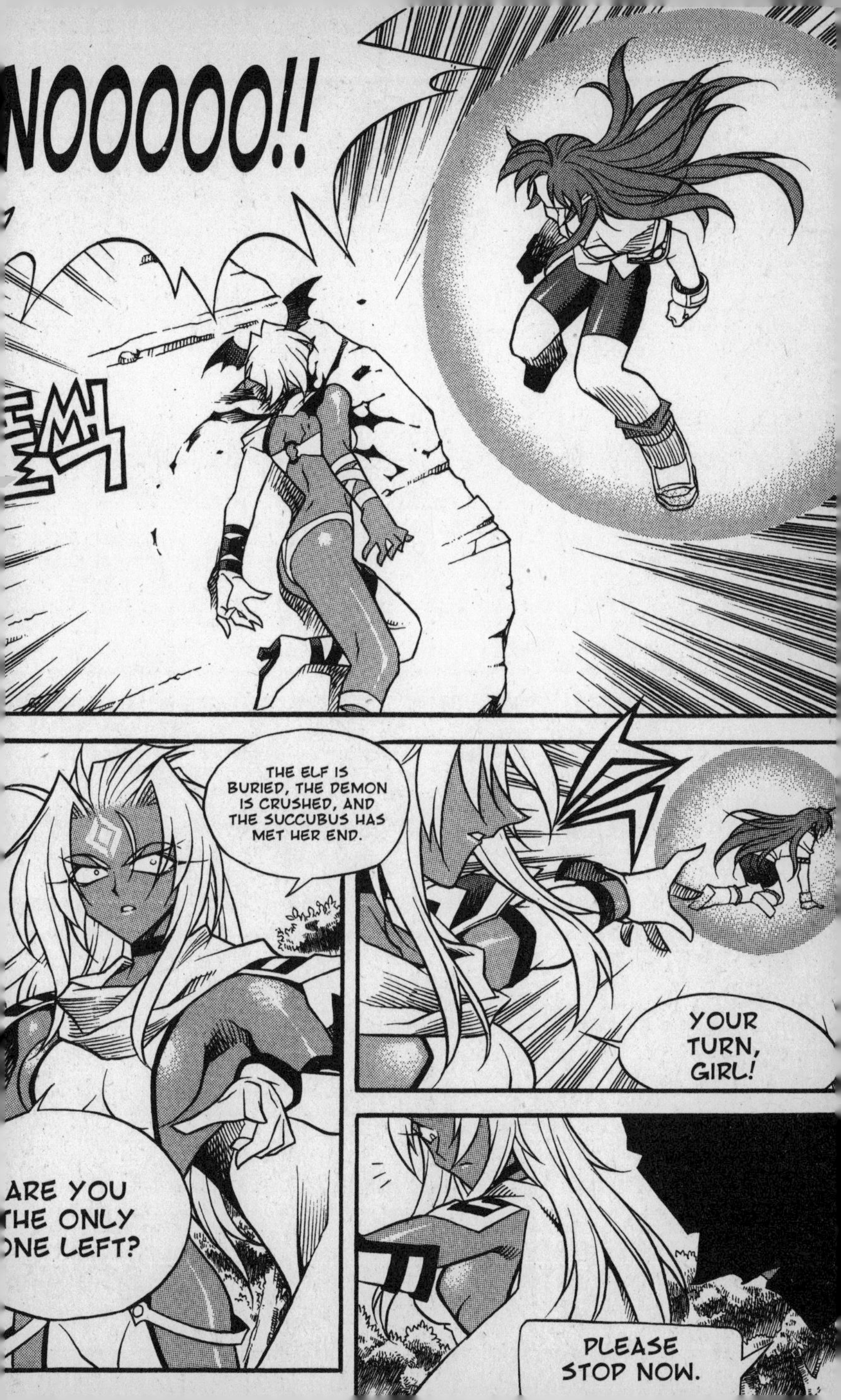
NOOOOO!!
THE ELF IS BURIED, THE DEMON IS CRUSHED, AND THE SUCCUBUS HAS MET HER END.
ARE YOU THE ONLY ONE LEFT?
YOUR TURN, GIRL!
PLEASE STOP NOW.

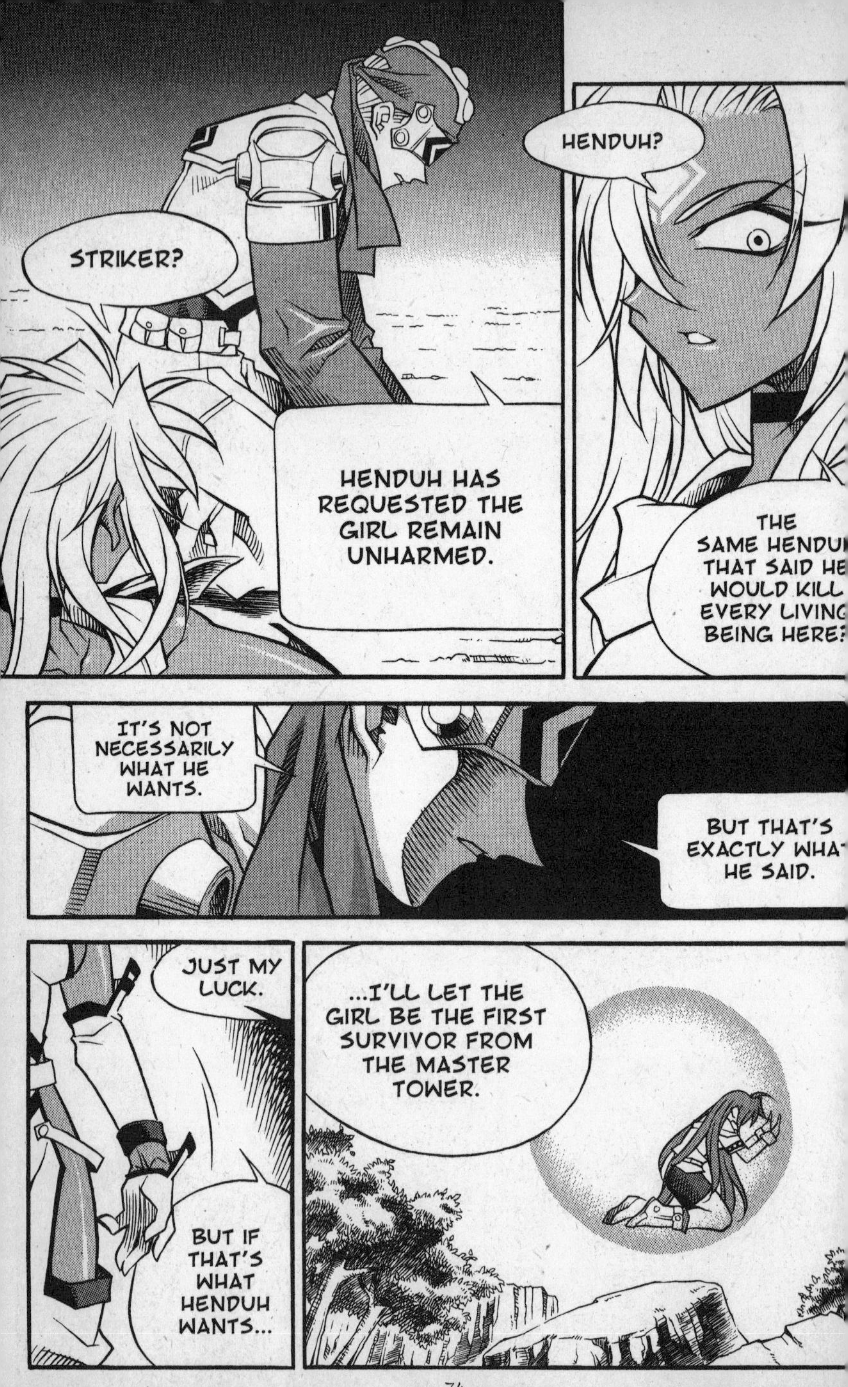
STRIKER?
HENDUH HAS REQUESTED THE GIRL REMAIN UNHARMED.
HENDUH?
THE SAME HENDUH THAT SAID HE WOULD KILL EVERY LIVING BEING HERE?
IT'S NOT NECESSARILY WHAT HE WANTS.
BUT THAT'S EXACTLY WHAT HE SAID.
JUST MY LUCK.
BUT IF THAT'S WHAT HENDUH WANTS...
...I'LL LET THE GIRL BE THE FIRST SURVIVOR FROM THE MASTER TOWER.

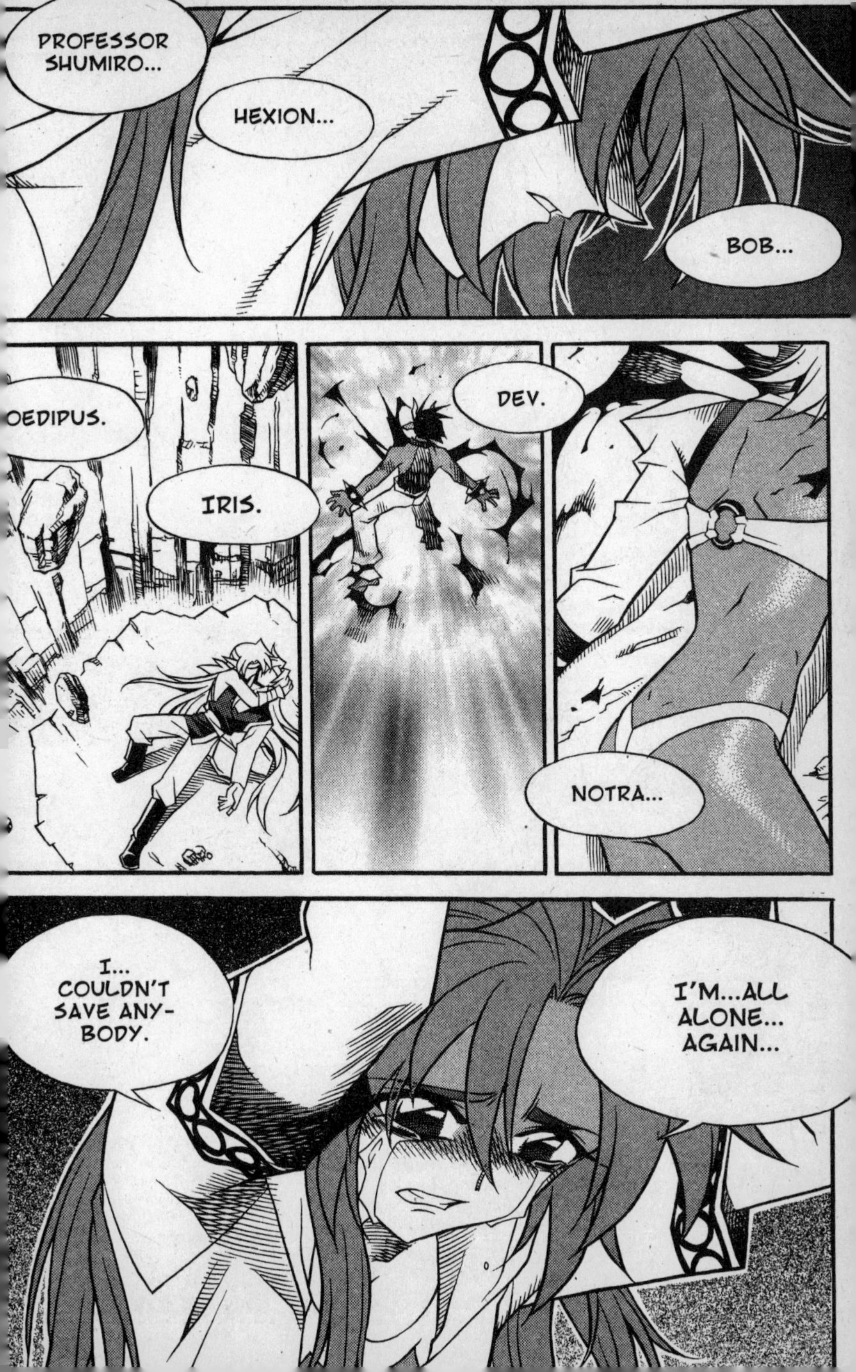
PROFESSOR SHUMIRO...
HEXION...
BOB...
OEDIPUS.
IRIS.
DEV.
NOTRA...
I... COULDN'T SAVE ANY-BODY.
I'M...ALL ALONE... AGAIN...

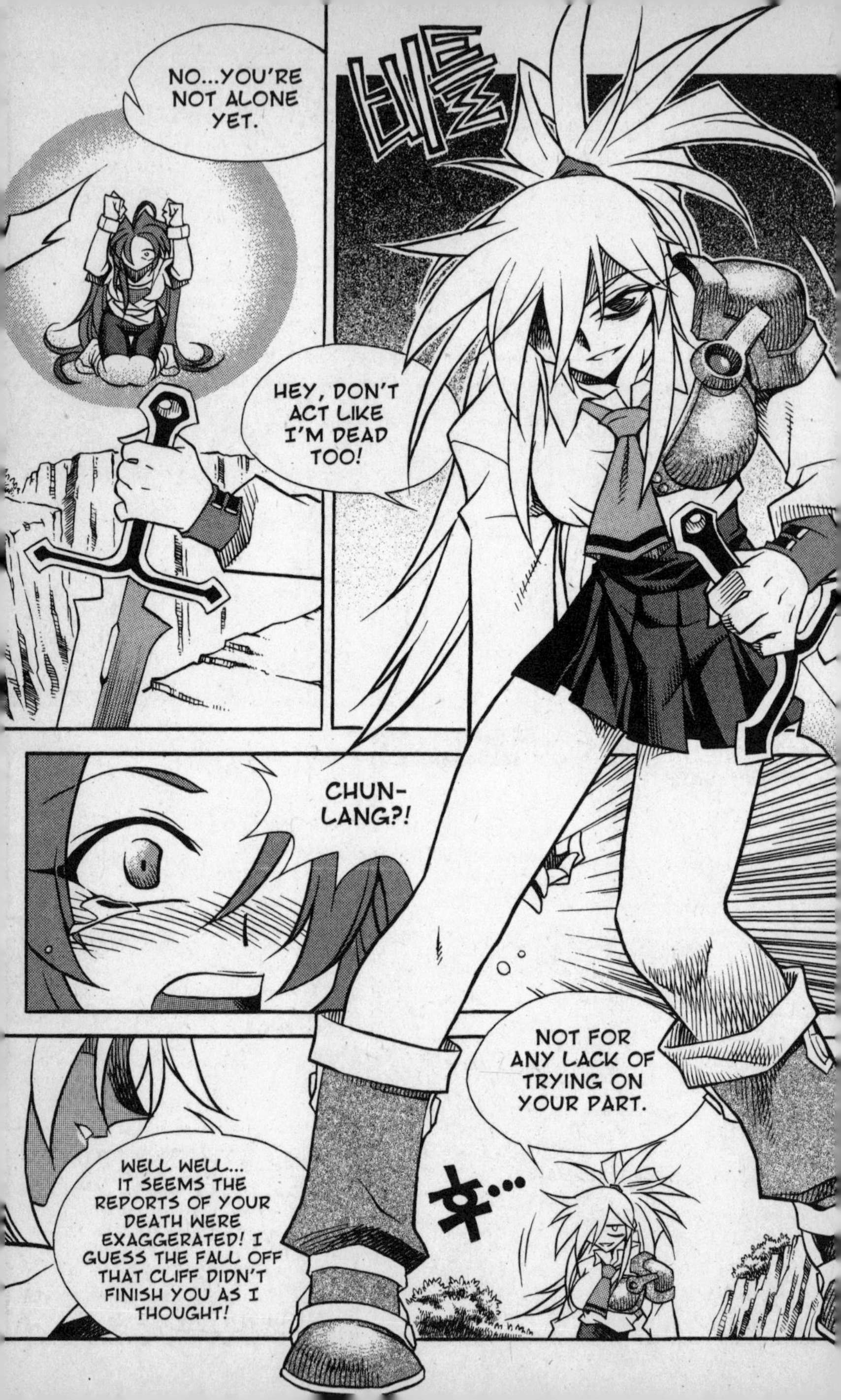

NO...YOU'RE NOT ALONE YET.
HEY, DON'T ACT LIKE I'M DEAD TOO!
CHUN-LANG?!
WELL WELL... IT SEEMS THE REPORTS OF YOUR DEATH WERE EXAGGERATED! I GUESS THE FALL OFF THAT CLIFF DIDN'T FINISH YOU AS I THOUGHT!
NOT FOR ANY LACK OF TRYING ON YOUR PART.

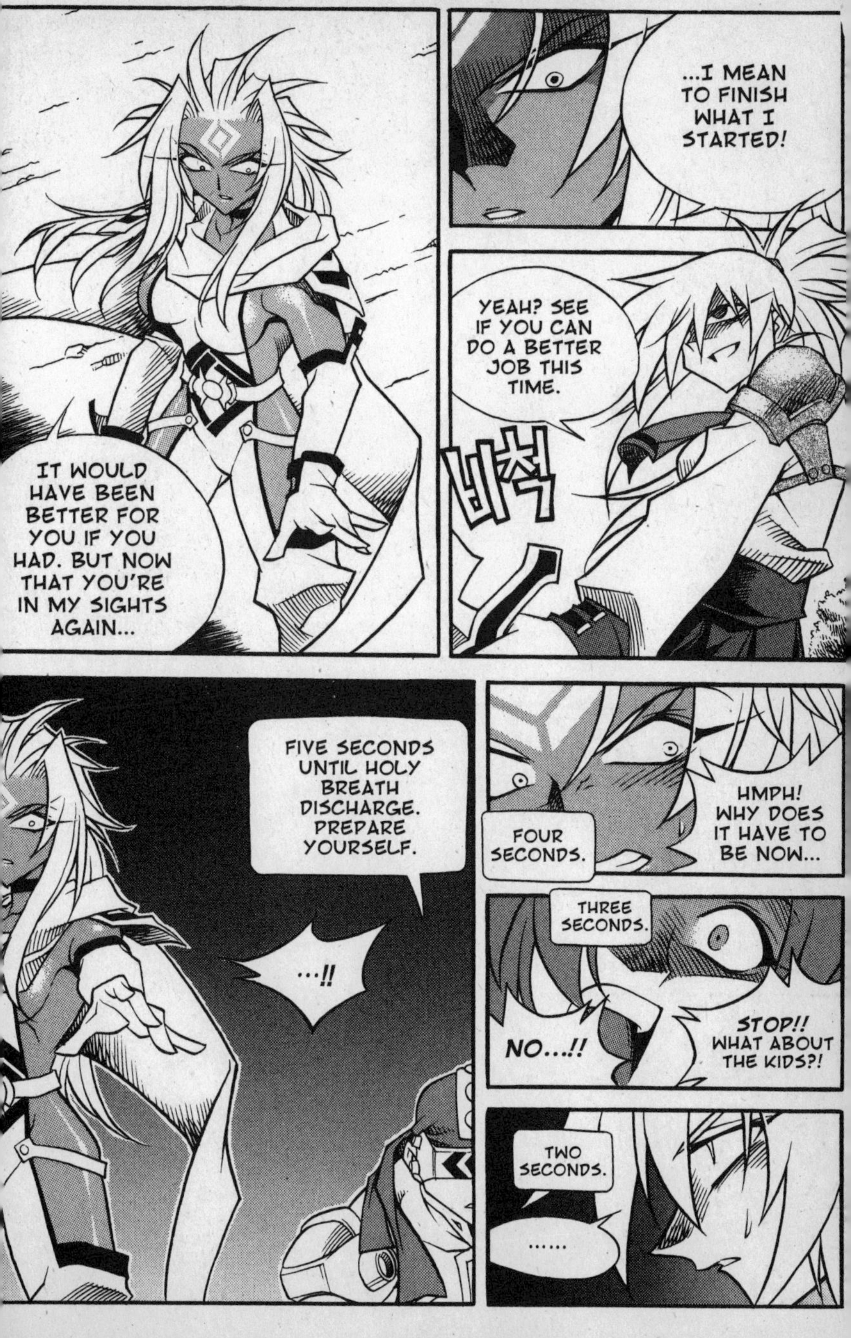
IT WOULD HAVE BEEN BETTER FOR YOU IF YOU HAD. BUT NOW THAT YOU'RE IN MY SIGHTS AGAIN...
...I MEAN TO FINISH WHAT I STARTED!
YEAH? SEE IF YOU CAN DO A BETTER JOB THIS TIME.
비척
FIVE SECONDS UNTIL HOLY BREATH DISCHARGE. PREPARE YOURSELF.
...!!
FOUR SECONDS.
HMPH! WHY DOES IT HAVE TO BE NOW...
THREE SECONDS.
NO...!!
STOP!! WHAT ABOUT THE KIDS?!
TWO SECONDS.
......

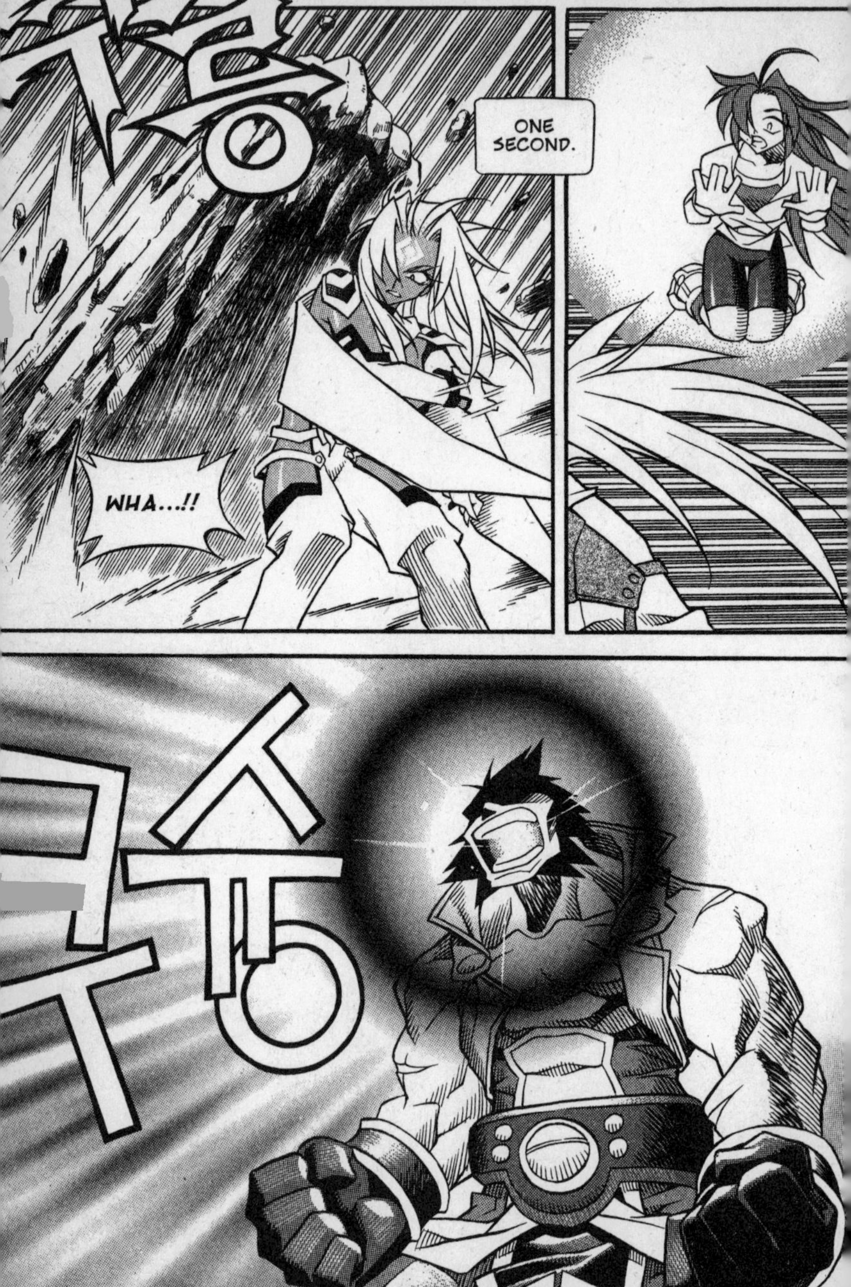
ONE SECOND.
WHA...!!

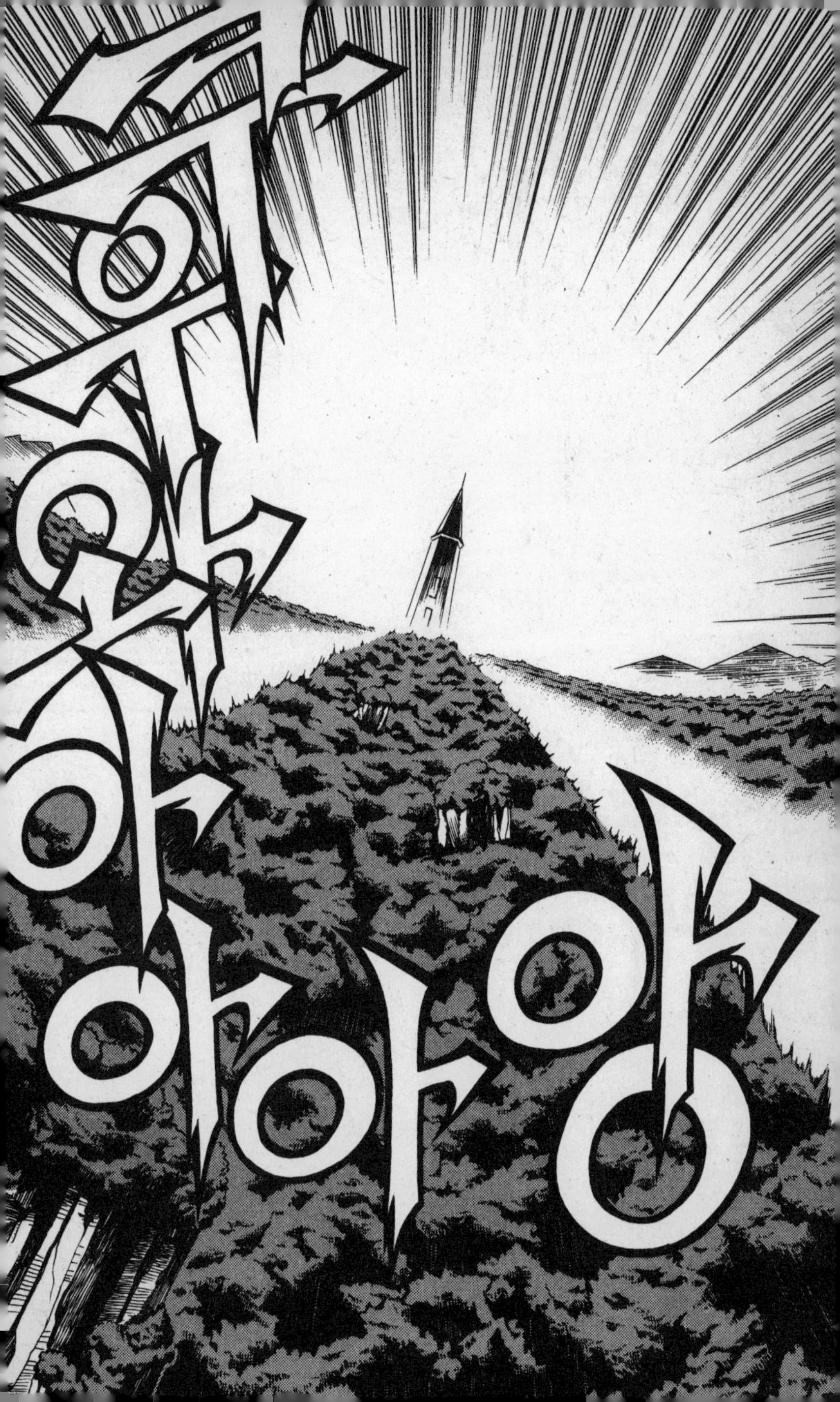

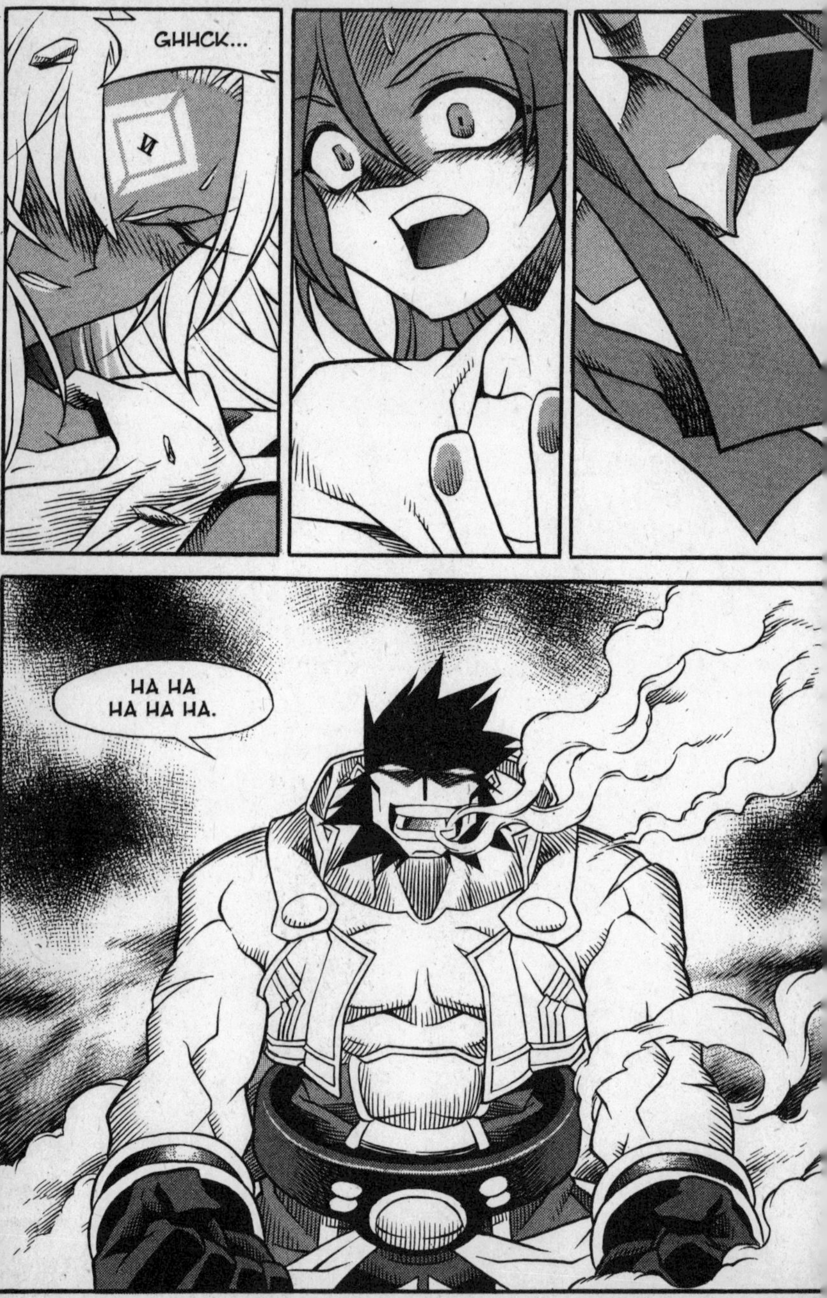
GHHCK...
HA HA
HA HA HA.

Quest 72

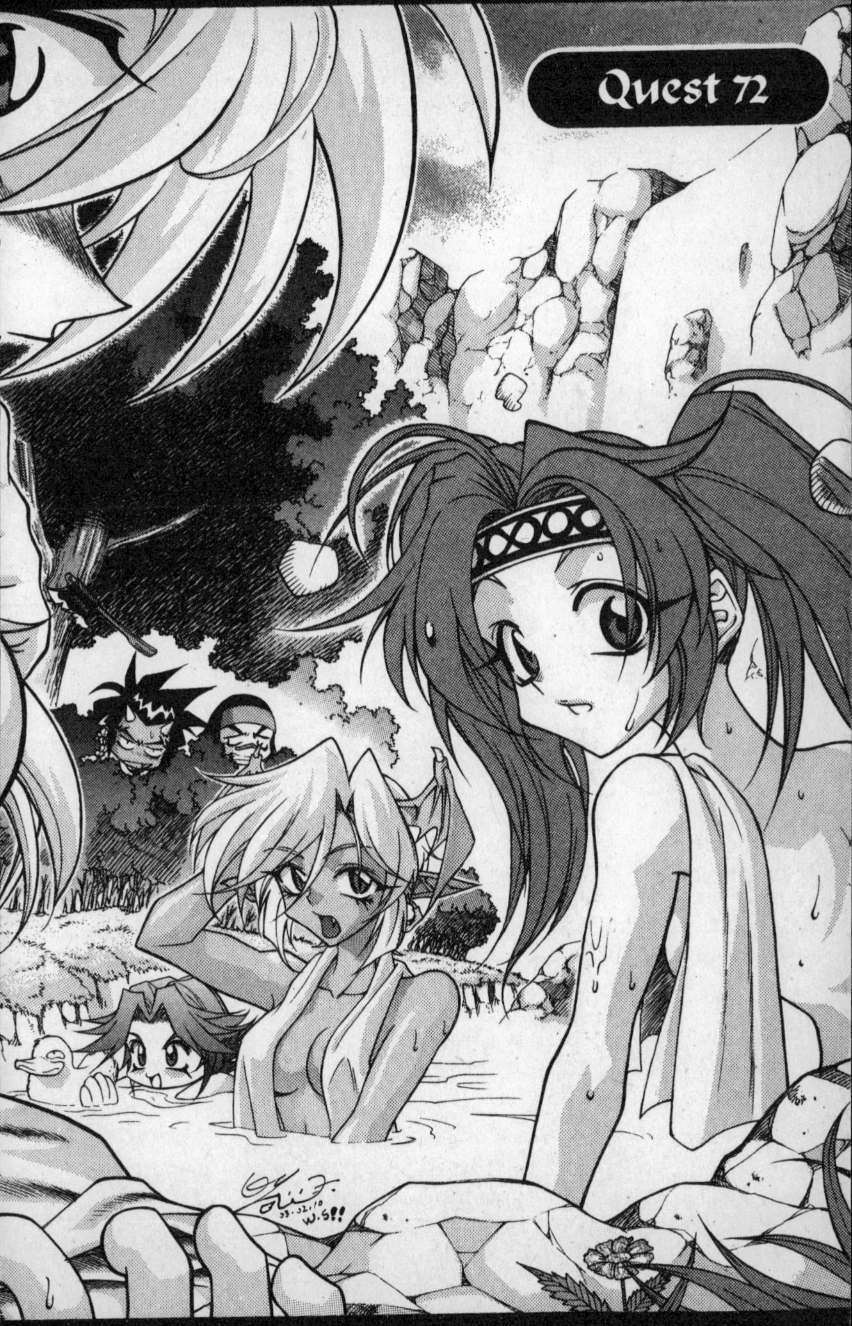

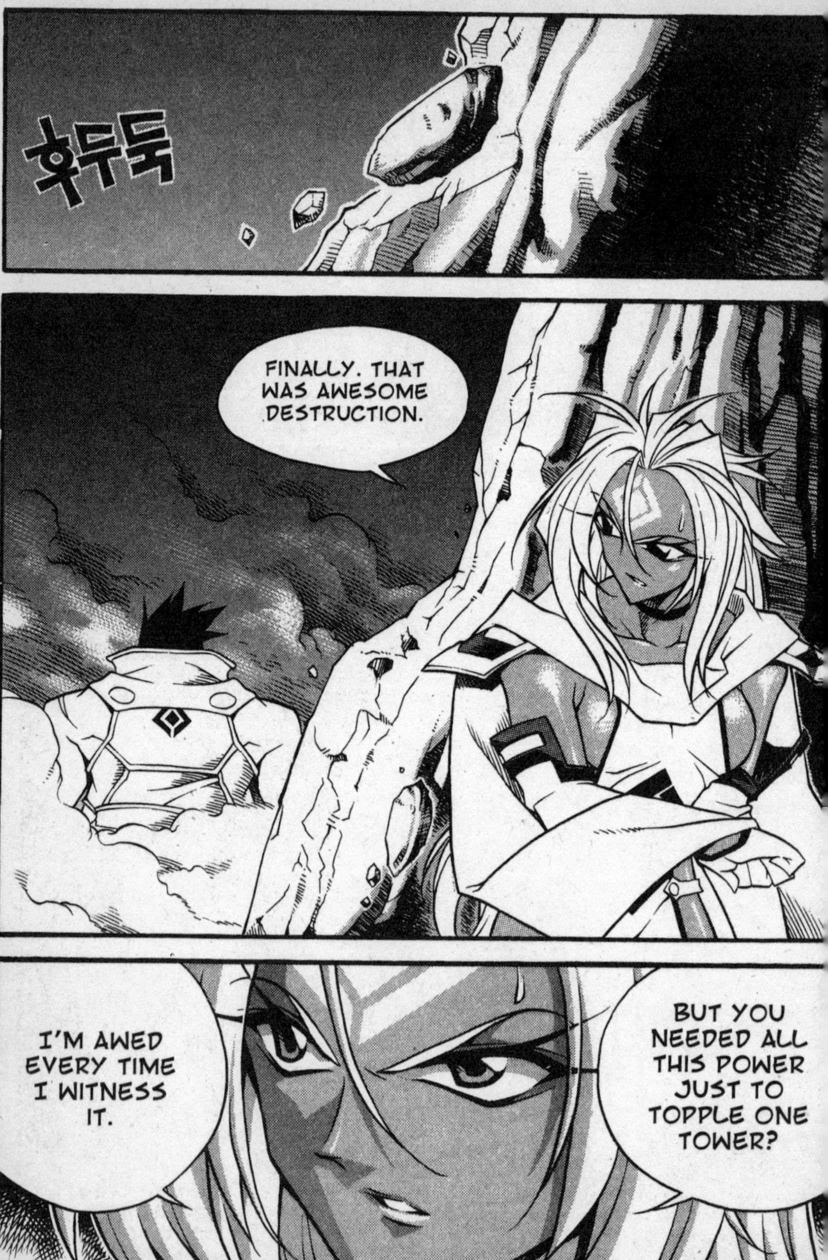
후두둑
FINALLY. THAT WAS AWESOME DESTRUCTION.
I'M AWED EVERY TIME I WITNESS IT.
BUT YOU NEEDED ALL THIS POWER JUST TO TOPPLE ONE TOWER?

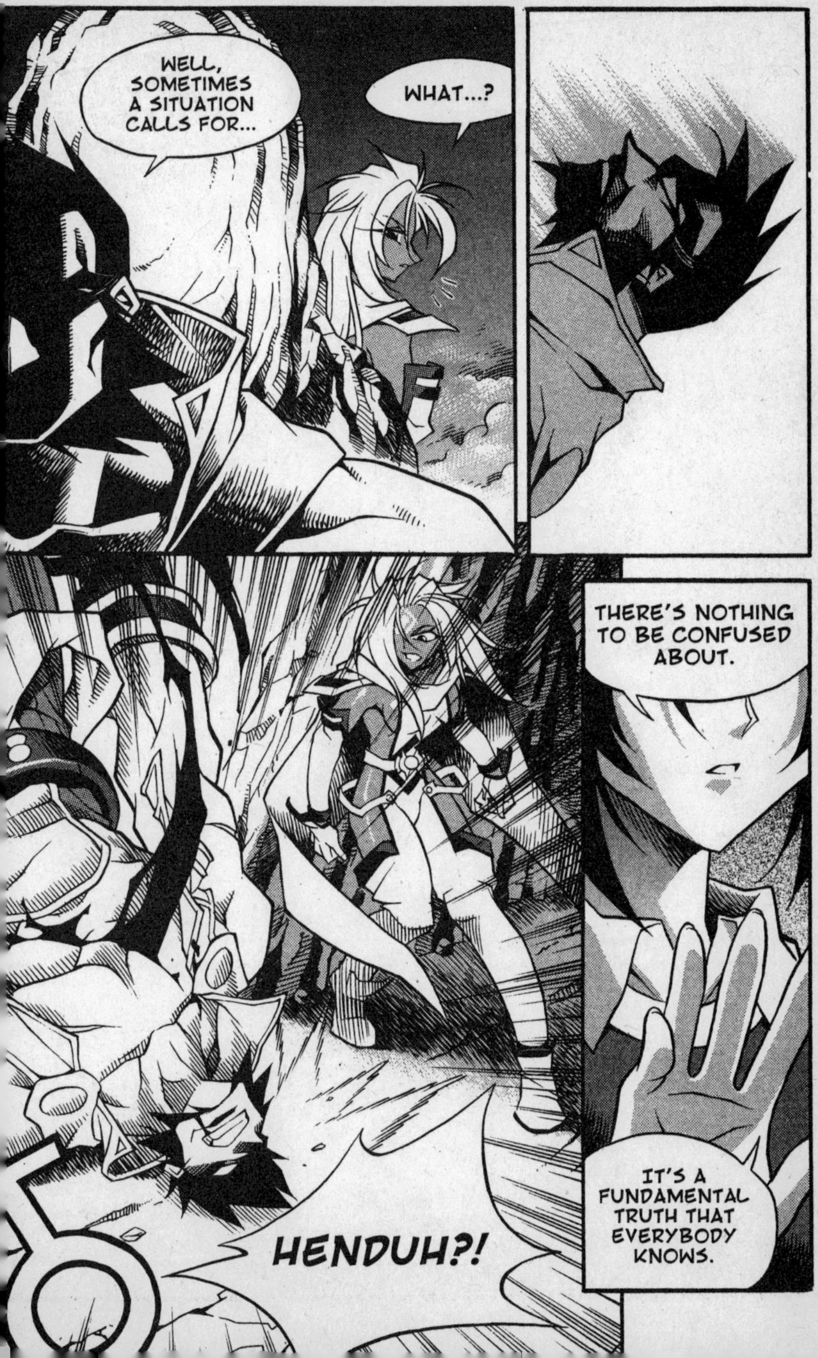
WELL, SOMETIMES A SITUATION CALLS FOR...
WHAT...?
HENDUH?!
THERE'S NOTHING TO BE CONFUSED ABOUT.
IT'S A FUNDAMENTAL TRUTH THAT EVERYBODY KNOWS.

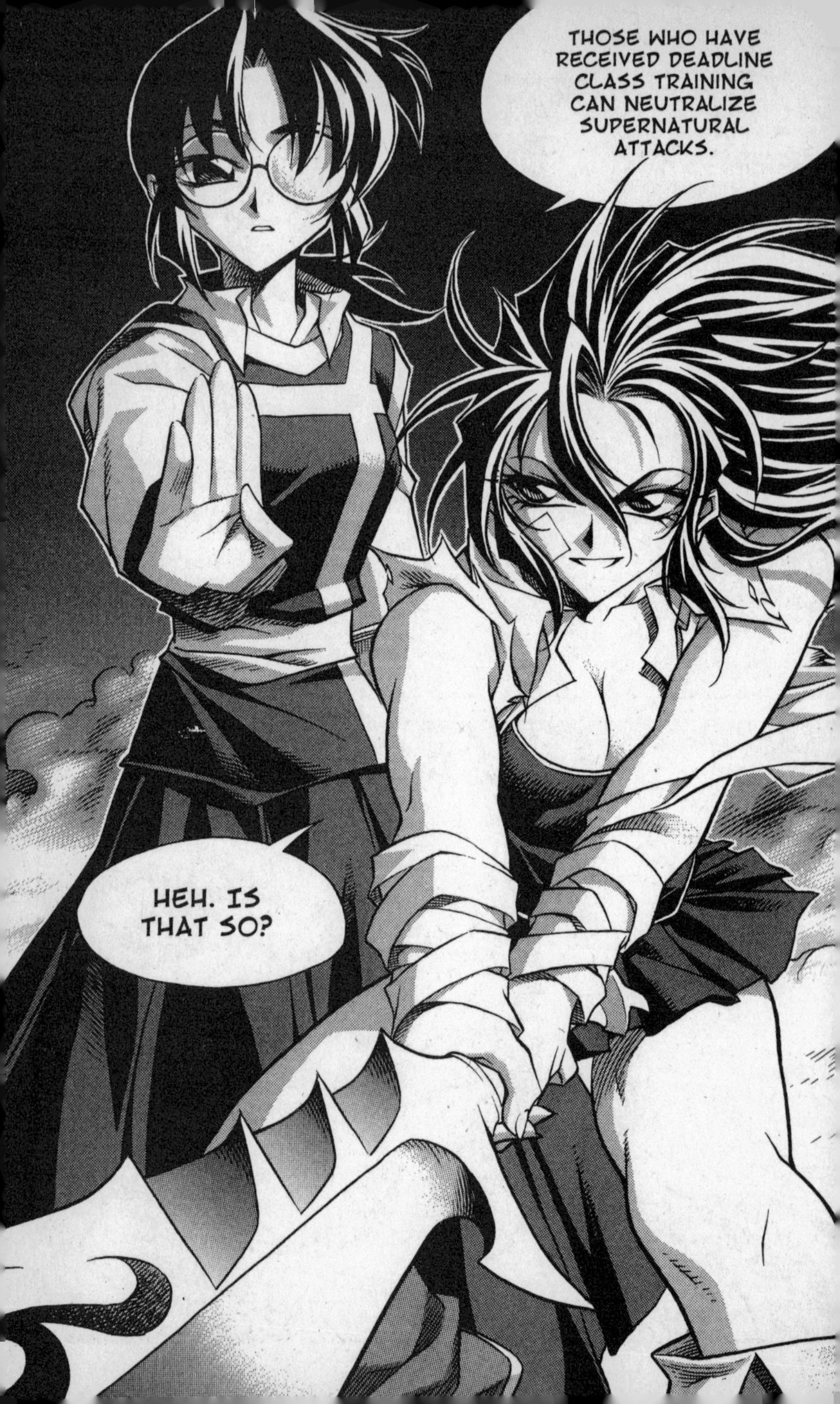
THOSE WHO HAVE RECEIVED DEADLINE CLASS TRAINING CAN NEUTRALIZE SUPERNATURAL ATTACKS.
HEH. IS THAT SO?

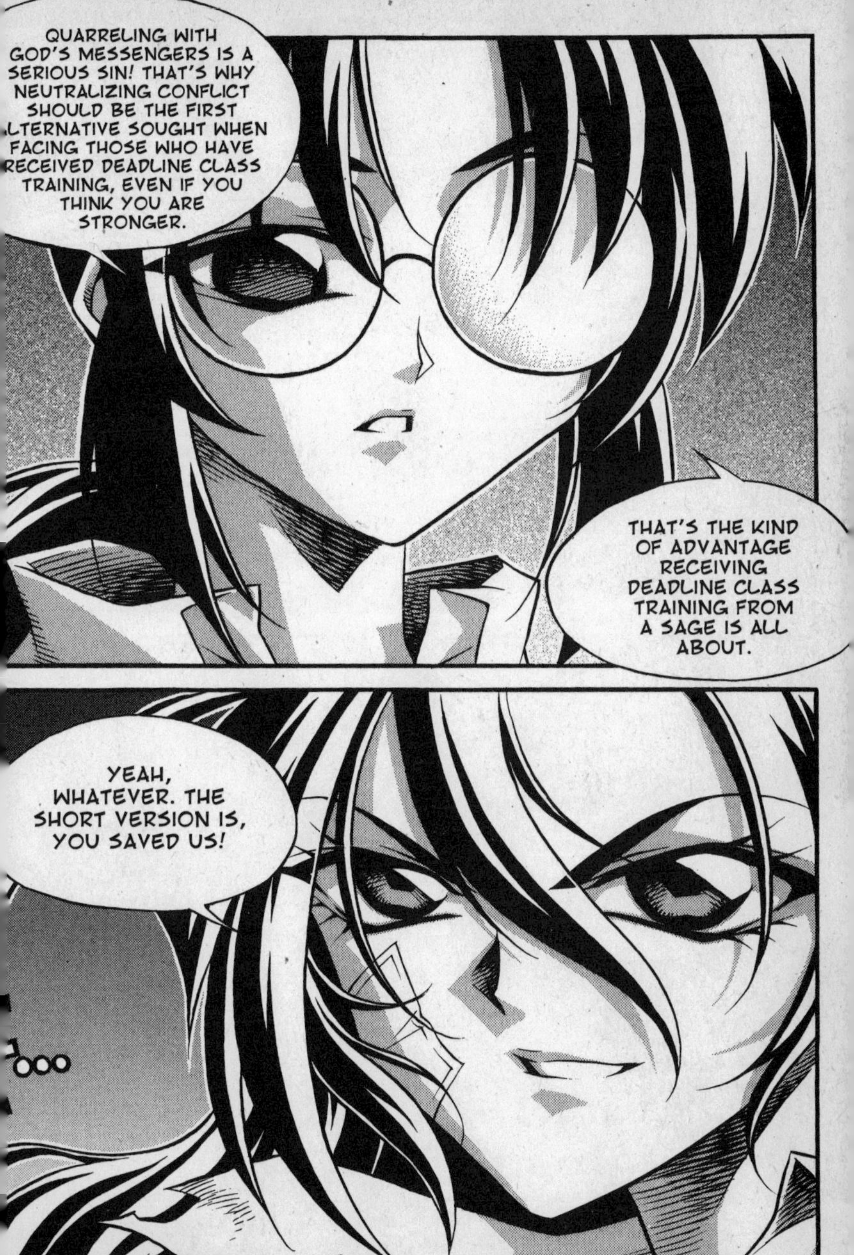
QUARRELING WITH GOD'S MESSENGERS IS A SERIOUS SIN! THAT'S WHY NEUTRALIZING CONFLICT SHOULD BE THE FIRST LTERNATIVE SOUGHT WHEN FACING THOSE WHO HAVE RECEIVED DEADLINE CLASS TRAINING, EVEN IF YOU THINK YOU ARE STRONGER.
THAT'S THE KIND OF ADVANTAGE RECEIVING DEADLINE CLASS TRAINING FROM A SAGE IS ALL ABOUT.
YEAH, WHATEVER. THE SHORT VERSION IS, YOU SAVED US!

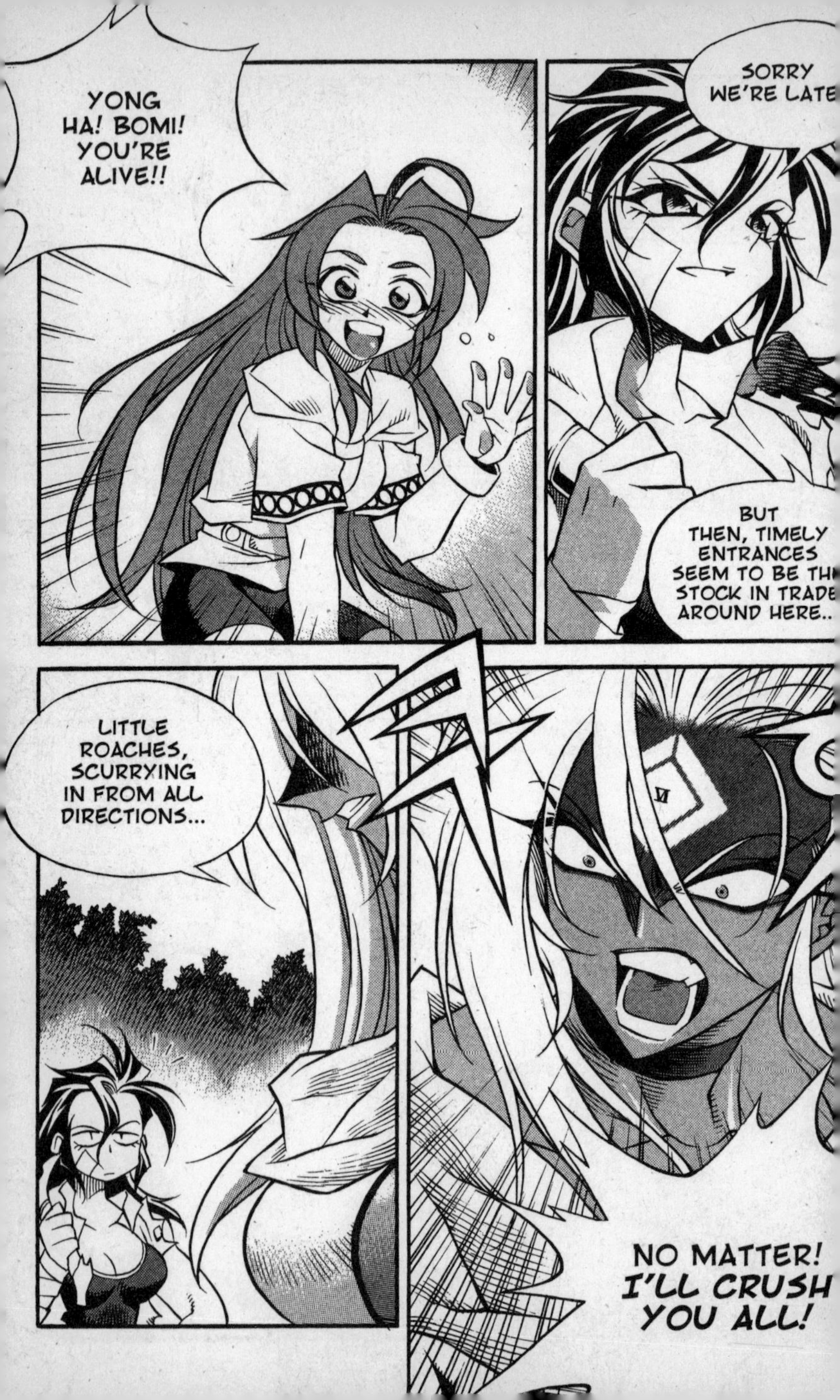

YONG HA! BOMI! YOU'RE ALIVE!!
SORRY WE'RE LATE
BUT THEN, TIMELY ENTRANCES SEEM TO BE THE STOCK IN TRADE AROUND HERE...
LITTLE ROACHES, SCURRYING IN FROM ALL DIRECTIONS...
NO MATTER! I'LL CRUSH YOU ALL!

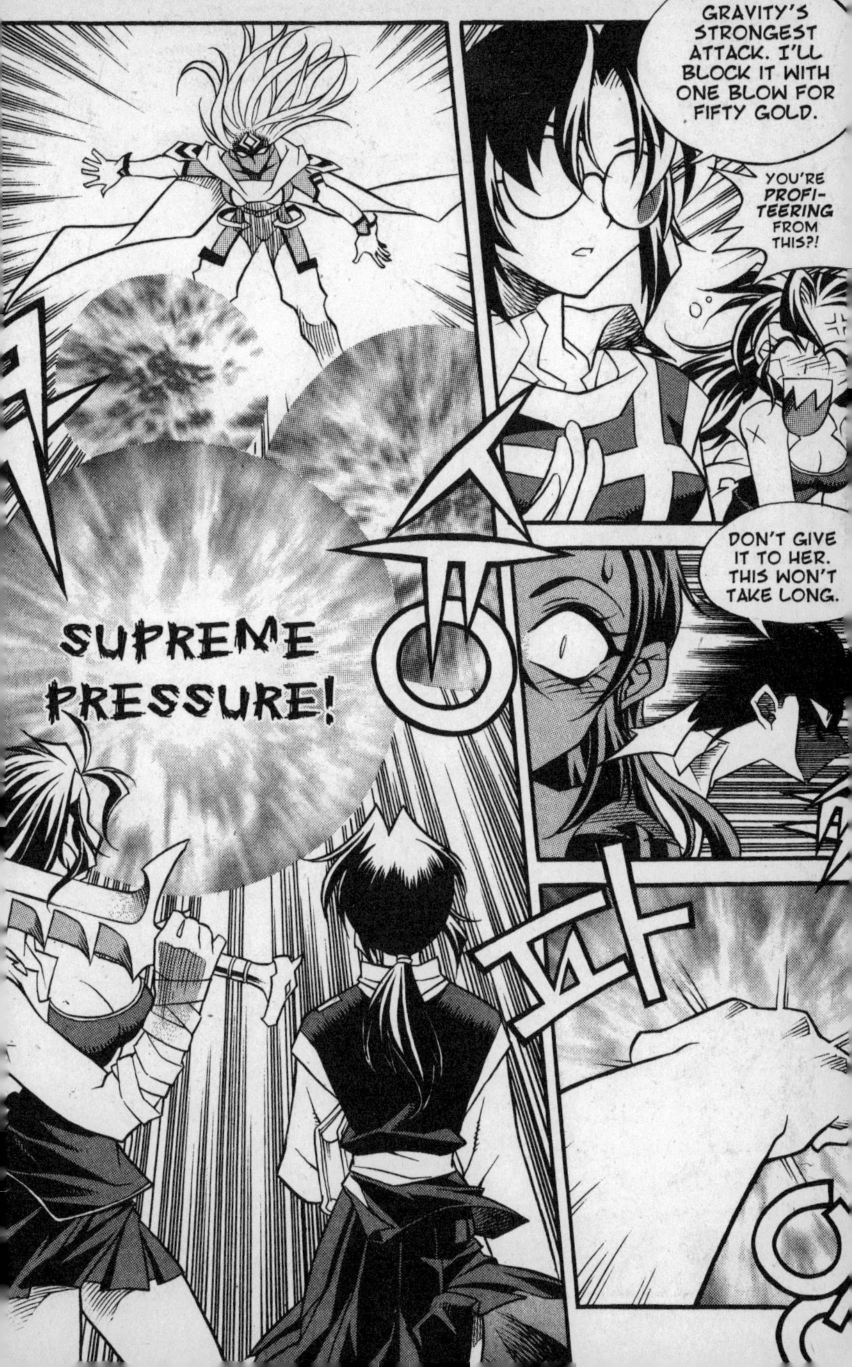
SUPREME PRESSURE!
GRAVITY'S STRONGEST ATTACK. I'LL BLOCK IT WITH ONE BLOW FOR FIFTY GOLD.
YOU'RE PROFITEERING FROM THIS?!
DON'T GIVE IT TO HER. THIS WON'T TAKE LONG.

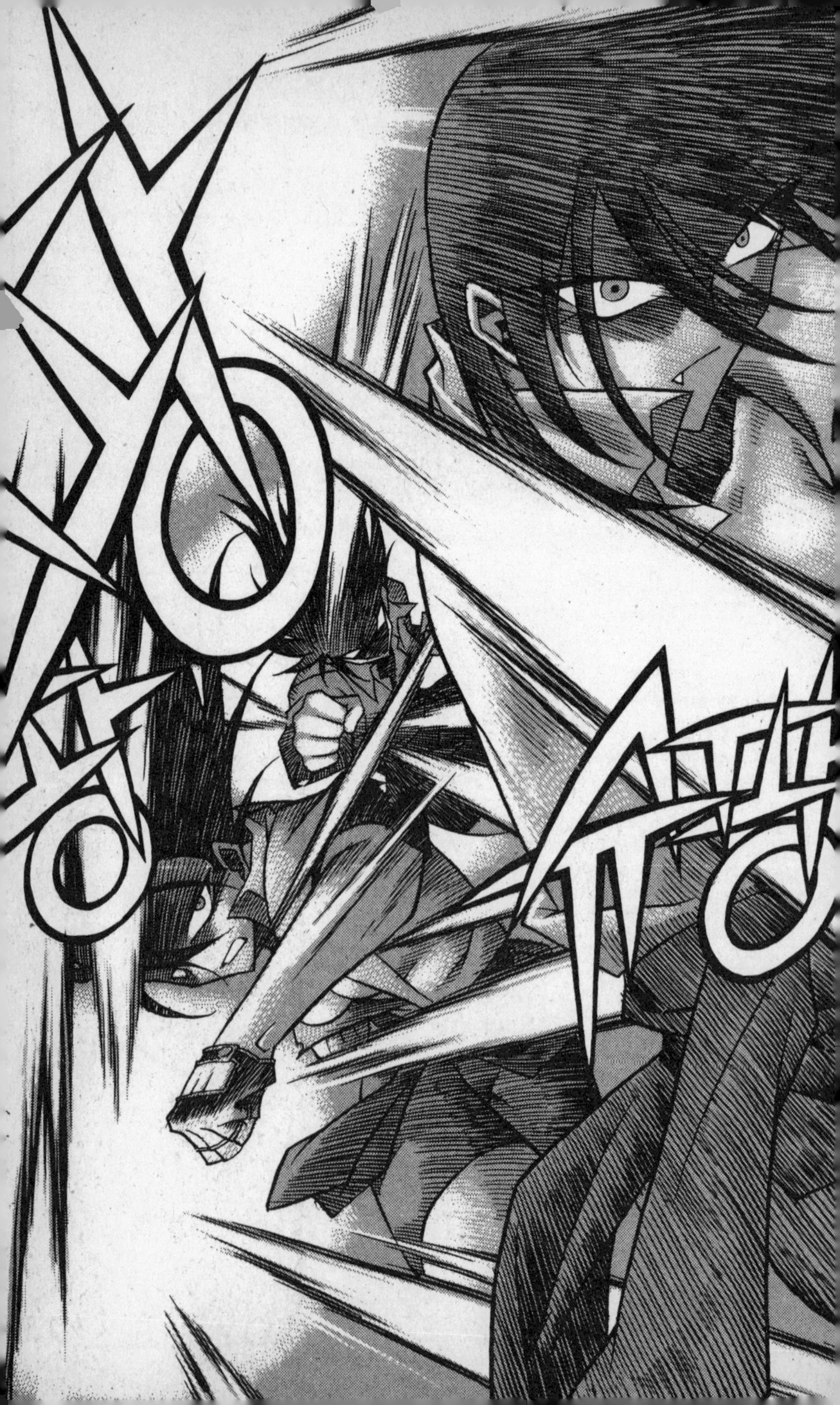

IMPOSSIBLE! HOW CAN HE DESTROY MY SUPREME PRESSURE WITH JUST A FIST...?

NO HUMAN ALIVE COULD...

IT DOESN'T MATTER IF YOU USE YOUR GRAVITY MAGIC ON ME, BECAUSE I CAN USE YOUR OWN GRAVITY TO STRIKE AGAINST IT!

YOUR ATTACKS ARE STRONG, BUT TO SOMEONE WHO UNDERSTANDS PHYSICS, THERE'S ALWAYS A COUNTER.

HEY GYO-HWE, YOU GOT THAT GRAVITY MAGIC INFORMATION FROM ME! INFORMATION FEE OF TEN GOLD!!

I BLOCKED HER ATTACK FROM HITTING YOU, SO I'D SAY YOU OWE ME. TAKE YOUR TEN AND GIVE ME MY CHANGE!

YOU'VE BECOME EVEN MORE INTRACTABLE DURING OUR SHORT TIME APART! To say nothing of your change in appearance...

HEY, I LEARNED FROM THE BEST!

These...idiots...

OH MY! ARE WE THE LAST ONES? YOU GUYS GOT HERE FIRST?

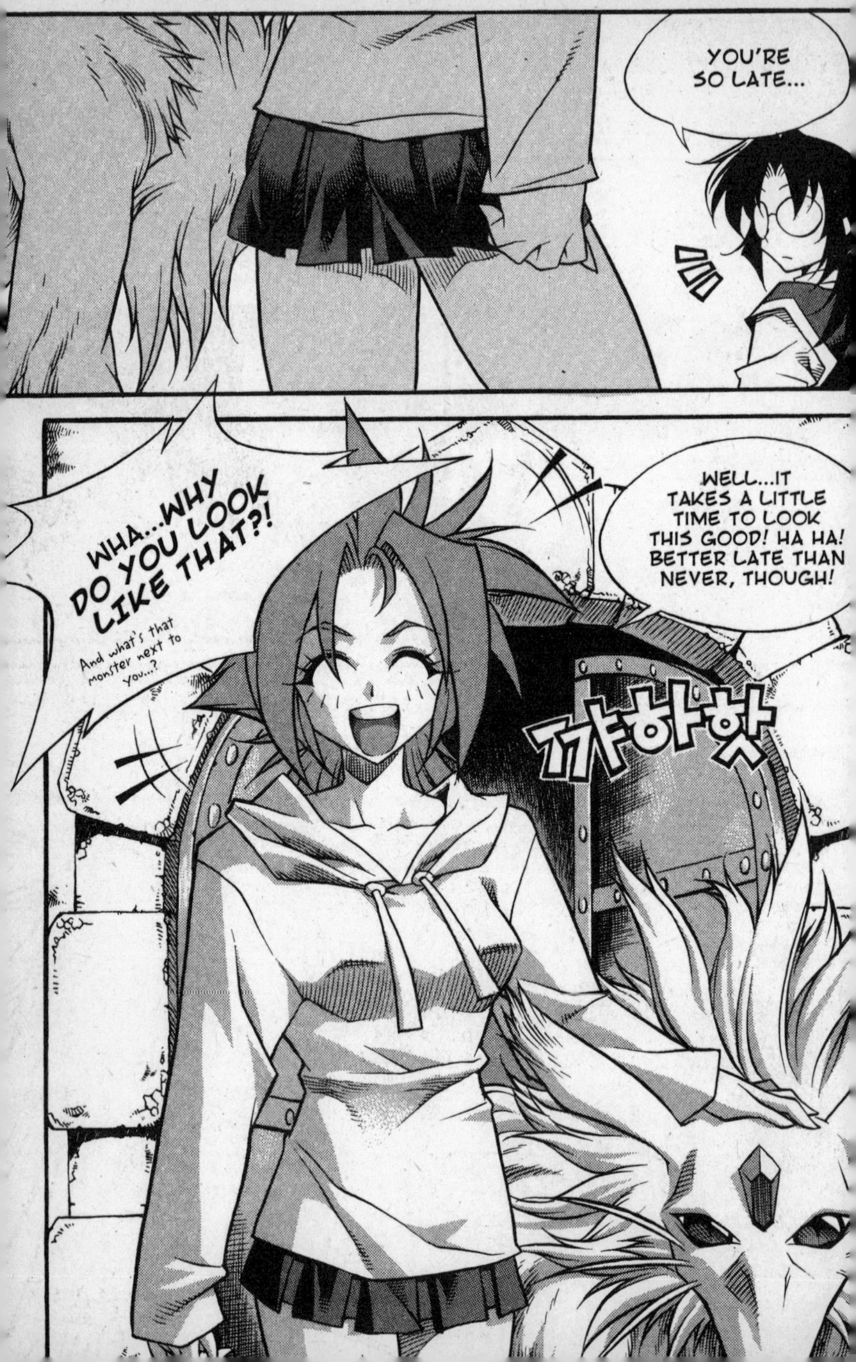
YOU'RE SO LATE...
WHA...WHY DO YOU LOOK LIKE THAT?!
And what's that monster next to you...?
WELL...IT TAKES A LITTLE TIME TO LOOK THIS GOOD! HA HA! BETTER LATE THAN NEVER, THOUGH!
꺄하핫

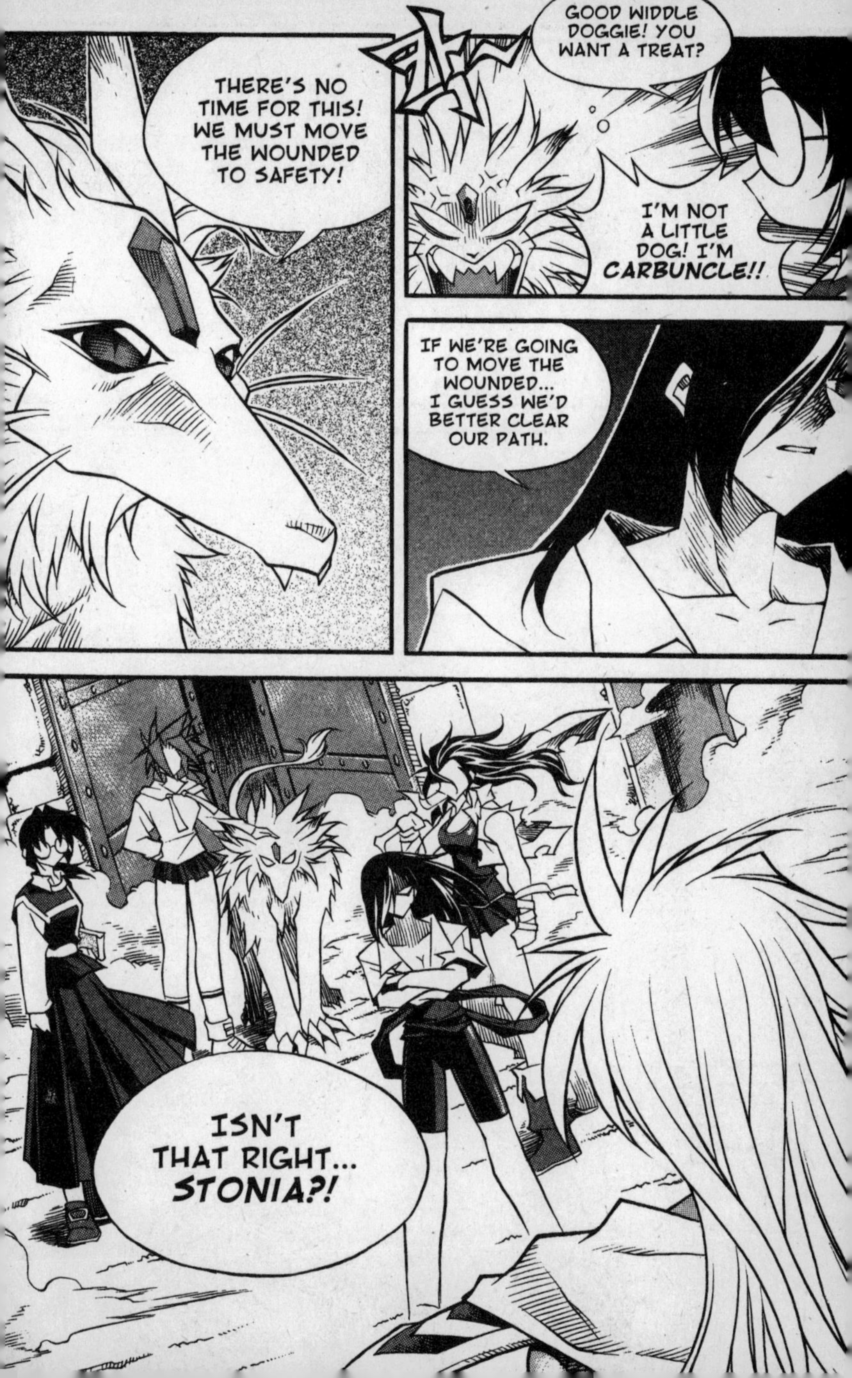
THERE'S NO TIME FOR THIS! WE MUST MOVE THE WOUNDED TO SAFETY!
GOOD WIDDLE DOGGIE! YOU WANT A TREAT?
I'M NOT A LITTLE DOG! I'M CARBUNCLE!!
IF WE'RE GOING TO MOVE THE WOUNDED... I GUESS WE'D BETTER CLEAR OUR PATH.
ISN'T THAT RIGHT... STONIA?!

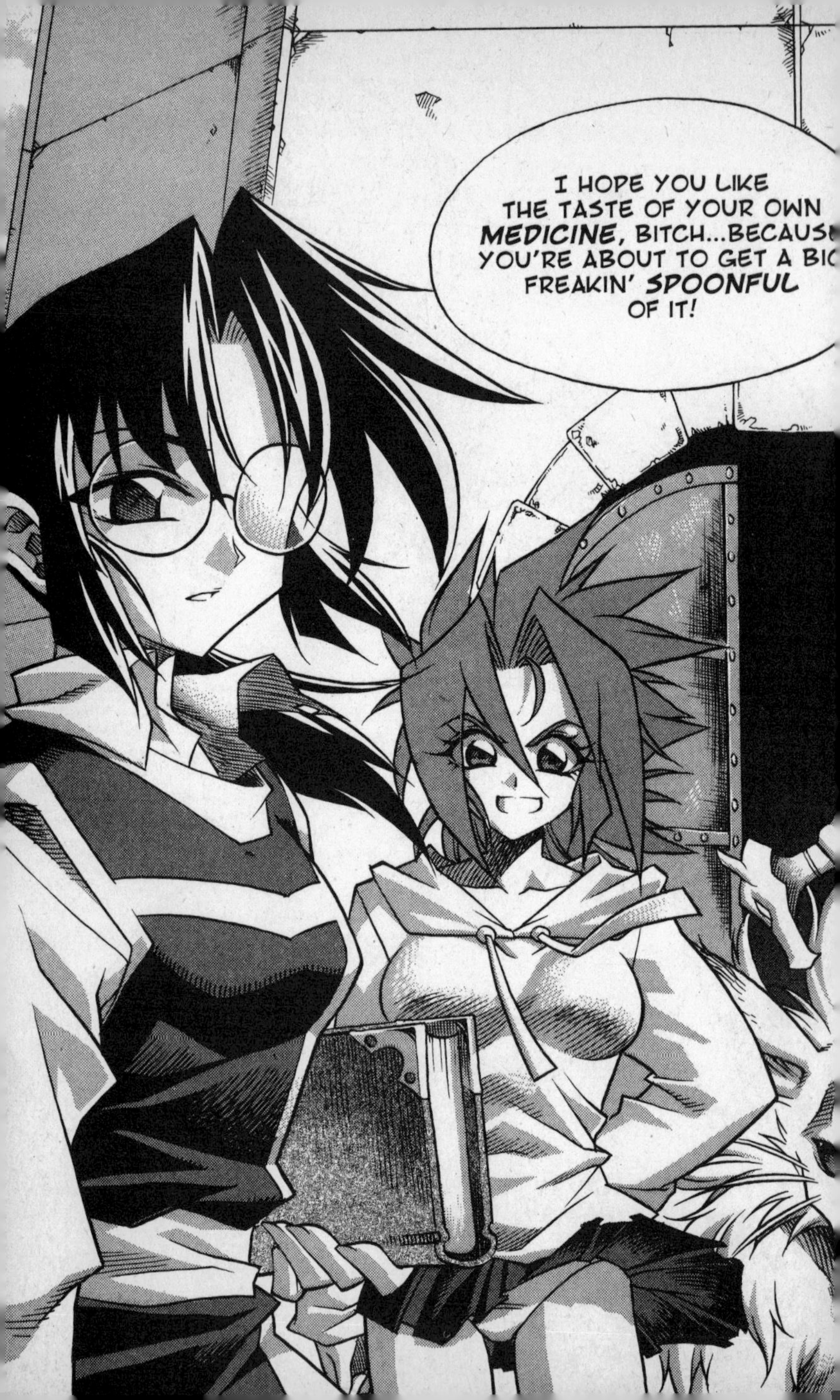
I HOPE YOU LIKE THE TASTE OF YOUR OWN MEDICINE, BITCH...BECAUS YOU'RE ABOUT TO GET A BI FREAKIN' SPOONFUL OF IT!

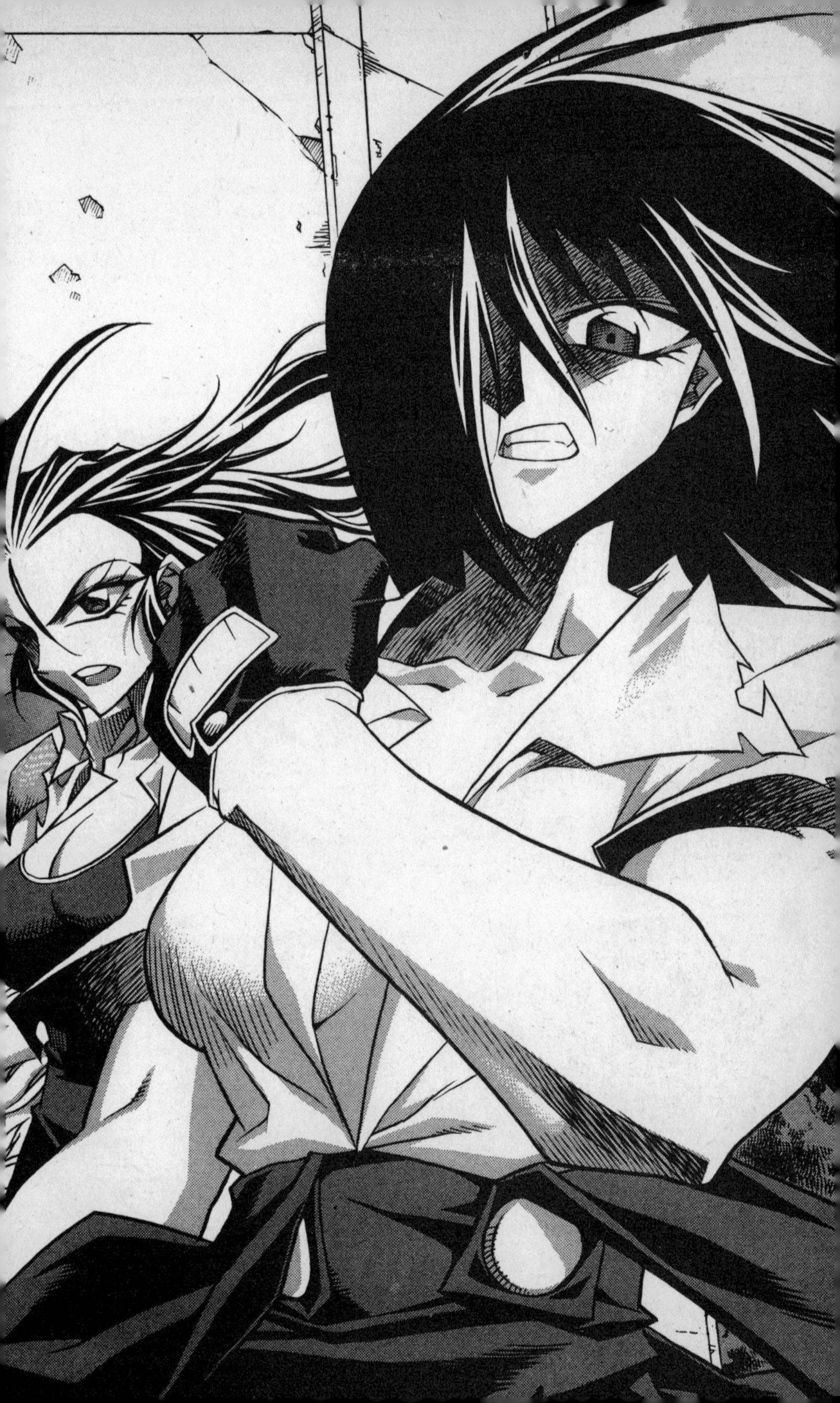

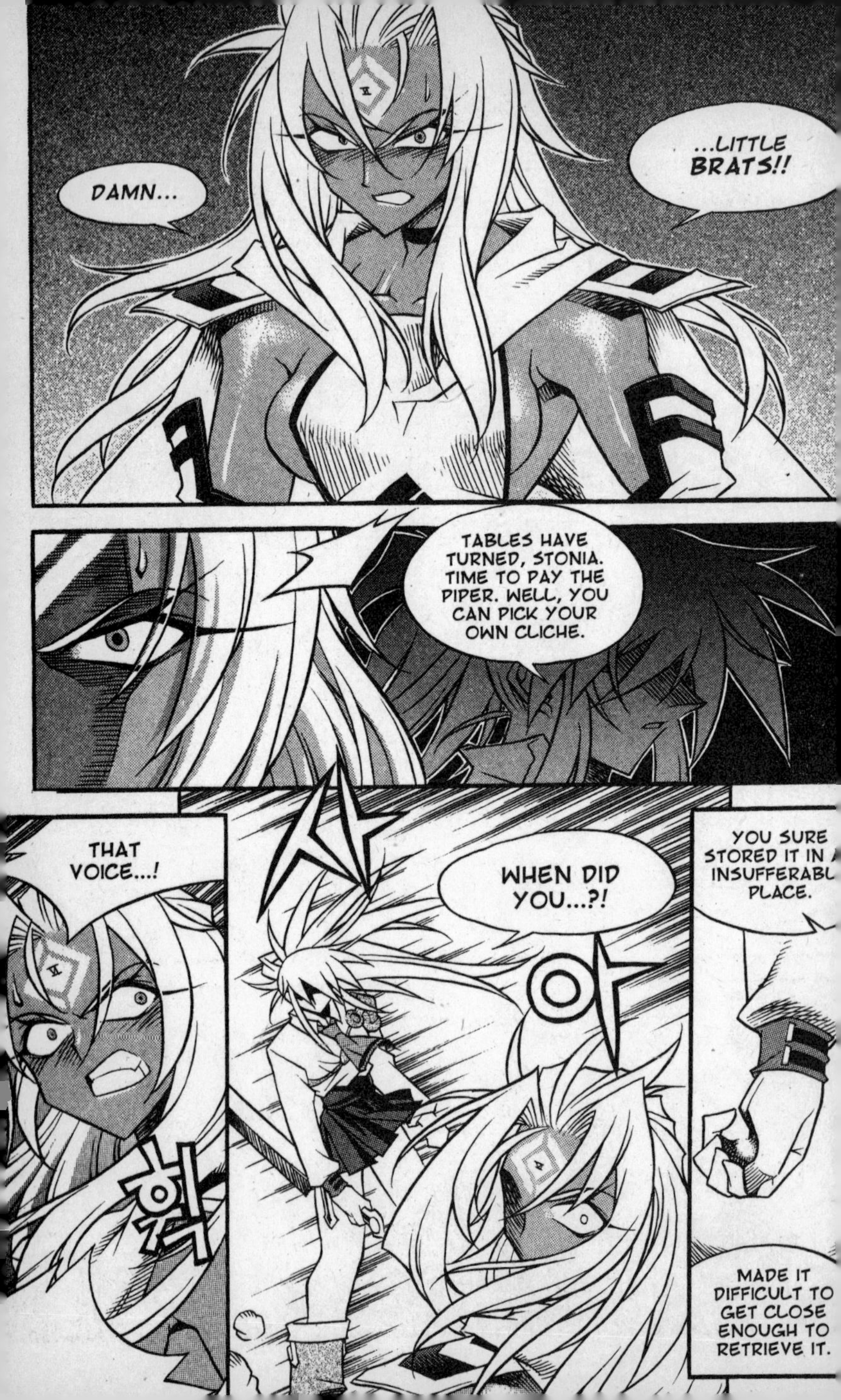
DAMN...
...LITTLE BRATS!!
TABLES HAVE TURNED, STONIA. TIME TO PAY THE PIPER. WELL, YOU CAN PICK YOUR OWN CLICHE.
THAT VOICE...!
WHEN DID YOU...?!
YOU SURE STORED IT IN A INSUFFERABL PLACE.
MADE IT DIFFICULT TO GET CLOSE ENOUGH TO RETRIEVE IT.

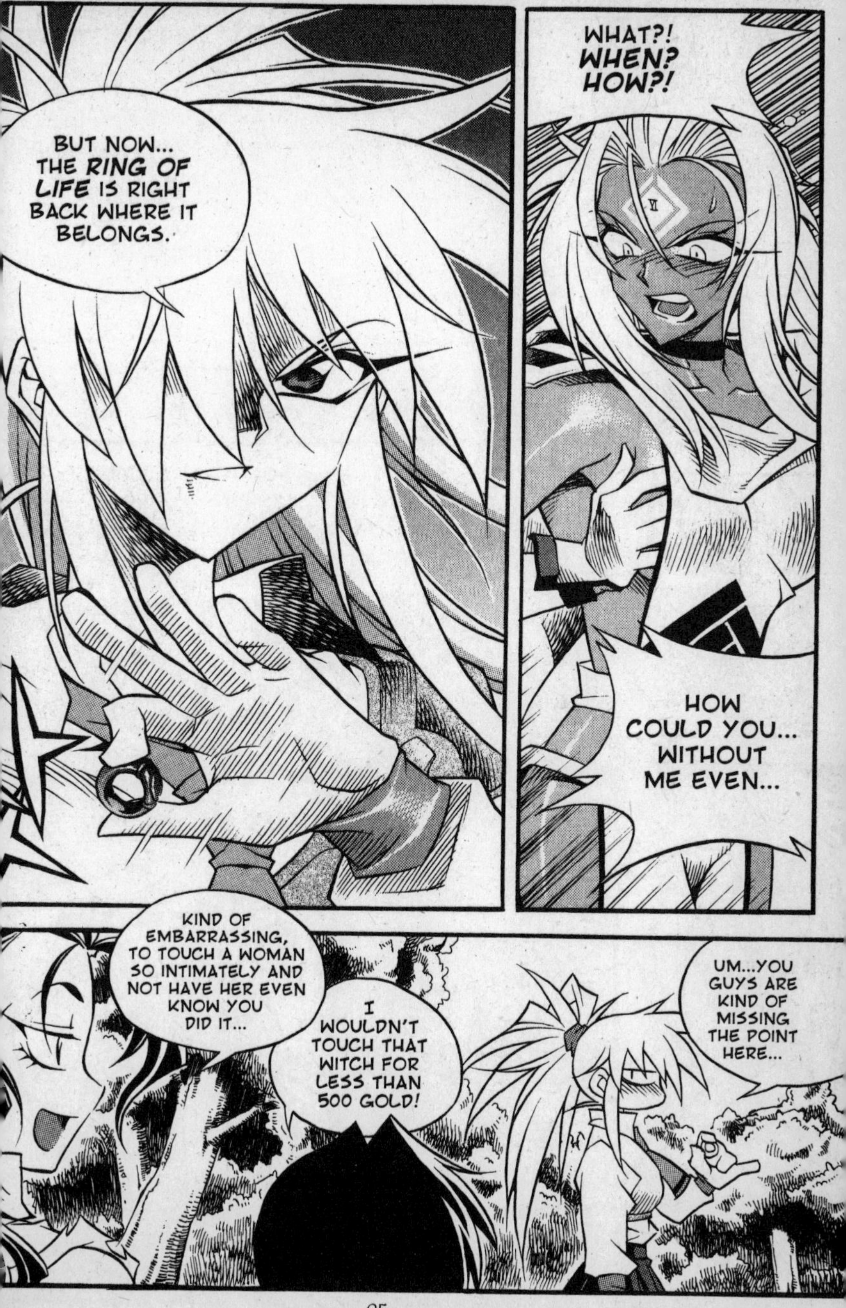
BUT NOW... THE RING OF LIFE IS RIGHT BACK WHERE IT BELONGS.
WHAT?! WHEN? HOW?!
HOW COULD YOU... WITHOUT ME EVEN...
KIND OF EMBARRASSING, TO TOUCH A WOMAN SO INTIMATELY AND NOT HAVE HER EVEN KNOW YOU DID IT...
I WOULDN'T TOUCH THAT WITCH FOR LESS THAN 500 GOLD!
UM...YOU GUYS ARE KIND OF MISSING THE POINT HERE...

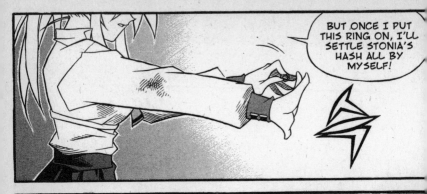

BUT ONCE I PUT THIS RING ON, I'LL SETTLE STONIA'S HASH ALL BY MYSELF!

GET READY, BITCH...

SWORD MASTER CHUN-LANG IS *BACK!*

Quest 73

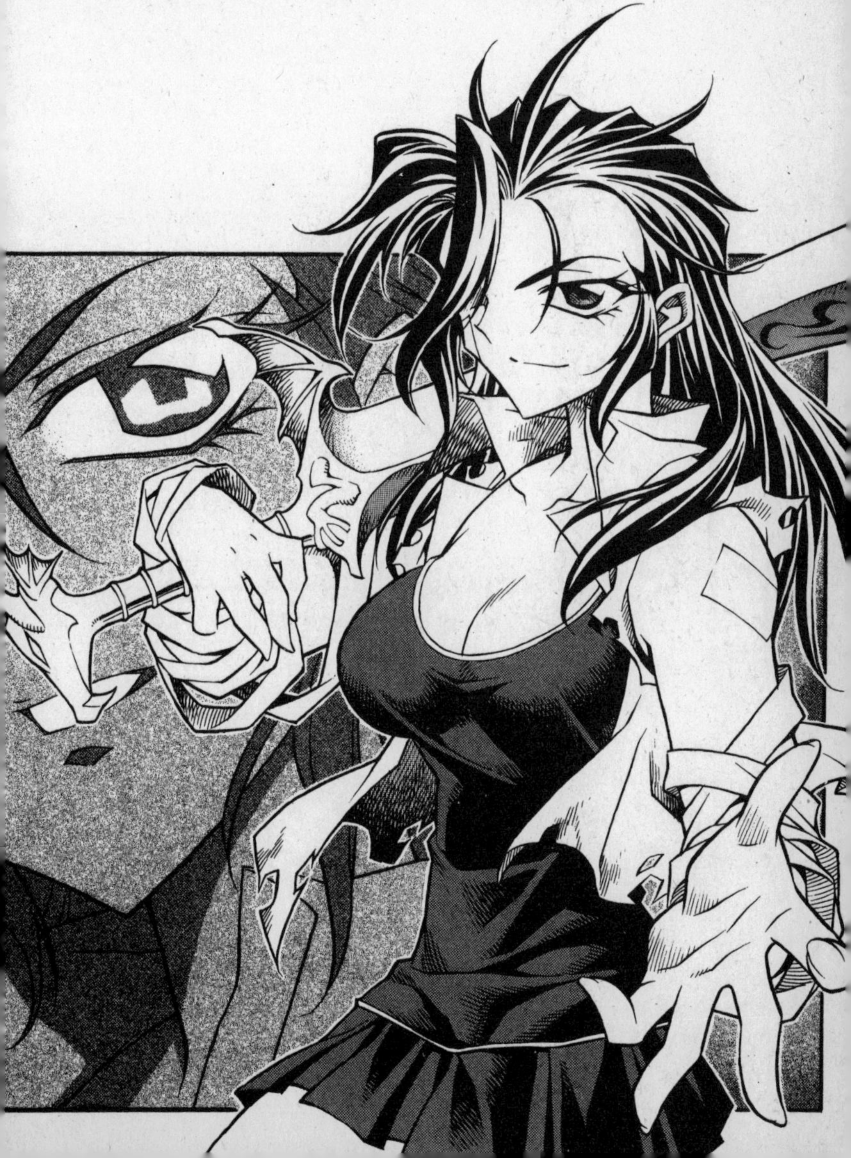

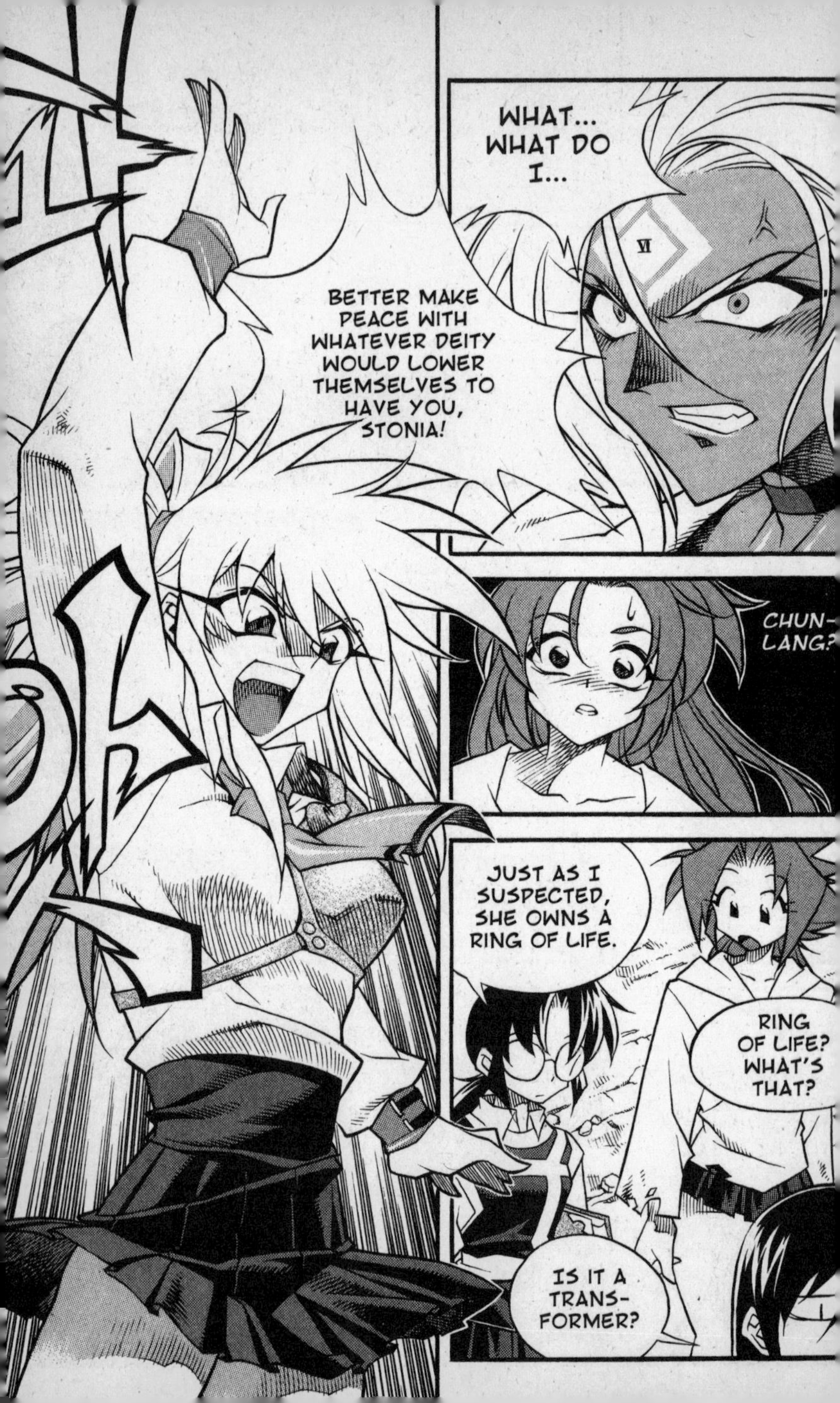
WHAT... WHAT DO I...
CHUN-LANG?
JUST AS I SUSPECTED, SHE OWNS A RING OF LIFE.
RING OF LIFE? WHAT'S THAT?
IS IT A TRANS-FORMER?
BETTER MAKE PEACE WITH WHATEVER DEITY WOULD LOWER THEMSELVES TO HAVE YOU, STONIA!

잠잠—

SILENCE

WHAT...WHAT'S GOING ON?! WHY AREN'T I CHANGING INTO A MAN?!

WELL. THAT WAS UNDERWHELMING.

I HAD SUCH HIGH EXPECTATIONS, TOO...

I'M POSITIVE IT'S MY RING... UNLESS IT'S AN IMITATION? DID SHE SWITCH IT?!

MPH! TO THINK I WAS WORRIED! THE RING OF LIFE DRAWS ITS STRENGTH FROM THE WEARER...

...AND SINCE THE RING'S LAST WEARER WAS SO MUCH MORE POWERFUL, YOU'RE NOT EVEN STRONG ENOUGH TO AWAKEN IT!

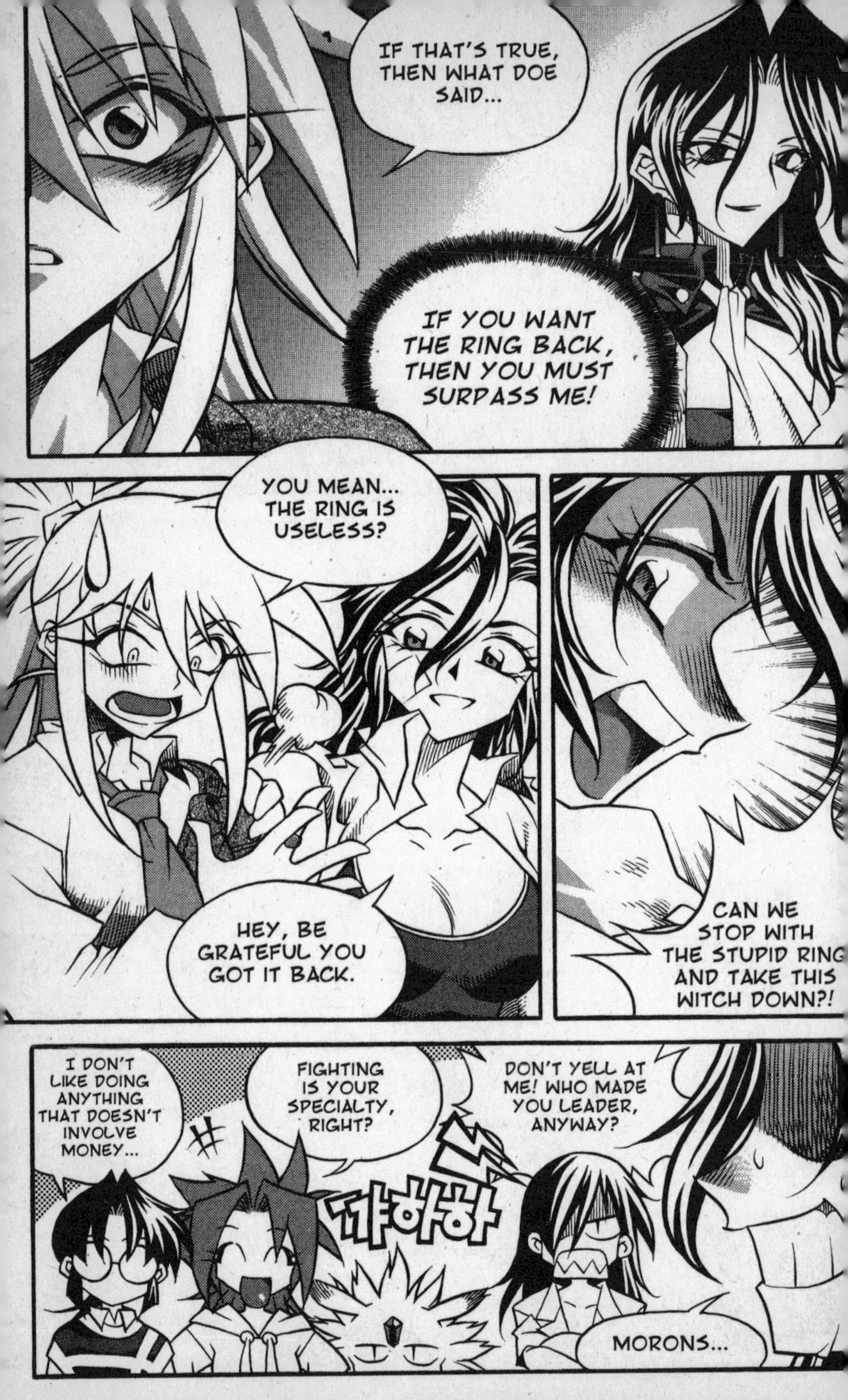
IF THAT'S TRUE, THEN WHAT DOE SAID...
IF YOU WANT THE RING BACK, THEN YOU MUST SURPASS ME!
YOU MEAN... THE RING IS USELESS?
HEY, BE GRATEFUL YOU GOT IT BACK.
CAN WE STOP WITH THE STUPID RING AND TAKE THIS WITCH DOWN?!
I DON'T LIKE DOING ANYTHING THAT DOESN'T INVOLVE MONEY...
FIGHTING IS YOUR SPECIALTY, RIGHT?
캬하하
DON'T YELL AT ME! WHO MADE YOU LEADER, ANYWAY?
MORONS...

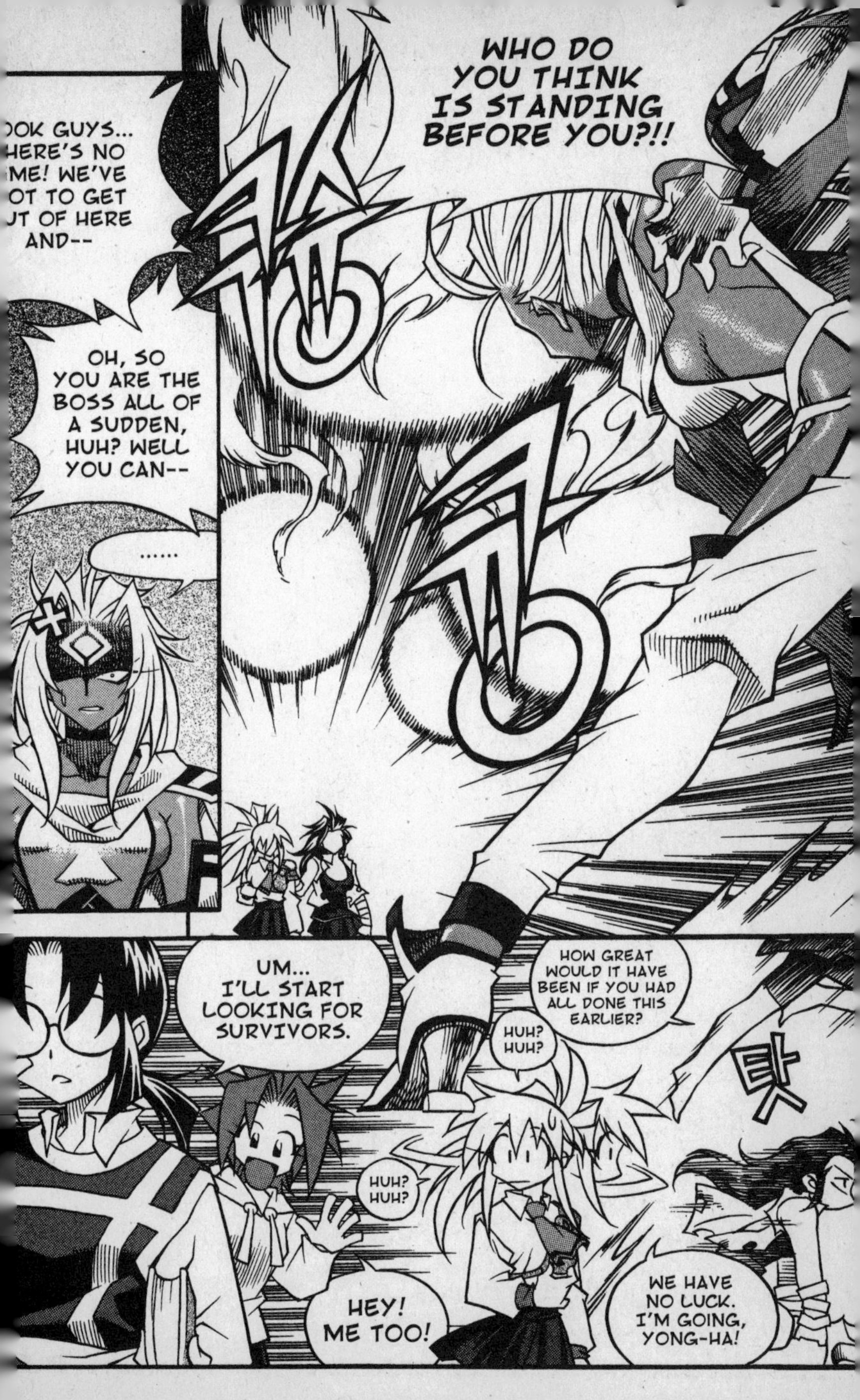

OOK GUYS... HERE'S NO ME! WE'VE OT TO GET UT OF HERE AND--
OH, SO YOU ARE THE BOSS ALL OF A SUDDEN, HUH? WELL YOU CAN--
......
WHO DO YOU THINK IS STANDING BEFORE YOU?!!
UM... I'LL START LOOKING FOR SURVIVORS.
HUH? HUH?
HOW GREAT WOULD IT HAVE BEEN IF YOU HAD ALL DONE THIS EARLIER?
HUH? HUH?
HEY! ME TOO!
WE HAVE NO LUCK. I'M GOING, YONG-HA!

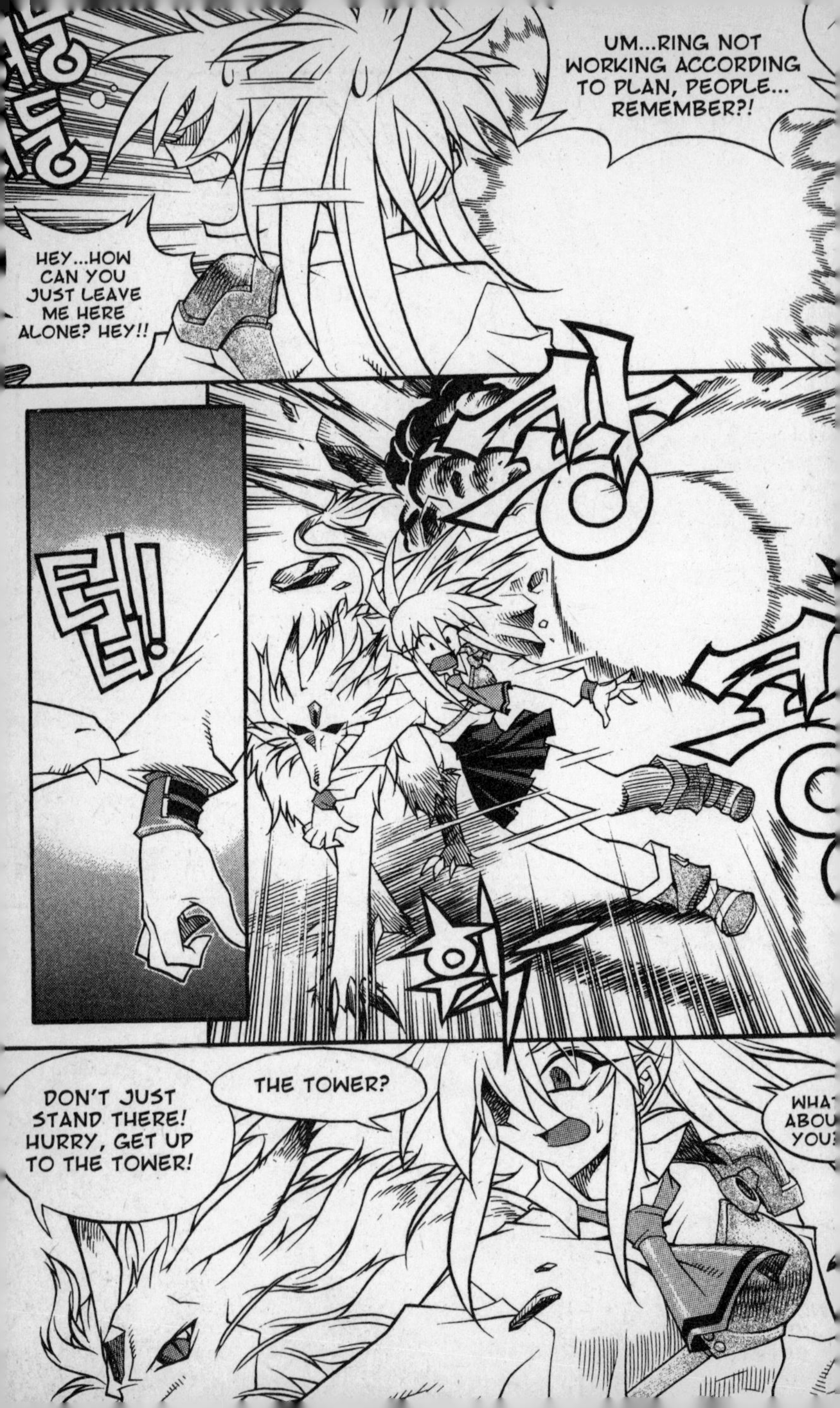
UM...RING NOT WORKING ACCORDING TO PLAN, PEOPLE... REMEMBER?!
HEY...HOW CAN YOU JUST LEAVE ME HERE ALONE? HEY!!
DON'T JUST STAND THERE! HURRY, GET UP TO THE TOWER!
THE TOWER?

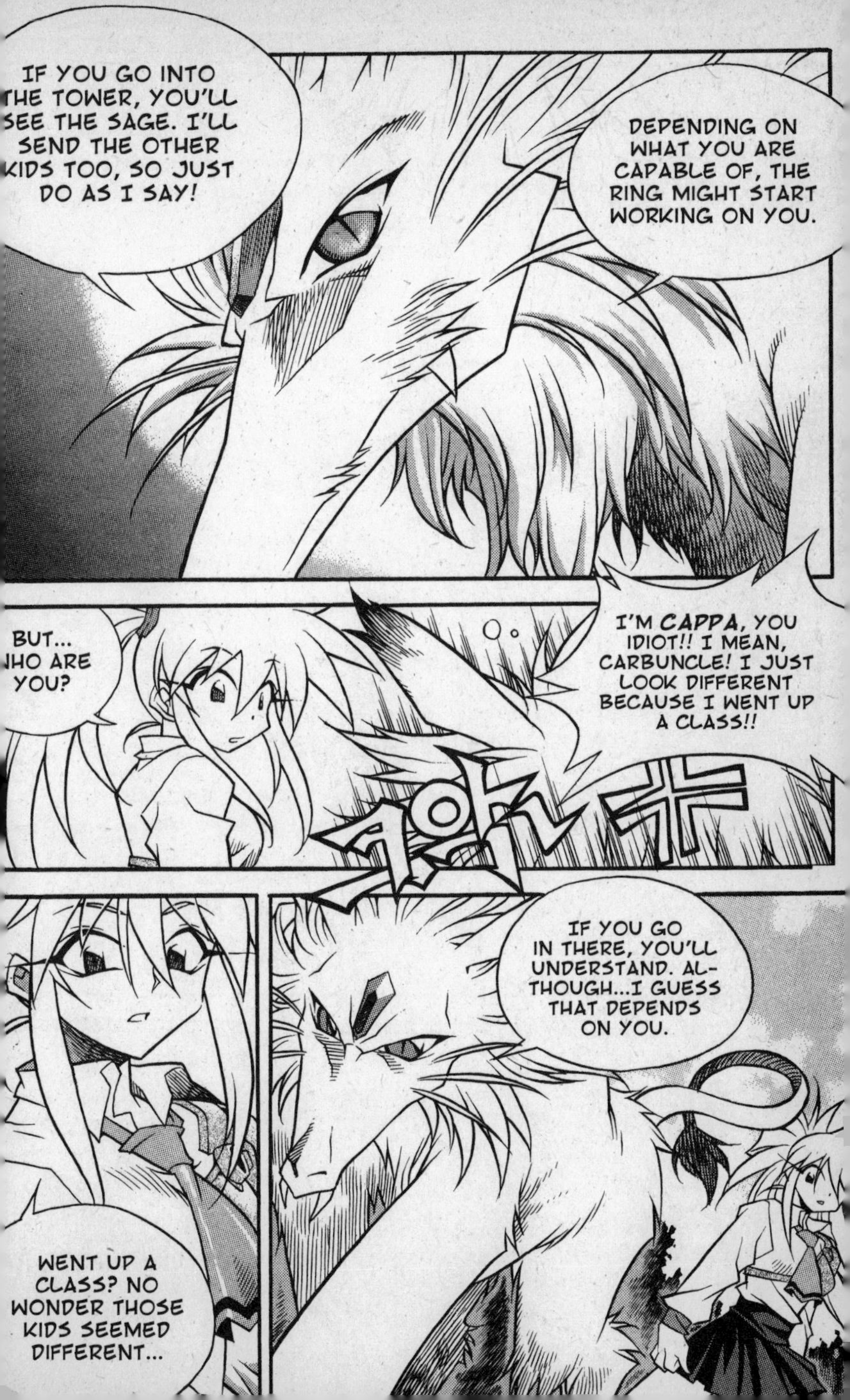
IF YOU GO INTO THE TOWER, YOU'LL SEE THE SAGE. I'LL SEND THE OTHER KIDS TOO, SO JUST DO AS I SAY!
DEPENDING ON WHAT YOU ARE CAPABLE OF, THE RING MIGHT START WORKING ON YOU.
BUT... WHO ARE YOU?
I'M ***CAPPA***, YOU IDIOT!! I MEAN, CARBUNCLE! I JUST LOOK DIFFERENT BECAUSE I WENT UP A CLASS!!
WENT UP A CLASS? NO WONDER THOSE KIDS SEEMED DIFFERENT...
IF YOU GO IN THERE, YOU'LL UNDERSTAND. ALTHOUGH...I GUESS THAT DEPENDS ON YOU.

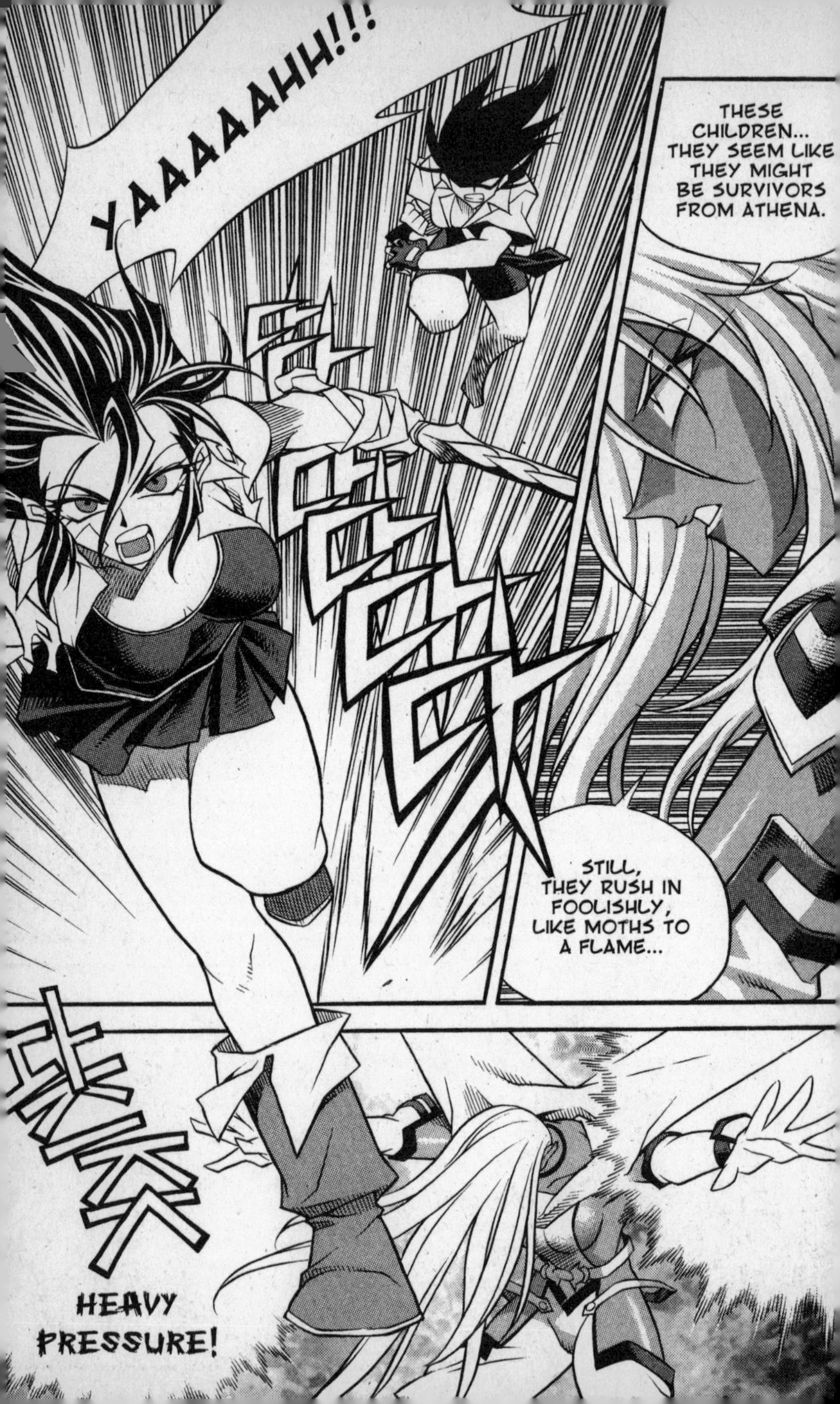
YAAAAAAHH!!!
THESE CHILDREN... THEY SEEM LIKE THEY MIGHT BE SURVIVORS FROM ATHENA.
STILL, THEY RUSH IN FOOLISHLY, LIKE MOTHS TO A FLAME...
HEAVY PRESSURE!

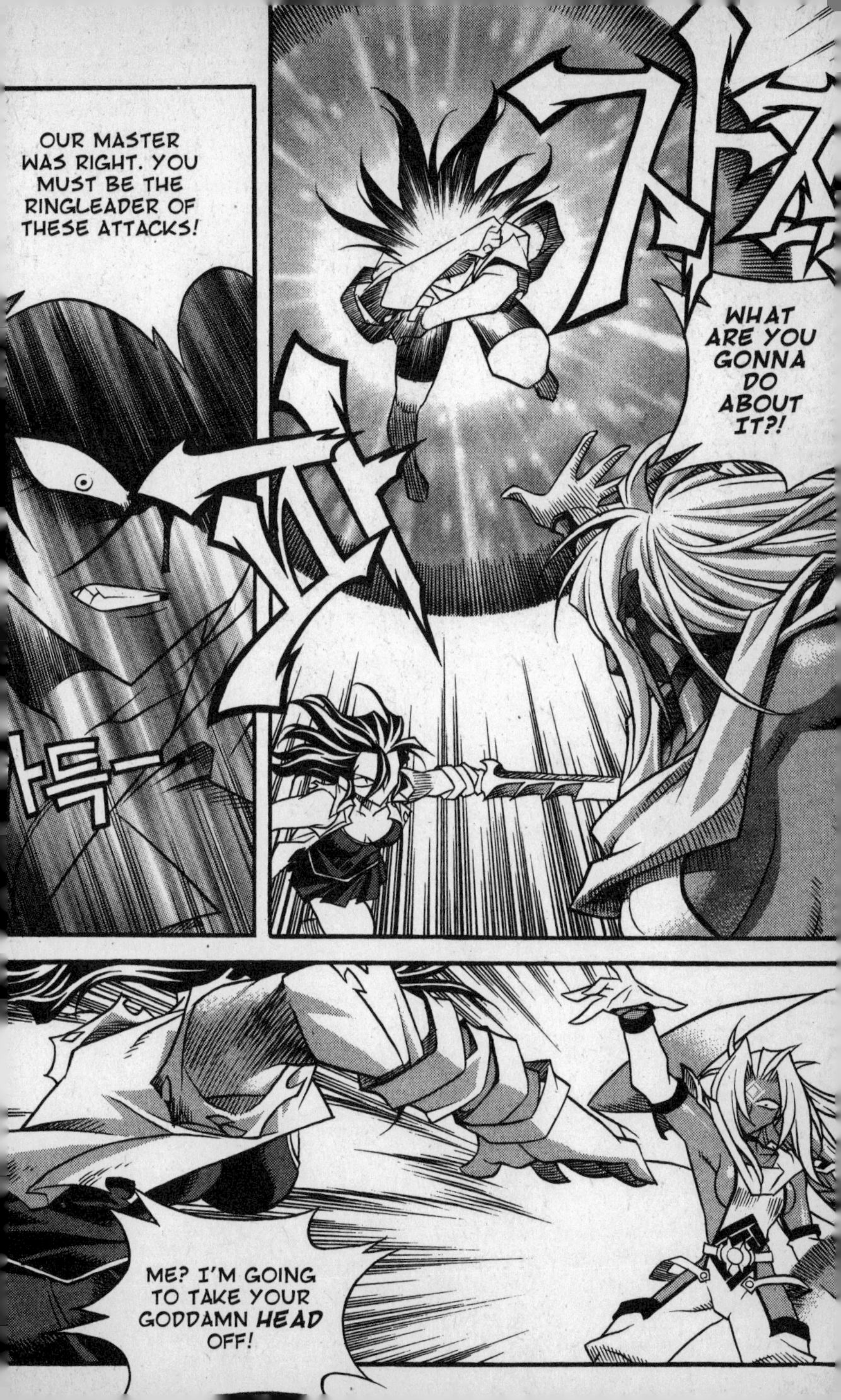
OUR MASTER WAS RIGHT. YOU MUST BE THE RINGLEADER OF THESE ATTACKS!
WHAT ARE YOU GONNA DO ABOUT IT?!
ME? I'M GOING TO TAKE YOUR GODDAMN **HEAD** OFF!

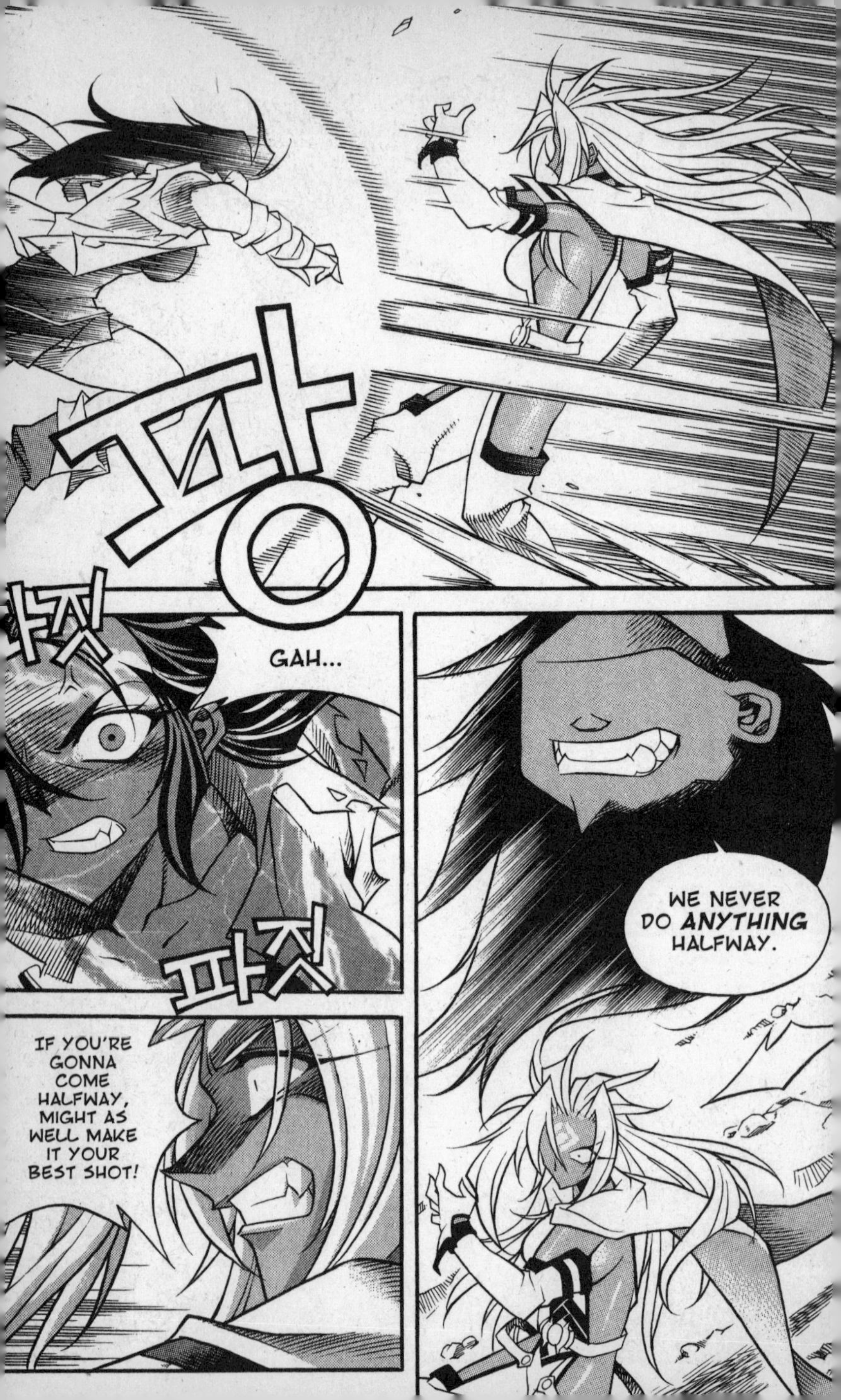
팡
GAH...
파짓
IF YOU'RE GONNA COME HALFWAY, MIGHT AS WELL MAKE IT YOUR BEST SHOT!
WE NEVER DO **ANYTHING** HALFWAY.

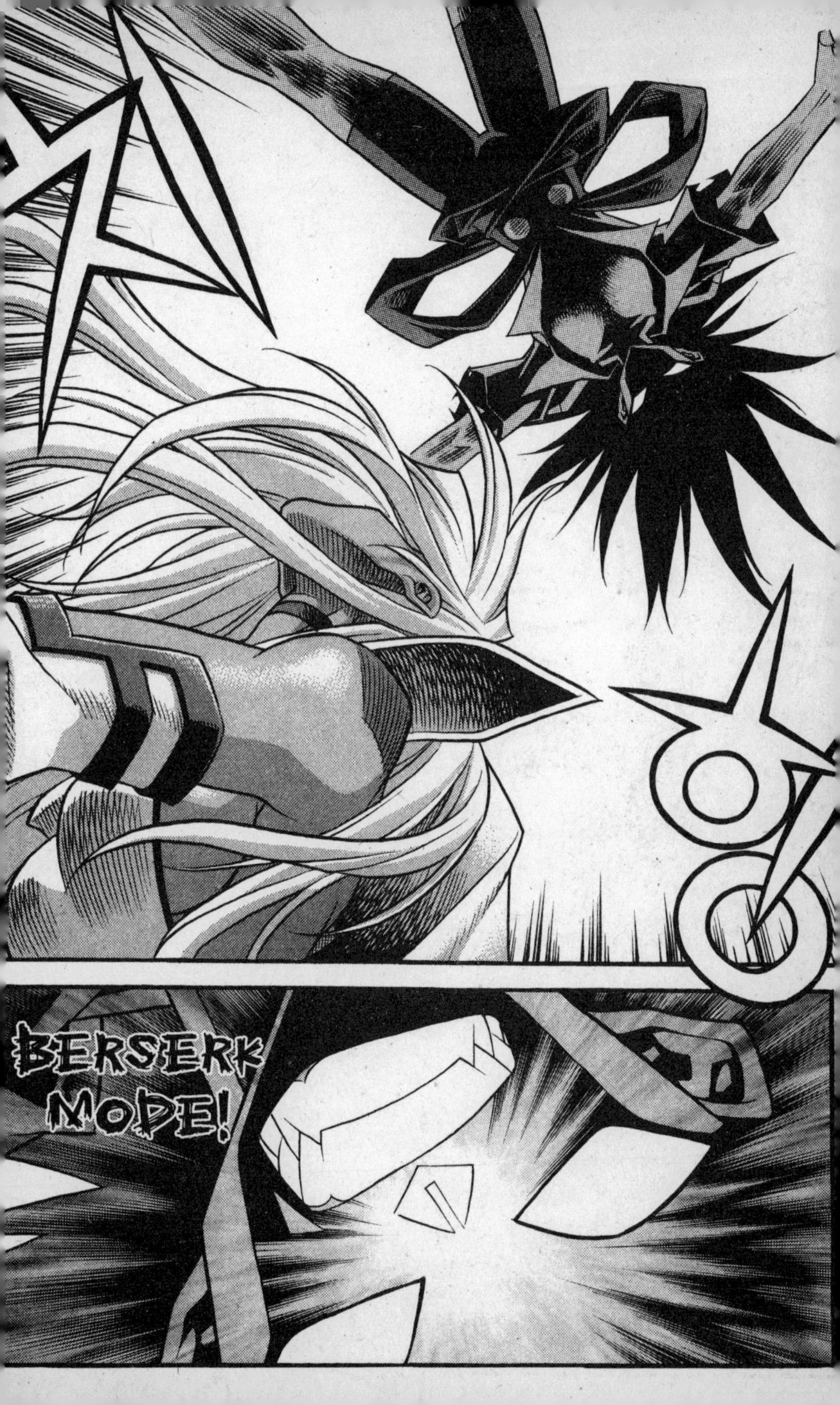
BERSERK MODE!

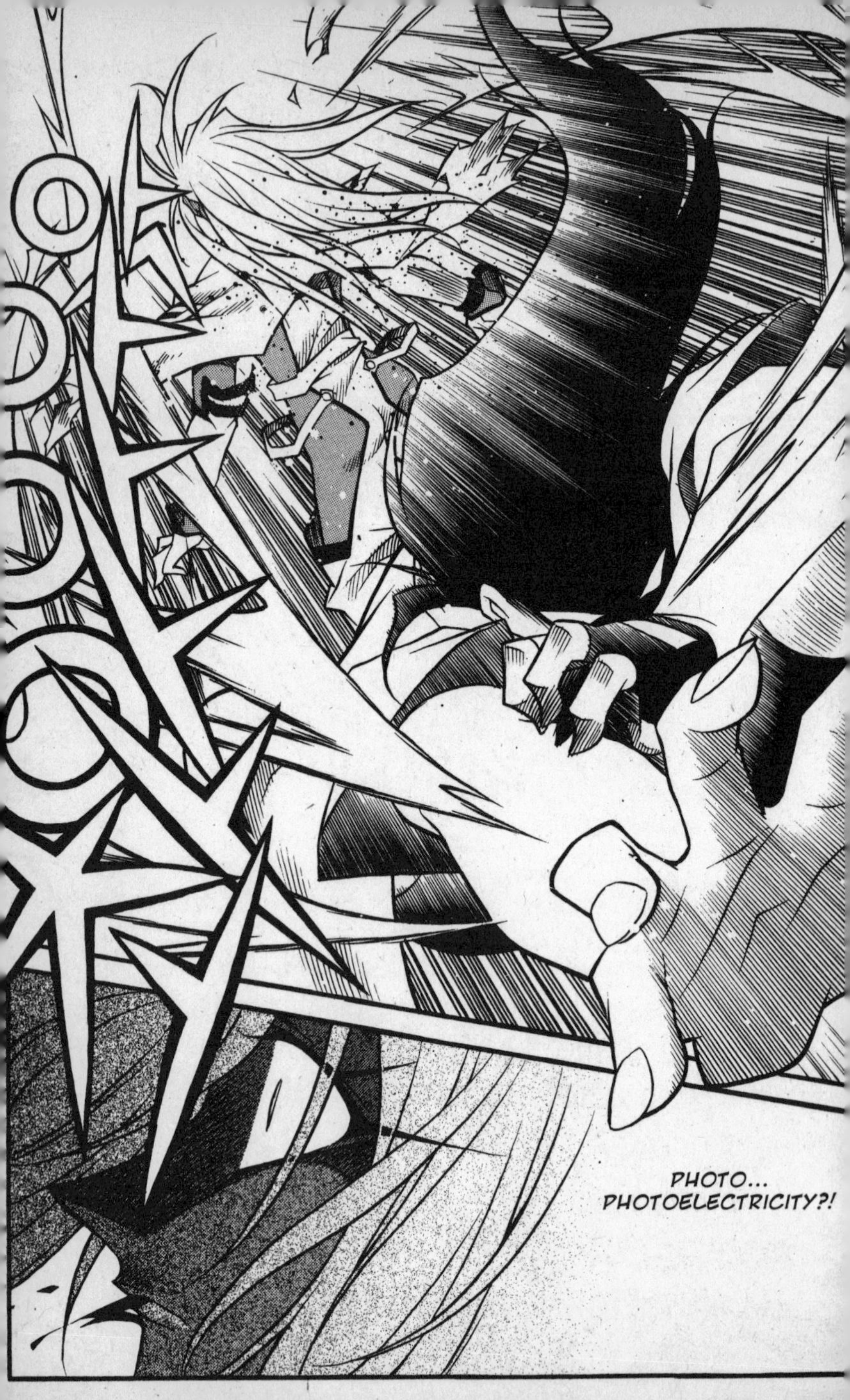
PHOTO...
PHOTOELECTRICITY?!

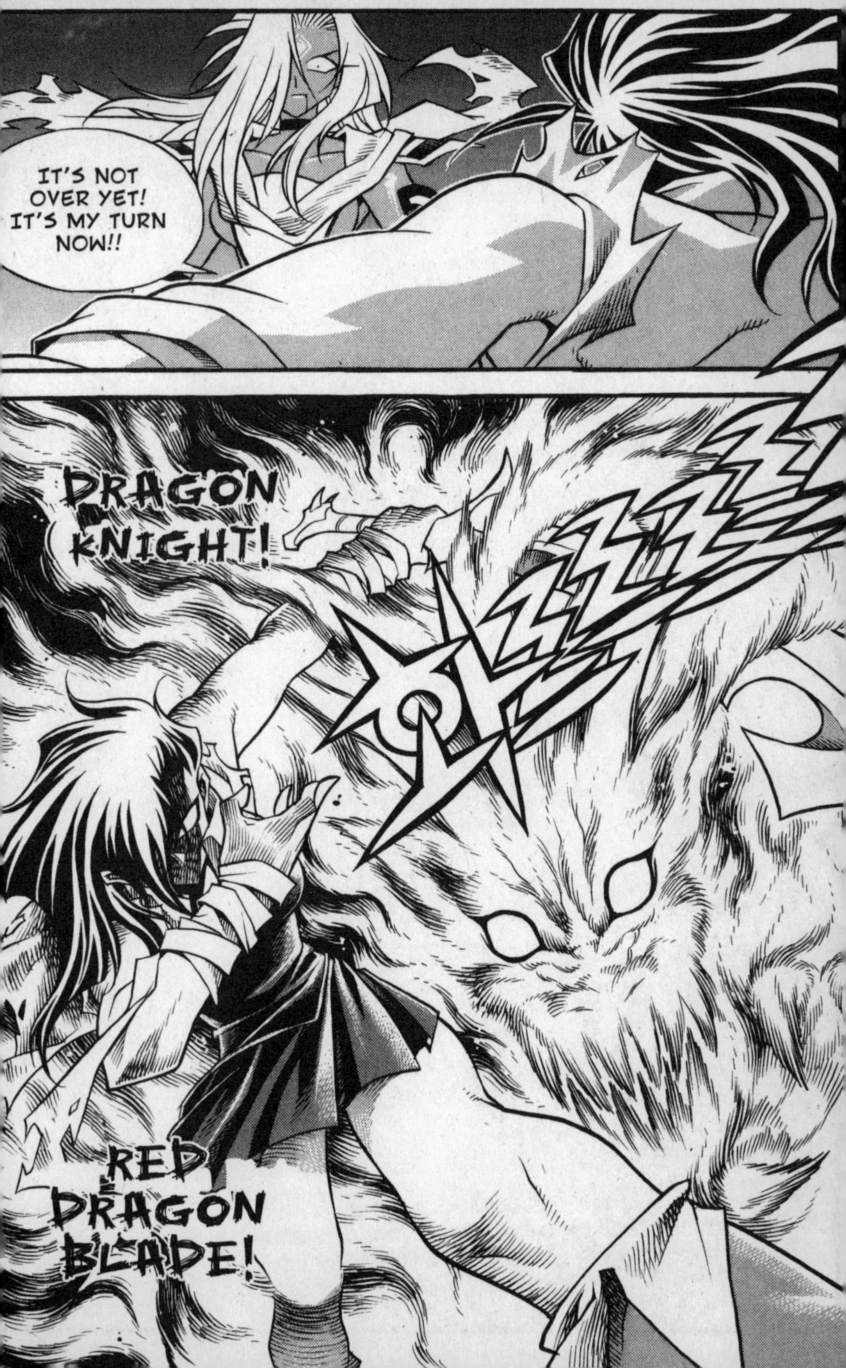
IT'S NOT OVER YET! IT'S MY TURN NOW!!
DRAGON KNIGHT!
RED DRAGON BLADE!

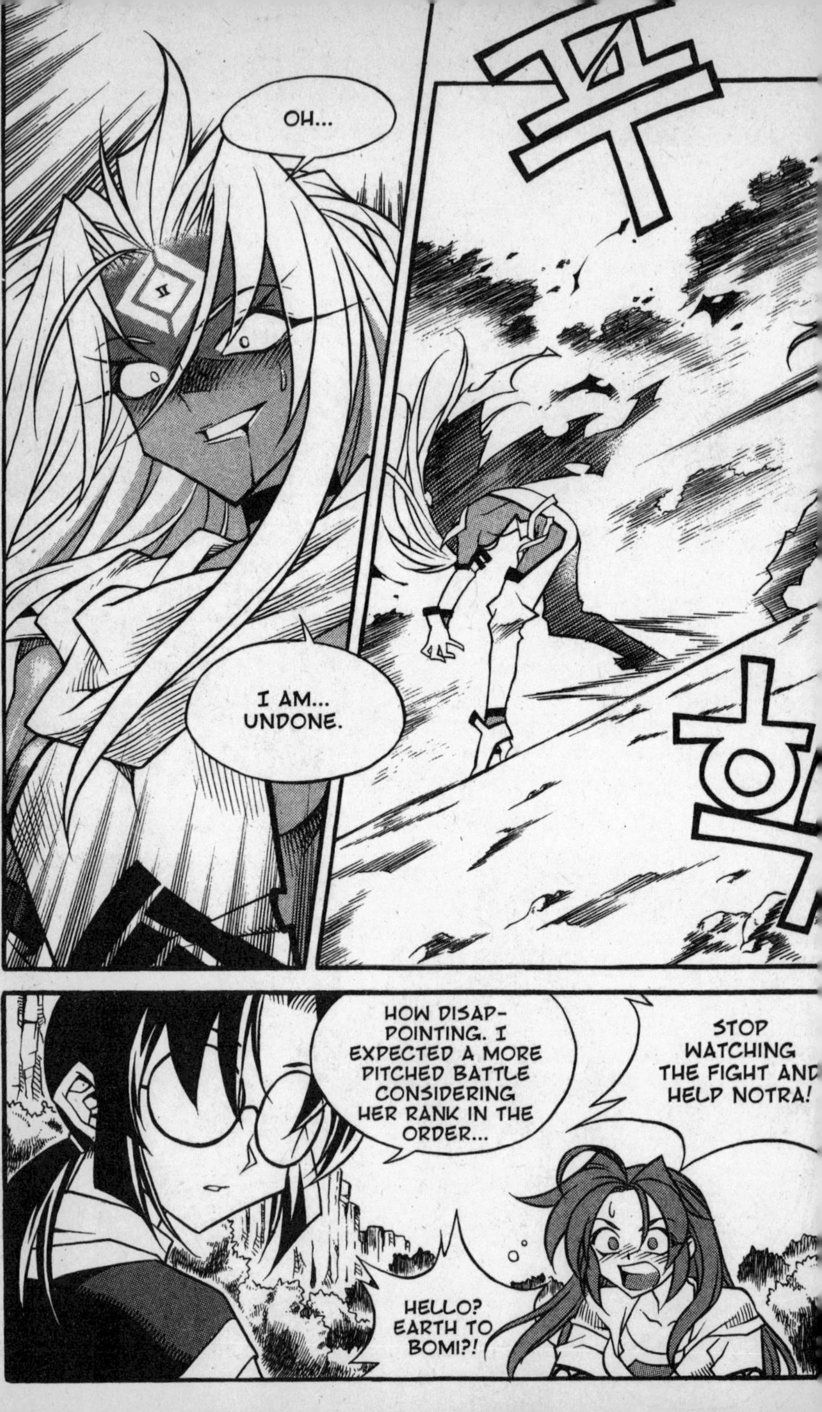
OH...
I AM... UNDONE.
푸
하
HOW DISAP-POINTING. I EXPECTED A MORE PITCHED BATTLE CONSIDERING HER RANK IN THE ORDER...
STOP WATCHING THE FIGHT AND HELP NOTRA!
HELLO? EARTH TO BOMI?!

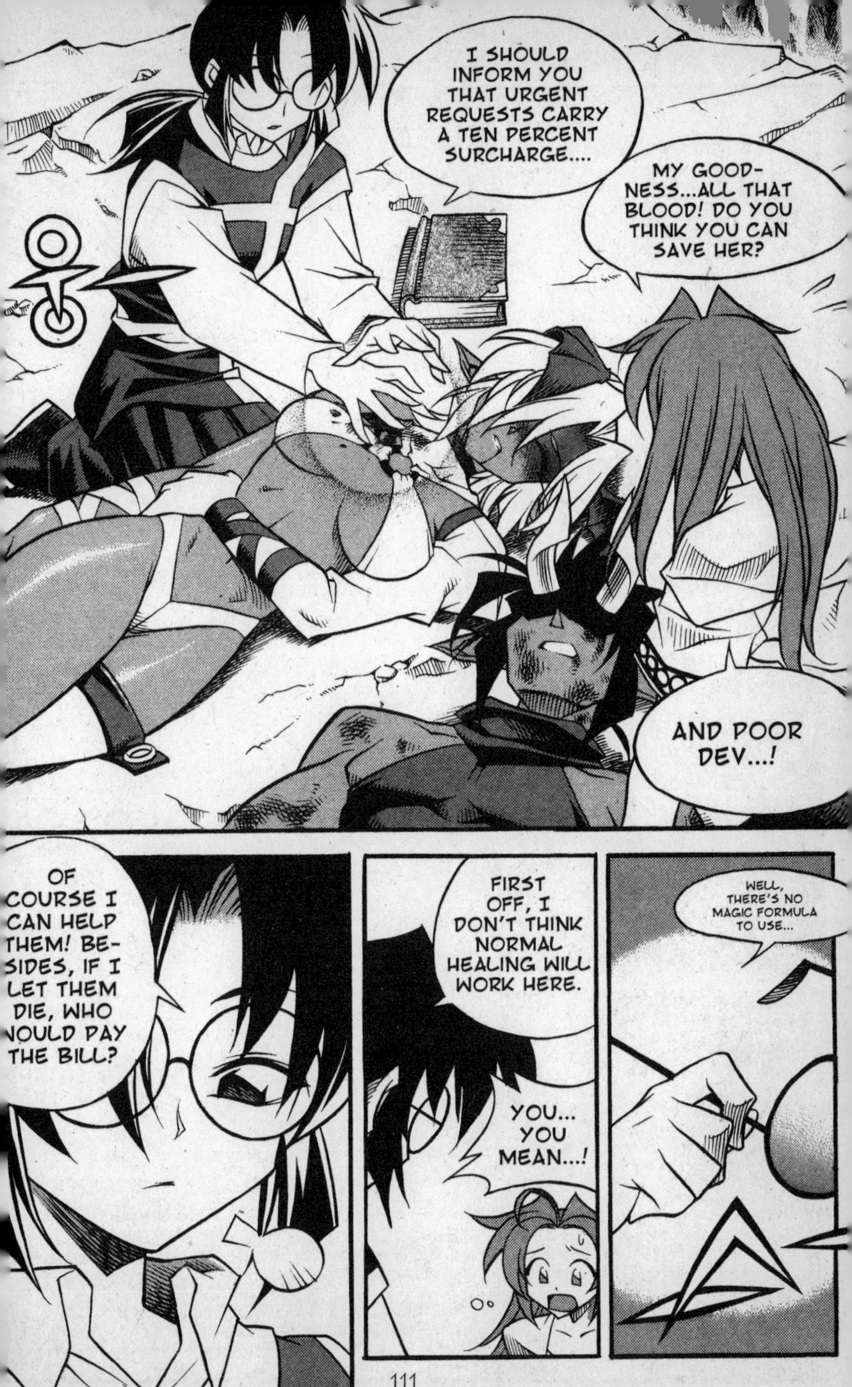
I SHOULD INFORM YOU THAT URGENT REQUESTS CARRY A TEN PERCENT SURCHARGE....
MY GOOD-NESS...ALL THAT BLOOD! DO YOU THINK YOU CAN SAVE HER?
AND POOR DEV...!
OF COURSE I CAN HELP THEM! BE-SIDES, IF I LET THEM DIE, WHO WOULD PAY THE BILL?
FIRST OFF, I DON'T THINK NORMAL HEALING WILL WORK HERE.
YOU... YOU MEAN...!
WELL, THERE'S NO MAGIC FORMULA TO USE...

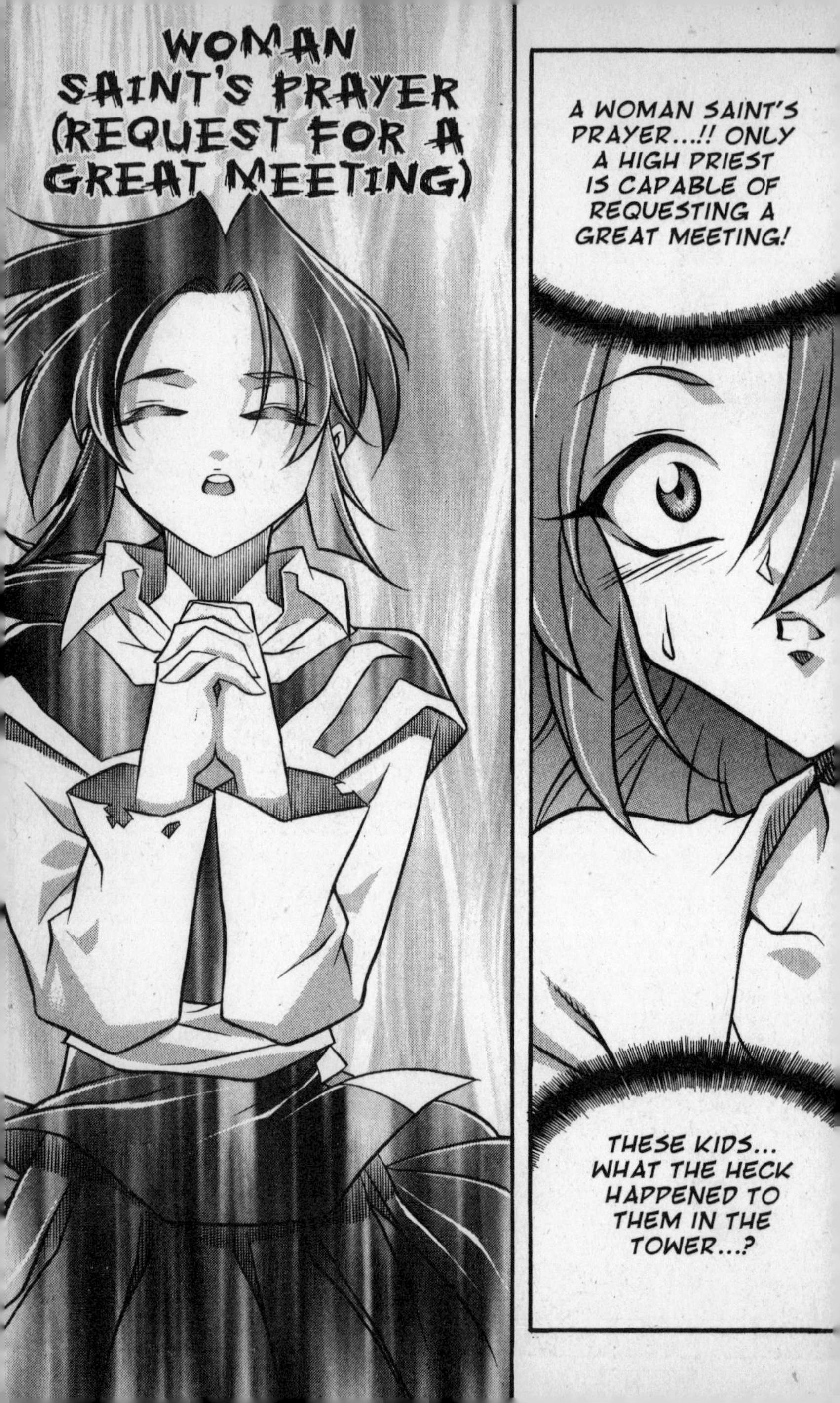
WOMAN SAINT'S PRAYER (REQUEST FOR A GREAT MEETING)
A WOMAN SAINT'S PRAYER...!! ONLY A HIGH PRIEST IS CAPABLE OF REQUESTING A GREAT MEETING!
THESE KIDS... WHAT THE HECK HAPPENED TO THEM IN THE TOWER...?

Quest 74

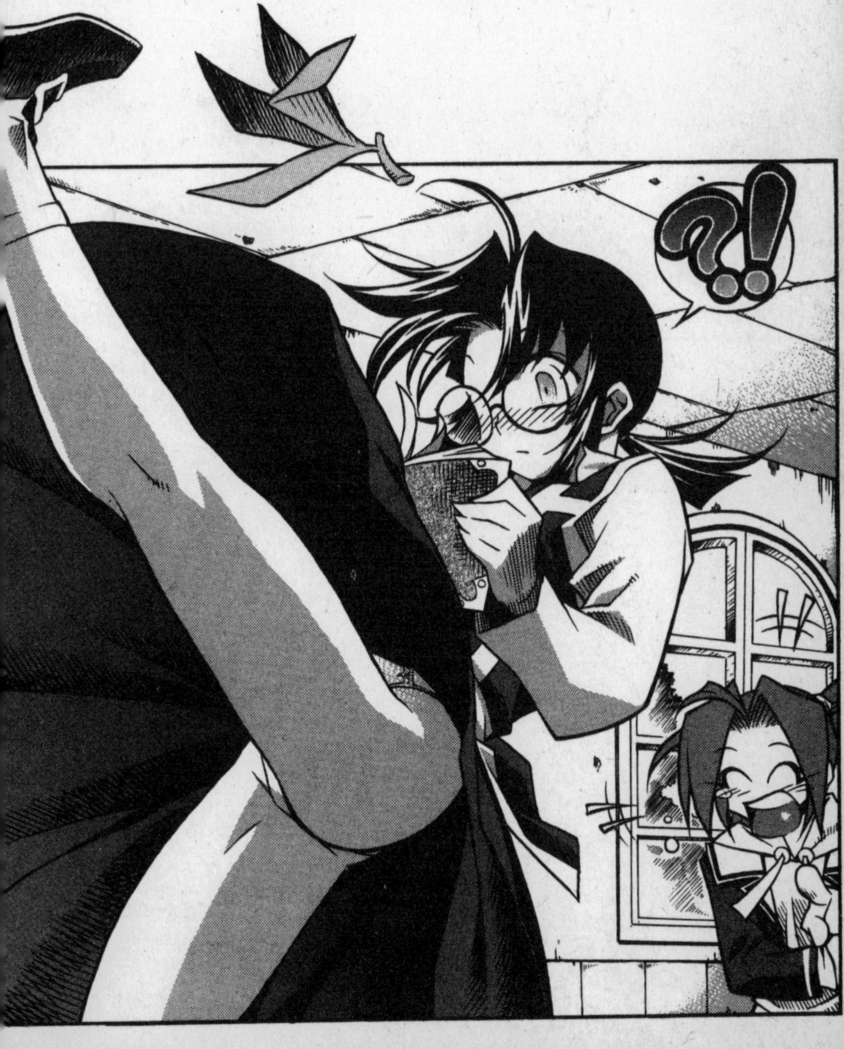
?!

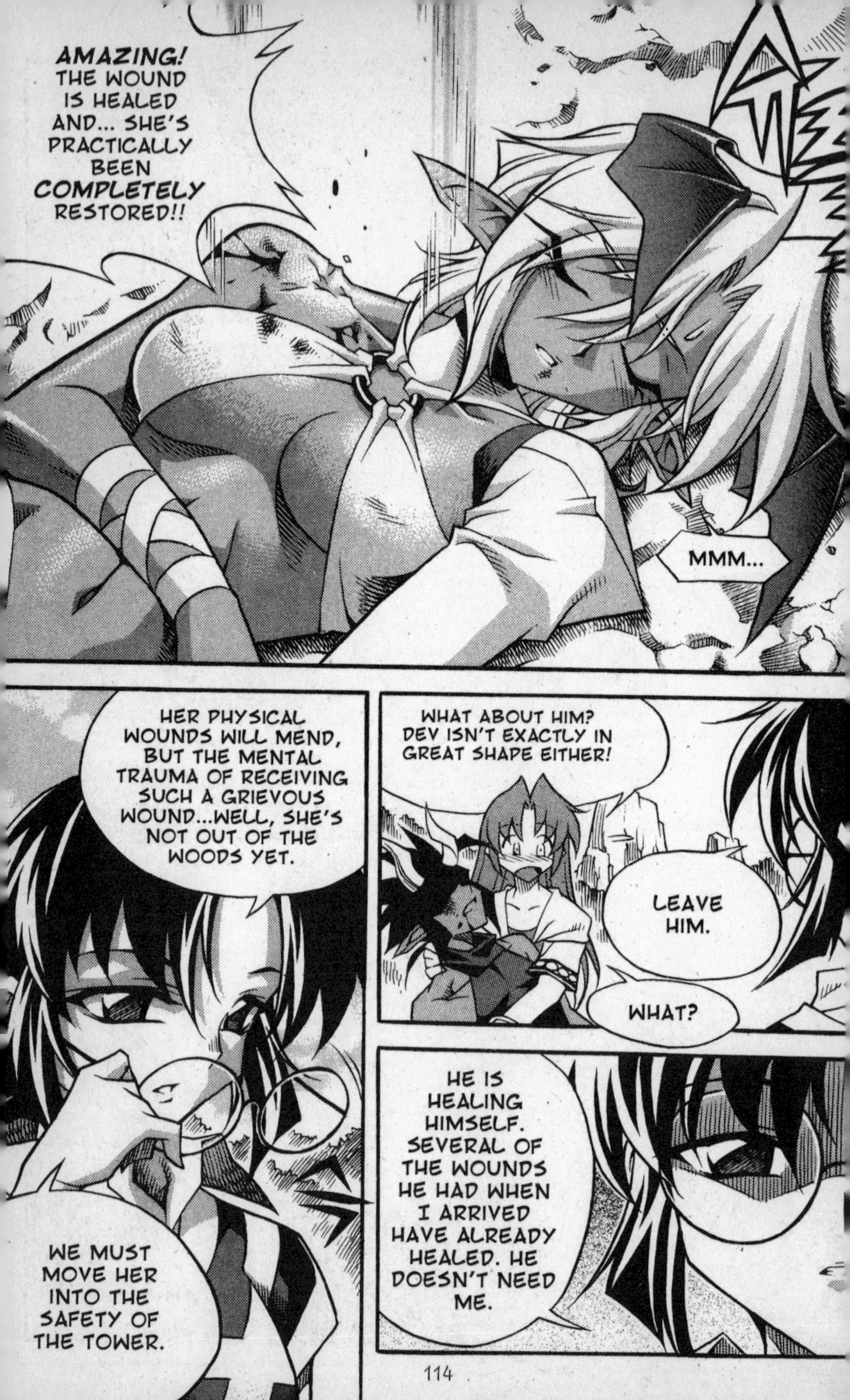

AMAZING! THE WOUND IS HEALED AND... SHE'S PRACTICALLY BEEN COMPLETELY RESTORED!!
MMM...
HER PHYSICAL WOUNDS WILL MEND, BUT THE MENTAL TRAUMA OF RECEIVING SUCH A GRIEVOUS WOUND...WELL, SHE'S NOT OUT OF THE WOODS YET.
WE MUST MOVE HER INTO THE SAFETY OF THE TOWER.
WHAT ABOUT HIM? DEV ISN'T EXACTLY IN GREAT SHAPE EITHER!
LEAVE HIM.
WHAT?
HE IS HEALING HIMSELF. SEVERAL OF THE WOUNDS HE HAD WHEN I ARRIVED HAVE ALREADY HEALED. HE DOESN'T NEED ME.

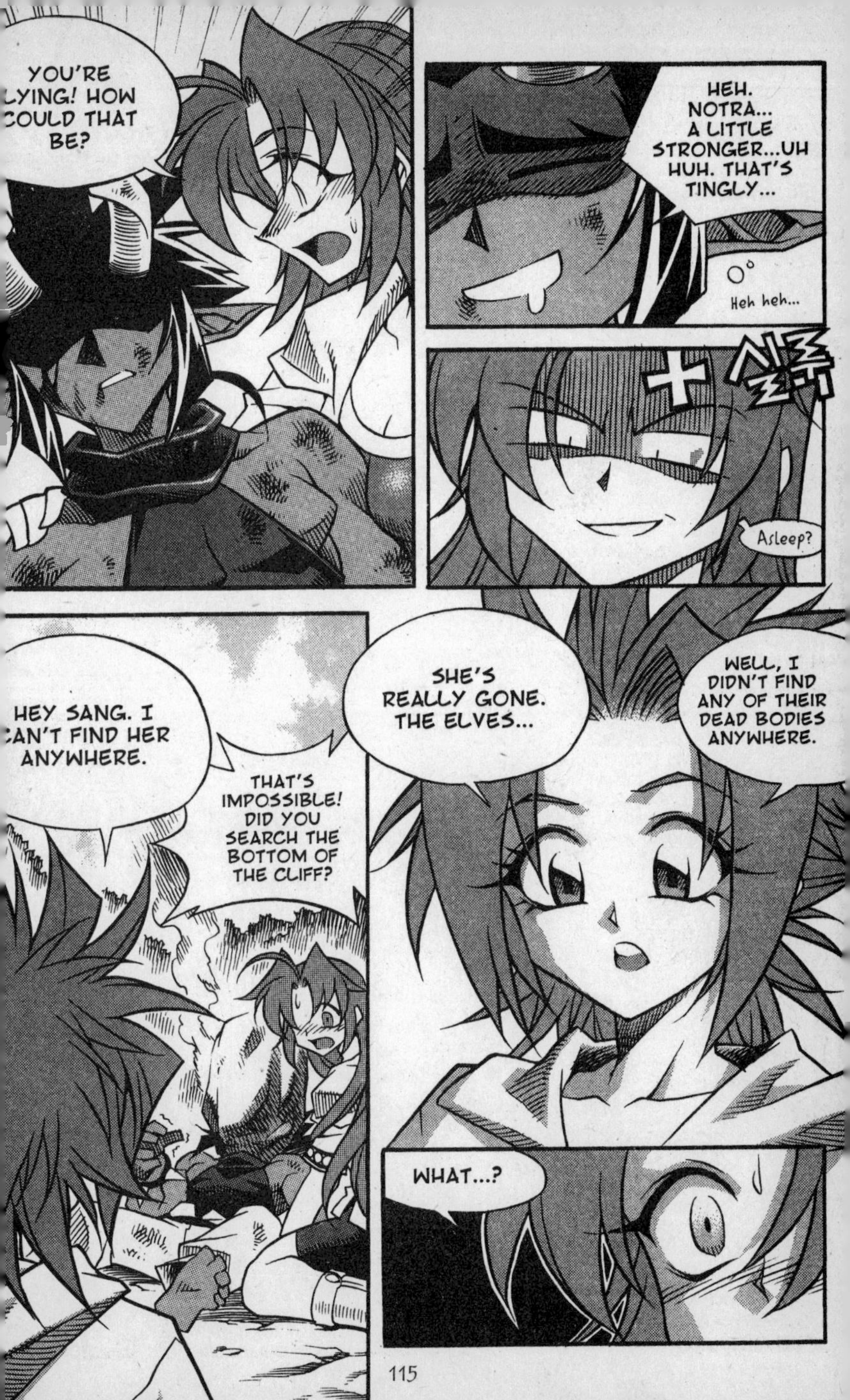

YOU'RE LYING! HOW COULD THAT BE?
HEH. NOTRA... A LITTLE STRONGER...UH HUH. THAT'S TINGLY...
Heh heh...
Asleep?
HEY SANG. I CAN'T FIND HER ANYWHERE.
THAT'S IMPOSSIBLE! DID YOU SEARCH THE BOTTOM OF THE CLIFF?
SHE'S REALLY GONE. THE ELVES...
WELL, I DIDN'T FIND ANY OF THEIR DEAD BODIES ANYWHERE.
WHAT...?

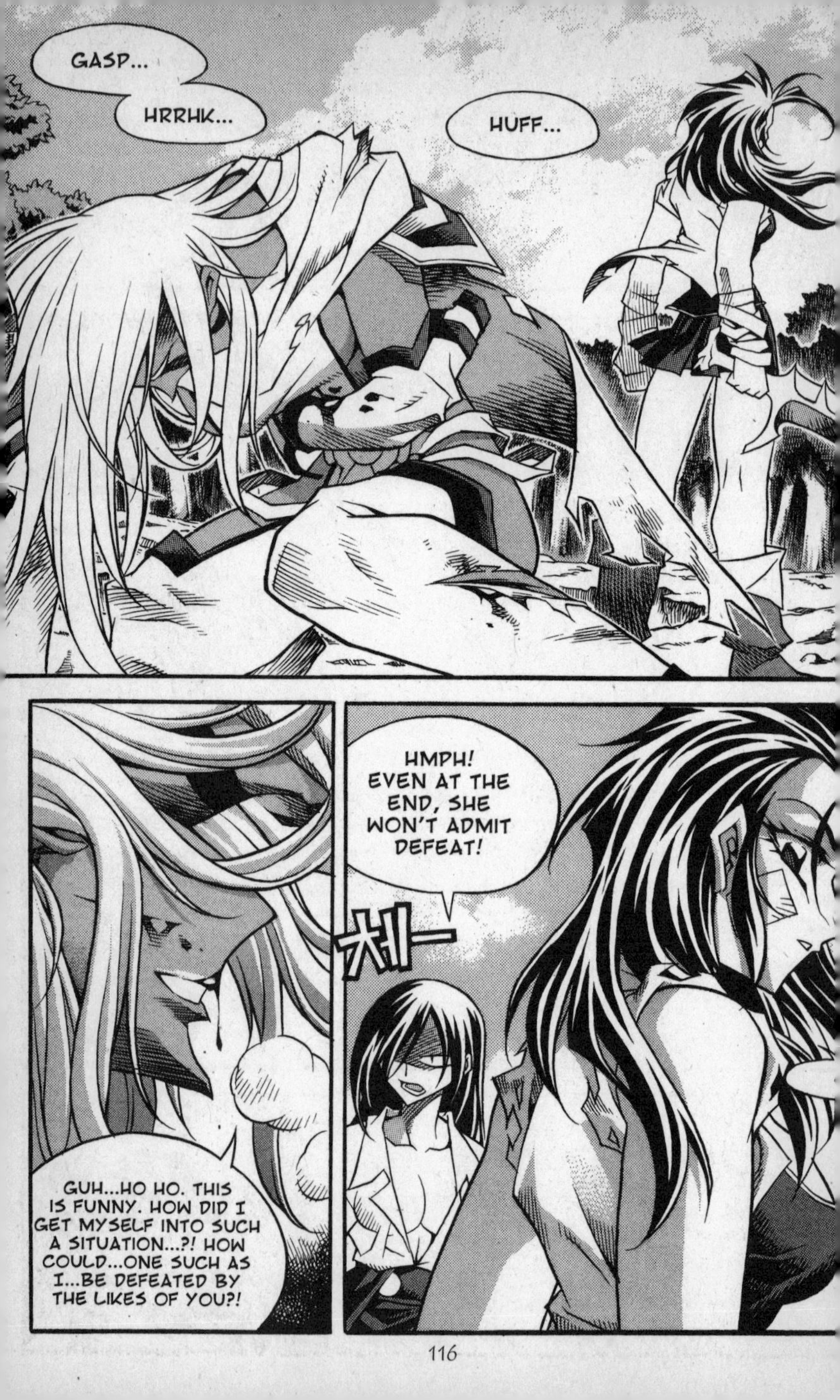
GASP...
HRRHK...
HUFF...
GUH...HO HO. THIS IS FUNNY. HOW DID I GET MYSELF INTO SUCH A SITUATION...?! HOW COULD...ONE SUCH AS I...BE DEFEATED BY THE LIKES OF YOU?!
HMPH! EVEN AT THE END, SHE WON'T ADMIT DEFEAT!

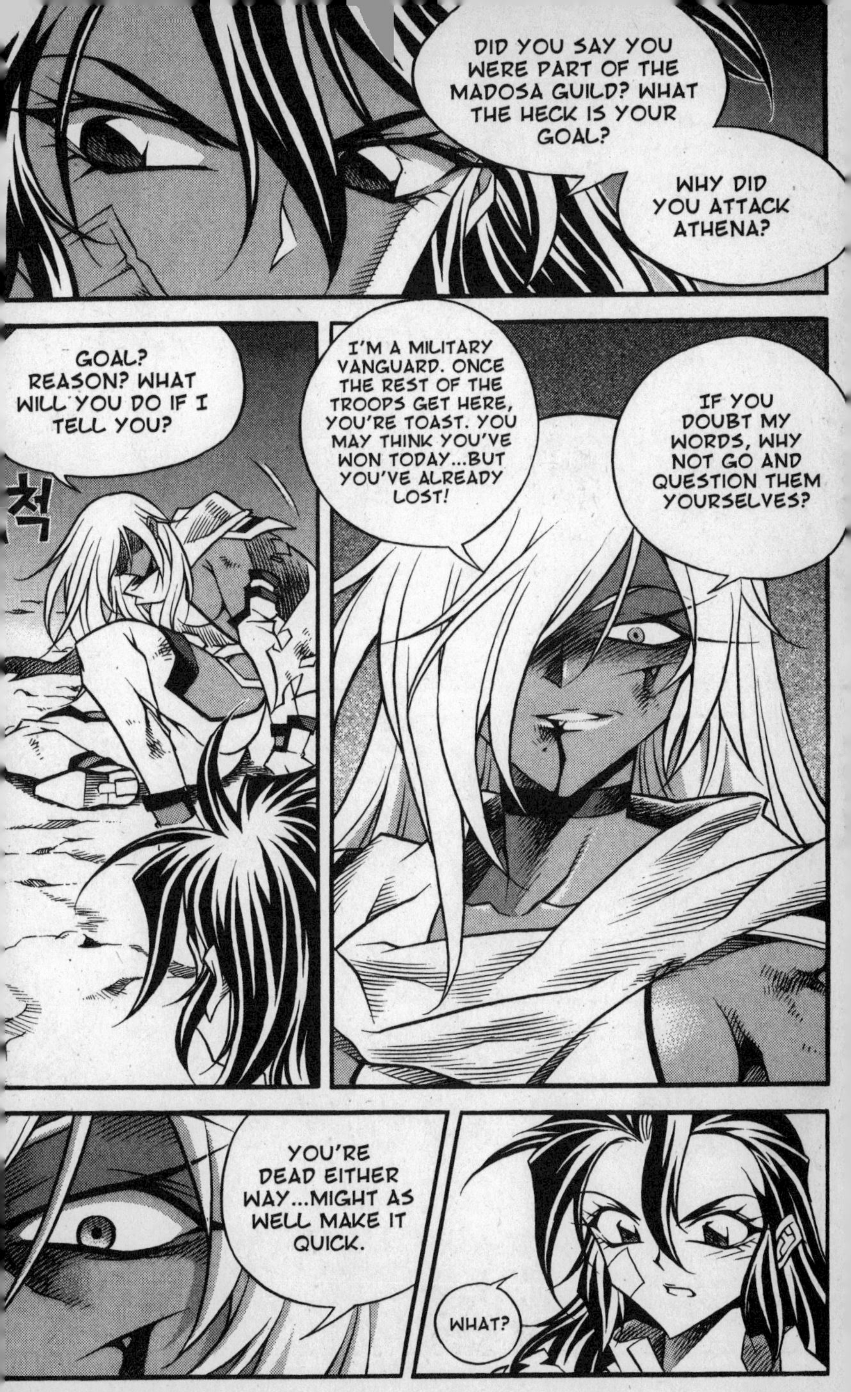
DID YOU SAY YOU WERE PART OF THE MADOSA GUILD? WHAT THE HECK IS YOUR GOAL?
WHY DID YOU ATTACK ATHENA?
GOAL? REASON? WHAT WILL YOU DO IF I TELL YOU?
척
I'M A MILITARY VANGUARD. ONCE THE REST OF THE TROOPS GET HERE, YOU'RE TOAST. YOU MAY THINK YOU'VE WON TODAY...BUT YOU'VE ALREADY LOST!
IF YOU DOUBT MY WORDS, WHY NOT GO AND QUESTION THEM YOURSELVES?
YOU'RE DEAD EITHER WAY...MIGHT AS WELL MAKE IT QUICK.
WHAT?

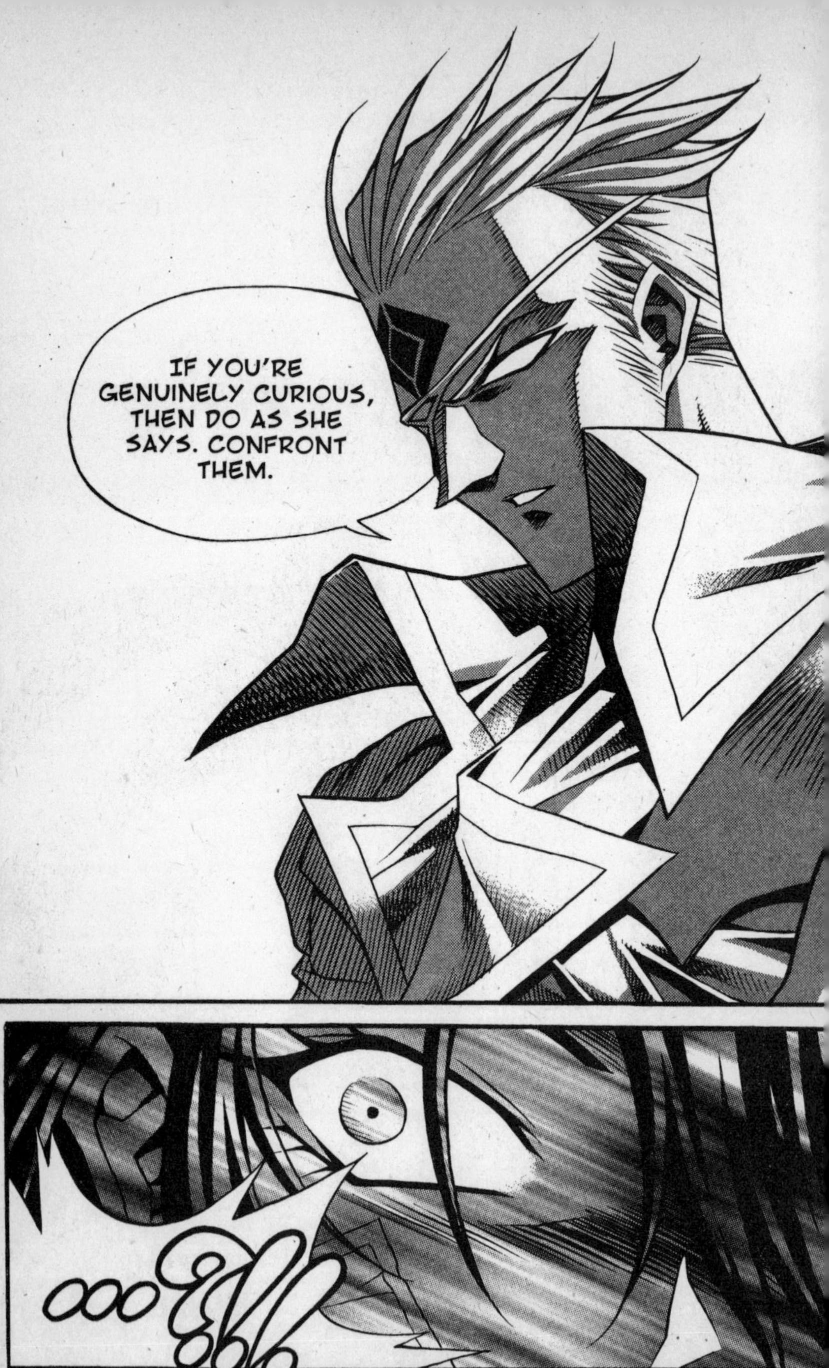
IF YOU'RE GENUINELY CURIOUS, THEN DO AS SHE SAYS. CONFRONT THEM.

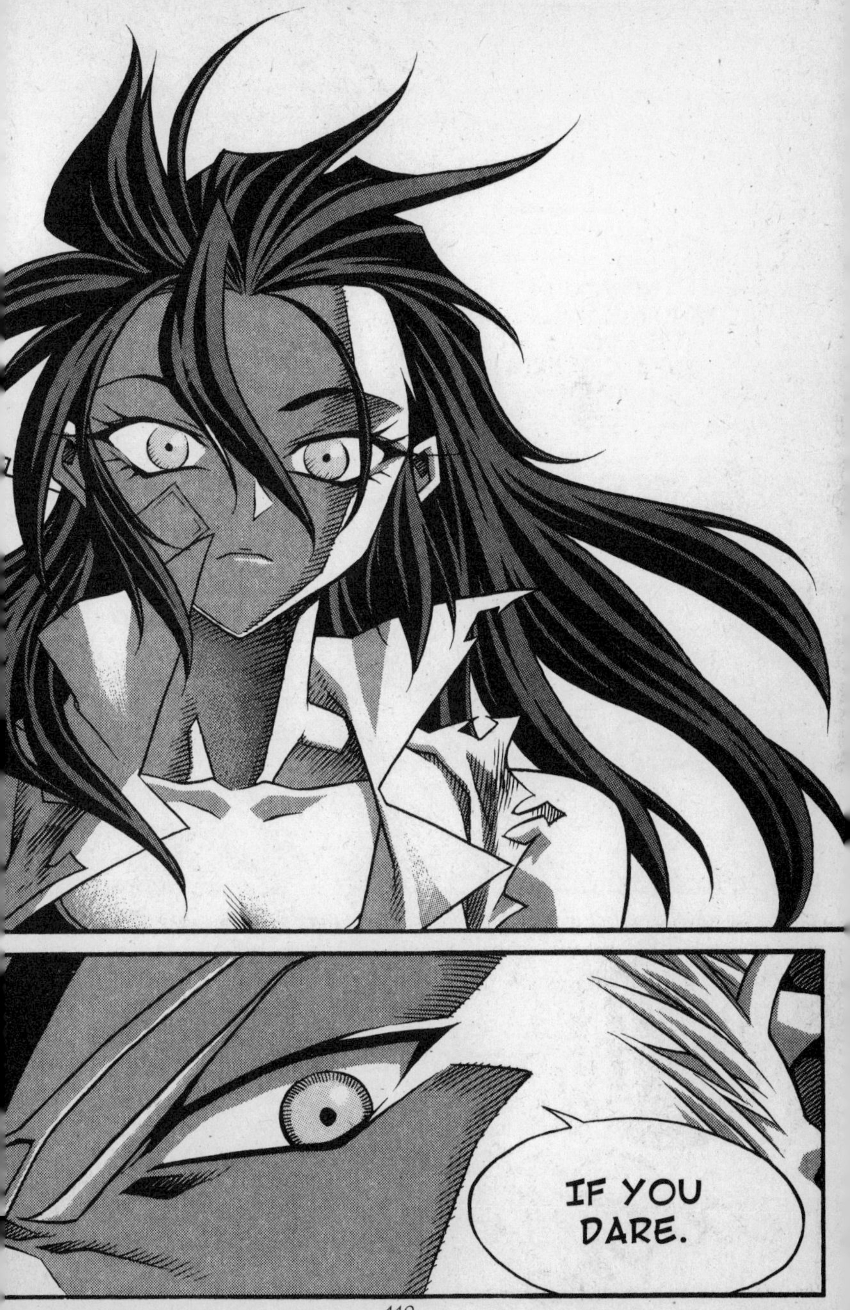
IF YOU DARE.

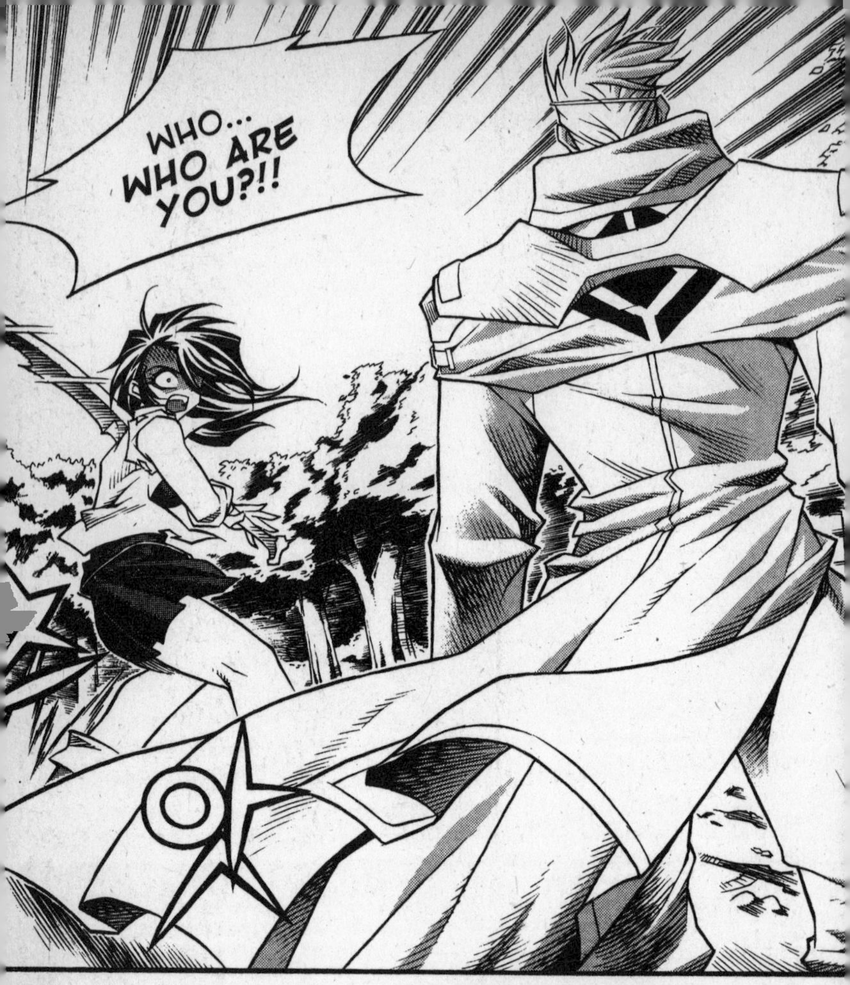
WHO... WHO ARE YOU?!!
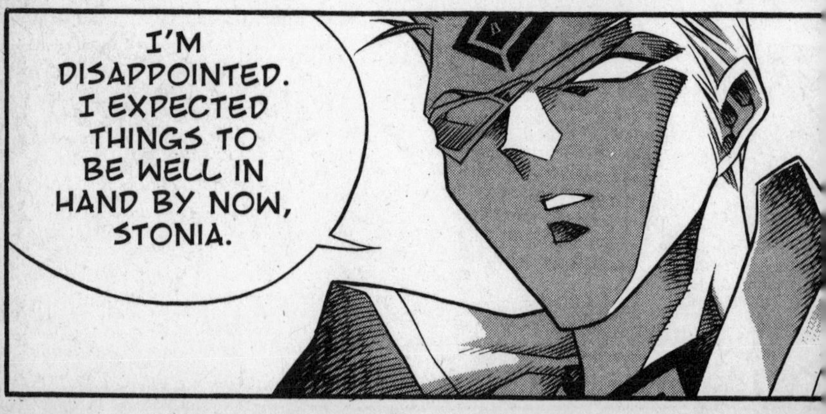
I'M DISAPPOINTED. I EXPECTED THINGS TO BE WELL IN HAND BY NOW, STONIA.

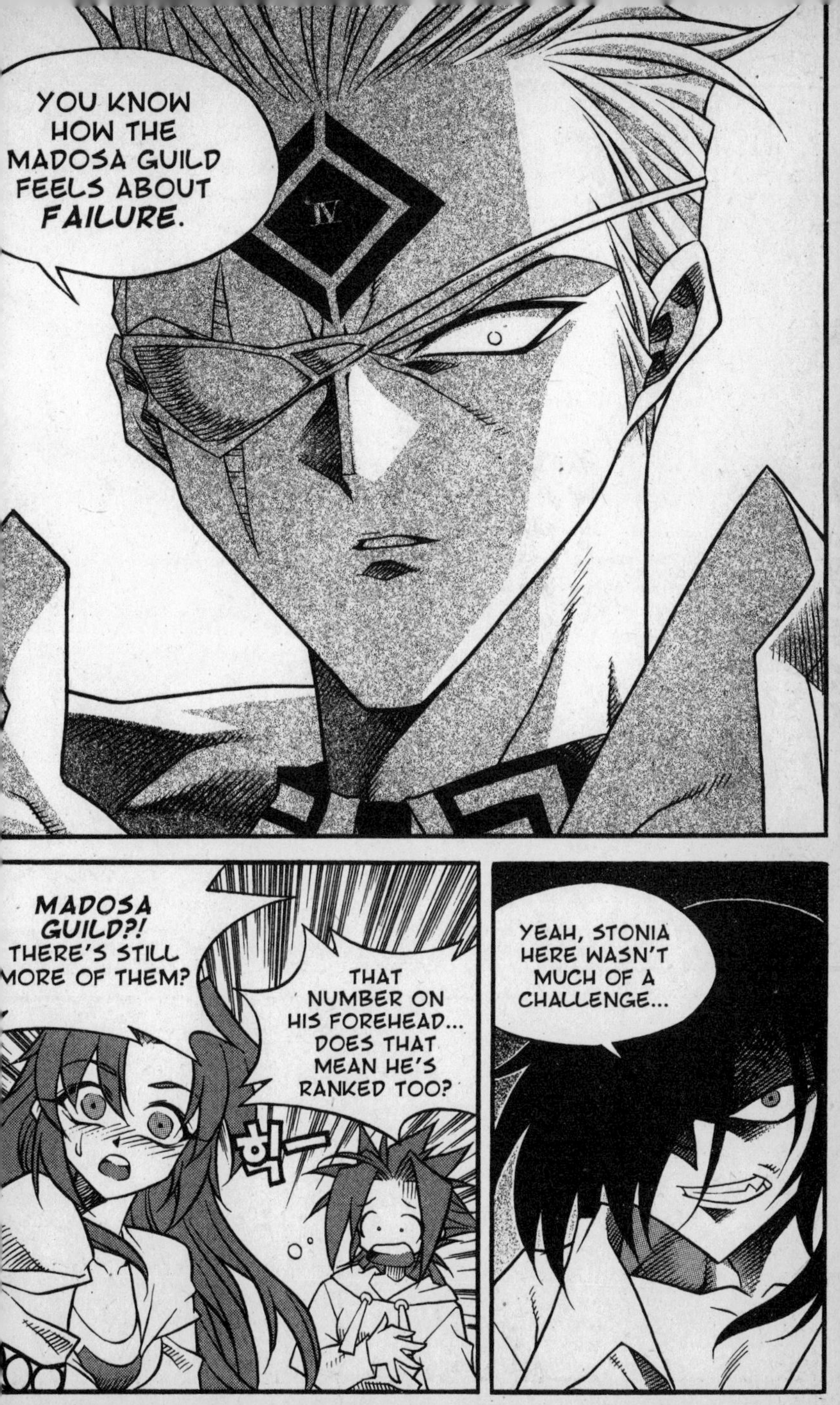
YOU KNOW HOW THE MADOSA GUILD FEELS ABOUT FAILURE.
MADOSA GUILD?! THERE'S STILL MORE OF THEM?
THAT NUMBER ON HIS FOREHEAD... DOES THAT MEAN HE'S RANKED TOO?
헉
YEAH, STONIA HERE WASN'T MUCH OF A CHALLENGE...

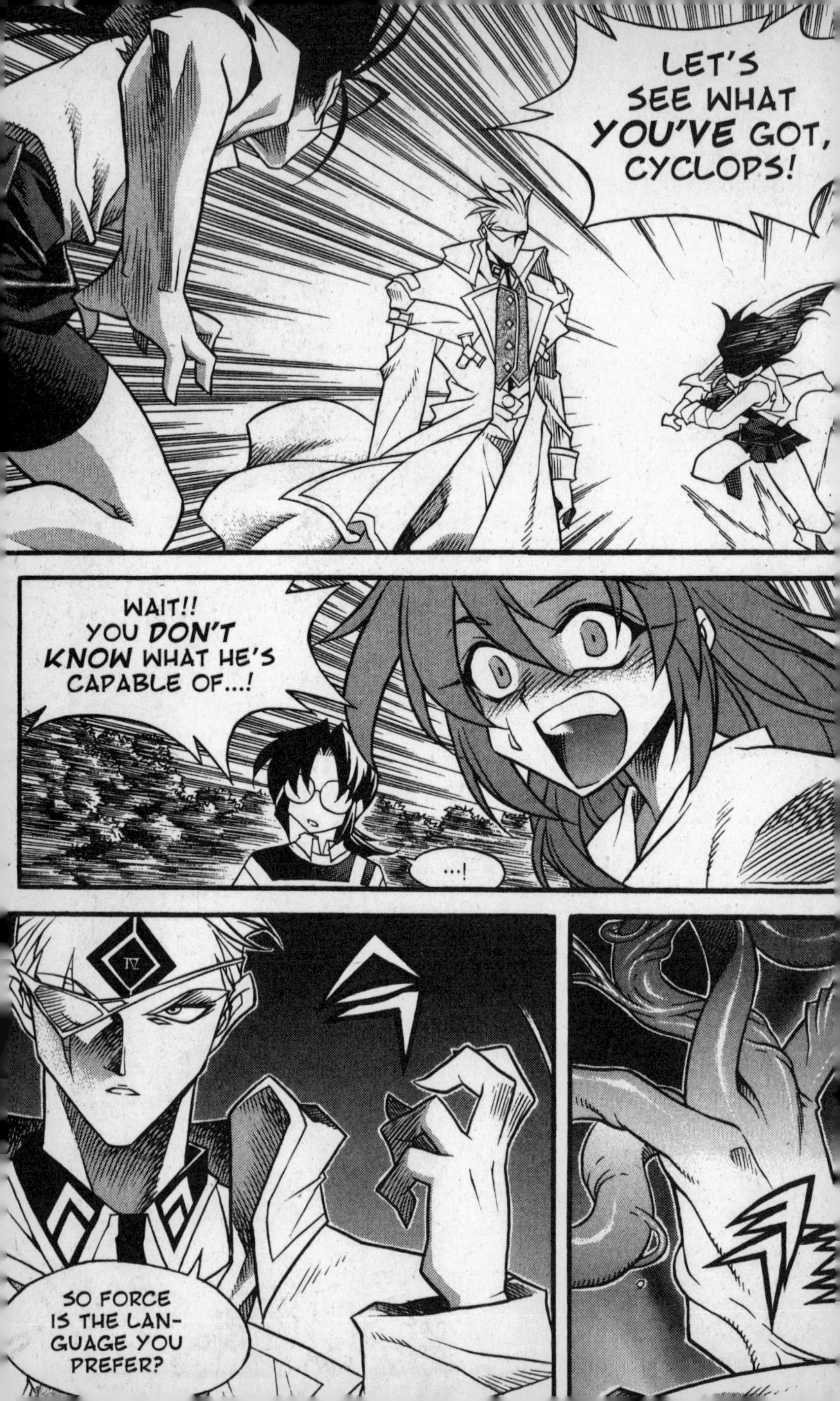
LET'S SEE WHAT YOU'VE GOT, CYCLOPS!
WAIT!! YOU DON'T KNOW WHAT HE'S CAPABLE OF...!
...!
SO FORCE IS THE LAN-GUAGE YOU PREFER?

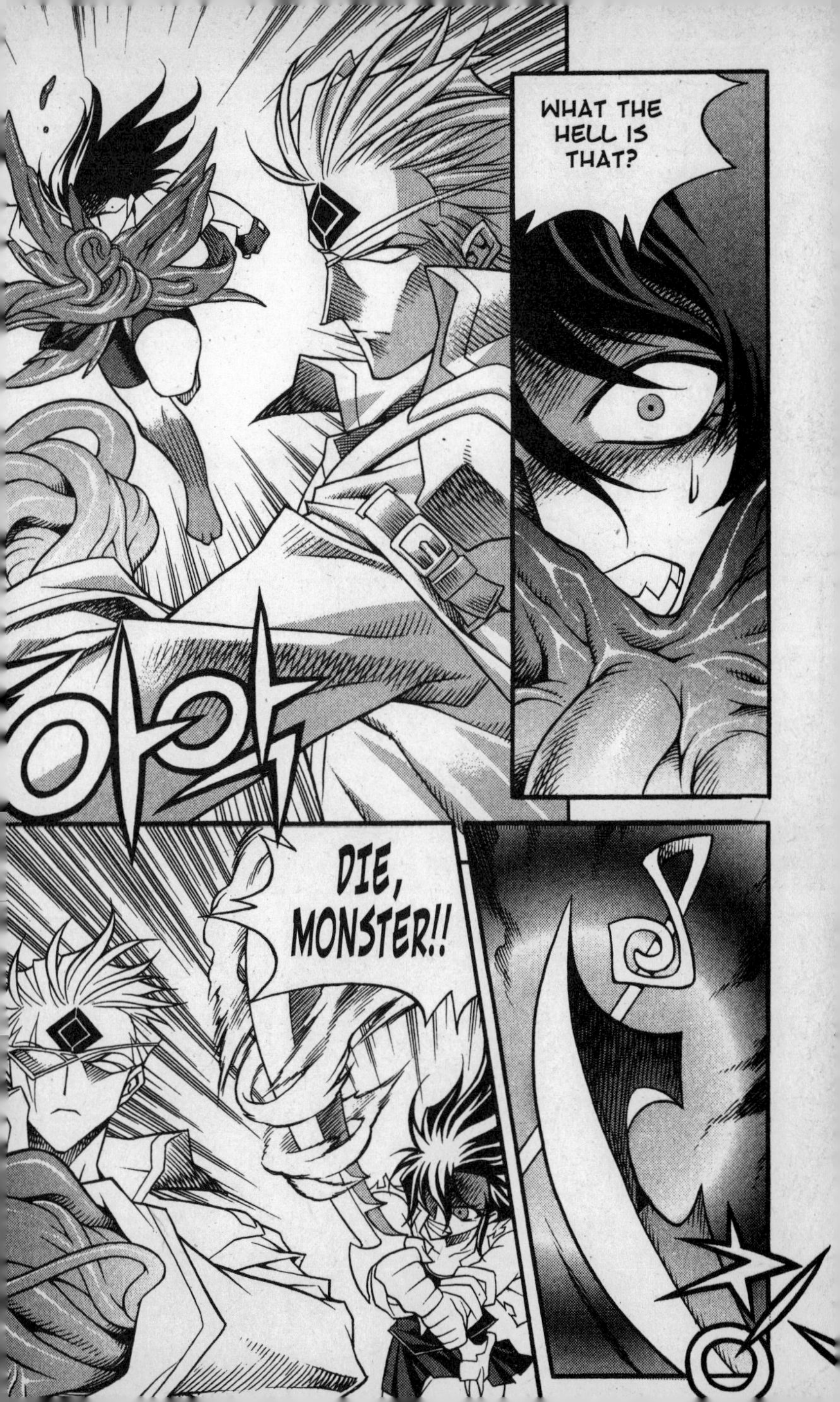
WHAT THE HELL IS THAT?
DIE, MONSTER!!

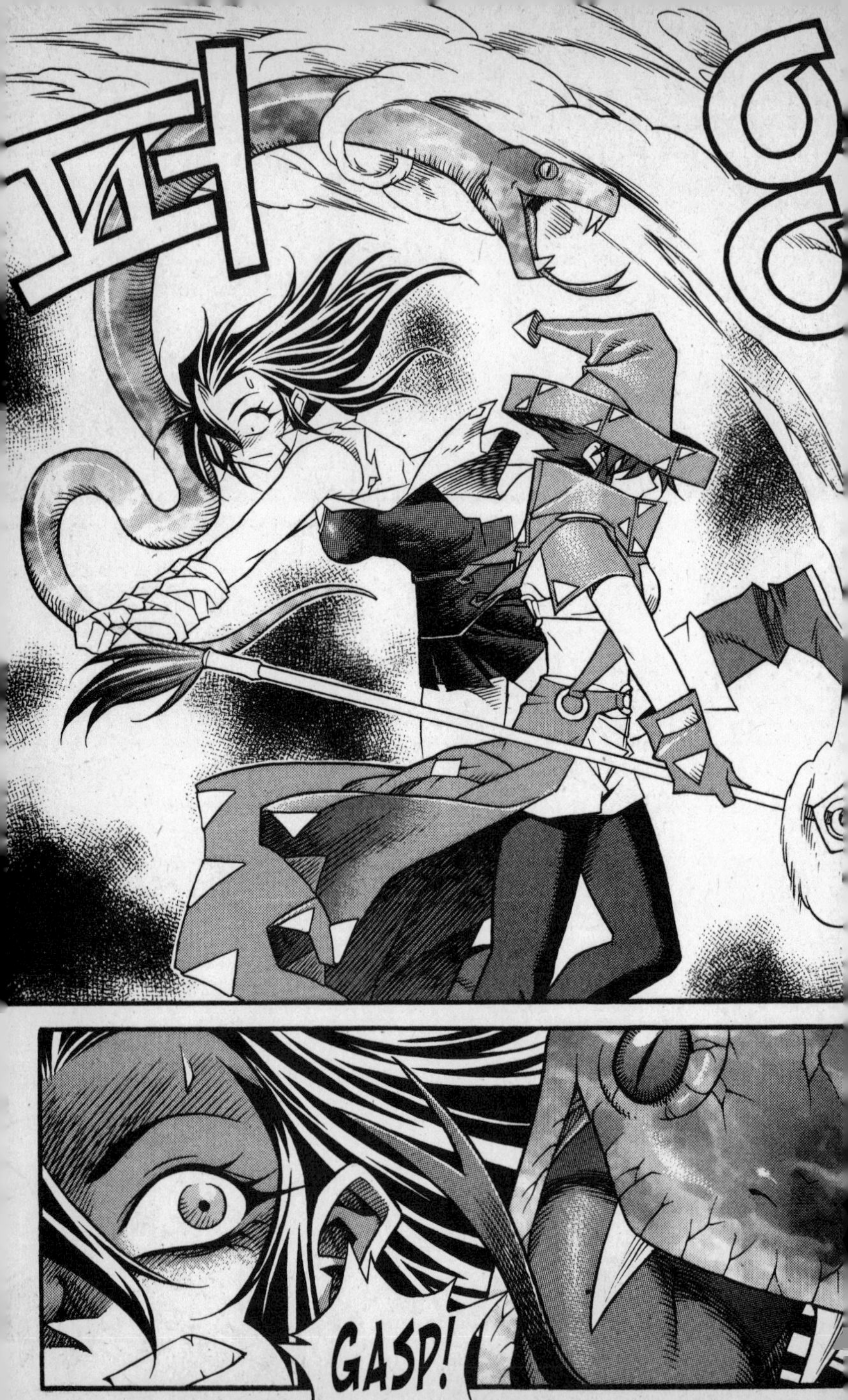
GASP!

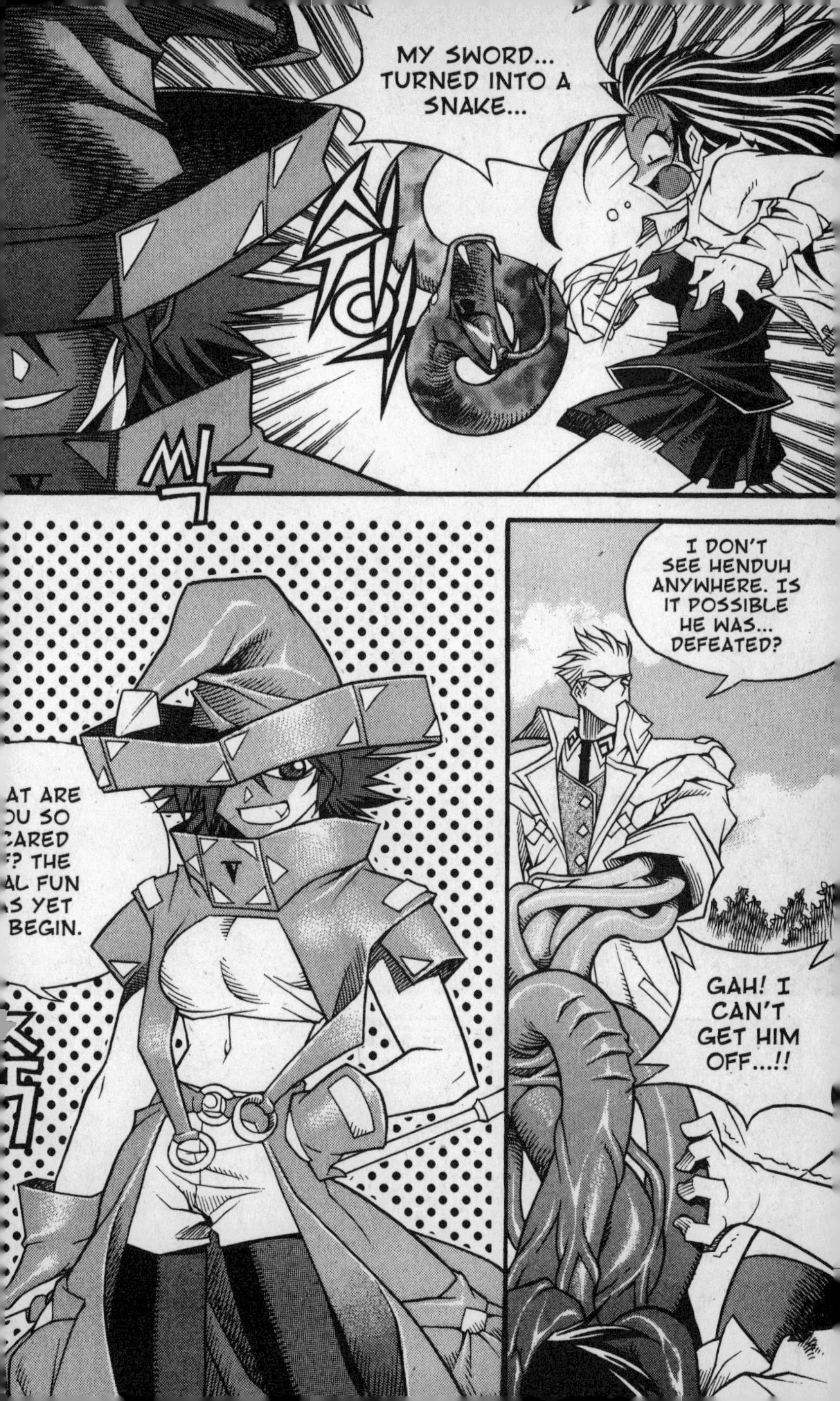
MY SWORD... TURNED INTO A SNAKE...
AT ARE OU SO CARED F? THE AL FUN AS YET BEGIN.
I DON'T SEE HENDUH ANYWHERE. IS IT POSSIBLE HE WAS... DEFEATED?
GAH! I CAN'T GET HIM OFF...!!

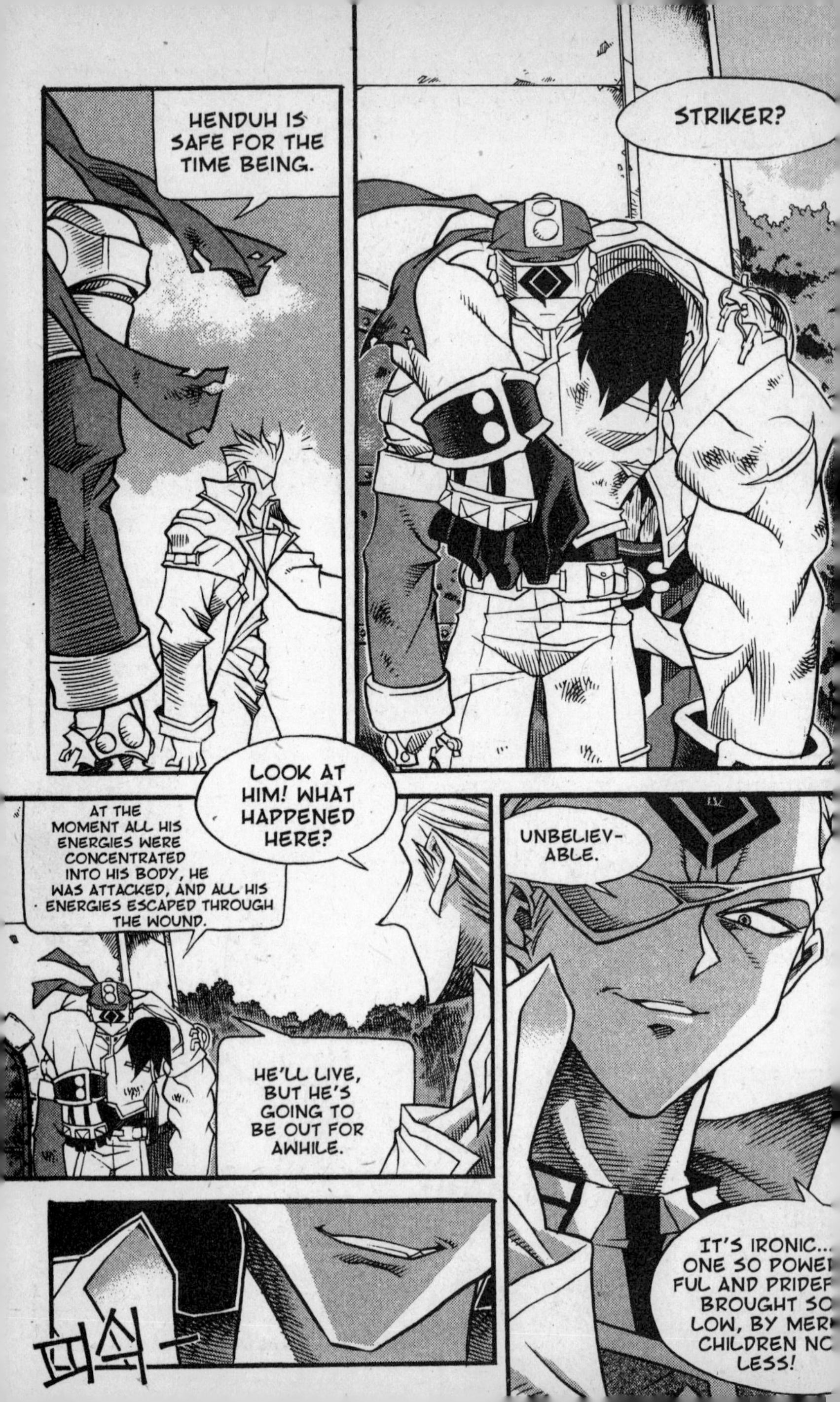
HENDUH IS SAFE FOR THE TIME BEING.
STRIKER?
LOOK AT HIM! WHAT HAPPENED HERE?
AT THE MOMENT ALL HIS ENERGIES WERE CONCENTRATED INTO HIS BODY, HE WAS ATTACKED, AND ALL HIS ENERGIES ESCAPED THROUGH THE WOUND.
HE'LL LIVE, BUT HE'S GOING TO BE OUT FOR AWHILE.
UNBELIEV-ABLE.
IT'S IRONIC... ONE SO POWE FUL AND PRIDEF BROUGHT SO LOW, BY MER CHILDREN NO LESS!

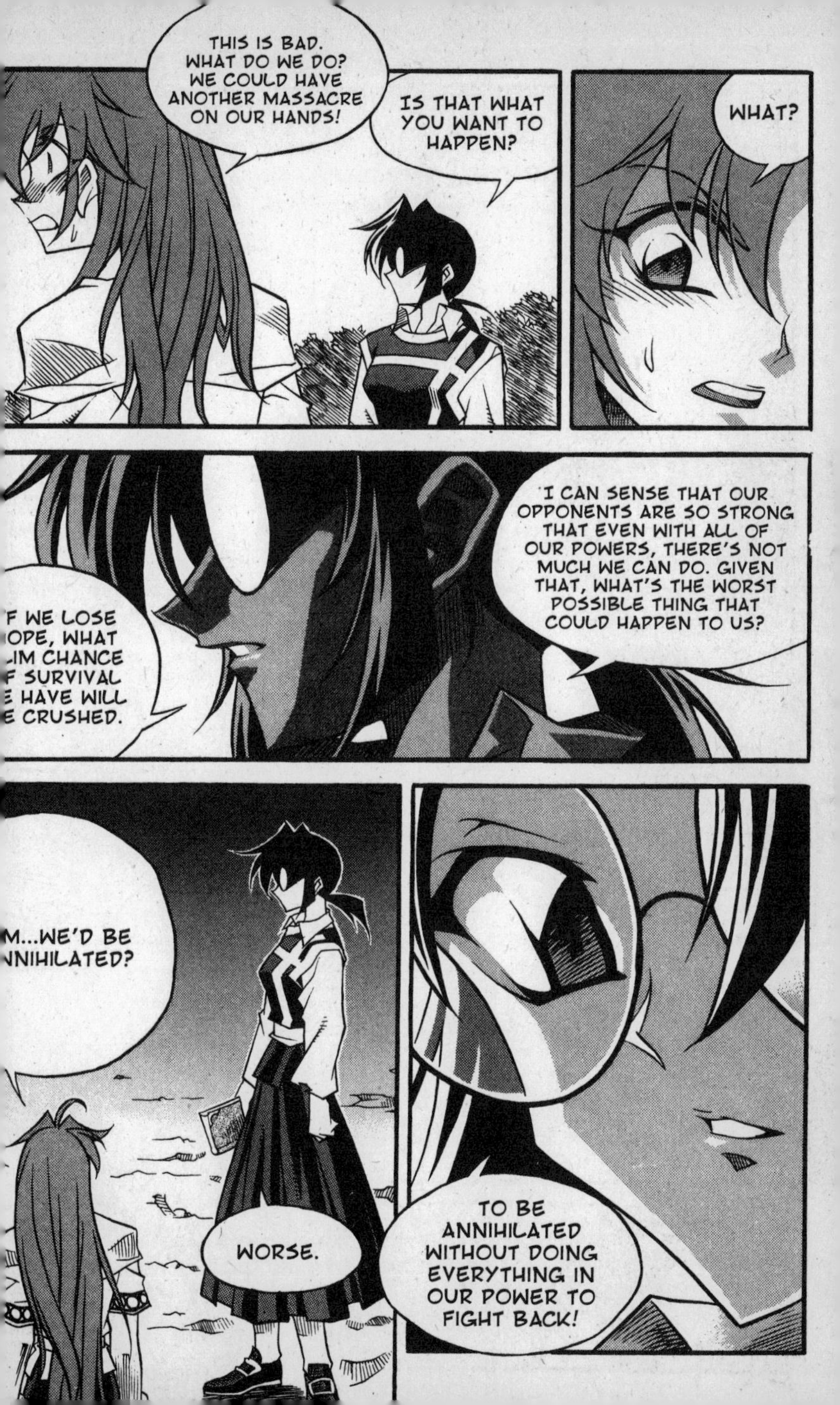

THIS IS BAD. WHAT DO WE DO? WE COULD HAVE ANOTHER MASSACRE ON OUR HANDS!
IS THAT WHAT YOU WANT TO HAPPEN?
WHAT?
F WE LOSE OPE, WHAT LIM CHANCE F SURVIVAL E HAVE WILL E CRUSHED.
I CAN SENSE THAT OUR OPPONENTS ARE SO STRONG THAT EVEN WITH ALL OF OUR POWERS, THERE'S NOT MUCH WE CAN DO. GIVEN THAT, WHAT'S THE WORST POSSIBLE THING THAT COULD HAPPEN TO US?
M...WE'D BE NNIHILATED?
WORSE.
TO BE ANNIHILATED WITHOUT DOING EVERYTHING IN OUR POWER TO FIGHT BACK!

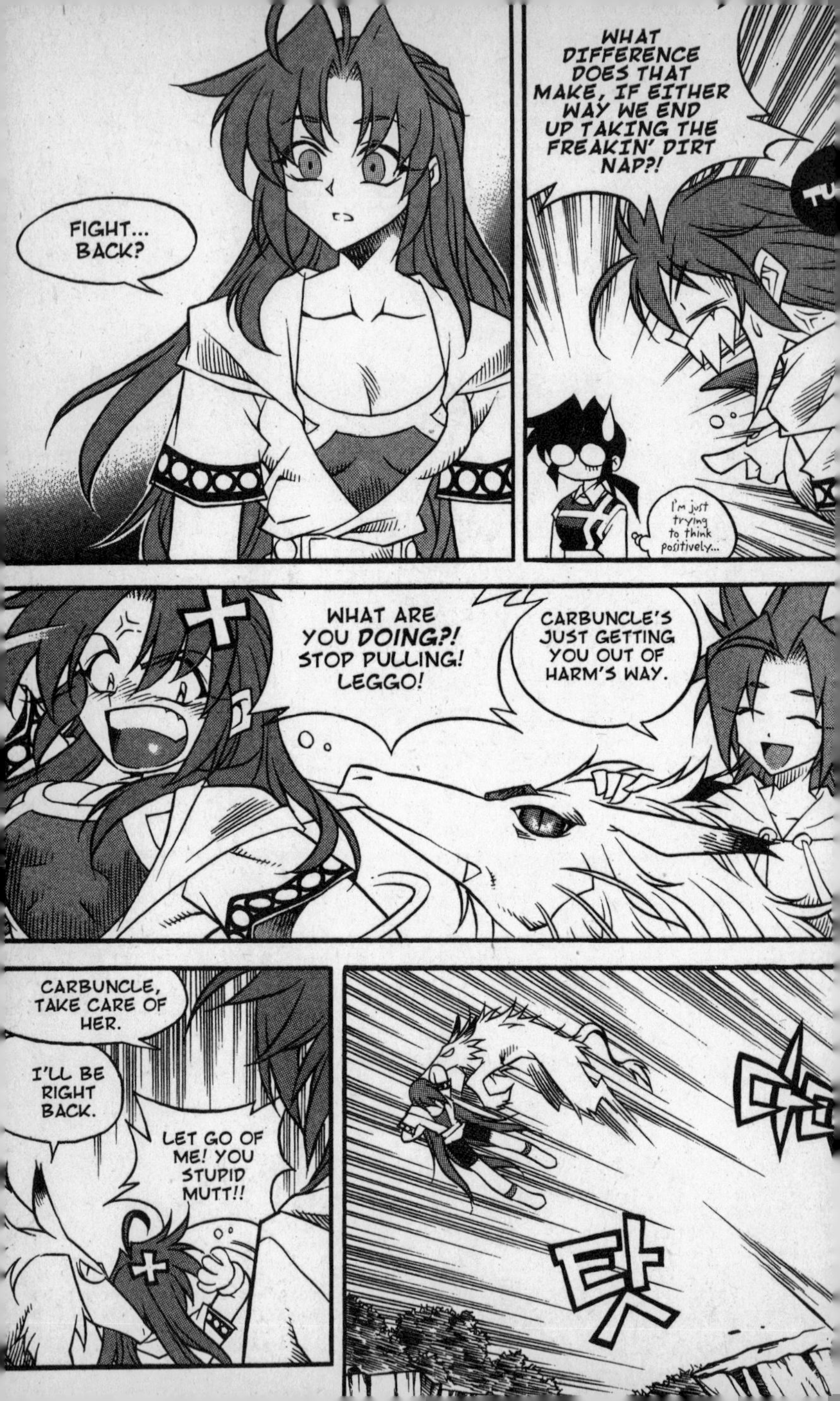
FIGHT... BACK?
WHAT DIFFERENCE DOES THAT MAKE, IF EITHER WAY WE END UP TAKING THE FREAKIN' DIRT NAP?!
I'm just trying to think positively...
WHAT ARE YOU DOING?! STOP PULLING! LEGGO!
CARBUNCLE'S JUST GETTING YOU OUT OF HARM'S WAY.
CARBUNCLE, TAKE CARE OF HER.
I'LL BE RIGHT BACK.
LET GO OF ME! YOU STUPID MUTT!!
탁

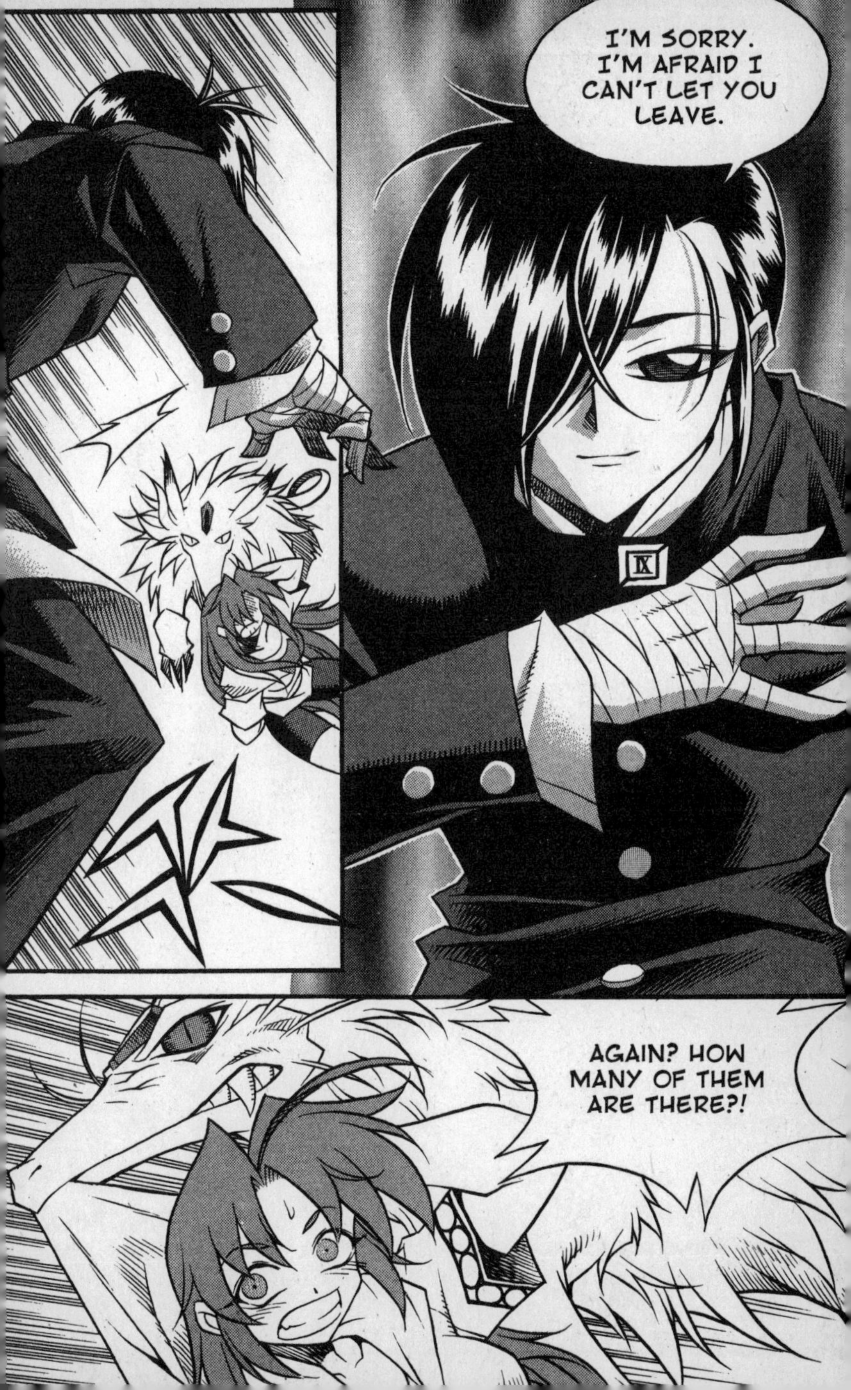
I'M SORRY. I'M AFRAID I CAN'T LET YOU LEAVE.
AGAIN? HOW MANY OF THEM ARE THERE?!

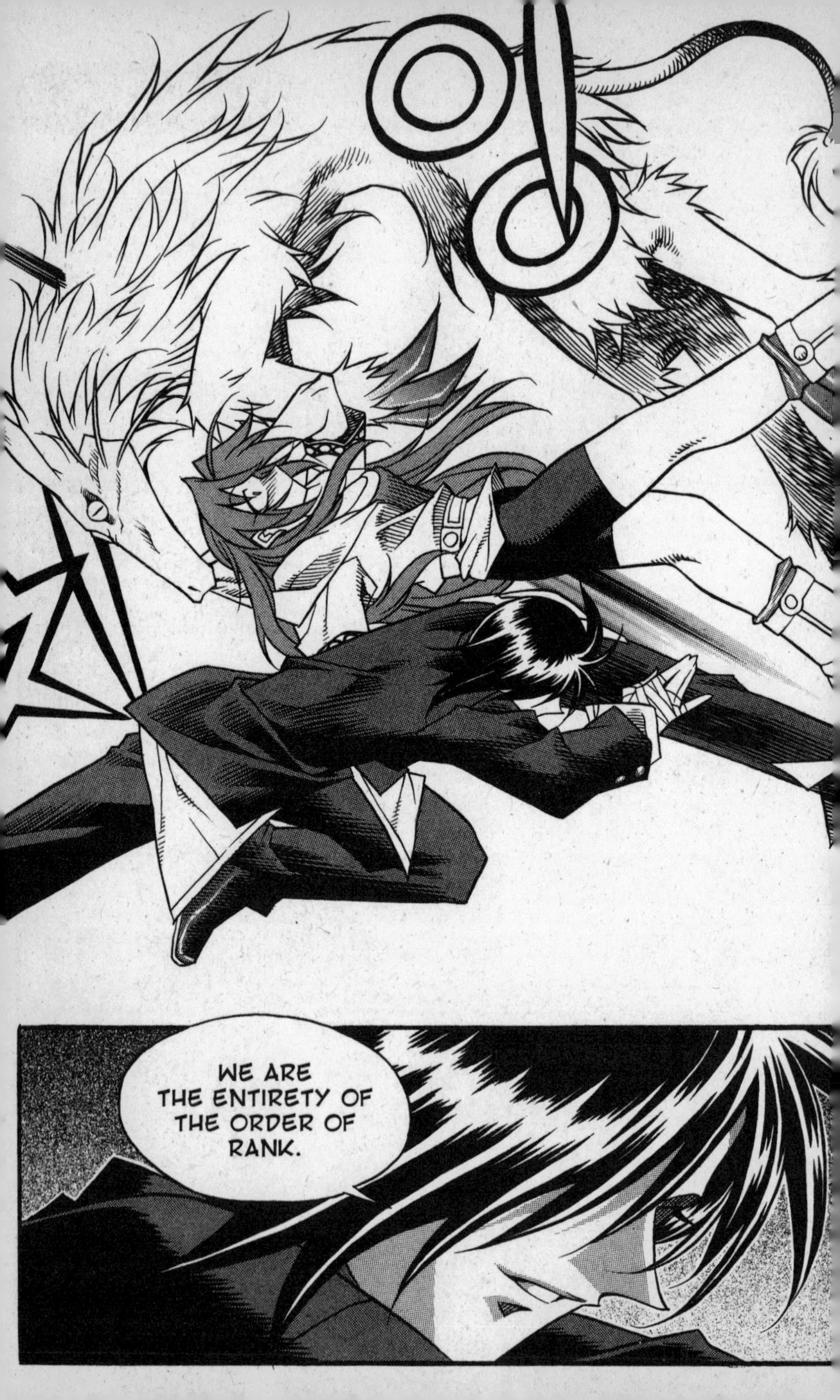
WE ARE THE ENTIRETY OF THE ORDER OF RANK.

Quest 75

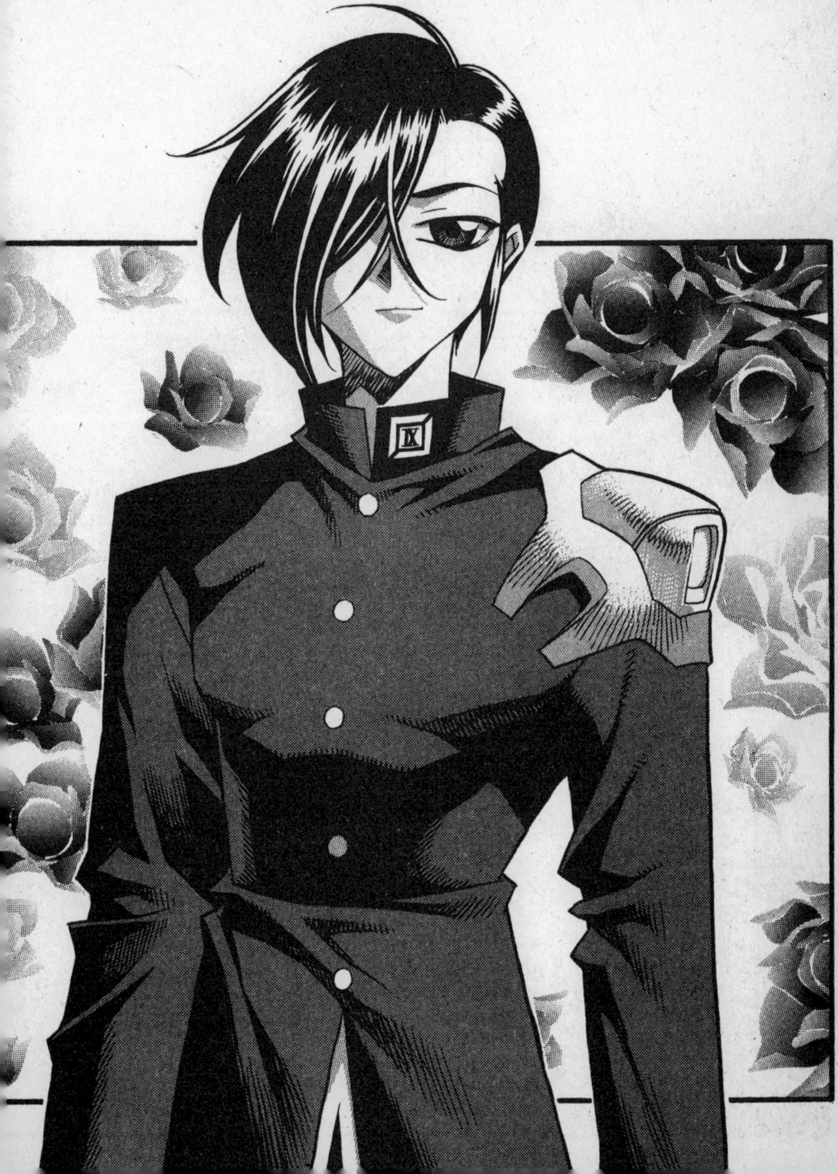

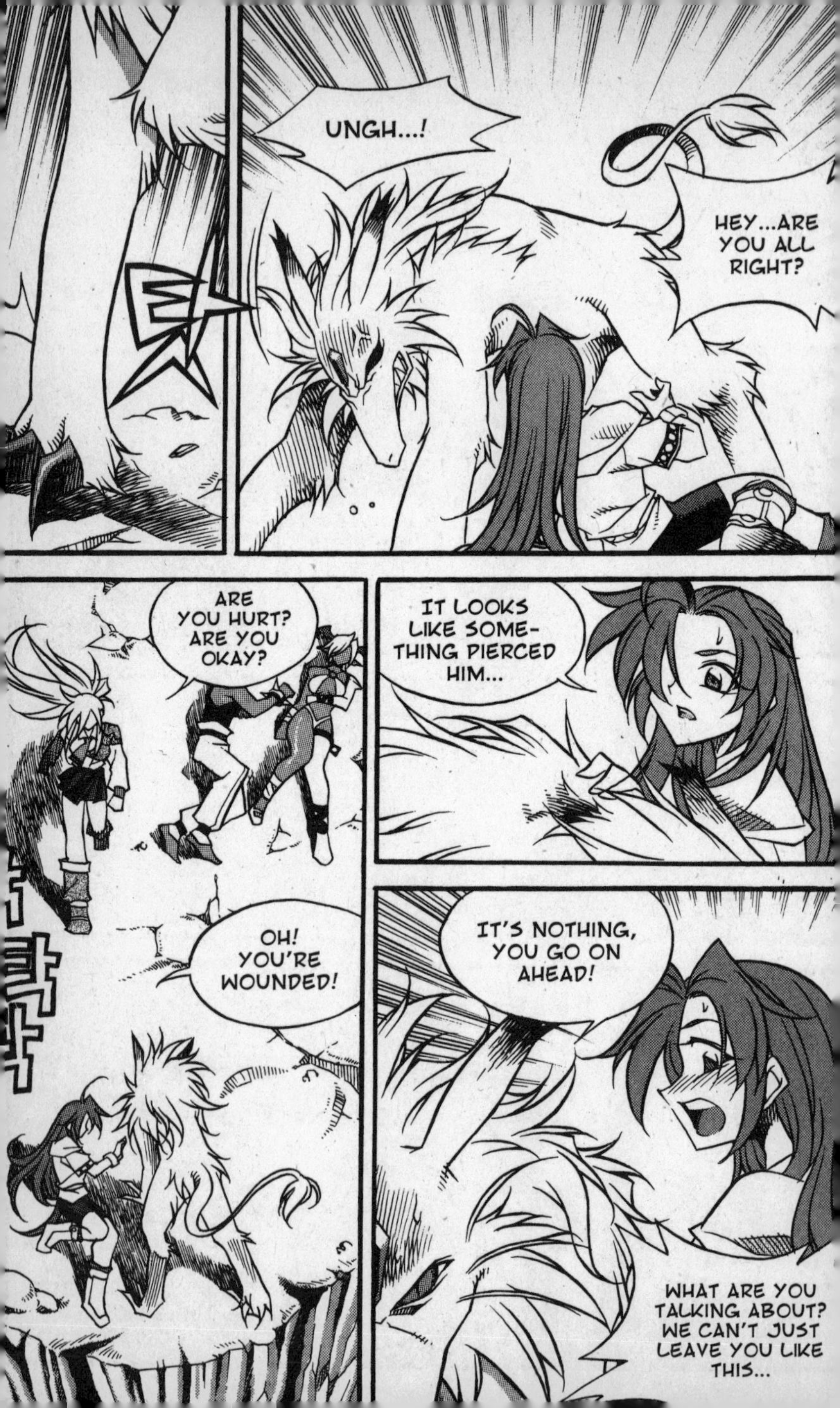
UNGH...!
HEY...ARE YOU ALL RIGHT?
ARE YOU HURT? ARE YOU OKAY?
OH! YOU'RE WOUNDED!
IT LOOKS LIKE SOME-THING PIERCED HIM...
IT'S NOTHING, YOU GO ON AHEAD!
WHAT ARE YOU TALKING ABOUT? WE CAN'T JUST LEAVE YOU LIKE THIS...

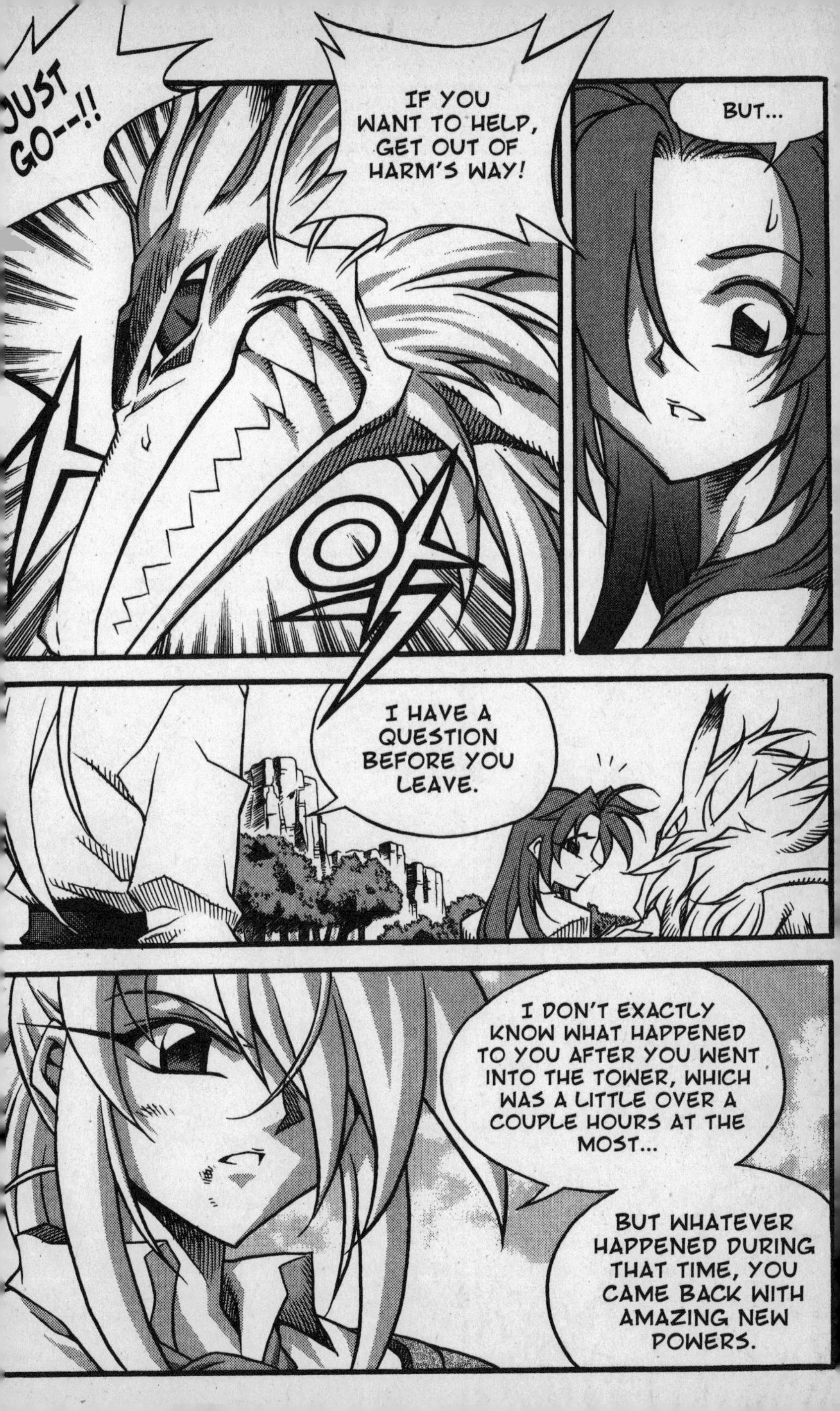
JUST GO--!!
IF YOU WANT TO HELP, GET OUT OF HARM'S WAY!
BUT...
I HAVE A QUESTION BEFORE YOU LEAVE.
I DON'T EXACTLY KNOW WHAT HAPPENED TO YOU AFTER YOU WENT INTO THE TOWER, WHICH WAS A LITTLE OVER A COUPLE HOURS AT THE MOST...
BUT WHATEVER HAPPENED DURING THAT TIME, YOU CAME BACK WITH AMAZING NEW POWERS.

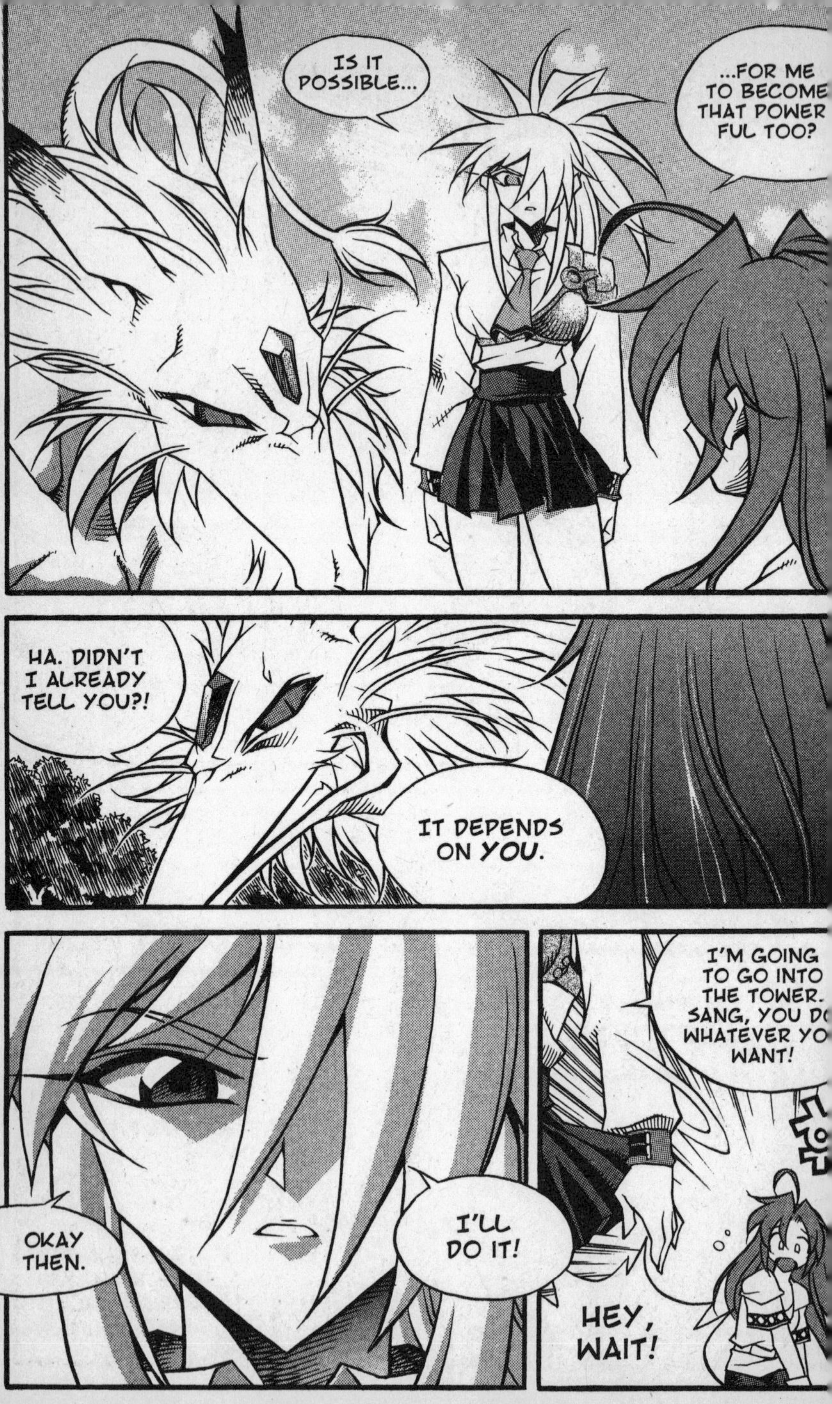
IS IT POSSIBLE...
...FOR ME TO BECOME THAT POWER FUL TOO?
HA. DIDN'T I ALREADY TELL YOU?!
IT DEPENDS ON *YOU*.
OKAY THEN.
I'LL DO IT!
I'M GOING TO GO INTO THE TOWER. SANG, YOU DO WHATEVER YOU WANT!
HEY, WAIT!

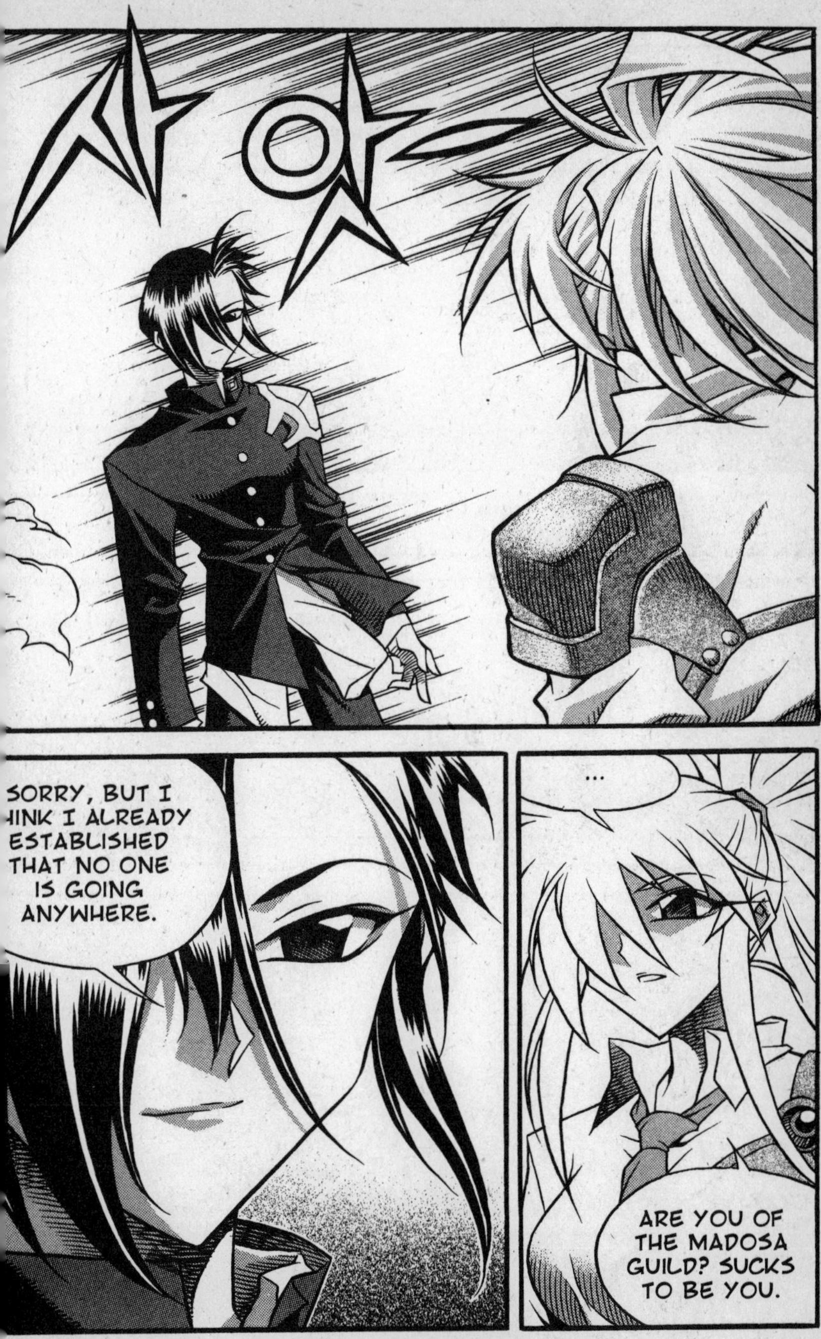
SORRY, BUT I HINK I ALREADY ESTABLISHED THAT NO ONE IS GOING ANYWHERE.
...
ARE YOU OF THE MADOSA GUILD? SUCKS TO BE YOU.

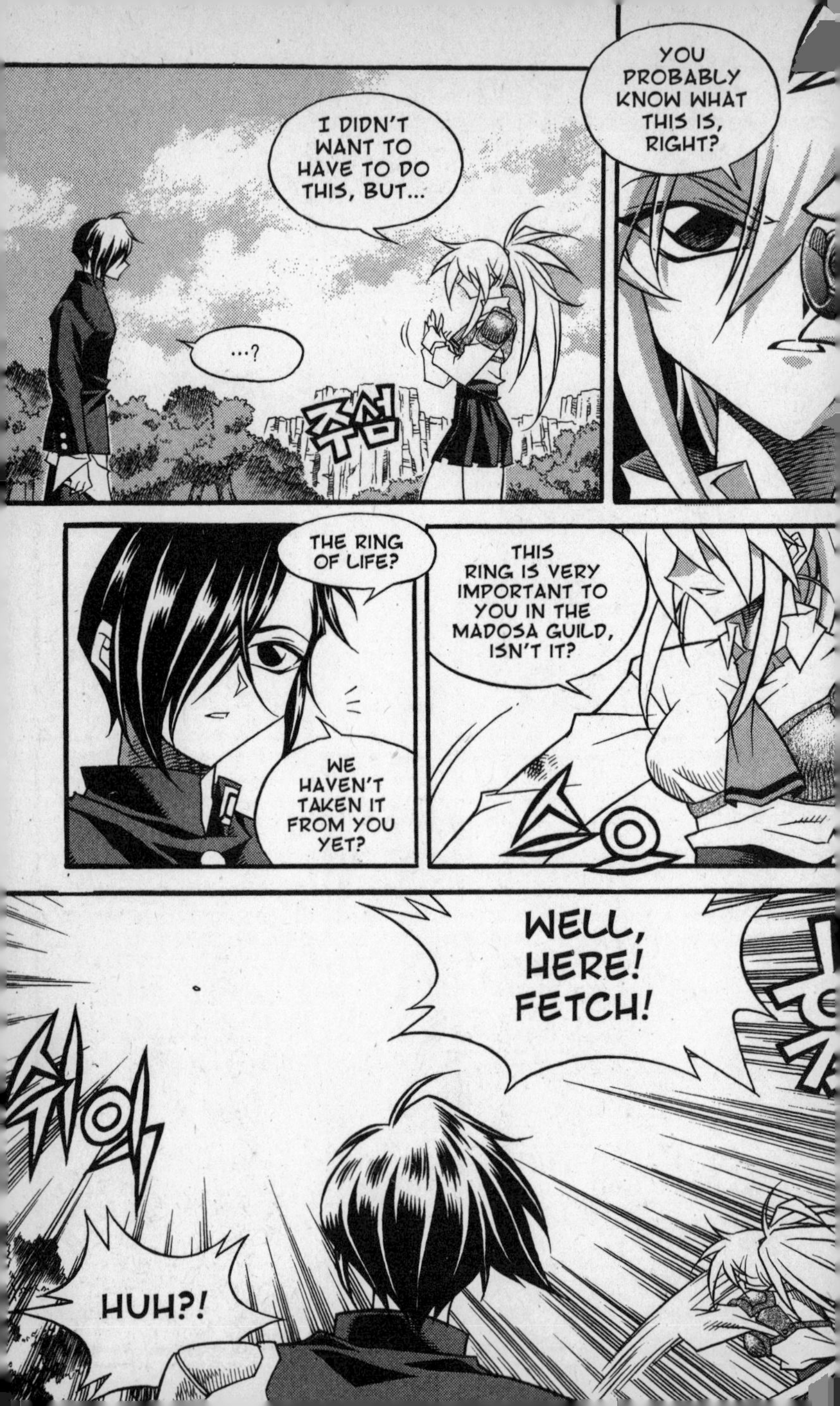
I DIDN'T WANT TO HAVE TO DO THIS, BUT...
...?
주섬
YOU PROBABLY KNOW WHAT THIS IS, RIGHT?
THE RING OF LIFE?
WE HAVEN'T TAKEN IT FROM YOU YET?
THIS RING IS VERY IMPORTANT TO YOU IN THE MADOSA GUILD, ISN'T IT?
WELL, HERE! FETCH!
HUH?!

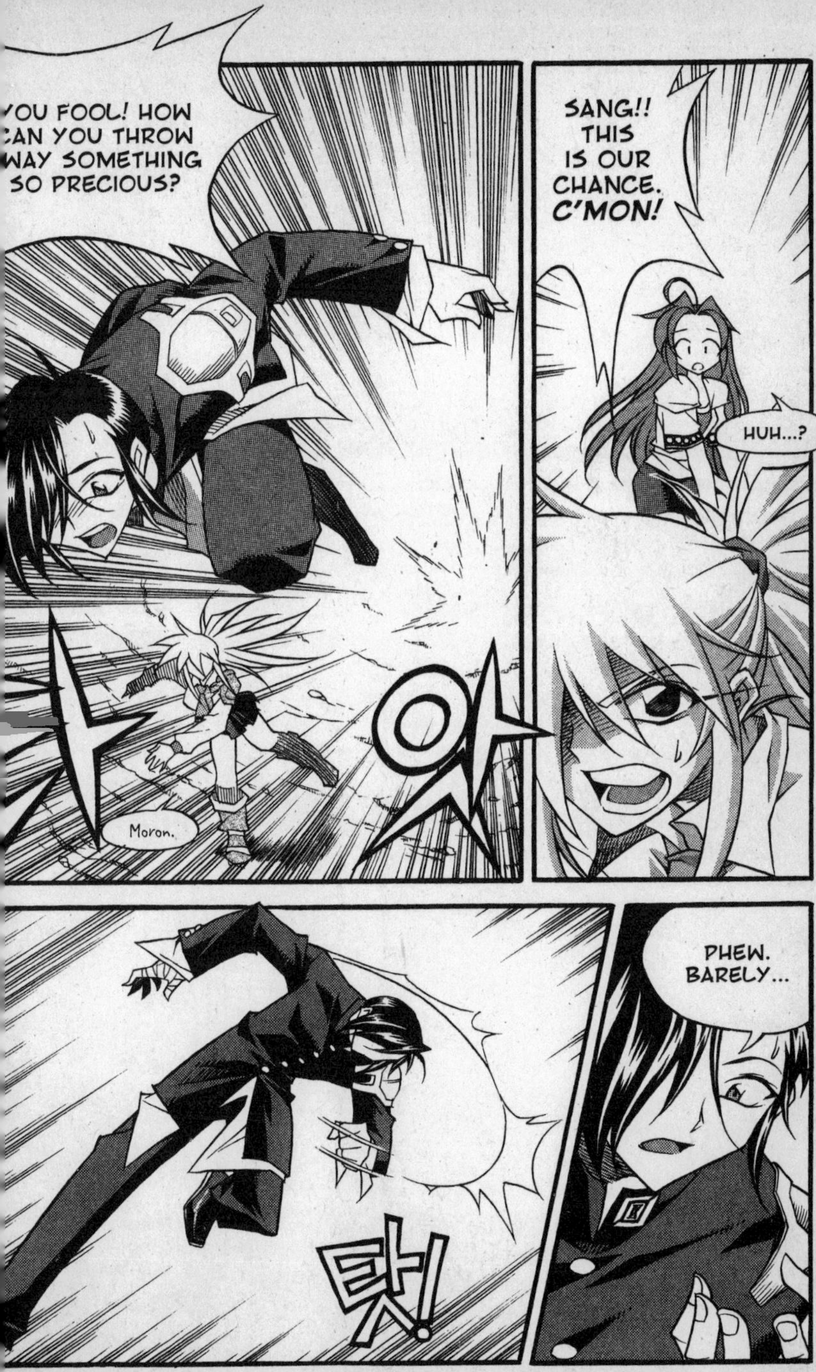

YOU FOOL! HOW CAN YOU THROW WAY SOMETHING SO PRECIOUS?
Moron.
SANG!! THIS IS OUR CHANCE. C'MON!
HUH...?
탓!
PHEW. BARELY...

......
SLAM
콰직
HA HA...
DAMN.

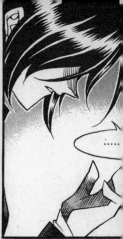

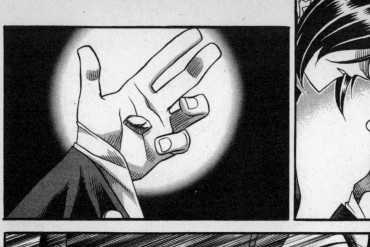

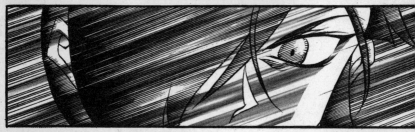

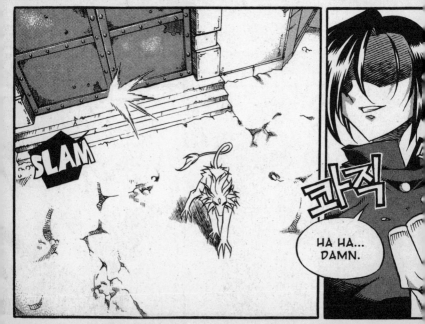

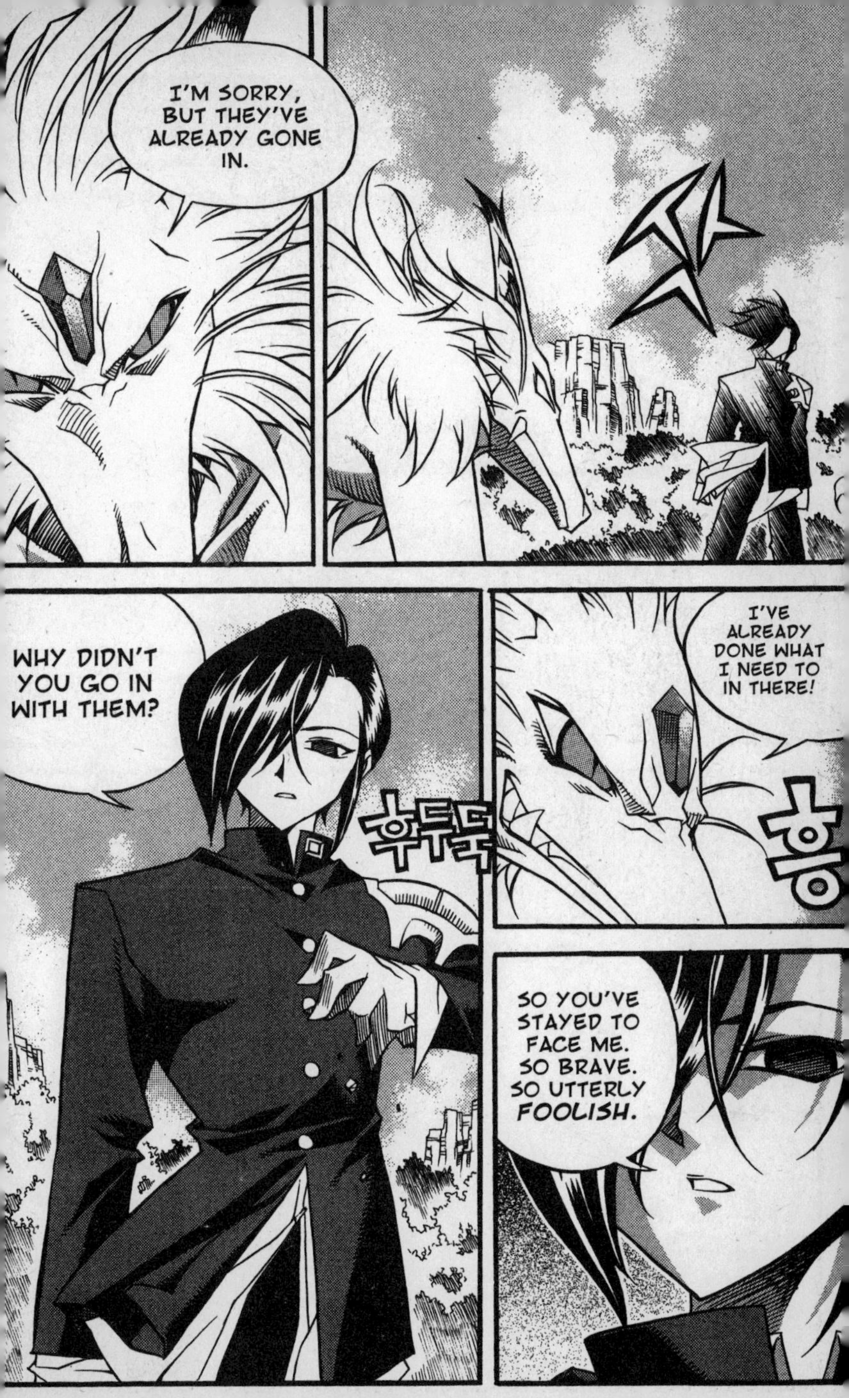
I'M SORRY, BUT THEY'VE ALREADY GONE IN.
WHY DIDN'T YOU GO IN WITH THEM?
I'VE ALREADY DONE WHAT I NEED TO IN THERE!
흥
SO YOU'VE STAYED TO FACE ME. SO BRAVE. SO UTTERLY **FOOLISH**.

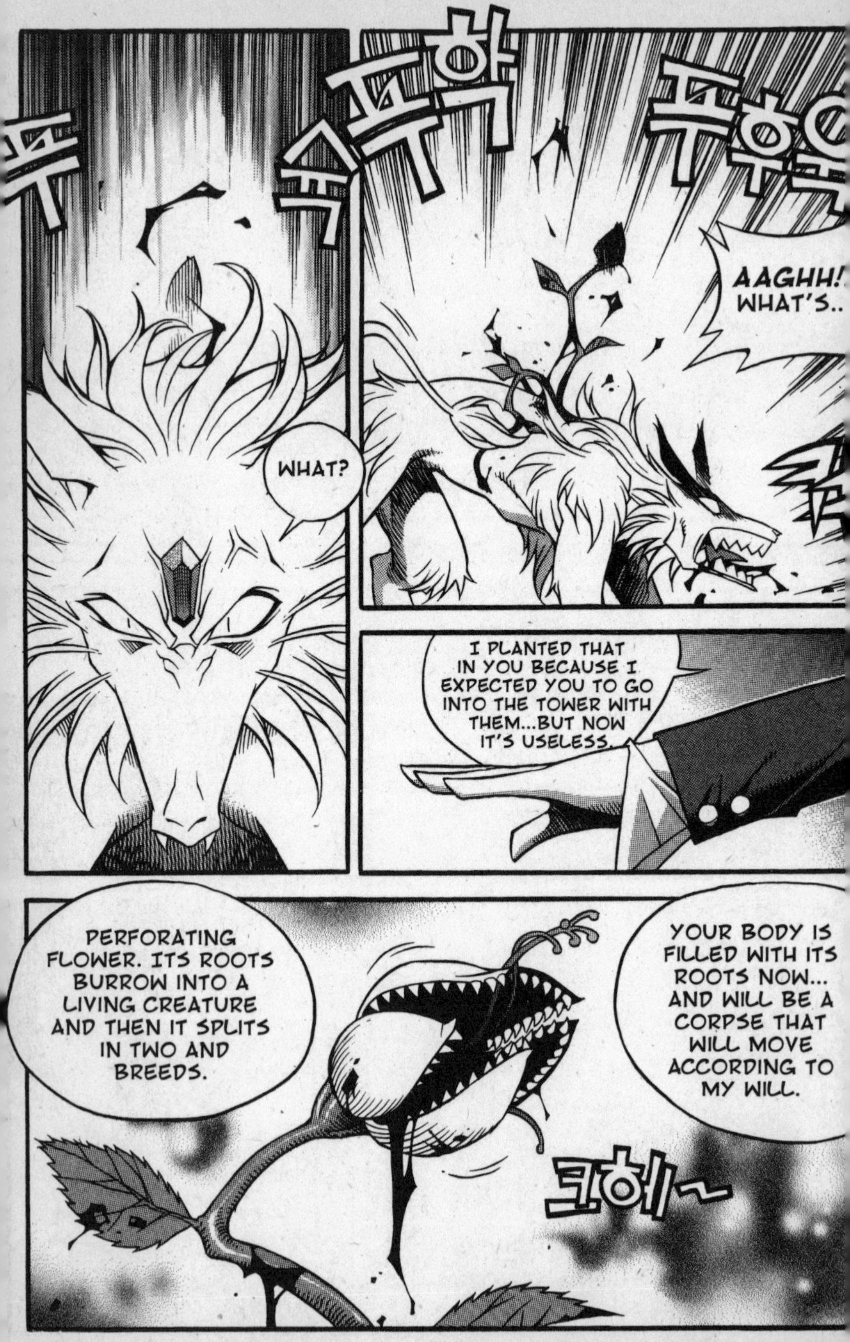
WHAT?
AAGHH! WHAT'S..
I PLANTED THAT IN YOU BECAUSE I EXPECTED YOU TO GO INTO THE TOWER WITH THEM...BUT NOW IT'S USELESS.
PERFORATING FLOWER. ITS ROOTS BURROW INTO A LIVING CREATURE AND THEN IT SPLITS IN TWO AND BREEDS.
YOUR BODY IS FILLED WITH ITS ROOTS NOW... AND WILL BE A CORPSE THAT WILL MOVE ACCORDING TO MY WILL.
코헤~

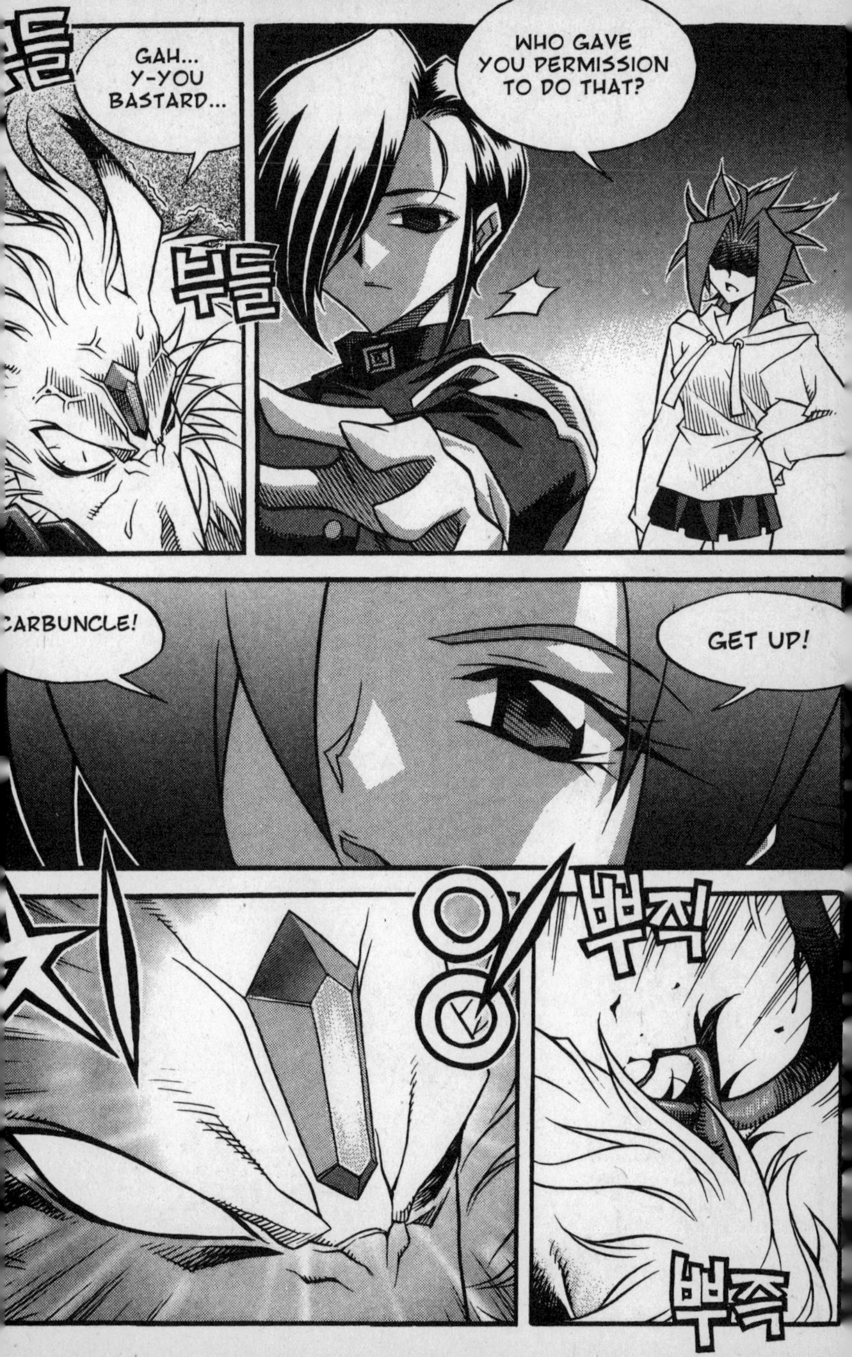
GAH... Y-YOU BASTARD...
부들
WHO GAVE YOU PERMISSION TO DO THAT?
CARBUNCLE!
GET UP!
뿌직
뿌죽

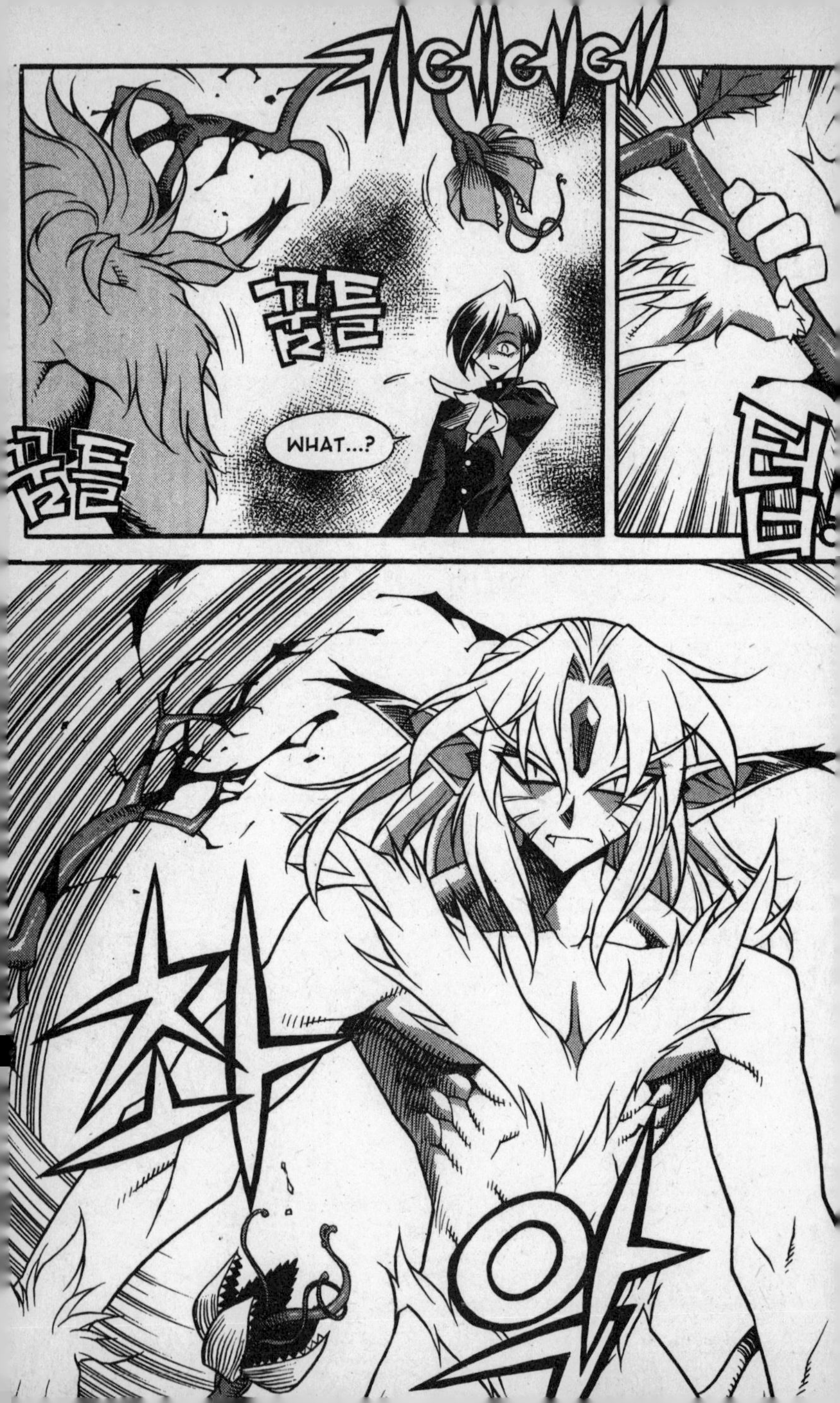
WHAT...?

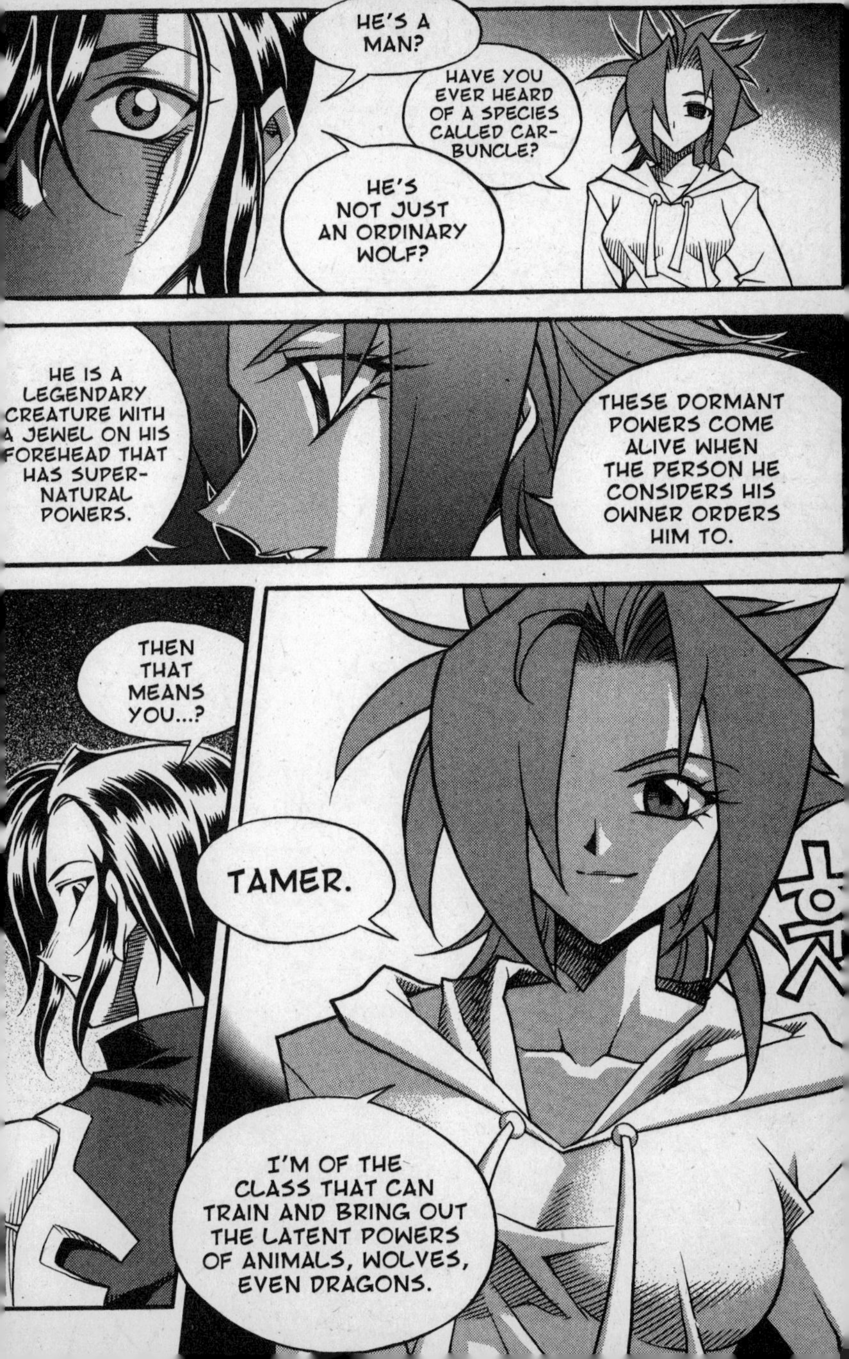
HE'S A MAN?
HAVE YOU EVER HEARD OF A SPECIES CALLED CAR-BUNCLE?
HE'S NOT JUST AN ORDINARY WOLF?
HE IS A LEGENDARY CREATURE WITH A JEWEL ON HIS FOREHEAD THAT HAS SUPER-NATURAL POWERS.
THESE DORMANT POWERS COME ALIVE WHEN THE PERSON HE CONSIDERS HIS OWNER ORDERS HIM TO.
THEN THAT MEANS YOU...?
TAMER.
I'M OF THE CLASS THAT CAN TRAIN AND BRING OUT THE LATENT POWERS OF ANIMALS, WOLVES, EVEN DRAGONS.

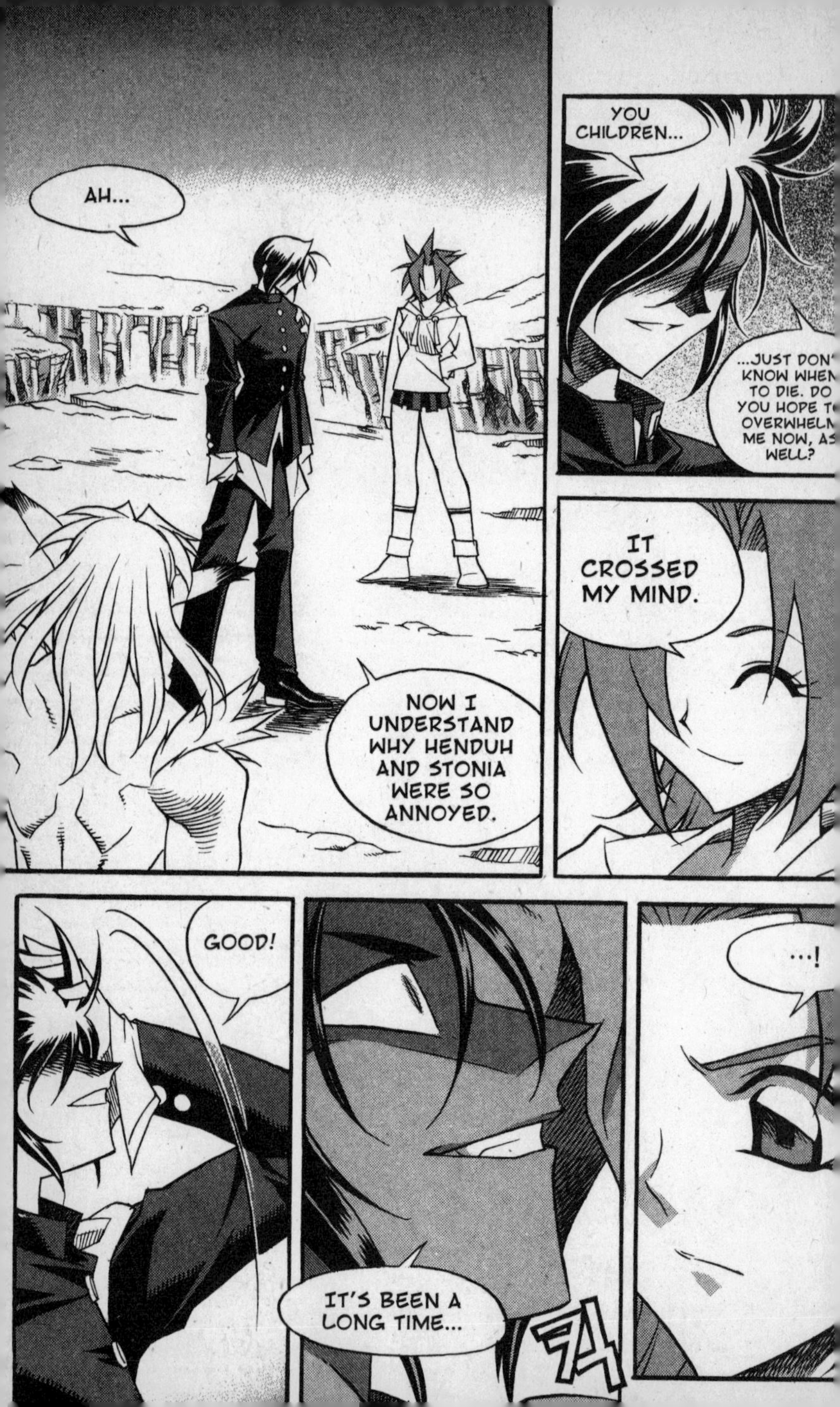
AH...
NOW I UNDERSTAND WHY HENDUH AND STONIA WERE SO ANNOYED.
YOU CHILDREN...
...JUST DON'T KNOW WHEN TO DIE. DO YOU HOPE TO OVERWHELM ME NOW, AS WELL?
IT CROSSED MY MIND.
GOOD!
IT'S BEEN A LONG TIME...
...!

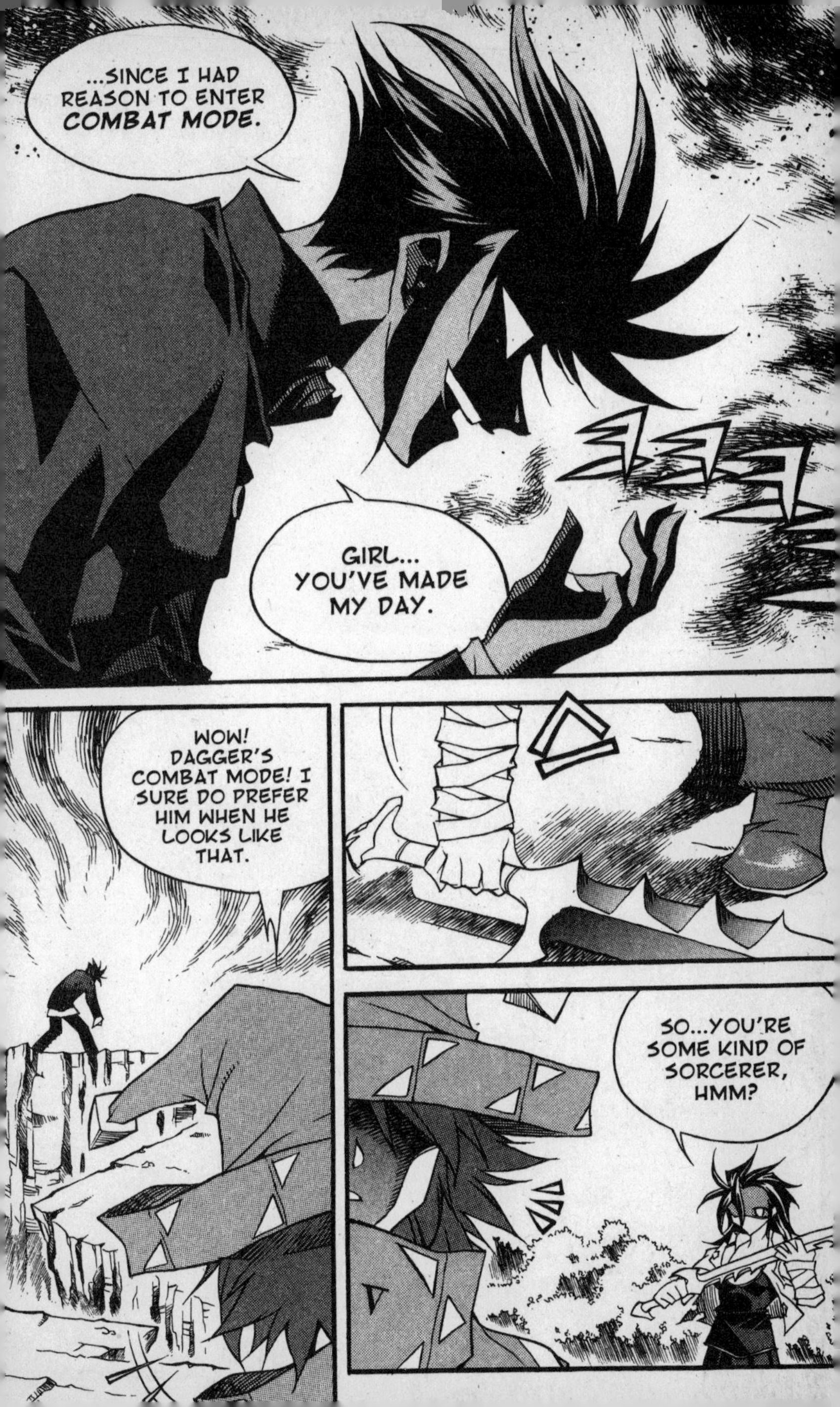
...SINCE I HAD REASON TO ENTER COMBAT MODE.
GIRL... YOU'VE MADE MY DAY.
WOW! DAGGER'S COMBAT MODE! I SURE DO PREFER HIM WHEN HE LOOKS LIKE THAT.
SO...YOU'RE SOME KIND OF SORCERER, HMM?

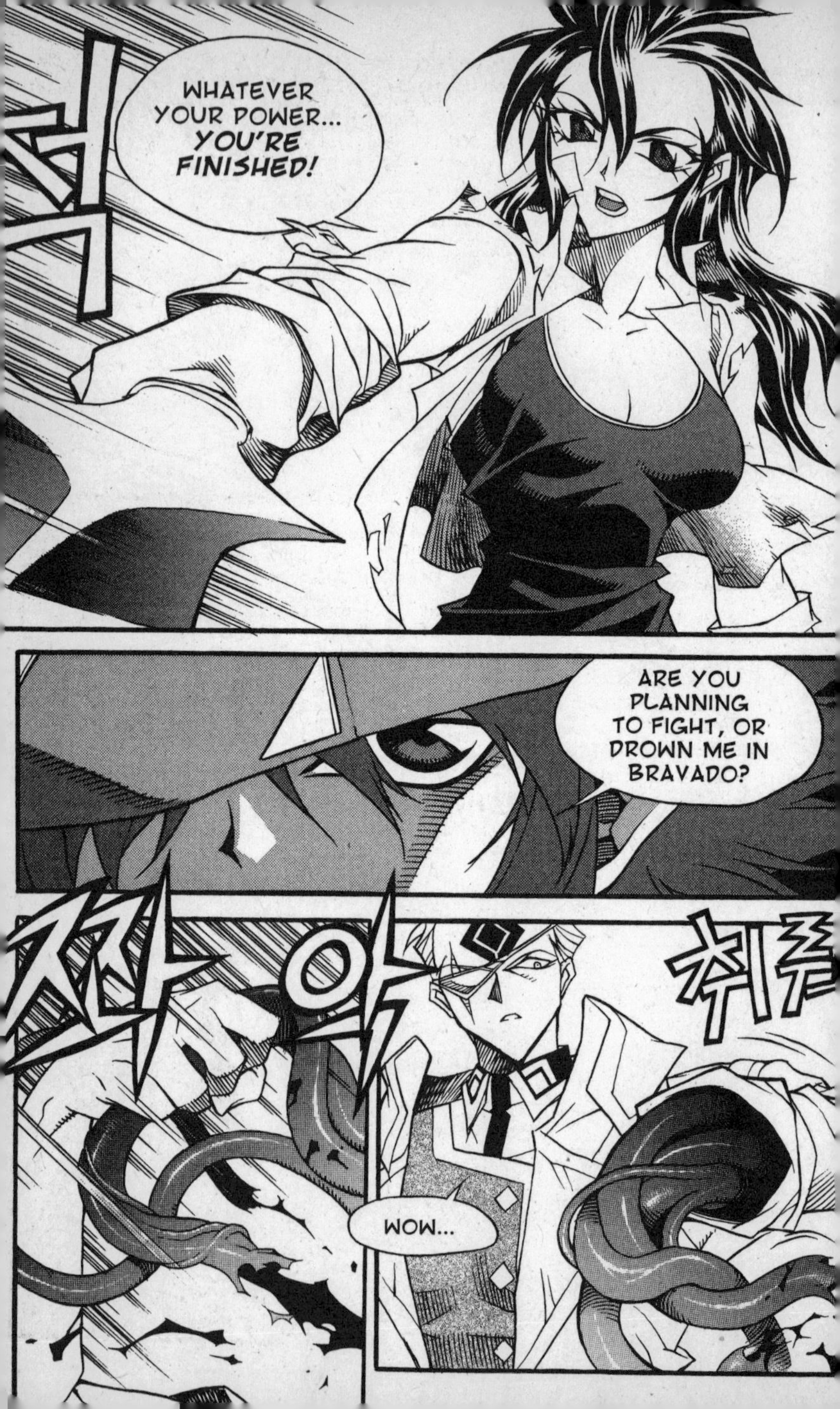
WHATEVER YOUR POWER... YOU'RE FINISHED!
ARE YOU PLANNING TO FIGHT, OR DROWN ME IN BRAVADO?
WOW...

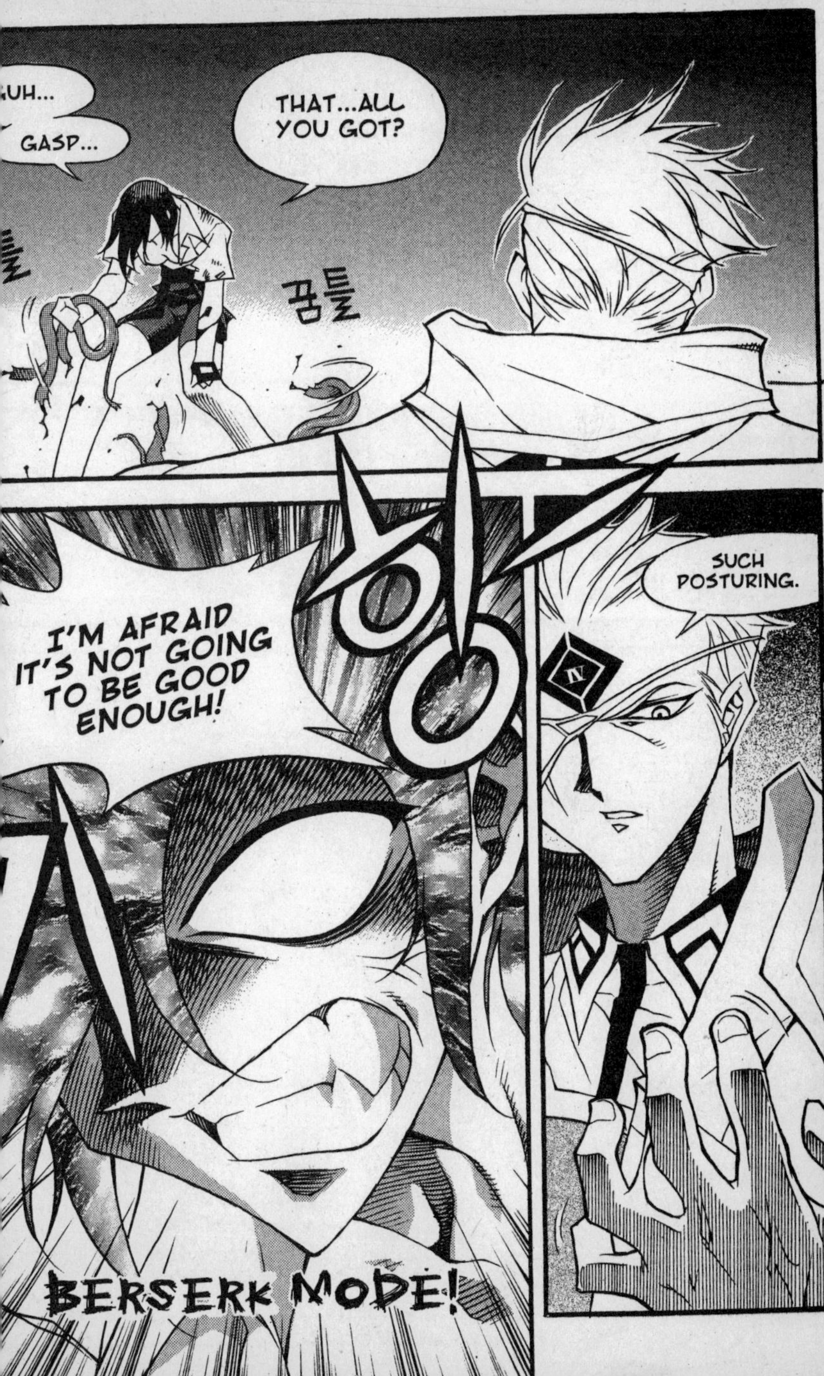
UH...
GASP...
THAT...ALL YOU GOT?
꿈틀
I'M AFRAID IT'S NOT GOING TO BE GOOD ENOUGH!
BERSERK MODE!
SUCH POSTURING.

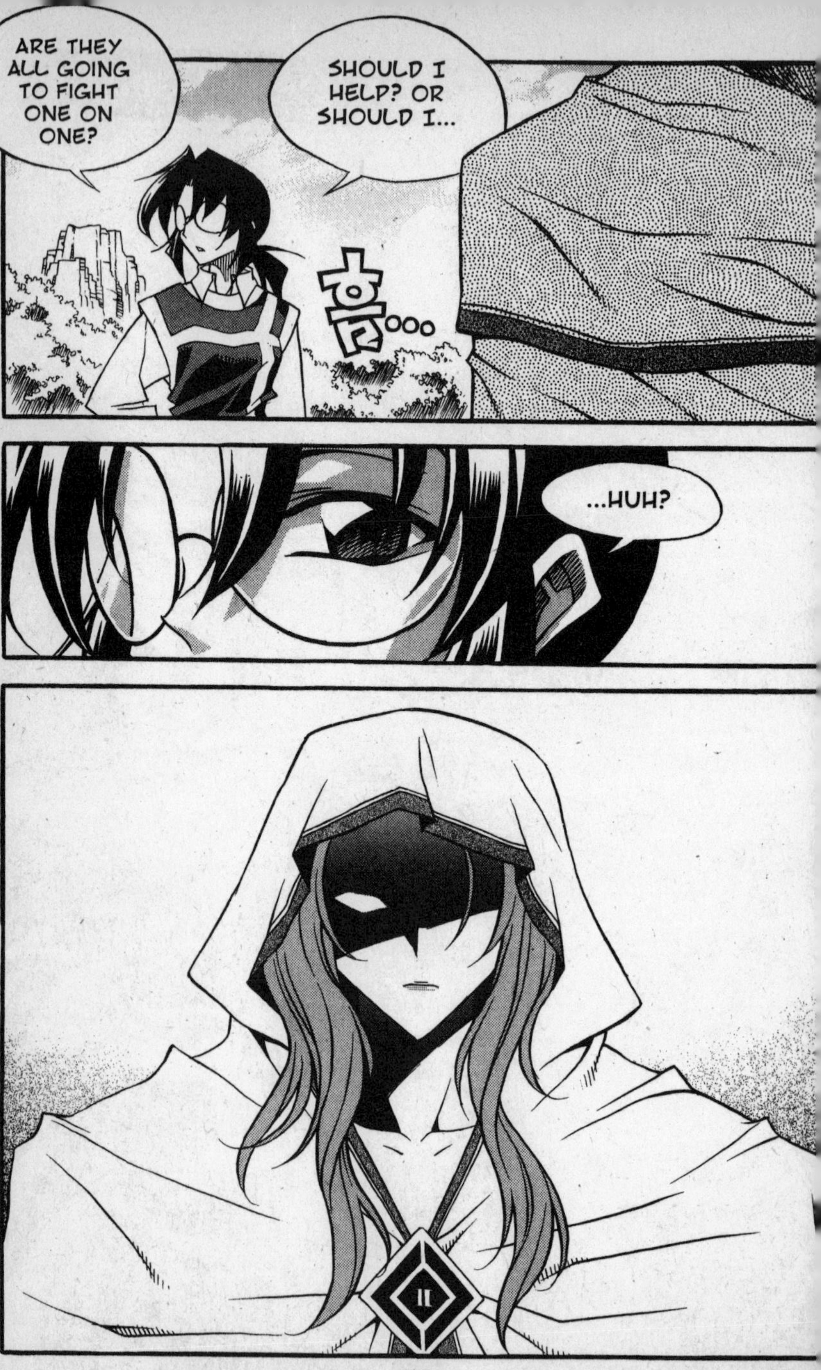
ARE THEY ALL GOING TO FIGHT ONE ON ONE?
SHOULD I HELP? OR SHOULD I...
흥ooo
...HUH?

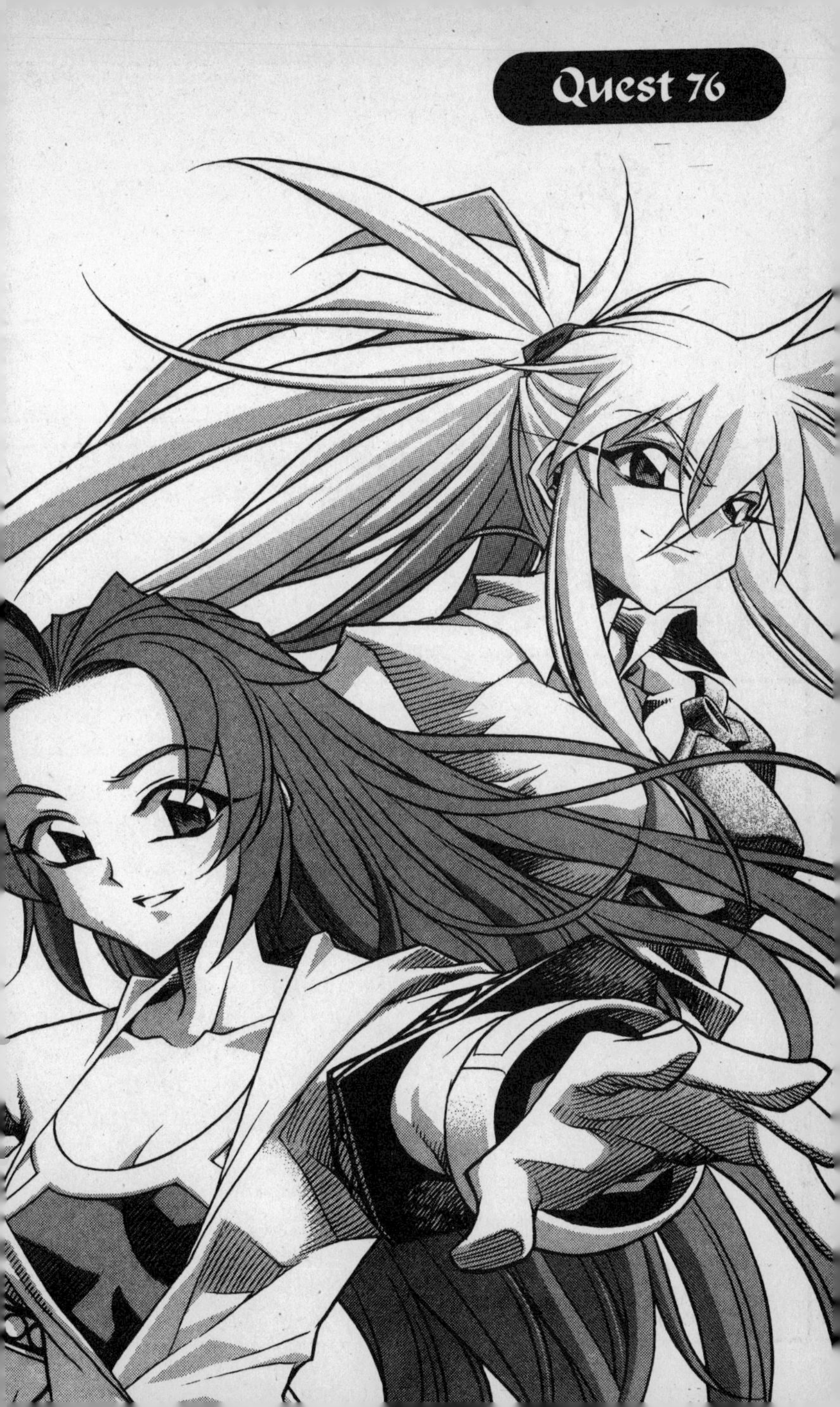
Quest 76

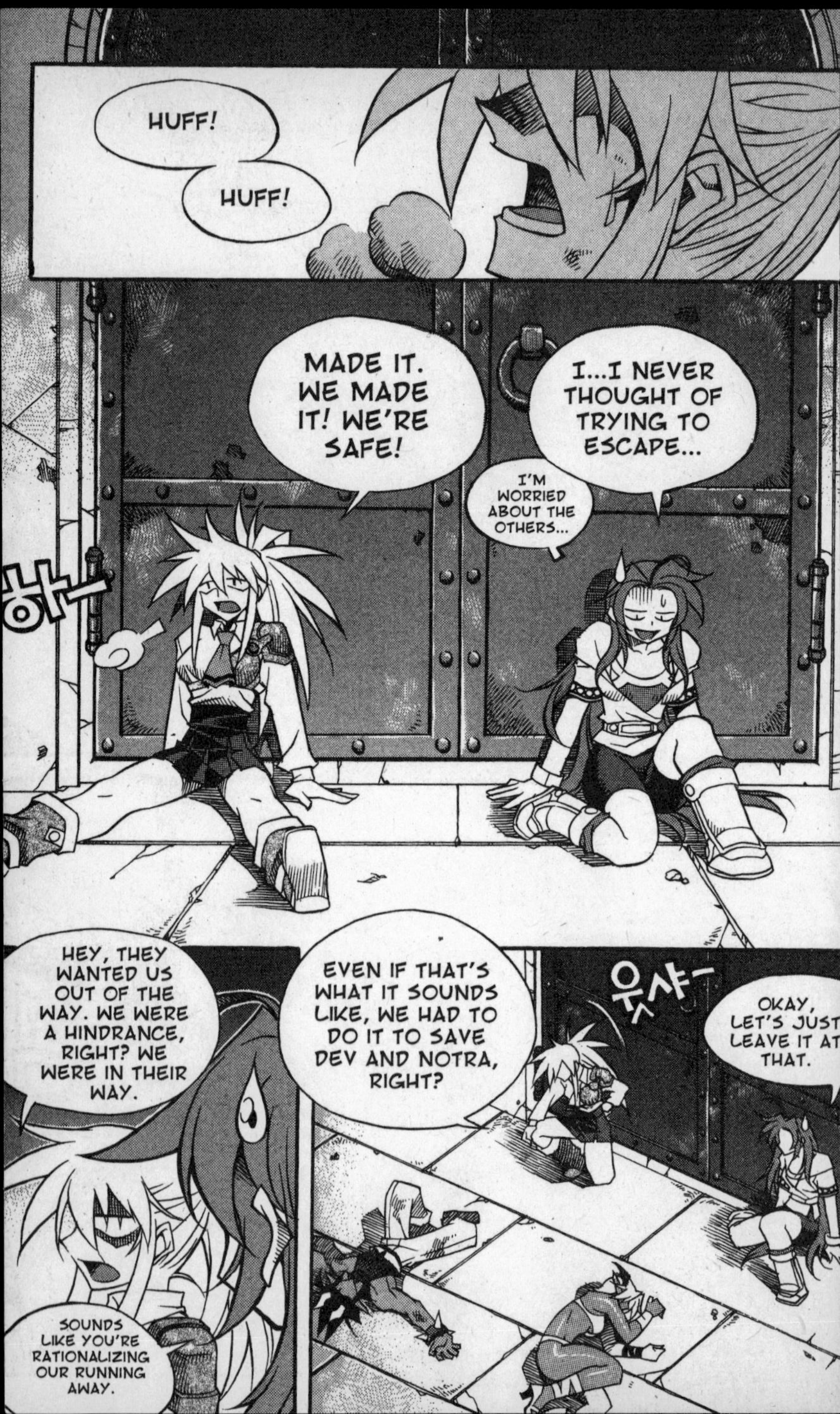
HUFF!
HUFF!
MADE IT. WE MADE IT! WE'RE SAFE!
I...I NEVER THOUGHT OF TRYING TO ESCAPE...
I'M WORRIED ABOUT THE OTHERS...
HEY, THEY WANTED US OUT OF THE WAY. WE WERE A HINDRANCE, RIGHT? WE WERE IN THEIR WAY.
SOUNDS LIKE YOU'RE RATIONALIZING OUR RUNNING AWAY.
EVEN IF THAT'S WHAT IT SOUNDS LIKE, WE HAD TO DO IT TO SAVE DEV AND NOTRA, RIGHT?
OKAY, LET'S JUST LEAVE IT AT THAT.

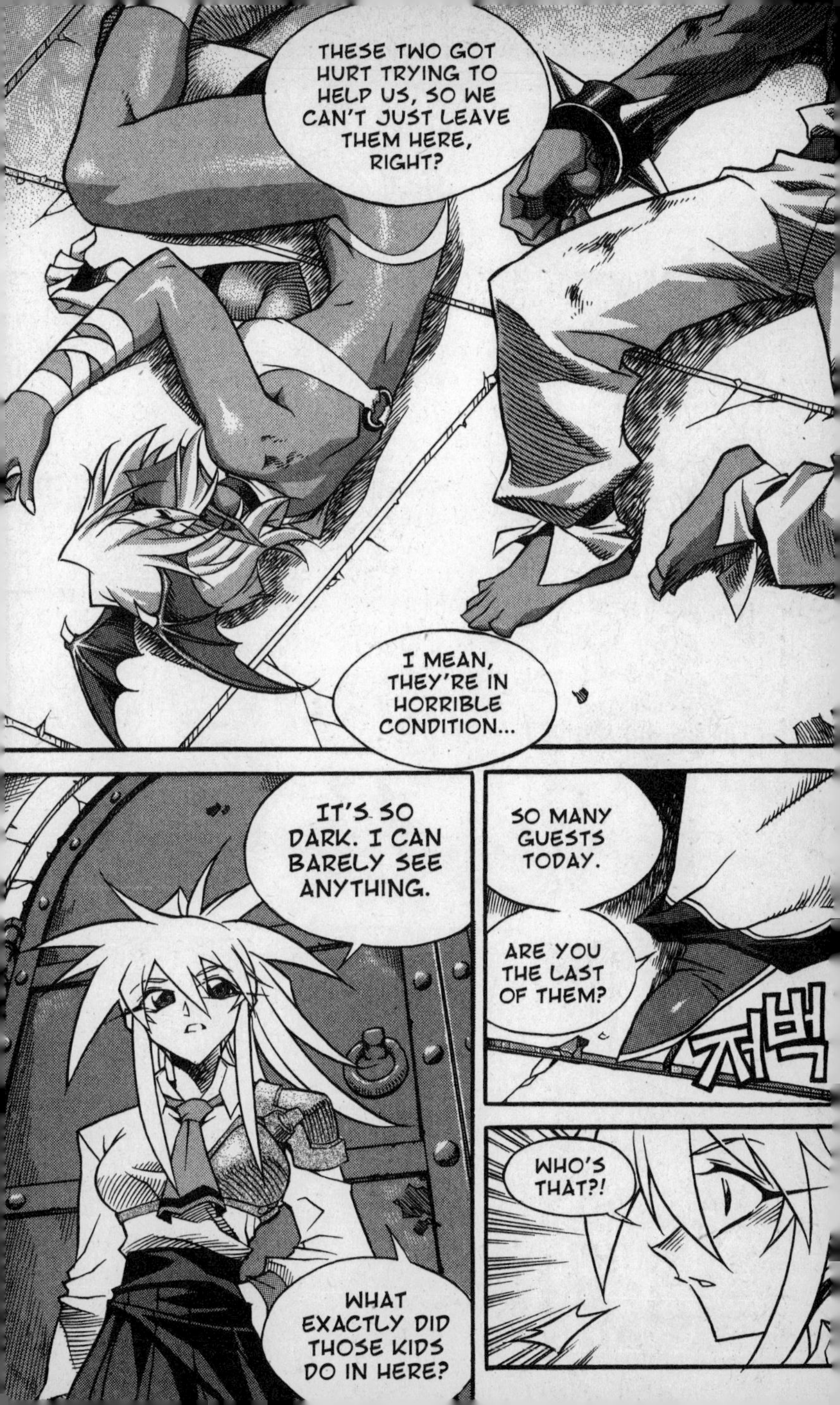
THESE TWO GOT HURT TRYING TO HELP US, SO WE CAN'T JUST LEAVE THEM HERE, RIGHT?
I MEAN, THEY'RE IN HORRIBLE CONDITION...
IT'S SO DARK. I CAN BARELY SEE ANYTHING.
WHAT EXACTLY DID THOSE KIDS DO IN HERE?
SO MANY GUESTS TODAY.
ARE YOU THE LAST OF THEM?
저벅
WHO'S THAT?!

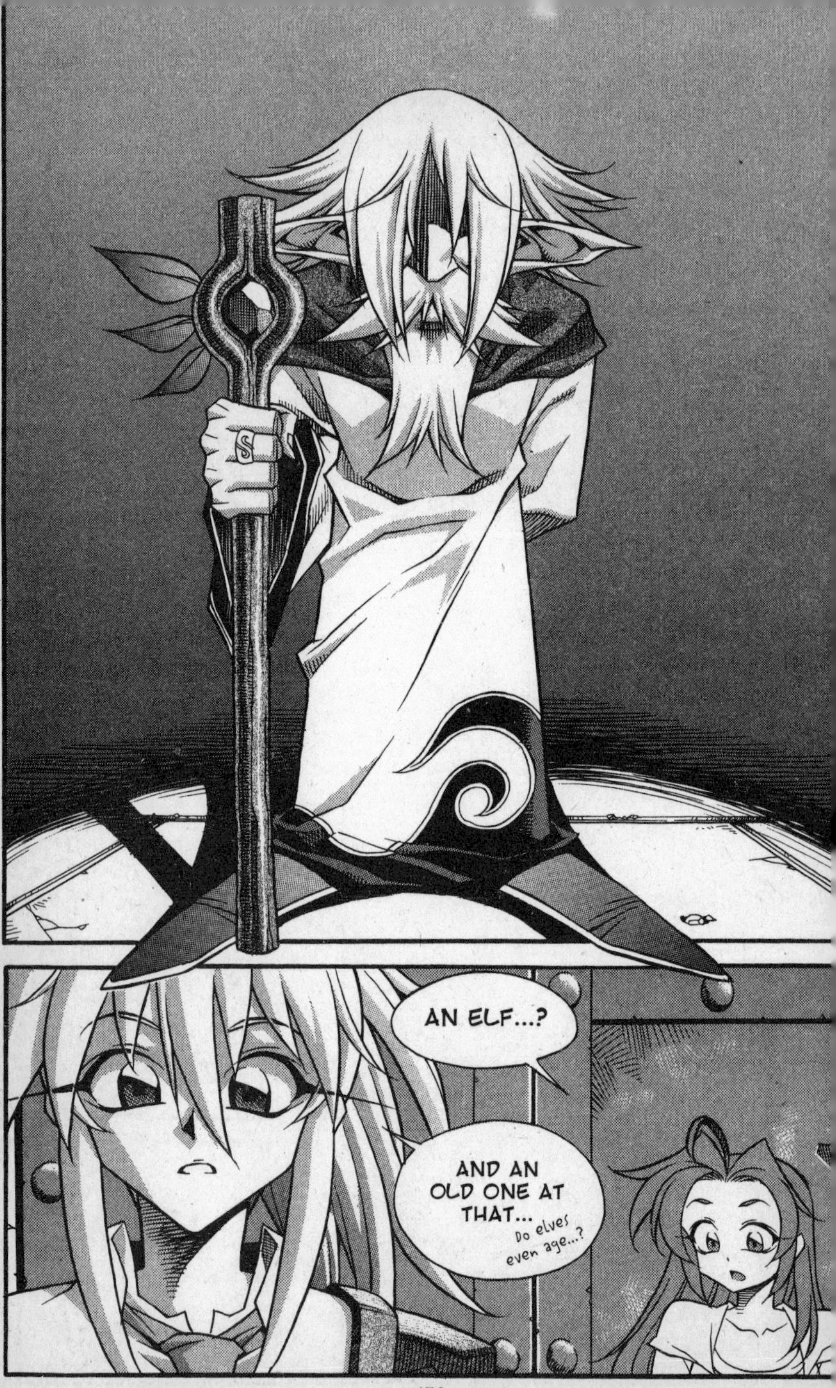
AN ELF...?
AND AN OLD ONE AT THAT...
Do elves even age...?

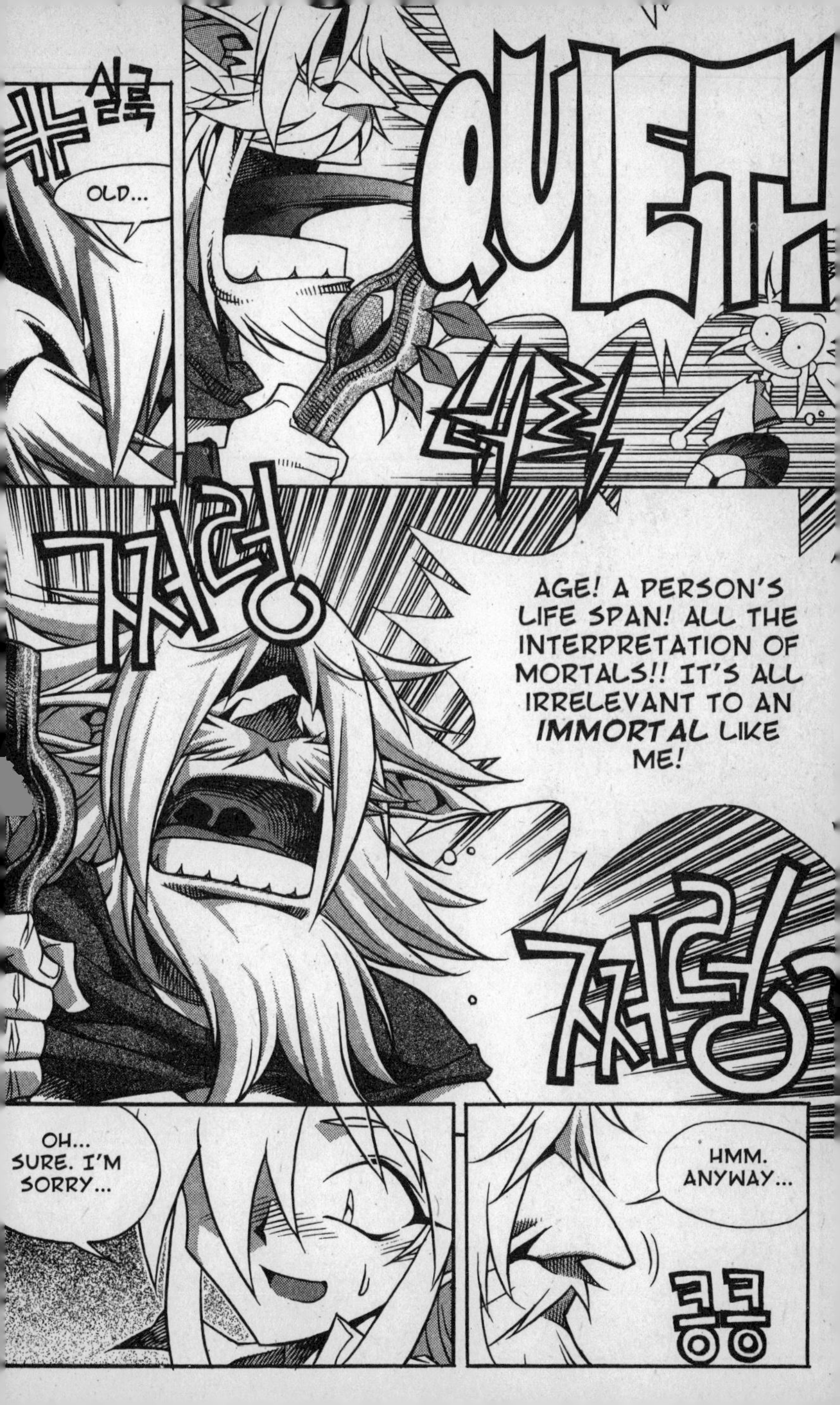
실룩
OLD...
QUIET!
AGE! A PERSON'S LIFE SPAN! ALL THE INTERPRETATION OF MORTALS!! IT'S ALL IRRELEVANT TO AN *IMMORTAL* LIKE ME!
OH... SURE. I'M SORRY...
HMM. ANYWAY...
킁킁

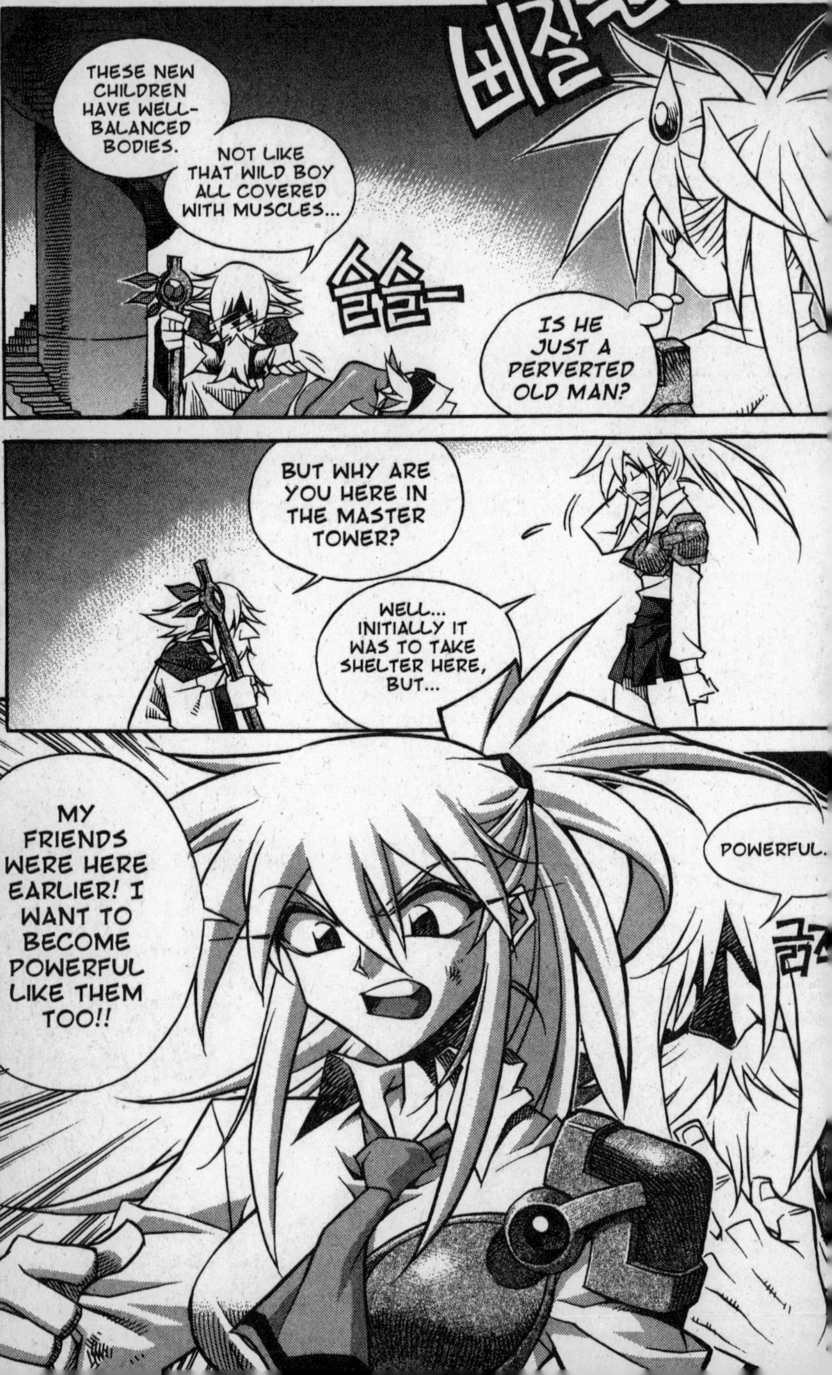
THESE NEW CHILDREN HAVE WELL-BALANCED BODIES.
NOT LIKE THAT WILD BOY ALL COVERED WITH MUSCLES...
삐질~
슬슬~
IS HE JUST A PERVERTED OLD MAN?
BUT WHY ARE YOU HERE IN THE MASTER TOWER?
WELL... INITIALLY IT WAS TO TAKE SHELTER HERE, BUT...
MY FRIENDS WERE HERE EARLIER! I WANT TO BECOME POWERFUL LIKE THEM TOO!!
POWERFUL.

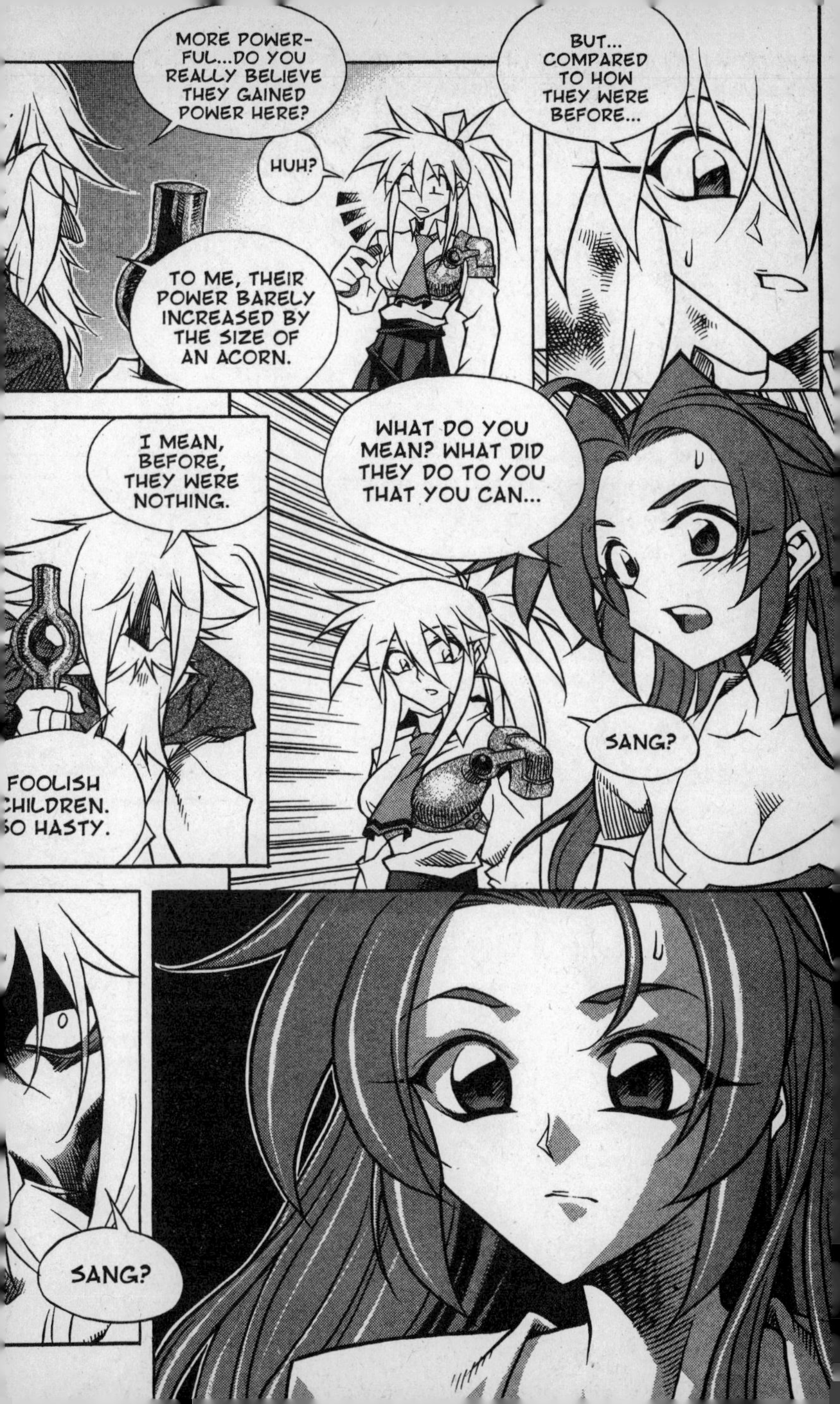
MORE POWER-FUL...DO YOU REALLY BELIEVE THEY GAINED POWER HERE?
HUH?
TO ME, THEIR POWER BARELY INCREASED BY THE SIZE OF AN ACORN.
BUT... COMPARED TO HOW THEY WERE BEFORE...
I MEAN, BEFORE, THEY WERE NOTHING.
FOOLISH CHILDREN. SO HASTY.
WHAT DO YOU MEAN? WHAT DID THEY DO TO YOU THAT YOU CAN...
SANG?
SANG?

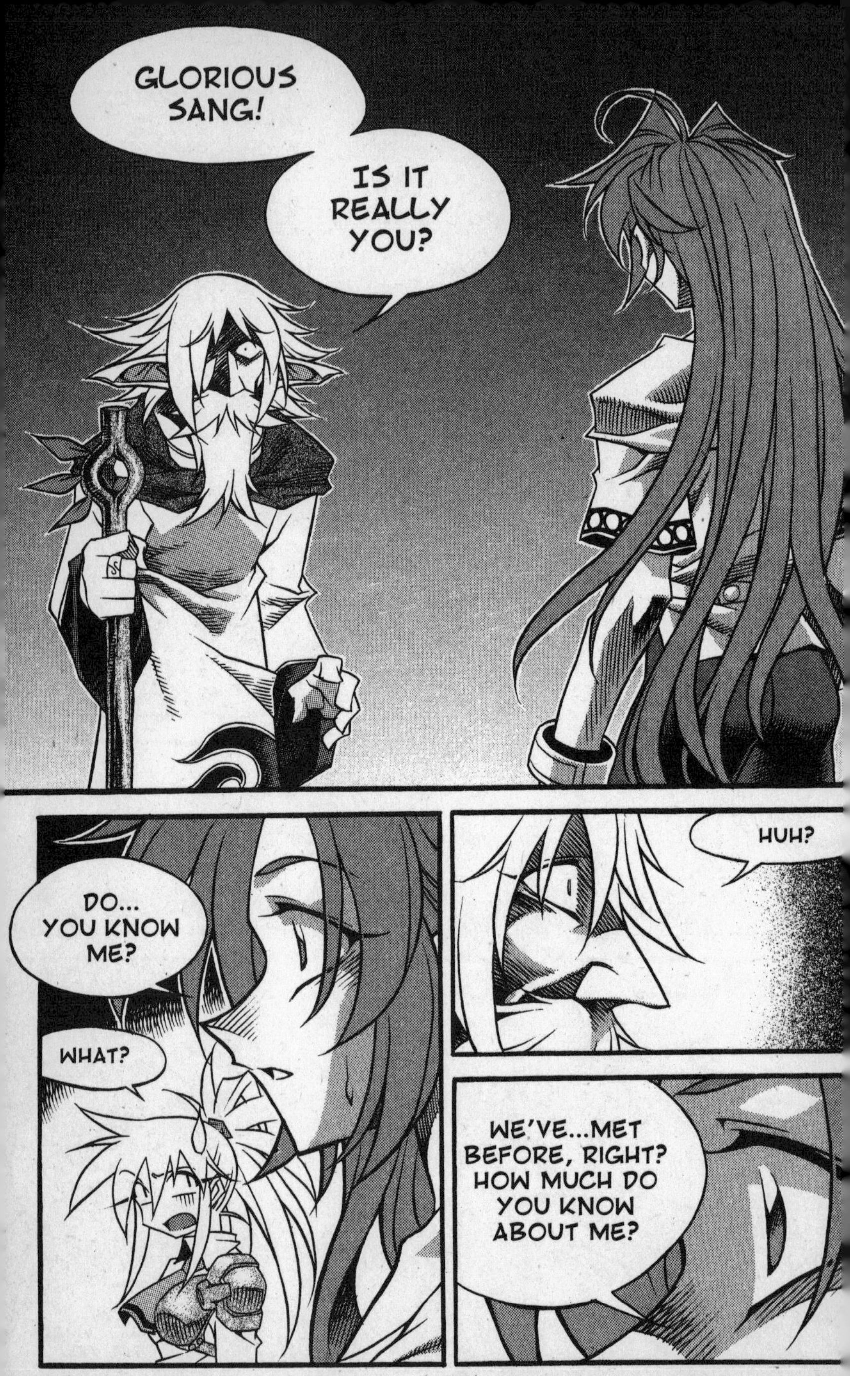
GLORIOUS SANG!
IS IT REALLY YOU?
DO... YOU KNOW ME?
WHAT?
HUH?
WE'VE...MET BEFORE, RIGHT? HOW MUCH DO YOU KNOW ABOUT ME?

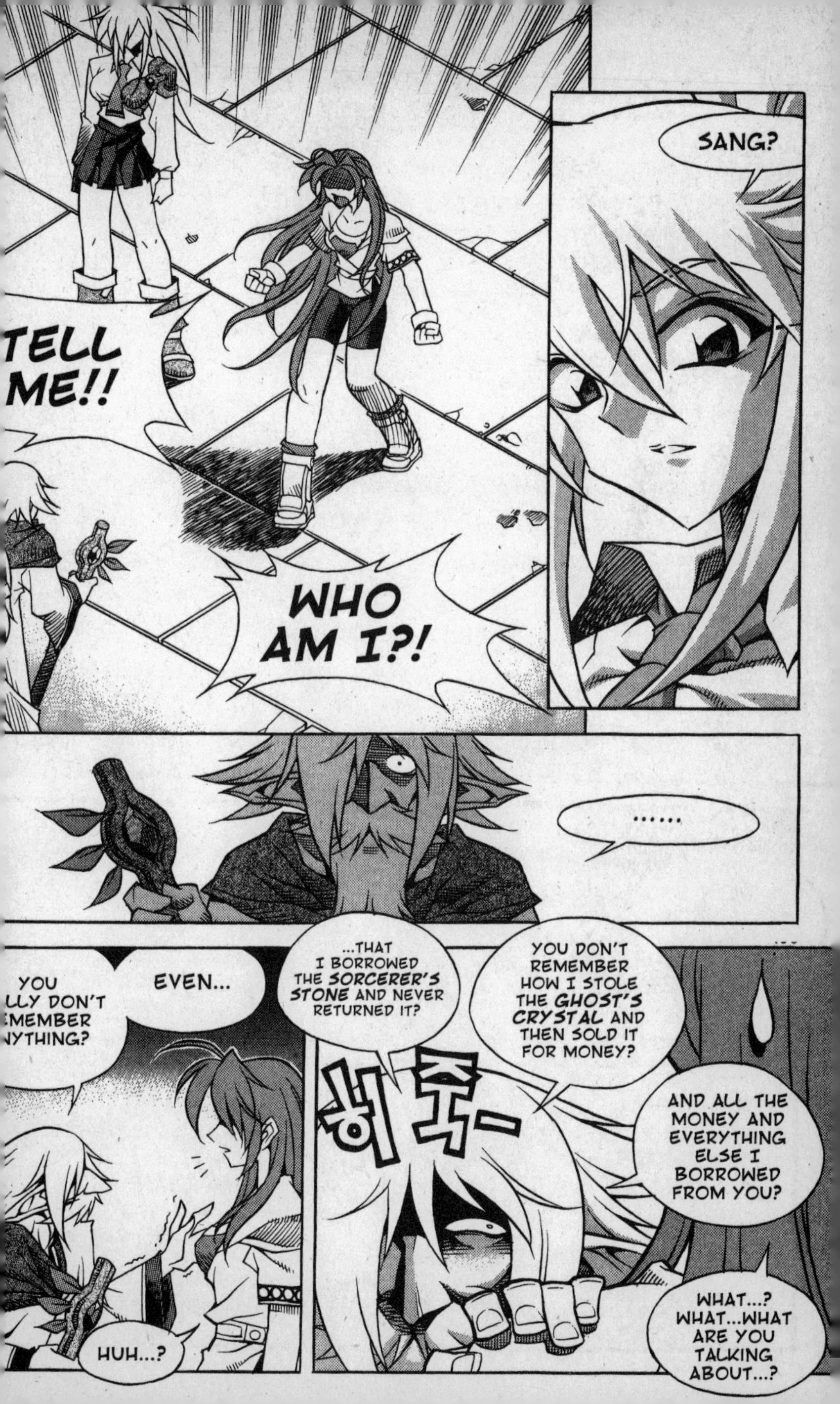

TELL ME!!
WHO AM I?!
SANG?
......
YOU LLY DON'T EMEMBER NYTHING?
EVEN...
HUH...?
...THAT I BORROWED THE SORCERER'S STONE AND NEVER RETURNED IT?
YOU DON'T REMEMBER HOW I STOLE THE GHOST'S CRYSTAL AND THEN SOLD IT FOR MONEY?
AND ALL THE MONEY AND EVERYTHING ELSE I BORROWED FROM YOU?
WHAT...? WHAT...WHAT ARE YOU TALKING ABOUT...?

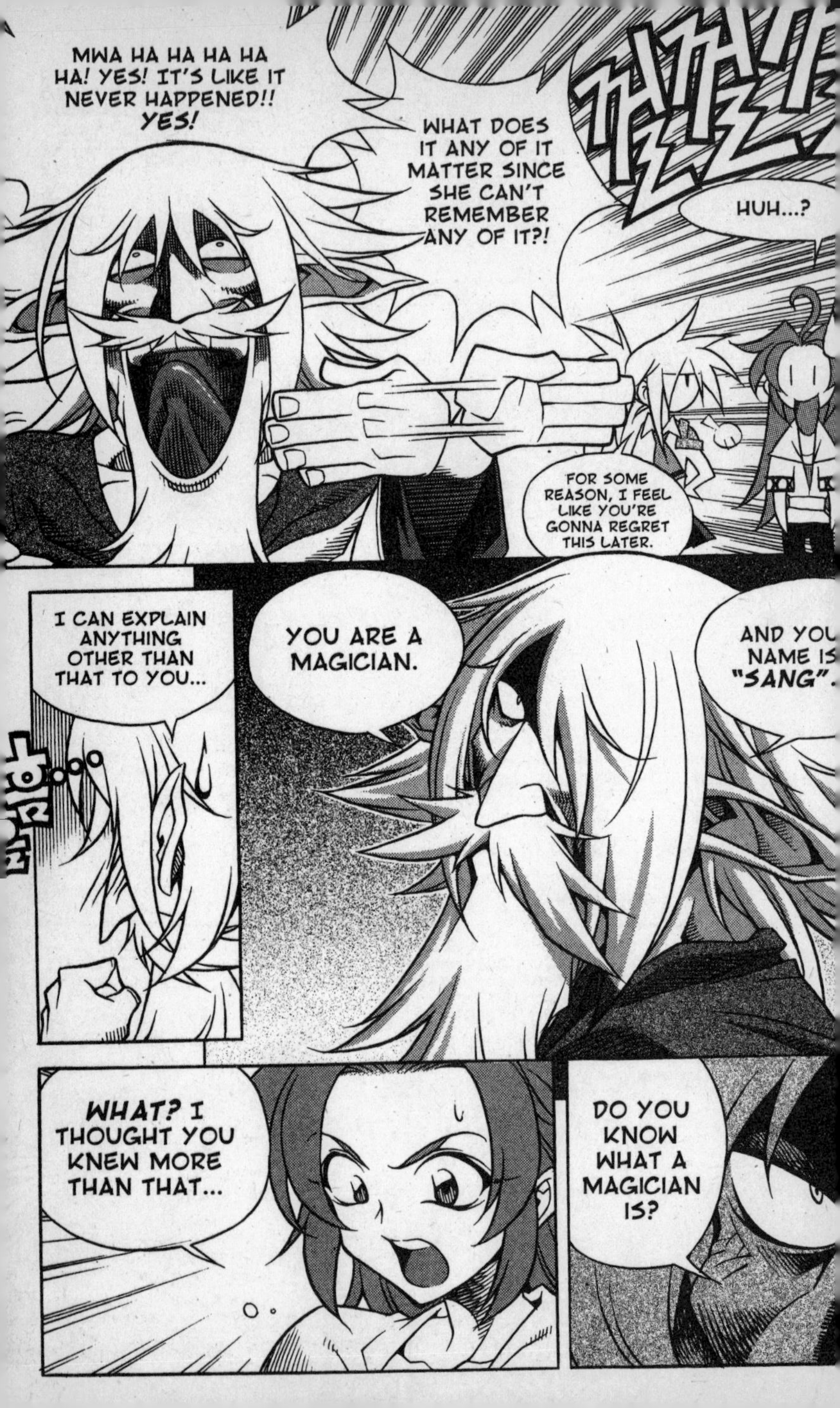
MWA HA HA HA HA HA! YES! IT'S LIKE IT NEVER HAPPENED!! *YES!*
WHAT DOES IT ANY OF IT MATTER SINCE SHE CAN'T REMEMBER ANY OF IT?!
HUH...?
FOR SOME REASON, I FEEL LIKE YOU'RE GONNA REGRET THIS LATER.
I CAN EXPLAIN ANYTHING OTHER THAN THAT TO YOU...
YOU ARE A MAGICIAN.
AND YOU NAME IS *"SANG"*.
WHAT? I THOUGHT YOU KNEW MORE THAN THAT...
DO YOU KNOW WHAT A MAGICIAN IS?

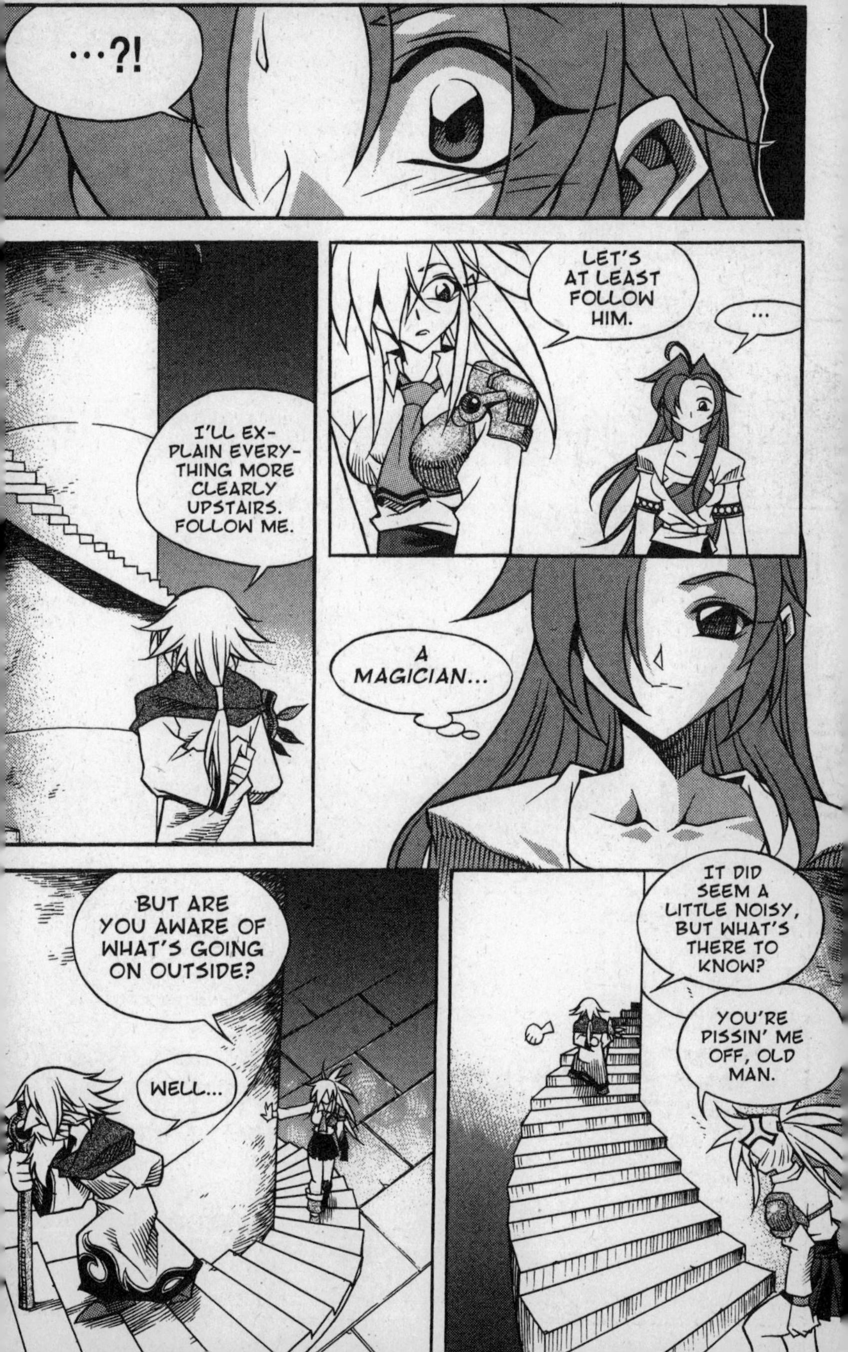
...?!
I'LL EX-PLAIN EVERY-THING MORE CLEARLY UPSTAIRS. FOLLOW ME.
LET'S AT LEAST FOLLOW HIM.
...
A MAGICIAN...
BUT ARE YOU AWARE OF WHAT'S GOING ON OUTSIDE?
WELL...
IT DID SEEM A LITTLE NOISY, BUT WHAT'S THERE TO KNOW?
YOU'RE PISSIN' ME OFF, OLD MAN.

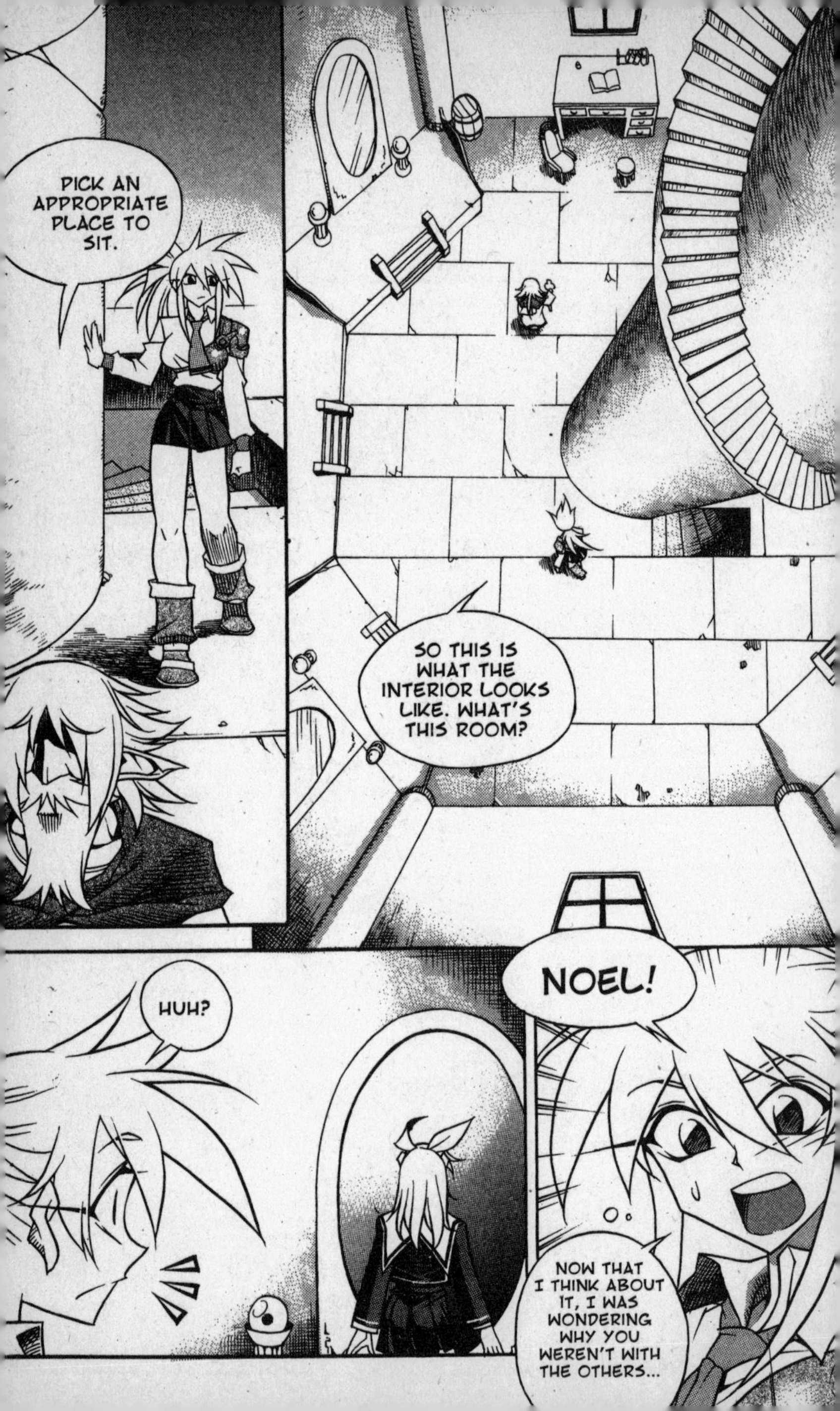
PICK AN APPROPRIATE PLACE TO SIT.
SO THIS IS WHAT THE INTERIOR LOOKS LIKE. WHAT'S THIS ROOM?
HUH?
NOEL!
NOW THAT I THINK ABOUT IT, I WAS WONDERING WHY YOU WEREN'T WITH THE OTHERS...

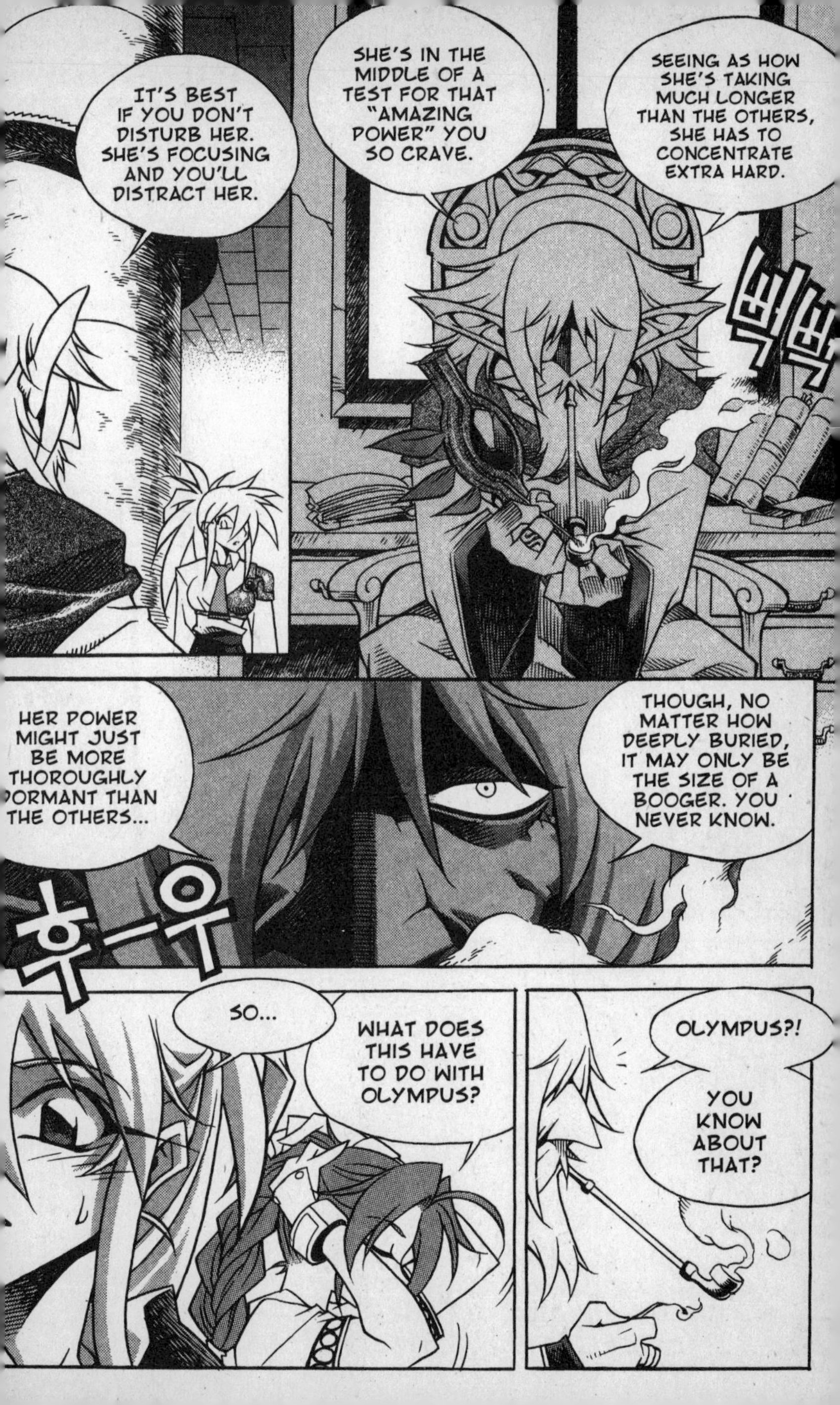
IT'S BEST IF YOU DON'T DISTURB HER. SHE'S FOCUSING AND YOU'LL DISTRACT HER.
SHE'S IN THE MIDDLE OF A TEST FOR THAT "AMAZING POWER" YOU SO CRAVE.
SEEING AS HOW SHE'S TAKING MUCH LONGER THAN THE OTHERS, SHE HAS TO CONCENTRATE EXTRA HARD.
HER POWER MIGHT JUST BE MORE THOROUGHLY DORMANT THAN THE OTHERS...
THOUGH, NO MATTER HOW DEEPLY BURIED, IT MAY ONLY BE THE SIZE OF A BOOGER. YOU NEVER KNOW.
후-우
SO...
WHAT DOES THIS HAVE TO DO WITH OLYMPUS?
OLYMPUS?!
YOU KNOW ABOUT THAT?

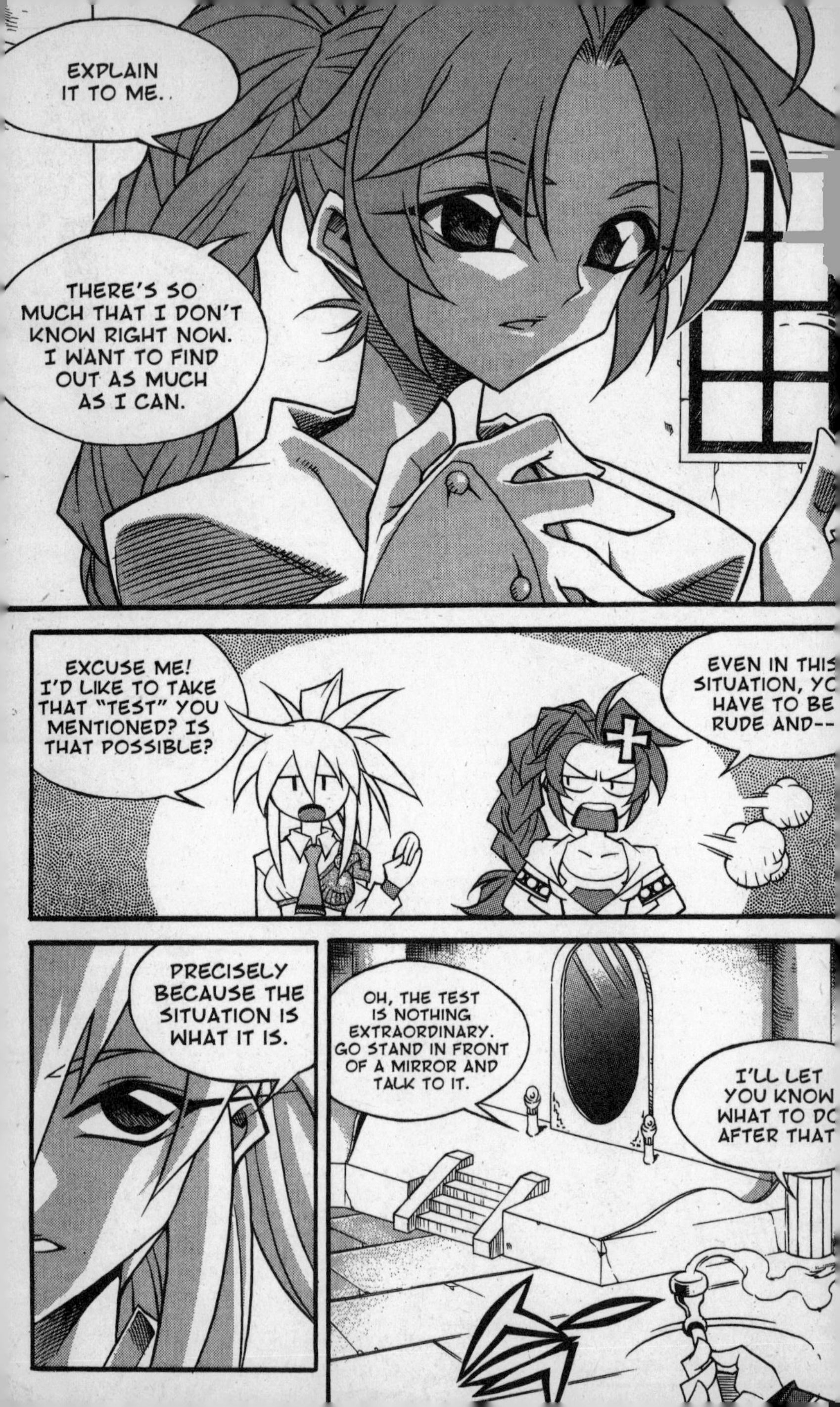
EXPLAIN IT TO ME..
THERE'S SO MUCH THAT I DON'T KNOW RIGHT NOW. I WANT TO FIND OUT AS MUCH AS I CAN.
EXCUSE ME! I'D LIKE TO TAKE THAT "TEST" YOU MENTIONED? IS THAT POSSIBLE?
EVEN IN THIS SITUATION, YO HAVE TO BE RUDE AND--
PRECISELY BECAUSE THE SITUATION IS WHAT IT IS.
OH, THE TEST IS NOTHING EXTRAORDINARY. GO STAND IN FRONT OF A MIRROR AND TALK TO IT.
I'LL LET YOU KNOW WHAT TO DO AFTER THAT

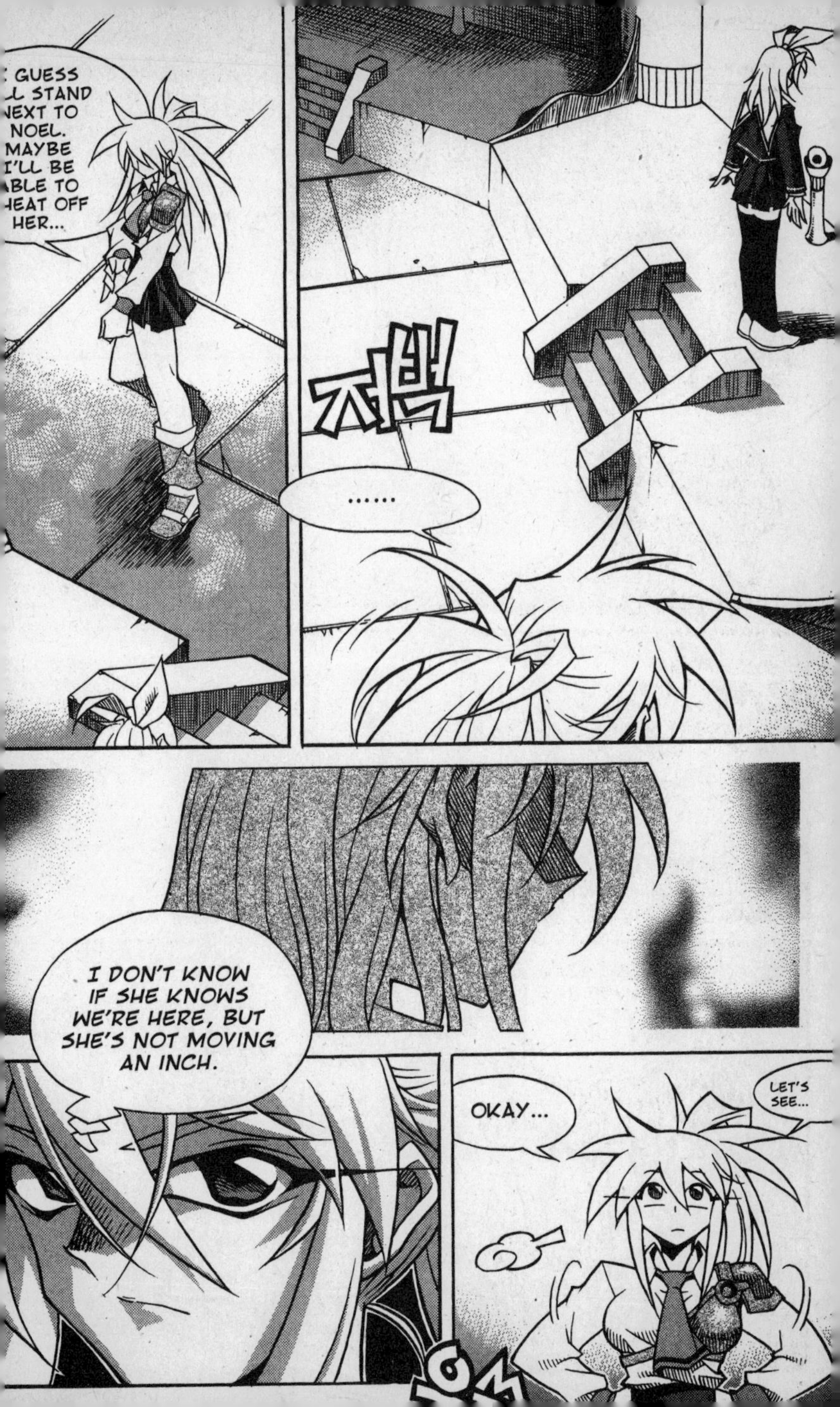
GUESS
L STAND
EXT TO
NOEL.
MAYBE
I'LL BE
BLE TO
HEAT OFF
HER...
저벅
......
I DON'T KNOW IF SHE KNOWS WE'RE HERE, BUT SHE'S NOT MOVING AN INCH.
OKAY...
LET'S SEE...

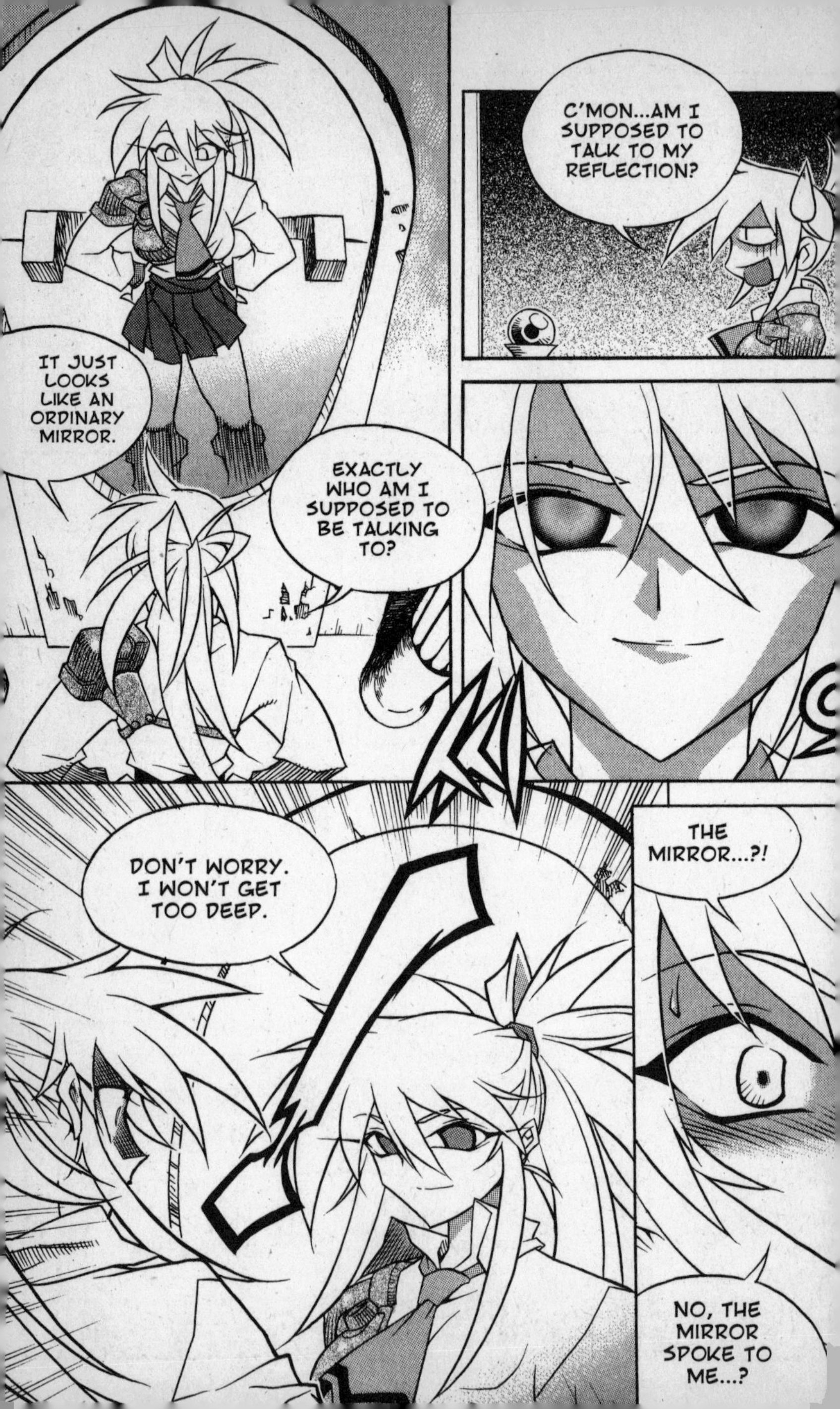
IT JUST LOOKS LIKE AN ORDINARY MIRROR.
EXACTLY WHO AM I SUPPOSED TO BE TALKING TO?
C'MON...AM I SUPPOSED TO TALK TO MY REFLECTION?
DON'T WORRY. I WON'T GET TOO DEEP.
THE MIRROR...?!
NO, THE MIRROR SPOKE TO ME...?

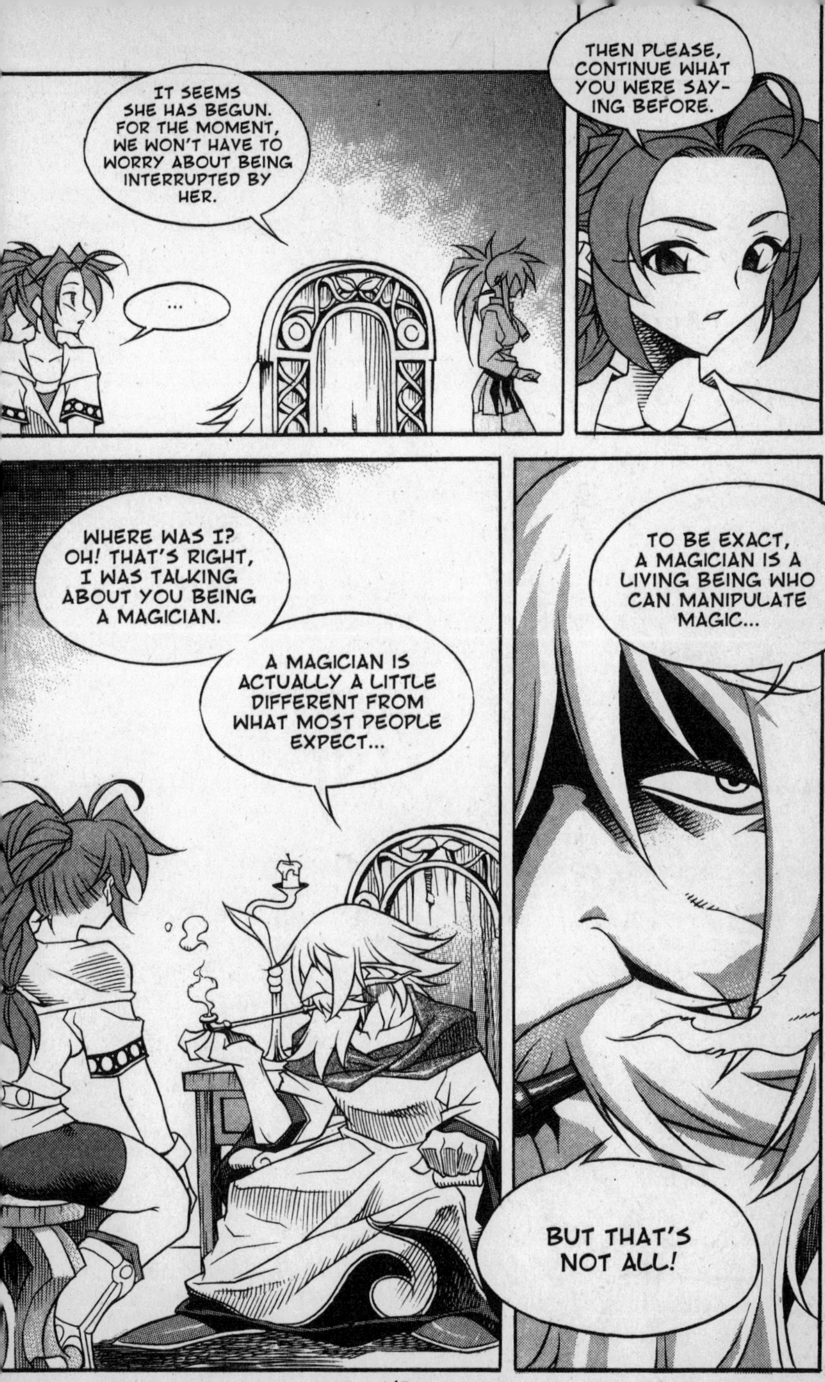
IT SEEMS SHE HAS BEGUN. FOR THE MOMENT, WE WON'T HAVE TO WORRY ABOUT BEING INTERRUPTED BY HER.
...
THEN PLEASE, CONTINUE WHAT YOU WERE SAY-ING BEFORE.
WHERE WAS I? OH! THAT'S RIGHT, I WAS TALKING ABOUT YOU BEING A MAGICIAN.
A MAGICIAN IS ACTUALLY A LITTLE DIFFERENT FROM WHAT MOST PEOPLE EXPECT...
TO BE EXACT, A MAGICIAN IS A LIVING BEING WHO CAN MANIPULATE MAGIC...
BUT THAT'S NOT ALL!

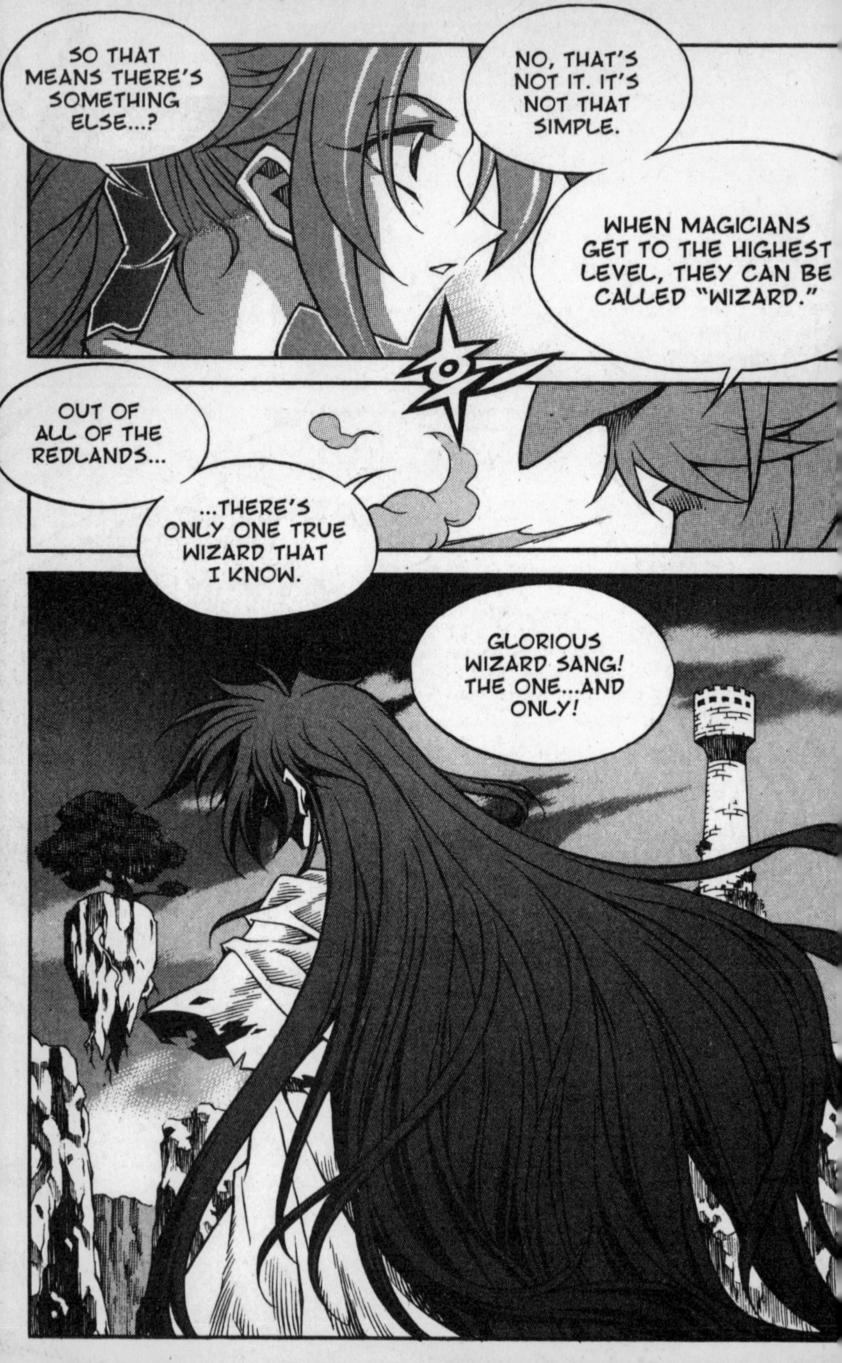
SO THAT MEANS THERE'S SOMETHING ELSE...?
NO, THAT'S NOT IT. IT'S NOT THAT SIMPLE.
WHEN MAGICIANS GET TO THE HIGHEST LEVEL, THEY CAN BE CALLED "WIZARD."
OUT OF ALL OF THE REDLANDS...
...THERE'S ONLY ONE TRUE WIZARD THAT I KNOW.
GLORIOUS WIZARD SANG! THE ONE...AND ONLY!

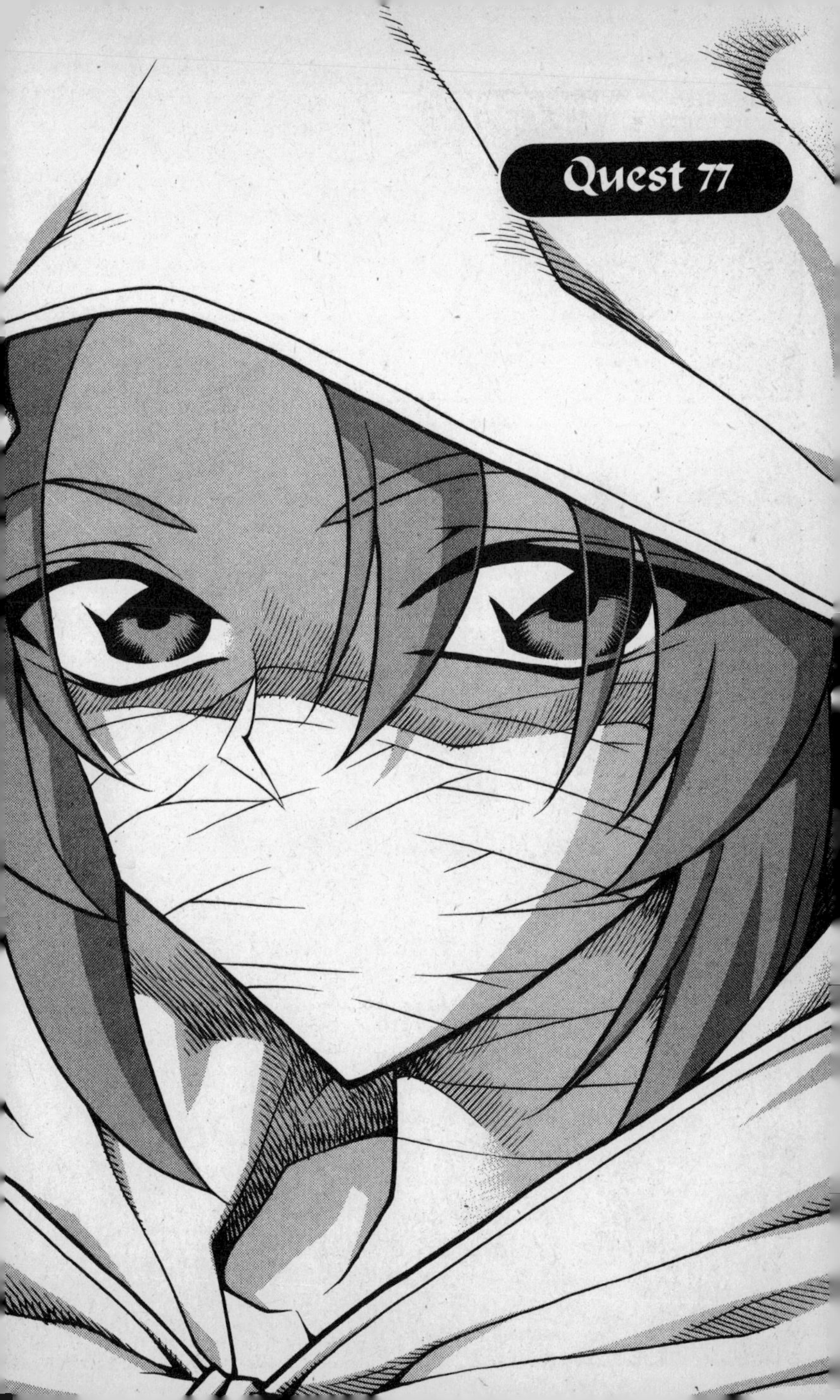
Quest 77

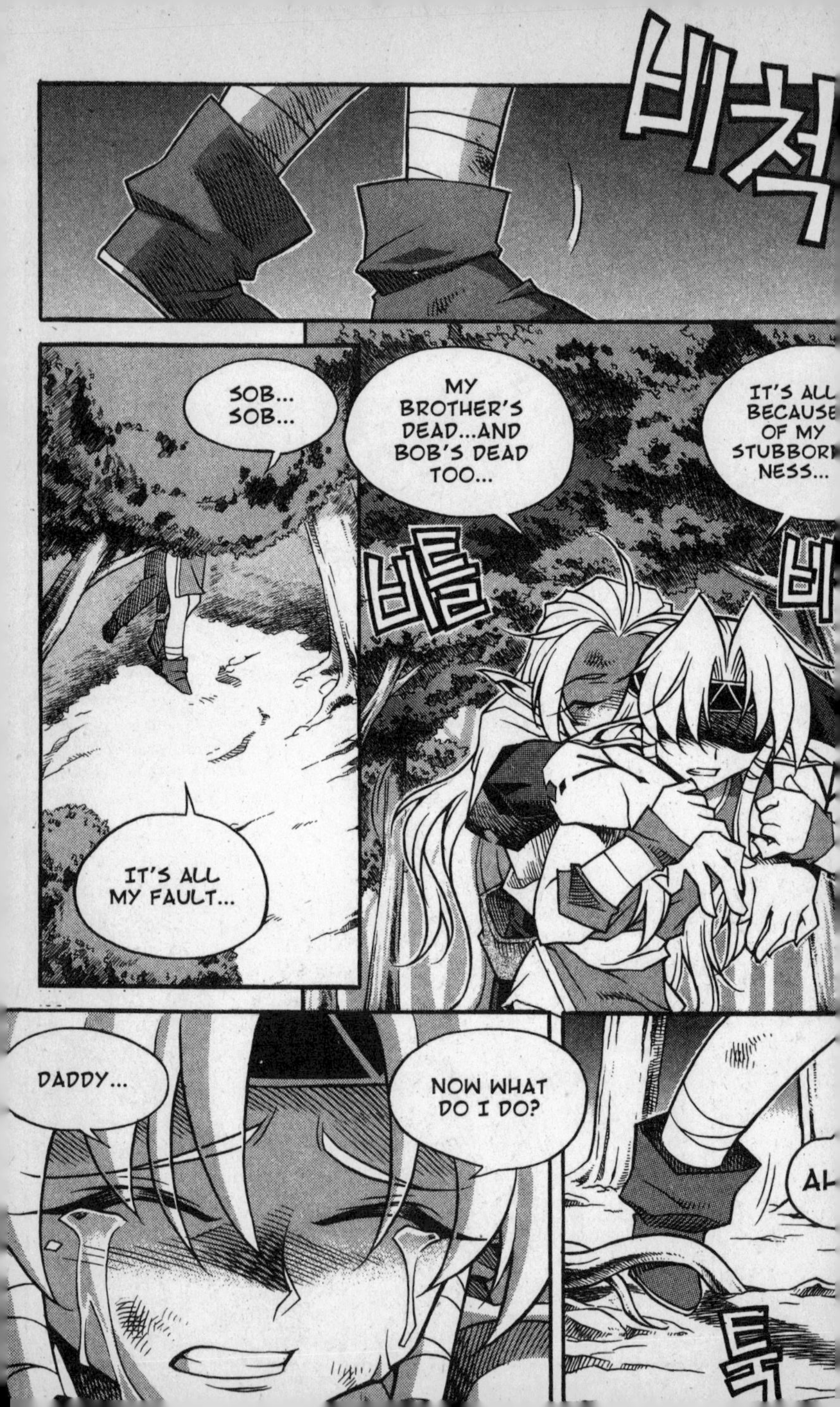
비척
SOB... SOB...
IT'S ALL MY FAULT...
MY BROTHER'S DEAD...AND BOB'S DEAD TOO...
비틀
IT'S ALL BECAUSE OF MY STUBBORN NESS...
DADDY...
NOW WHAT DO I DO?
툭

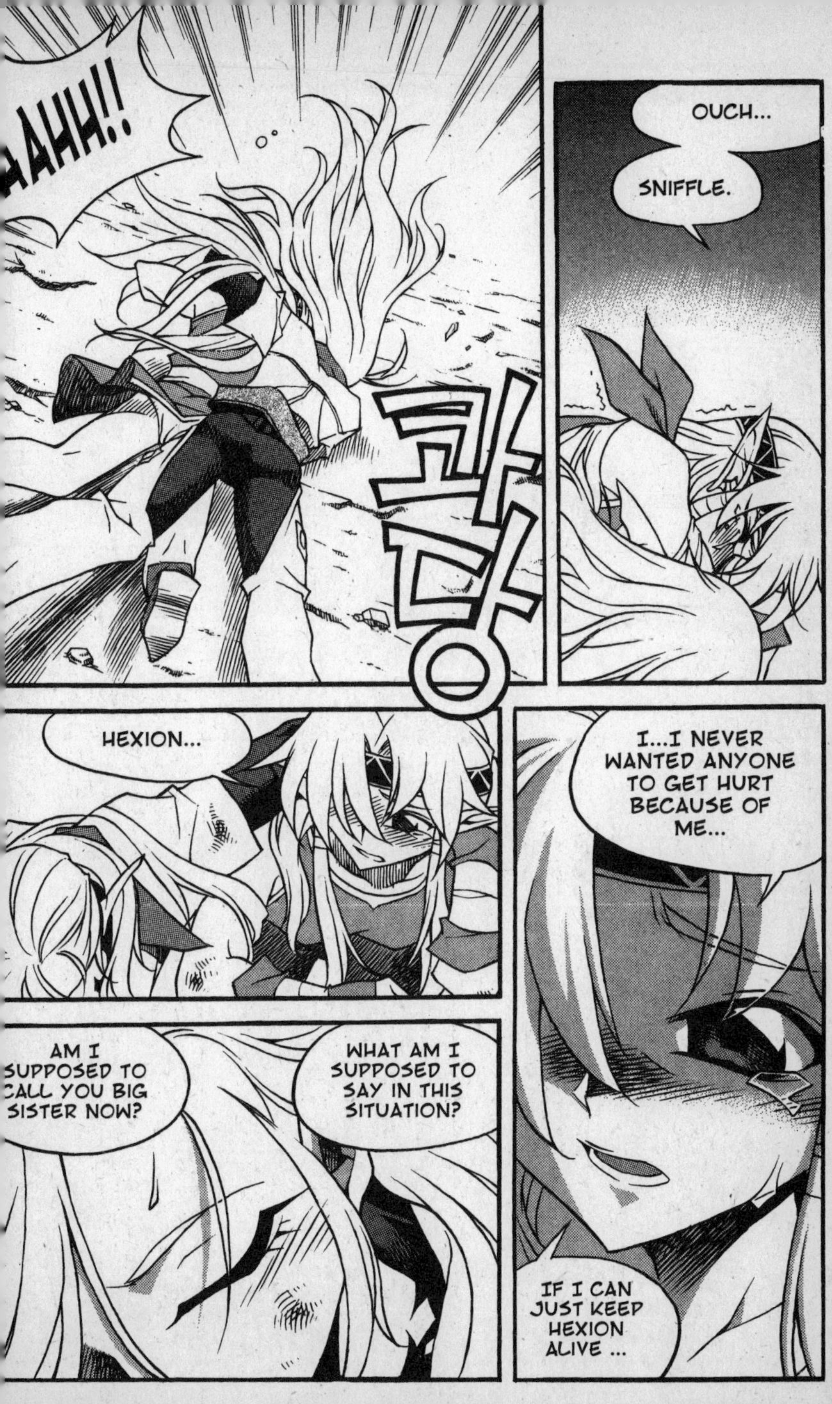
AAHH!!
콰당
OUCH...
SNIFFLE.
HEXION...
AM I SUPPOSED TO CALL YOU BIG SISTER NOW?
WHAT AM I SUPPOSED TO SAY IN THIS SITUATION?
I...I NEVER WANTED ANYONE TO GET HURT BECAUSE OF ME...
IF I CAN JUST KEEP HEXION ALIVE ...

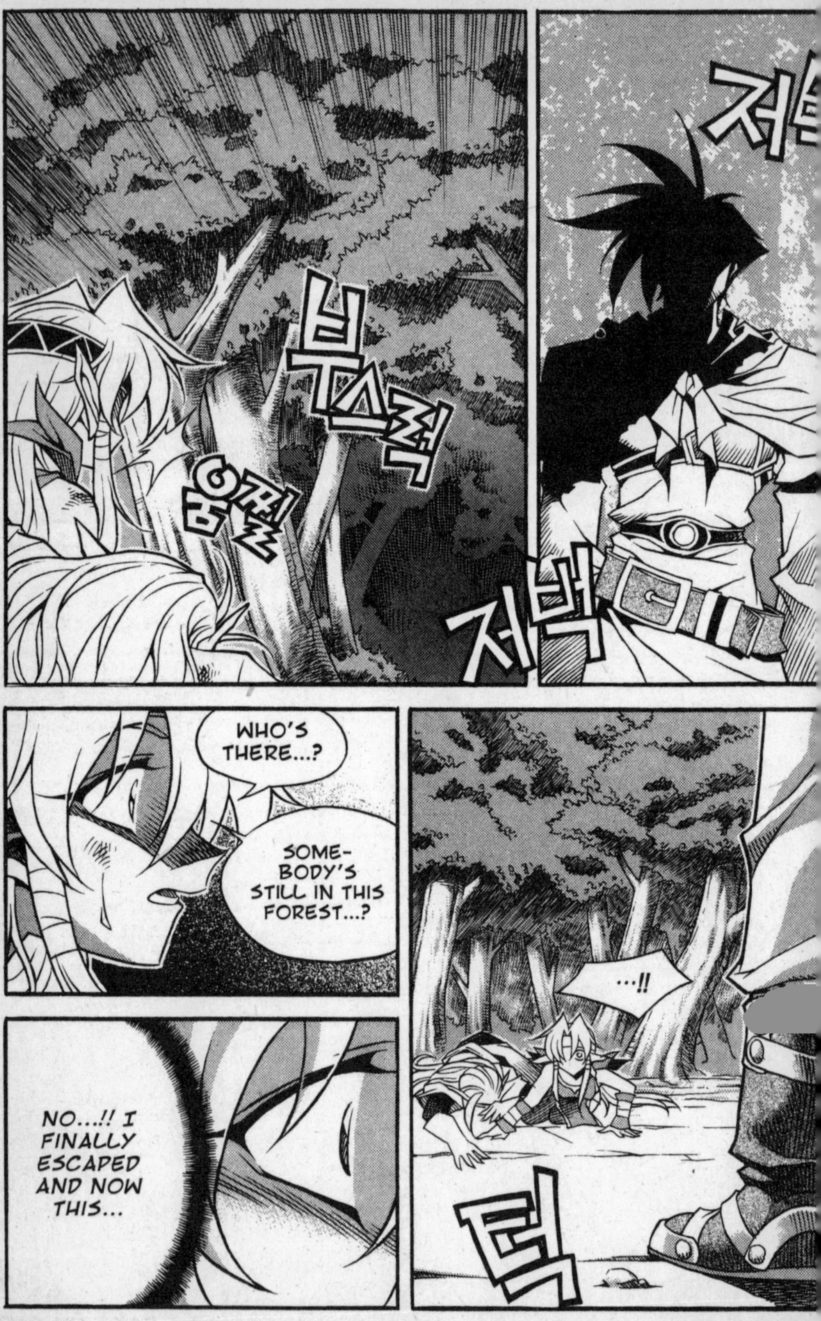
부스럭
움찔
저벅
WHO'S THERE...?
SOME-BODY'S STILL IN THIS FOREST...?
NO...!! I FINALLY ESCAPED AND NOW THIS...
...!!
턱

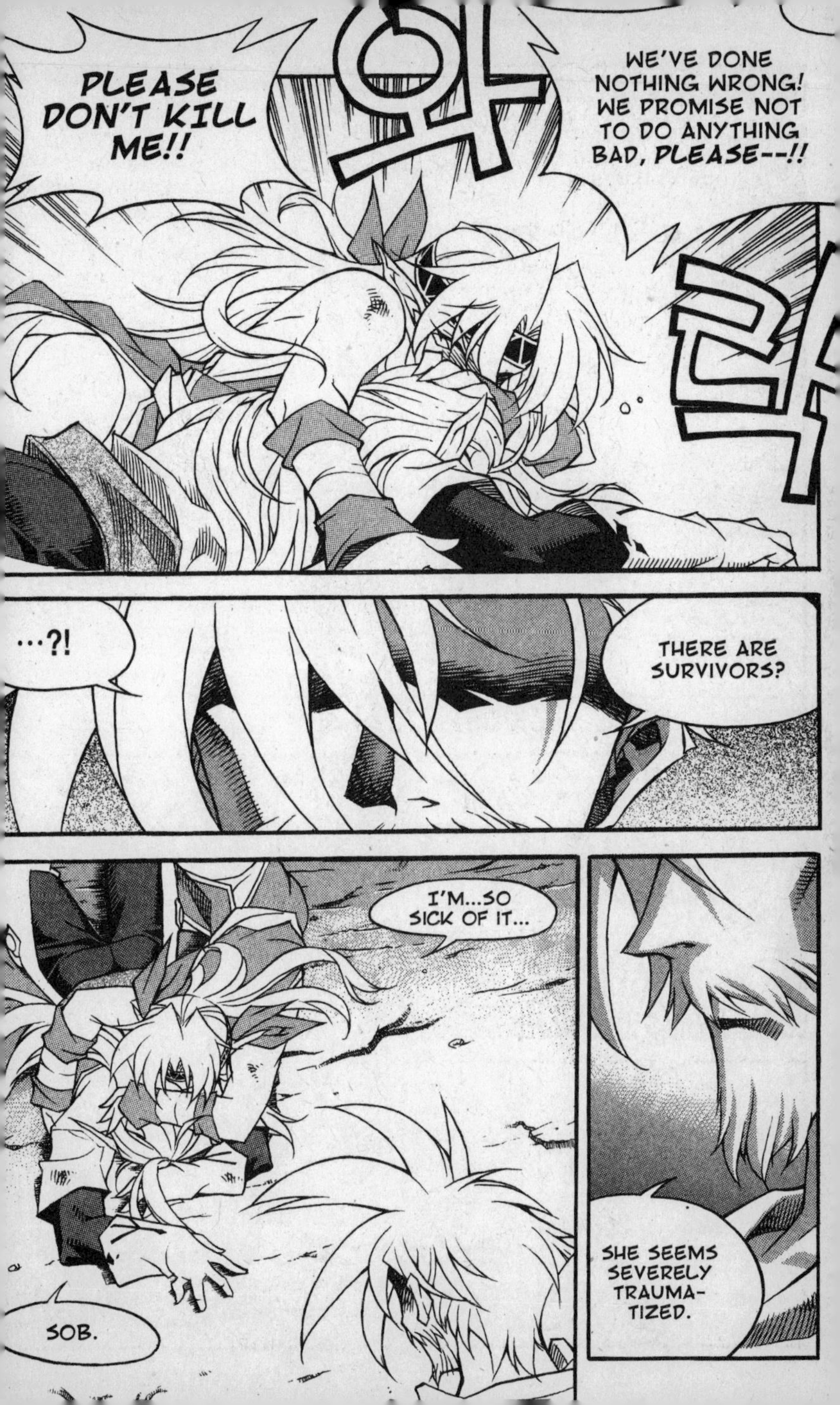
PLEASE DON'T KILL ME!!
WE'VE DONE NOTHING WRONG! WE PROMISE NOT TO DO ANYTHING BAD, PLEASE--!!
...?!
THERE ARE SURVIVORS?
I'M...SO SICK OF IT...
SOB.
SHE SEEMS SEVERELY TRAUMA-TIZED.

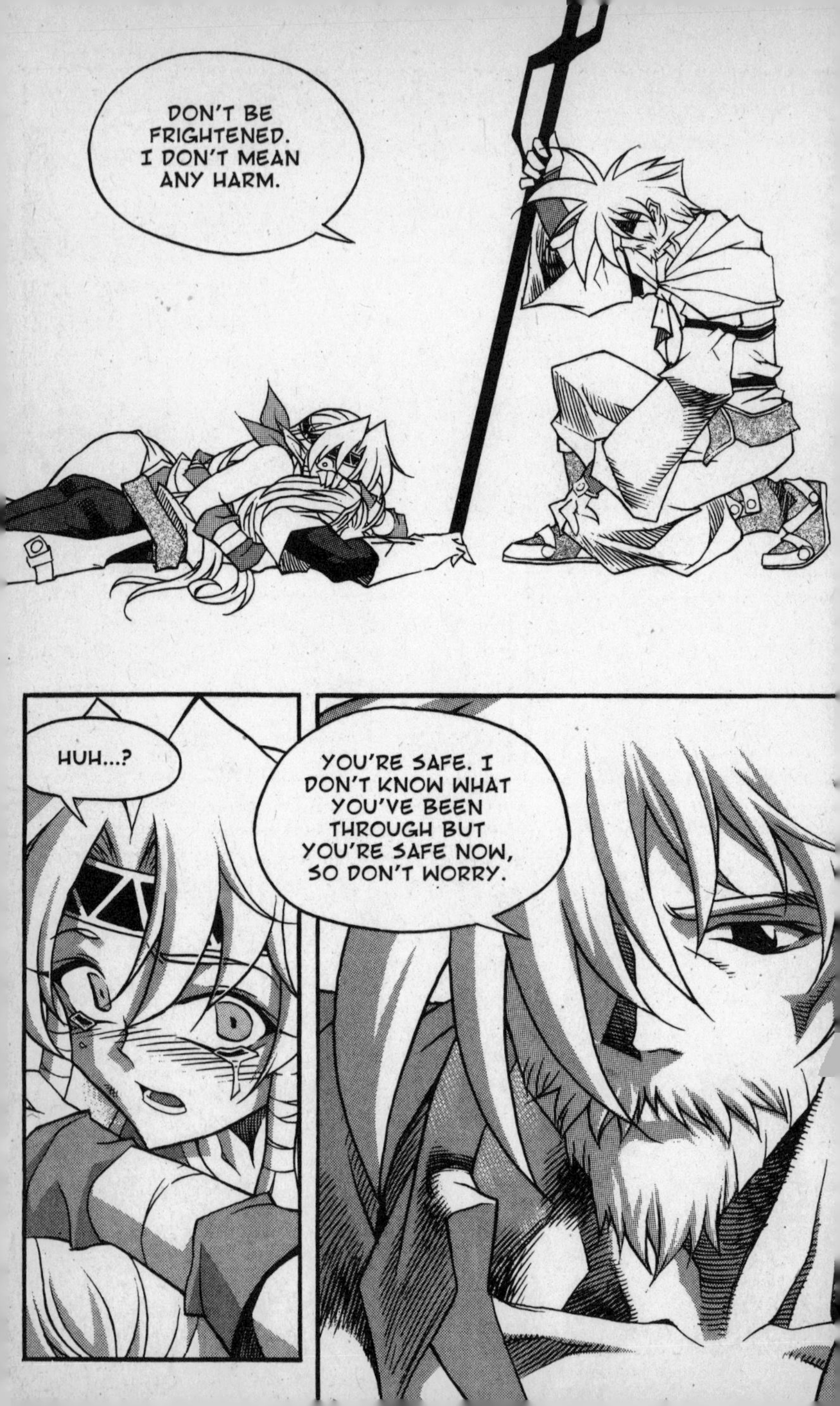
DON'T BE FRIGHTENED. I DON'T MEAN ANY HARM.
HUH...?
YOU'RE SAFE. I DON'T KNOW WHAT YOU'VE BEEN THROUGH BUT YOU'RE SAFE NOW, SO DON'T WORRY.

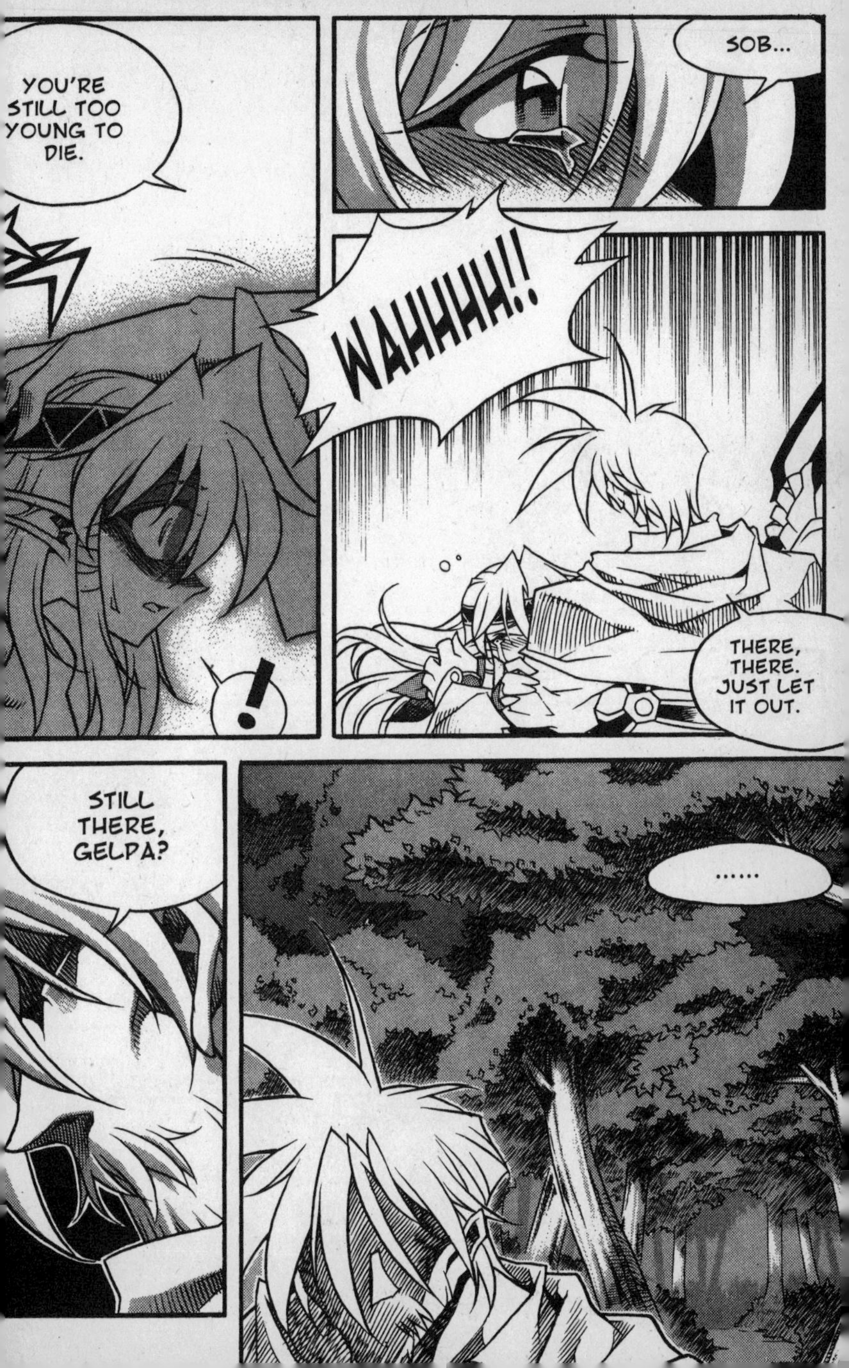
YOU'RE STILL TOO YOUNG TO DIE.
!
SOB...
WAHHHHH!!
THERE, THERE. JUST LET IT OUT.
STILL THERE, GELPA?
......

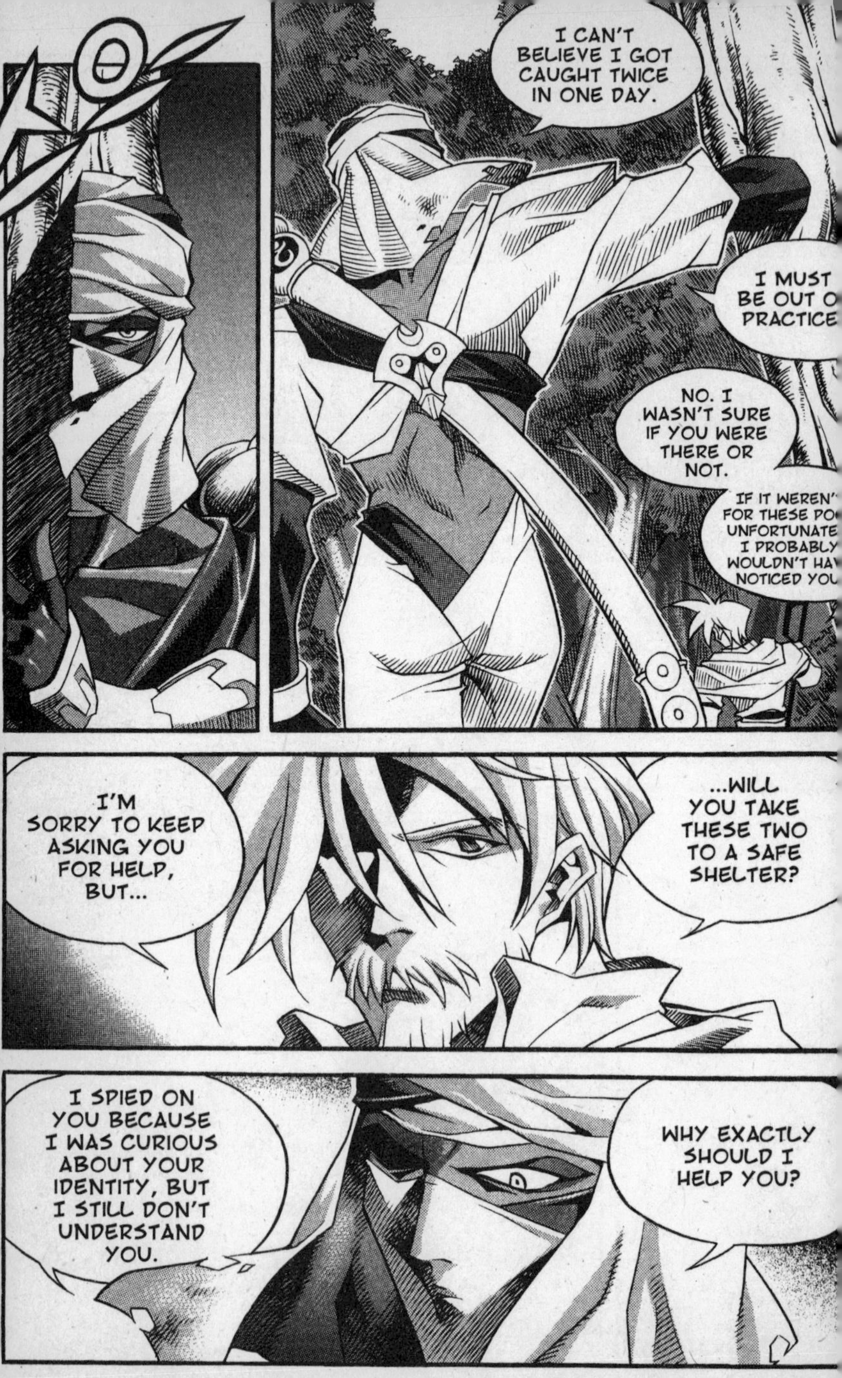
I CAN'T BELIEVE I GOT CAUGHT TWICE IN ONE DAY.
I MUST BE OUT O PRACTICE
NO. I WASN'T SURE IF YOU WERE THERE OR NOT.
IF IT WEREN'' FOR THESE PO UNFORTUNATE I PROBABLY WOULDN'T HA NOTICED YOU
I'M SORRY TO KEEP ASKING YOU FOR HELP, BUT...
...WILL YOU TAKE THESE TWO TO A SAFE SHELTER?
I SPIED ON YOU BECAUSE I WAS CURIOUS ABOUT YOUR IDENTITY, BUT I STILL DON'T UNDERSTAND YOU.
WHY EXACTLY SHOULD I HELP YOU?

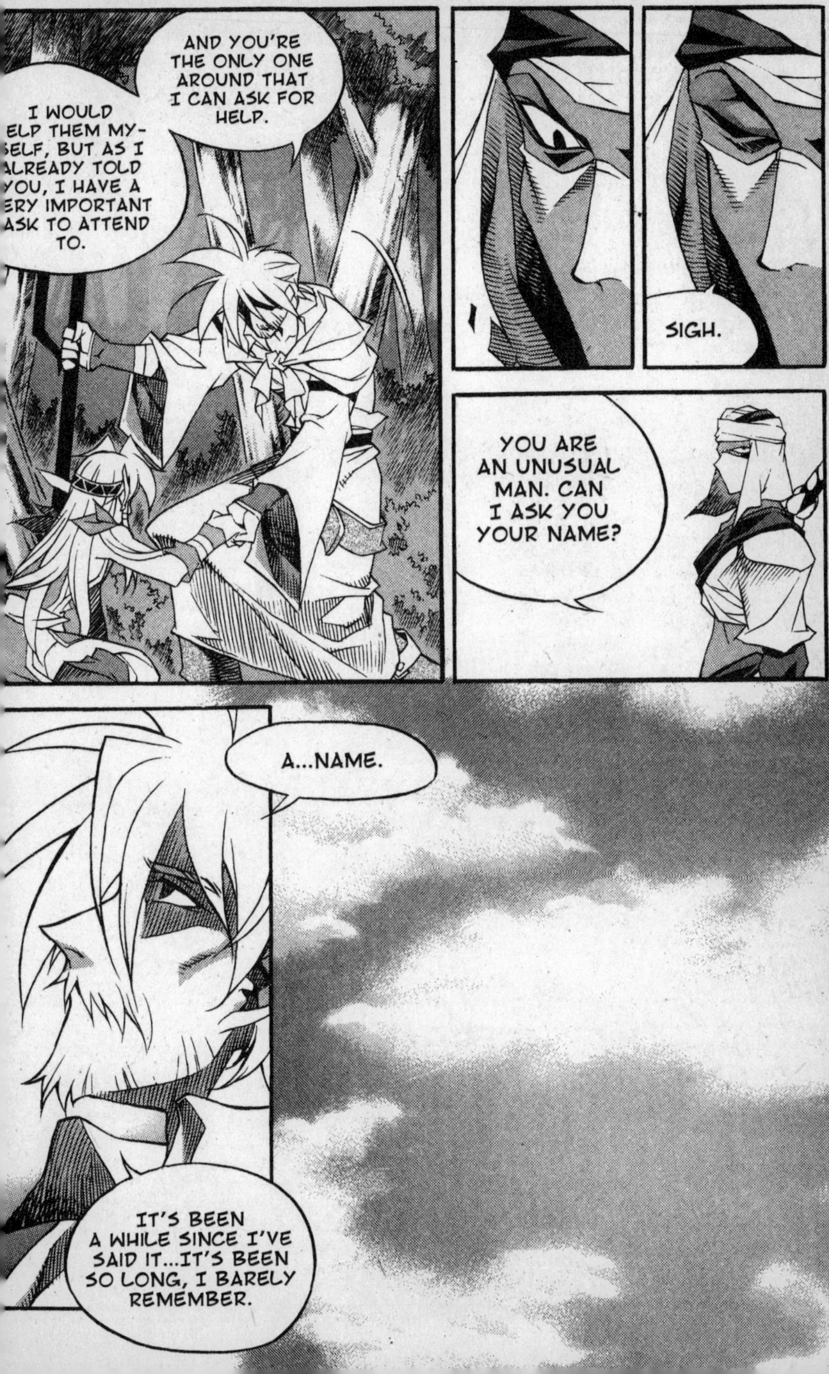
I WOULD ELP THEM MY-SELF, BUT AS I ALREADY TOLD YOU, I HAVE A ERY IMPORTANT ASK TO ATTEND TO.
AND YOU'RE THE ONLY ONE AROUND THAT I CAN ASK FOR HELP.
SIGH.
YOU ARE AN UNUSUAL MAN. CAN I ASK YOU YOUR NAME?
A...NAME.
IT'S BEEN A WHILE SINCE I'VE SAID IT...IT'S BEEN SO LONG, I BARELY REMEMBER.

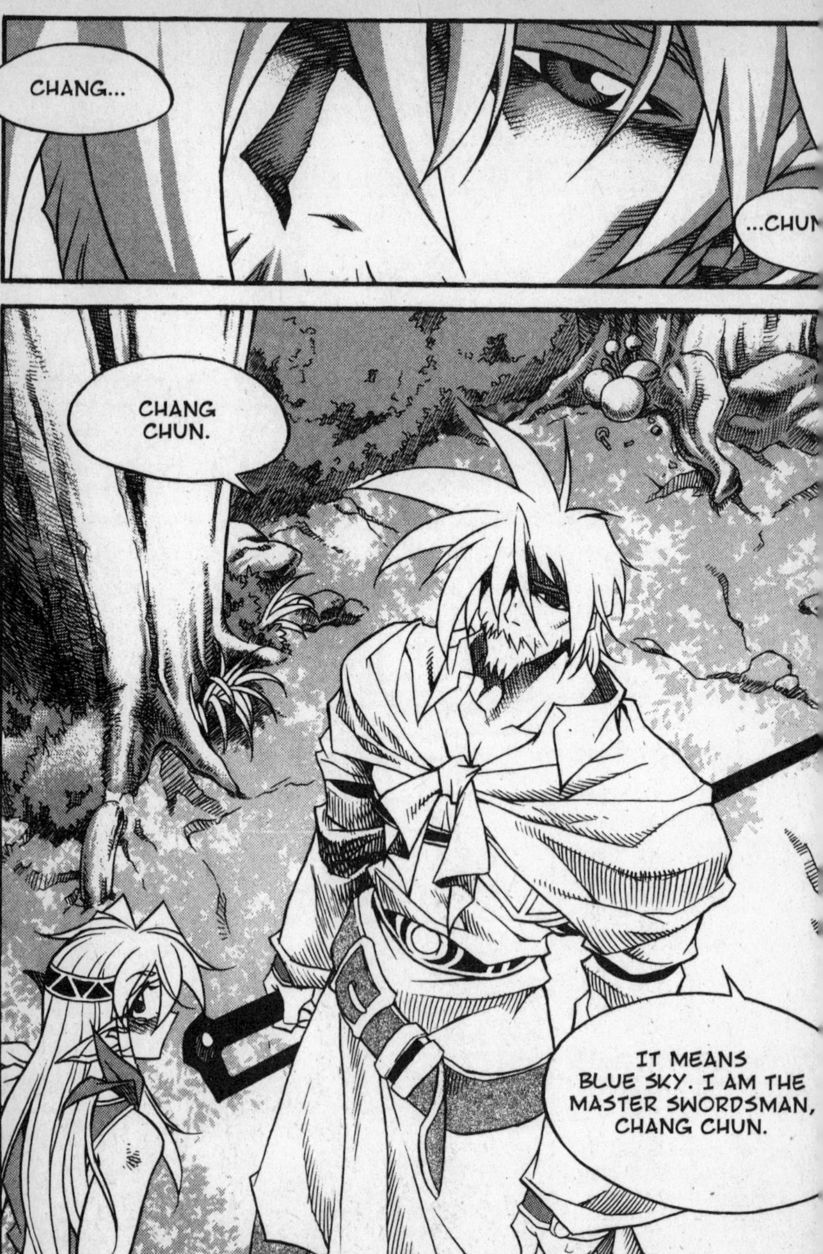
CHANG...
...CHUN
CHANG CHUN.
IT MEANS BLUE SKY. I AM THE MASTER SWORDSMAN, CHANG CHUN.

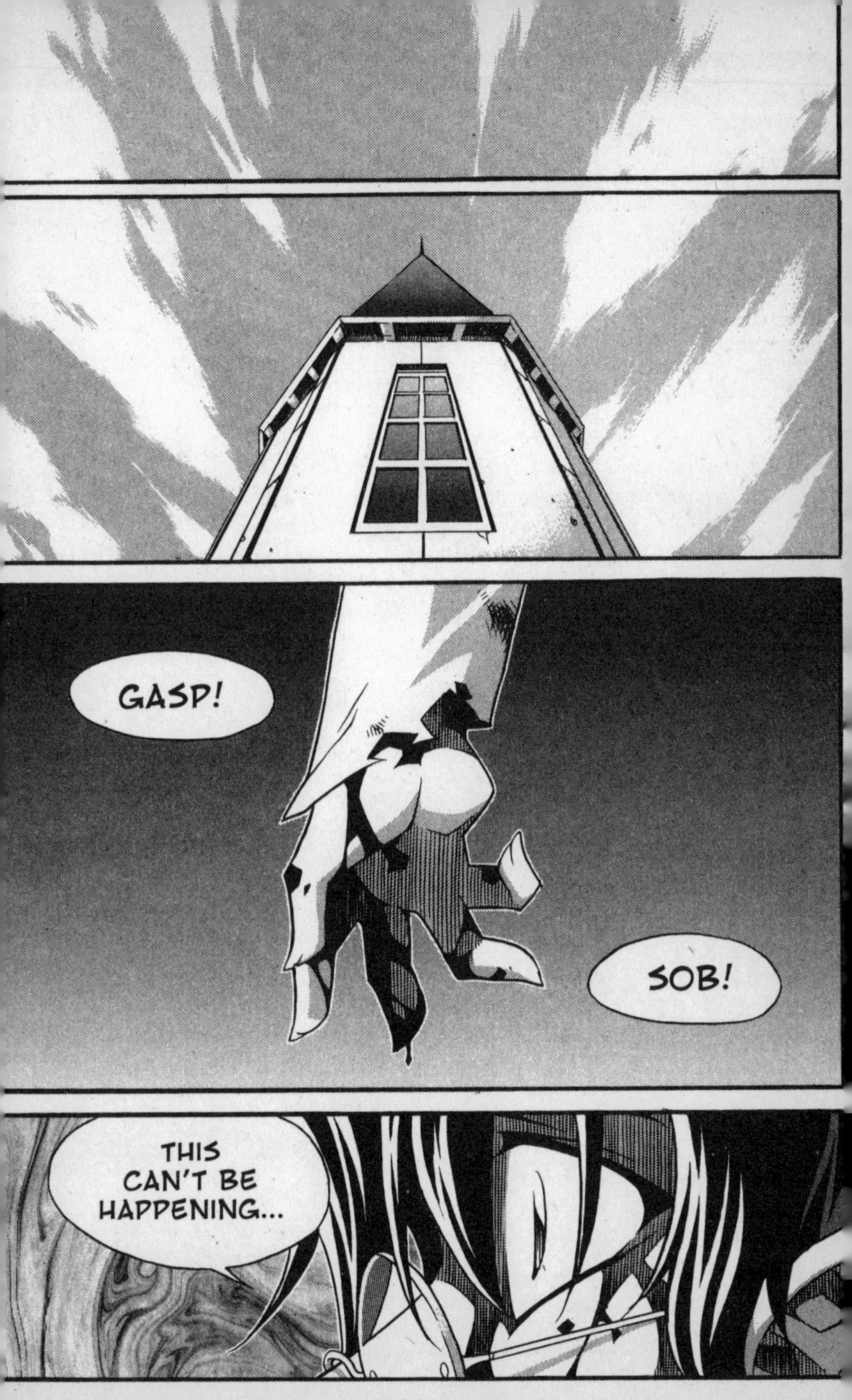
GASP!
SOB!
THIS CAN'T BE HAPPENING...

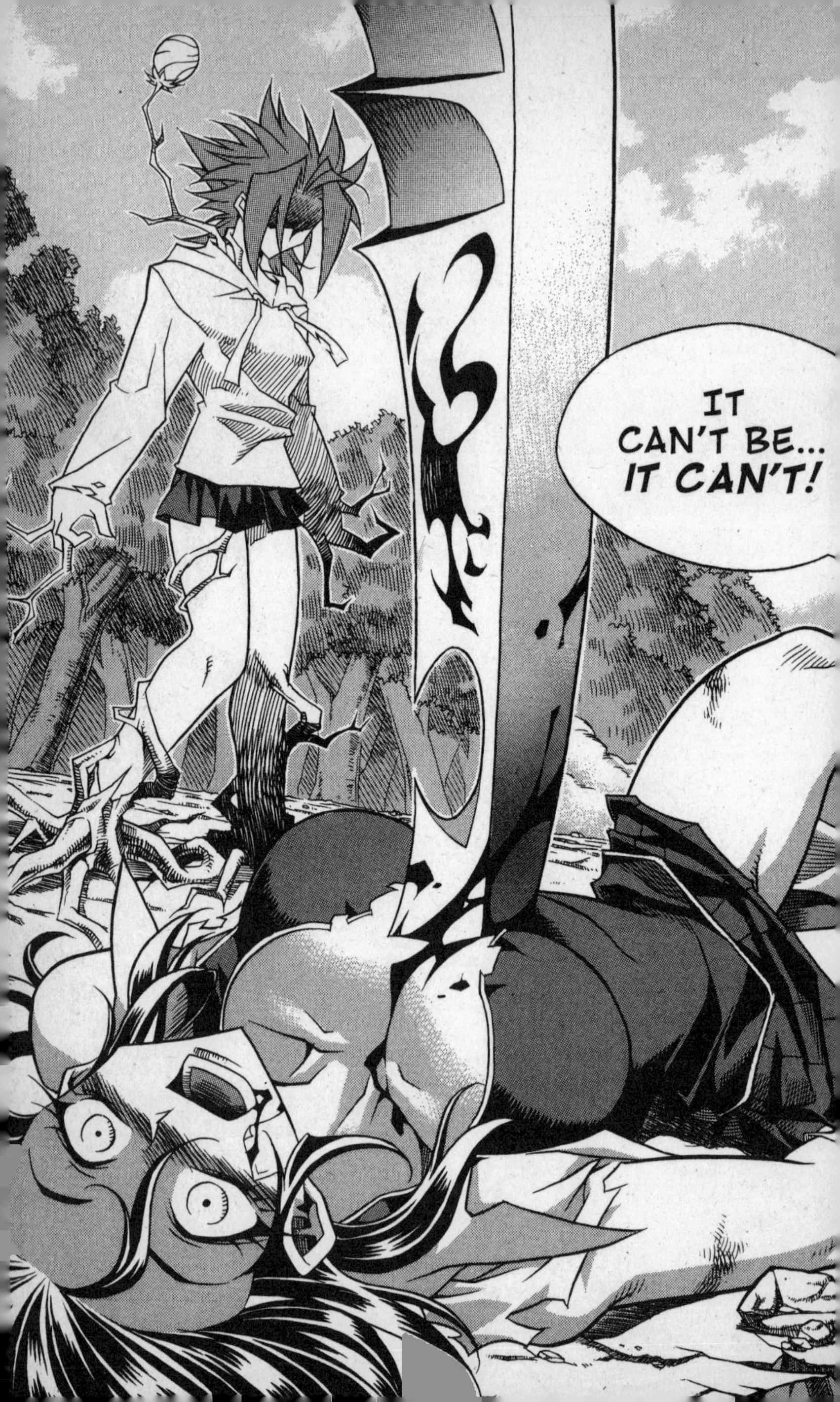
IT CAN'T BE... IT CAN'T!

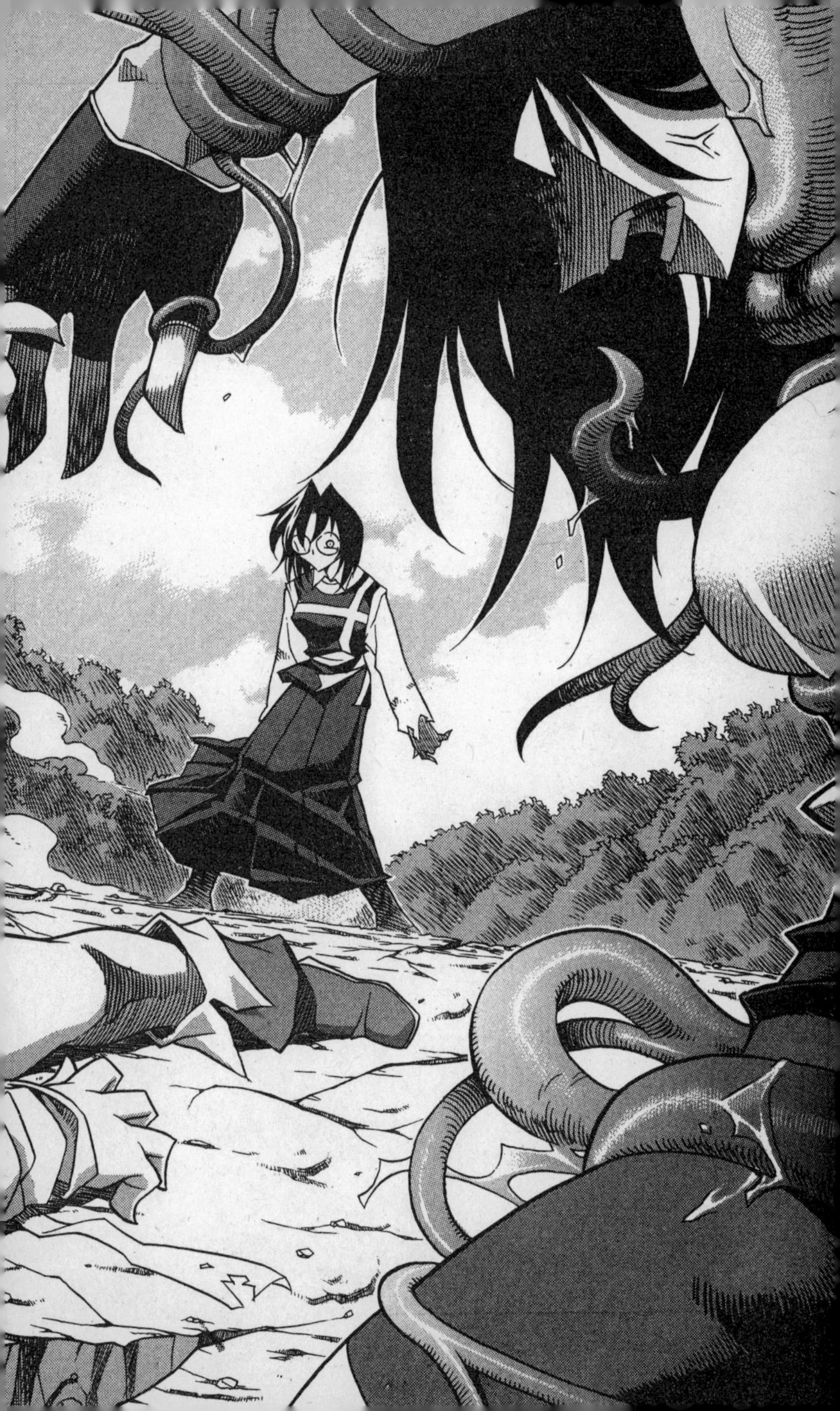

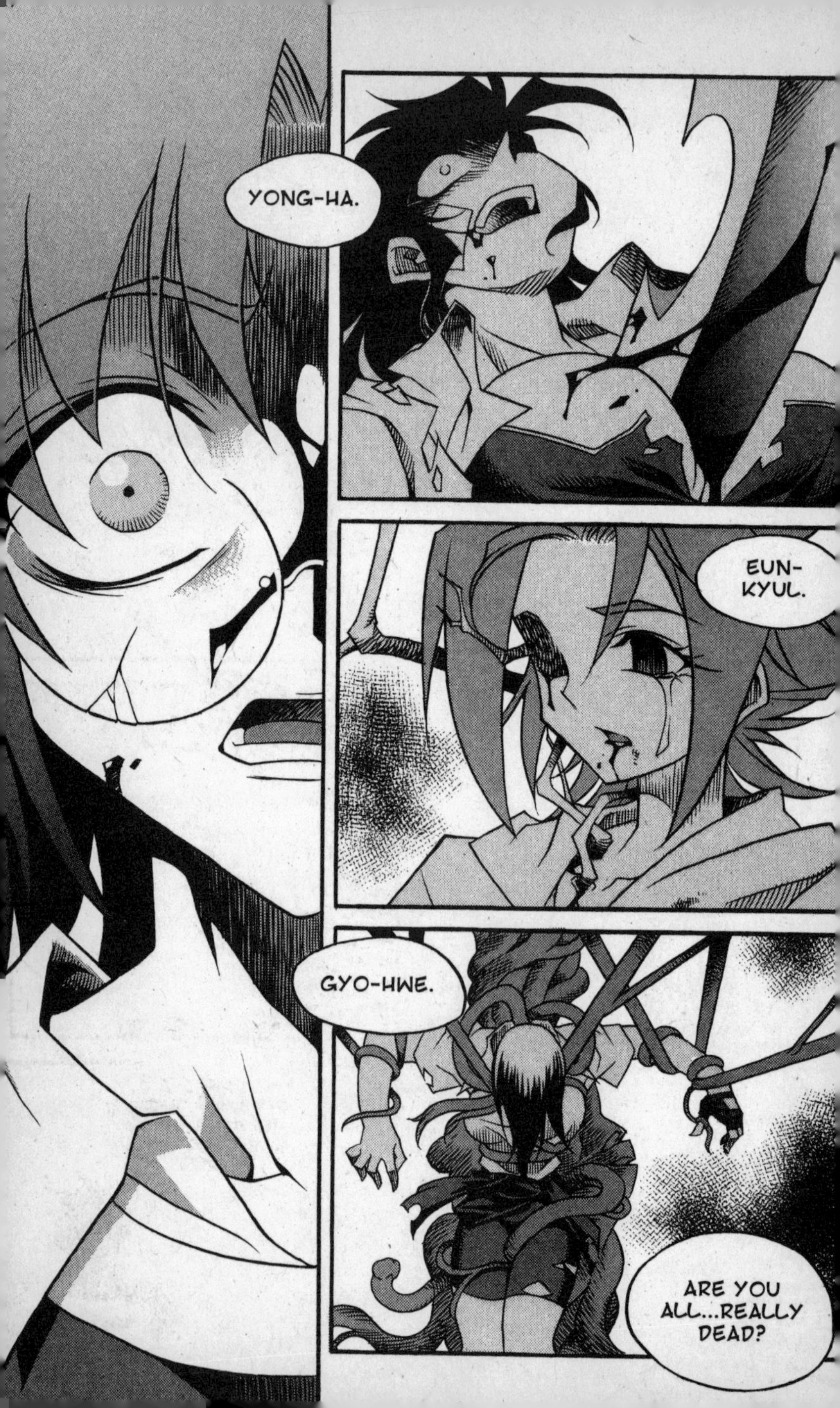
YONG-HA.
EUN-KYUL.
GYO-HWE.
ARE YOU ALL...REALLY DEAD?

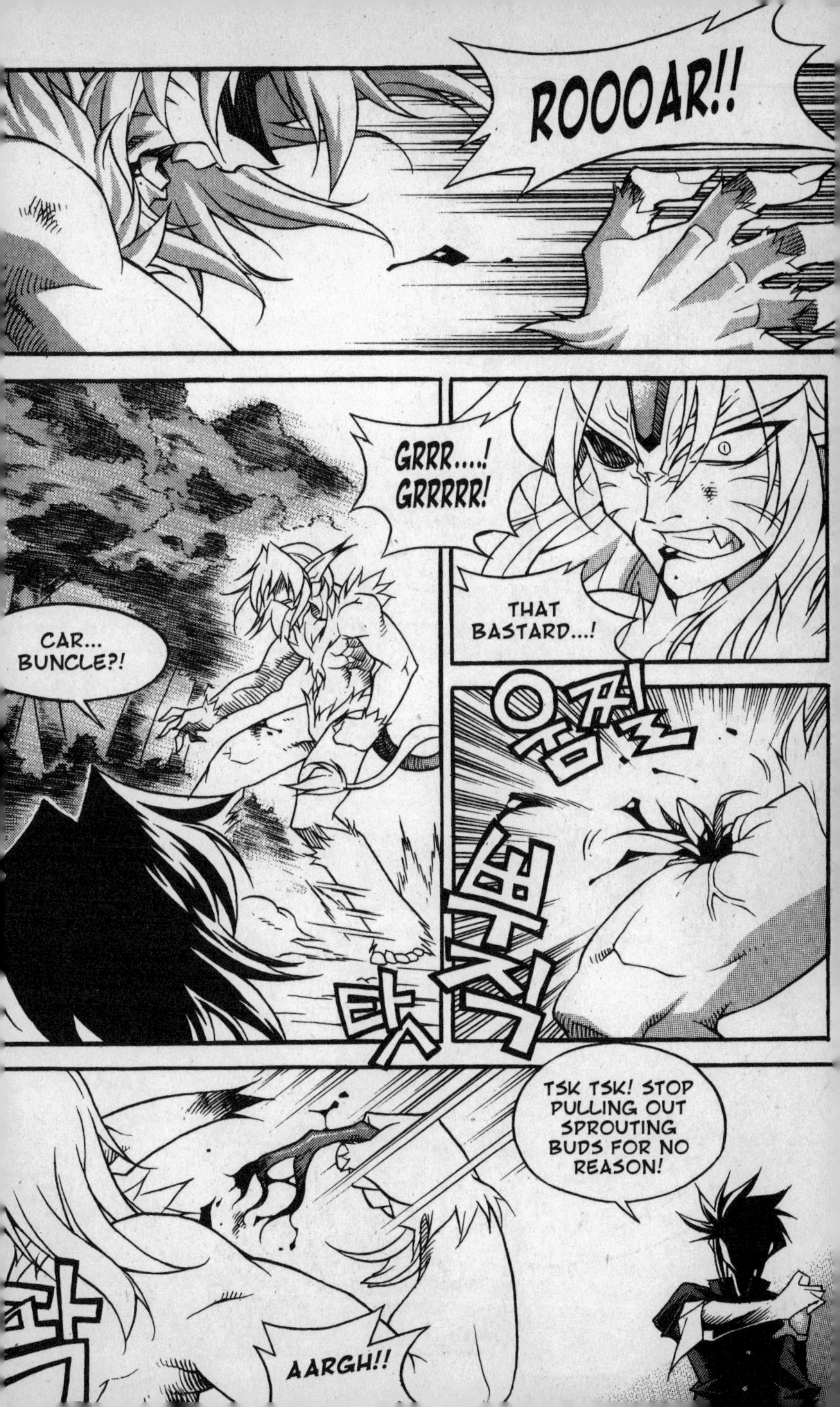
ROOOAR!!
GRRR....! GRRRRR!
CAR... BUNCLE?!
THAT BASTARD...!
TSK TSK! STOP PULLING OUT SPROUTING BUDS FOR NO REASON!
AARGH!!

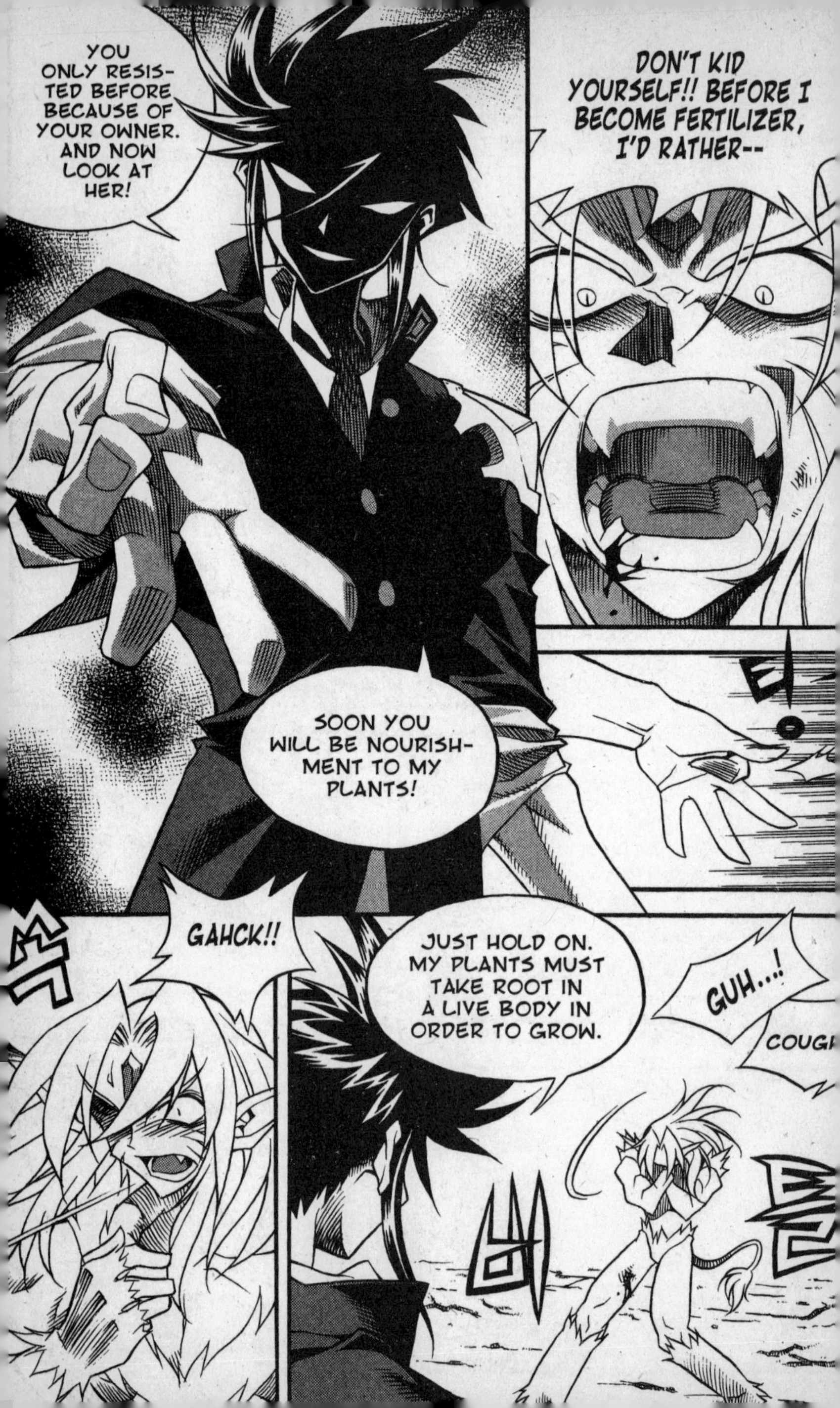
YOU ONLY RESIS-TED BEFORE BECAUSE OF YOUR OWNER. AND NOW LOOK AT HER!
SOON YOU WILL BE NOURISH-MENT TO MY PLANTS!
DON'T KID YOURSELF!! BEFORE I BECOME FERTILIZER, I'D RATHER--
GAHCK!!
JUST HOLD ON. MY PLANTS MUST TAKE ROOT IN A LIVE BODY IN ORDER TO GROW.
GUH...!
COUG

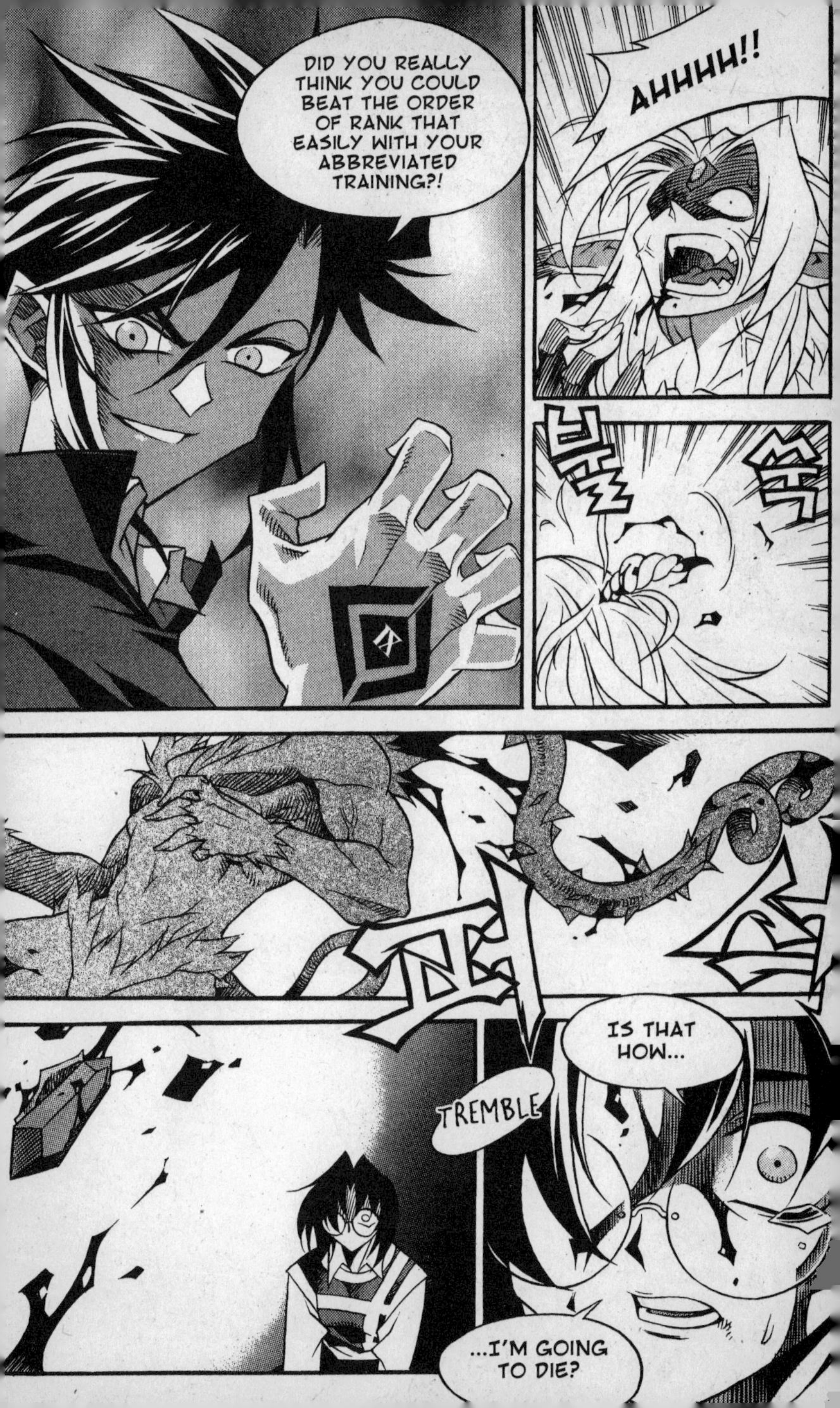
DID YOU REALLY THINK YOU COULD BEAT THE ORDER OF RANK THAT EASILY WITH YOUR ABBREVIATED TRAINING?!
AHHHH!!
TREMBLE
IS THAT HOW...
...I'M GOING TO DIE?

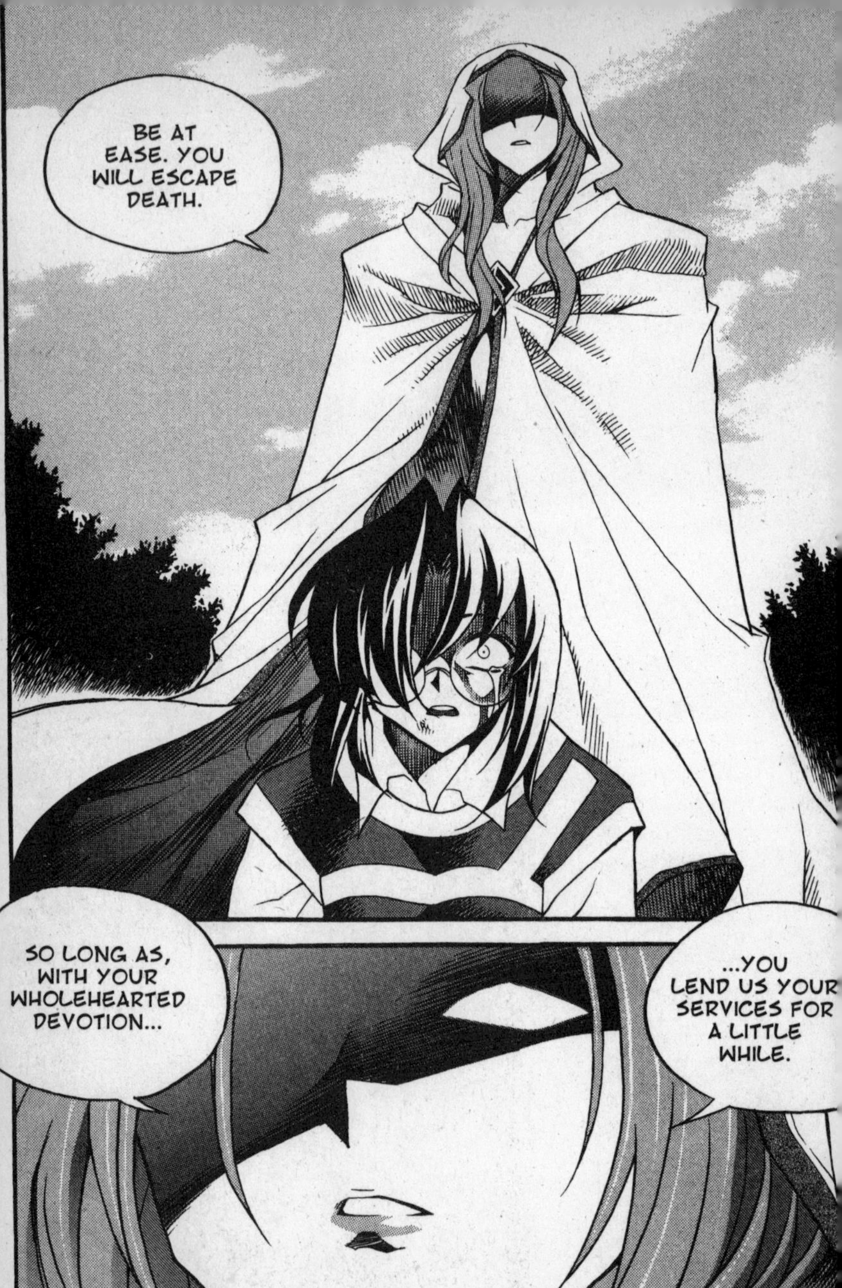
BE AT EASE. YOU WILL ESCAPE DEATH.
SO LONG AS, WITH YOUR WHOLEHEARTED DEVOTION...
...YOU LEND US YOUR SERVICES FOR A LITTLE WHILE.

To be continued in PhD: Phantasy Degree Volume 8!!

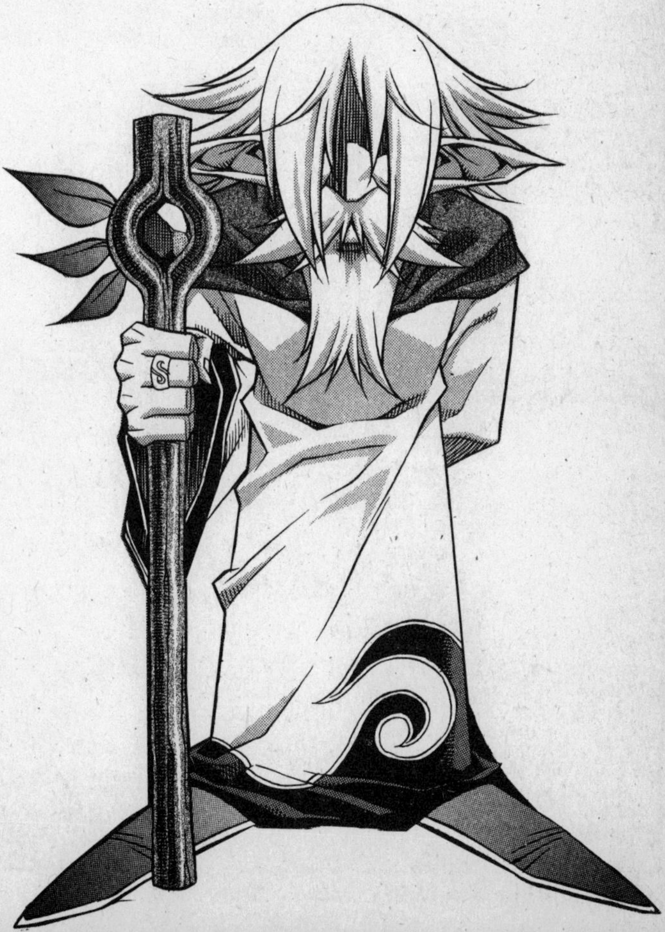

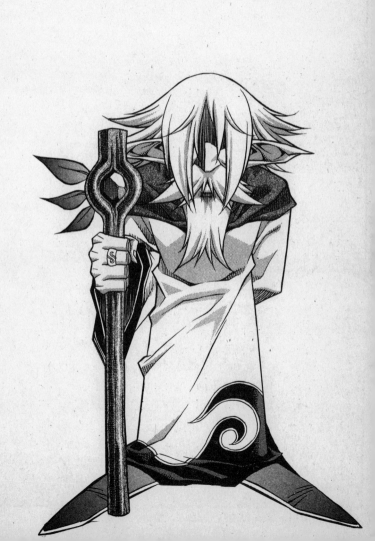

In the Next Volume of...

PHD
PHANTASY DEGREE

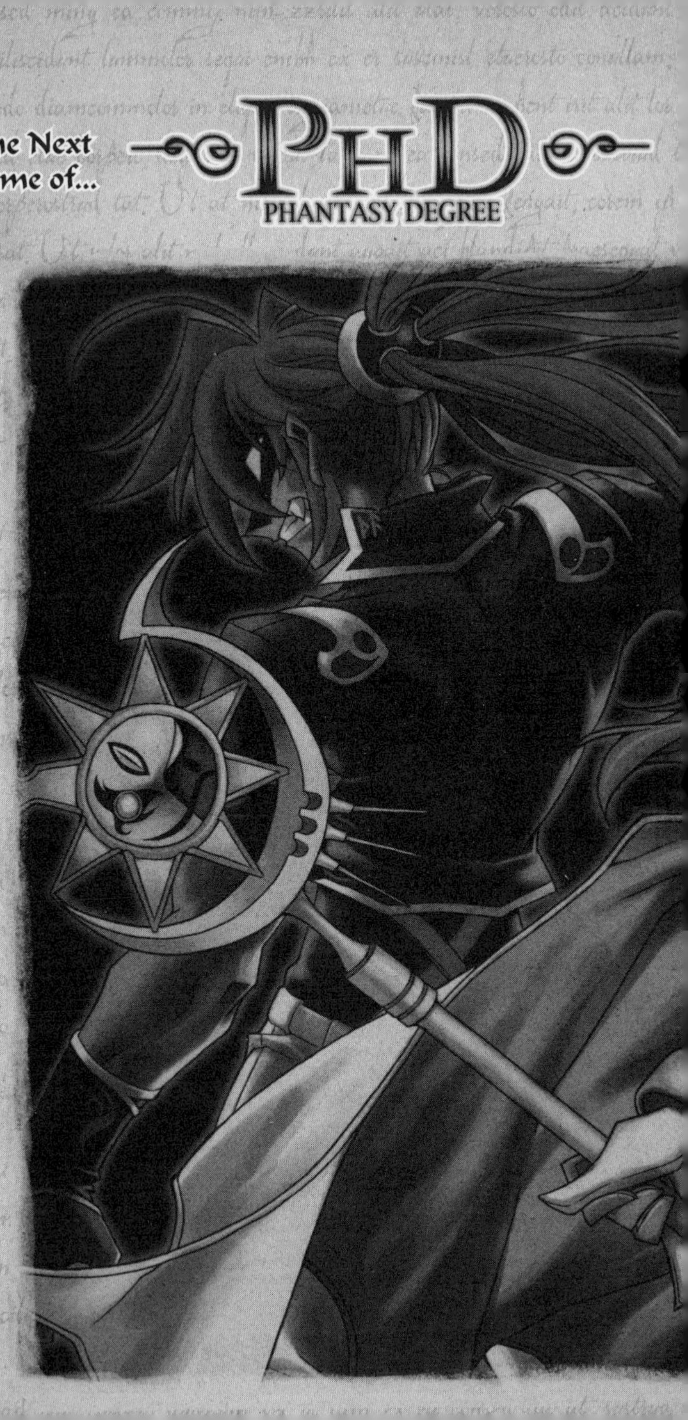

Available January 2007

Quest 78

Episode VIII: Wizard

How long would it take to get over...

losing the love of your life?

When Jackie's ex-lover Noah dies, she decides the quickest way to get over her is to hold a personal ritual with Noah's ashes. Jackie consumes the ashes in the form of smoothies for 12 days, hoping the pain will subside. But will that be enough?

From the internationally published illustrator June Kim

DRAMA

OT OLDER TEEN AGE 15+

© June Kim and TOKYOPOP Inc.

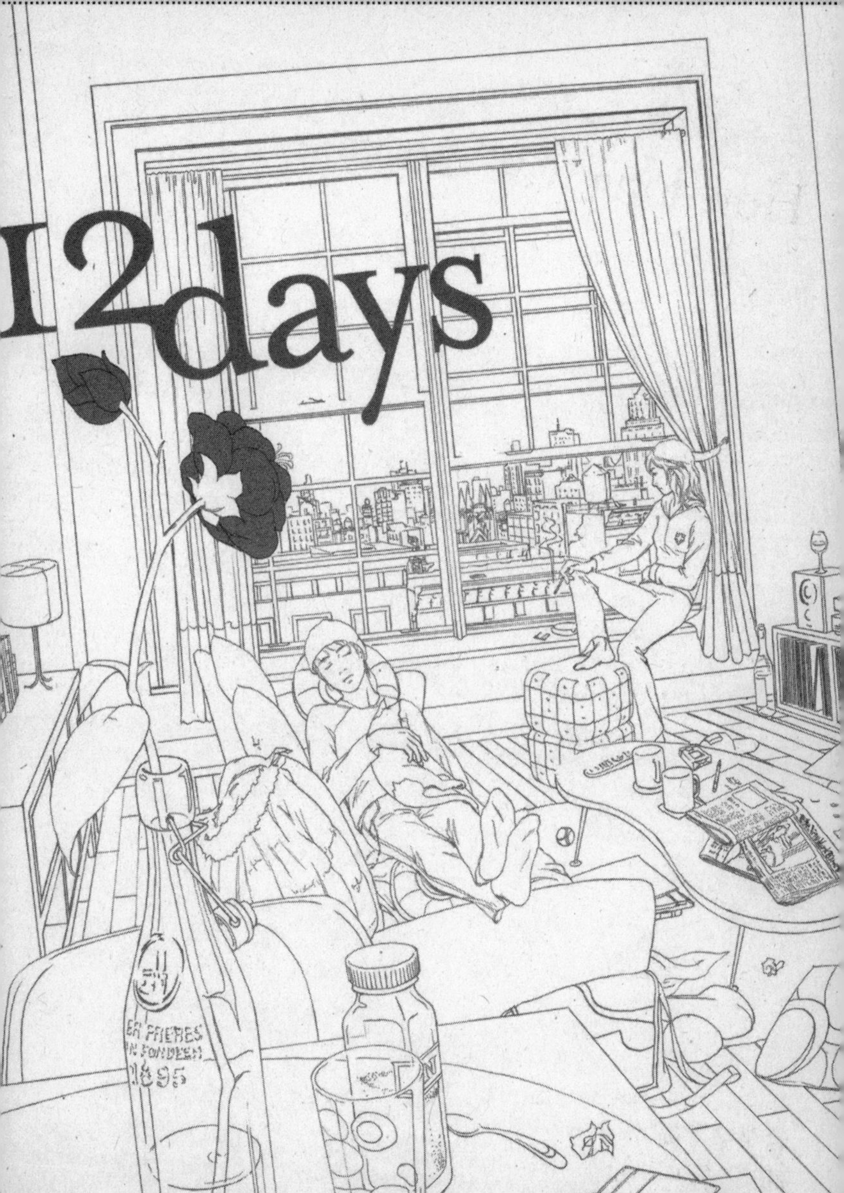
12days
FRERES
FONDEEN
1895

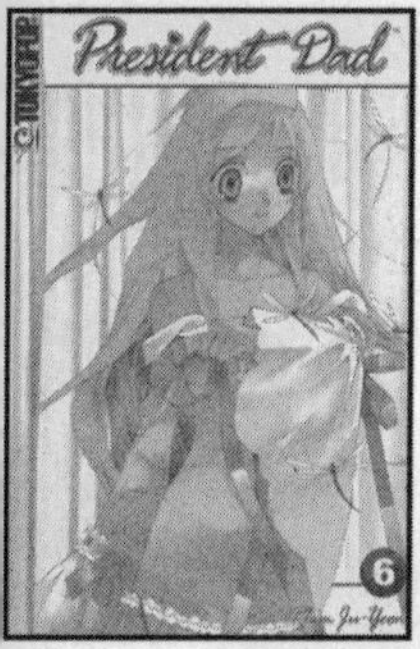
President Dad
6

COMEDY
TEEN AGE 13+

PRESIDENT DAD

BY JU-YEON RHIM

In spite of the kind of dorky title, this book is tremendously fun and stylish. The mix of romance and truly bizarre comedy won me over in a heartbeat. When young Ami's father becomes the new president of South Korea, suddenly she is forced into a limelight that she never looked for and isn't particularly excited about. She's got your typical teenage crushes on pop idols (and a mysterious boy from her past who may be a North Korean spy! Who'd have thought there'd be global politics thrown into a shojo series?!), and more than her fair share of crazy relatives, but now she's also got a super-tough bodyguard who can disguise himself as anyone you can possibly imagine, and the eyes of the nation are upon her! This underrated manhwa totally deserves a second look!

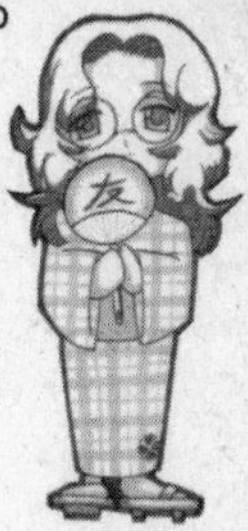

~Lillian Diaz-Pryzbyl, Editor

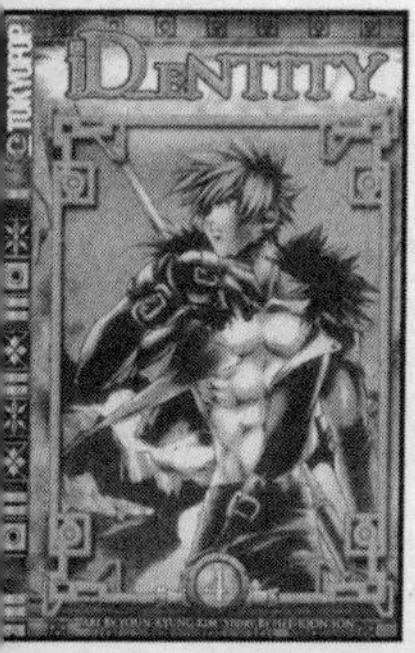
iDeNTITY

ACTION
TEEN AGE 13+

ID_ENTITY

BY HEE-JOON SON AND YOUN-KYUNG KIM

As a fan of online gaming, I've really been enjoying *iD_eNTITY.* Packed with action, intrigue and loads of laughs, *iD_eNTITY* is a raucous romp through a virtual world that's obviously written and illustrated by fellow gamers. Hee-Joon Son and Youn-Kyung Kim utilize gaming's terms and conventions while keeping the story simple and entertaining enough for noobs (a glossary of gaming terms is included in the back). Anyone else out there who has already absorbed *.hack* and is looking for a new gaming adventure to go on would do well to start here.

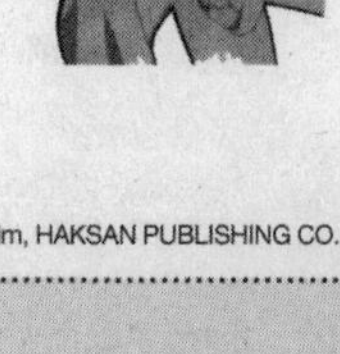

~Tim Beedle, Editor

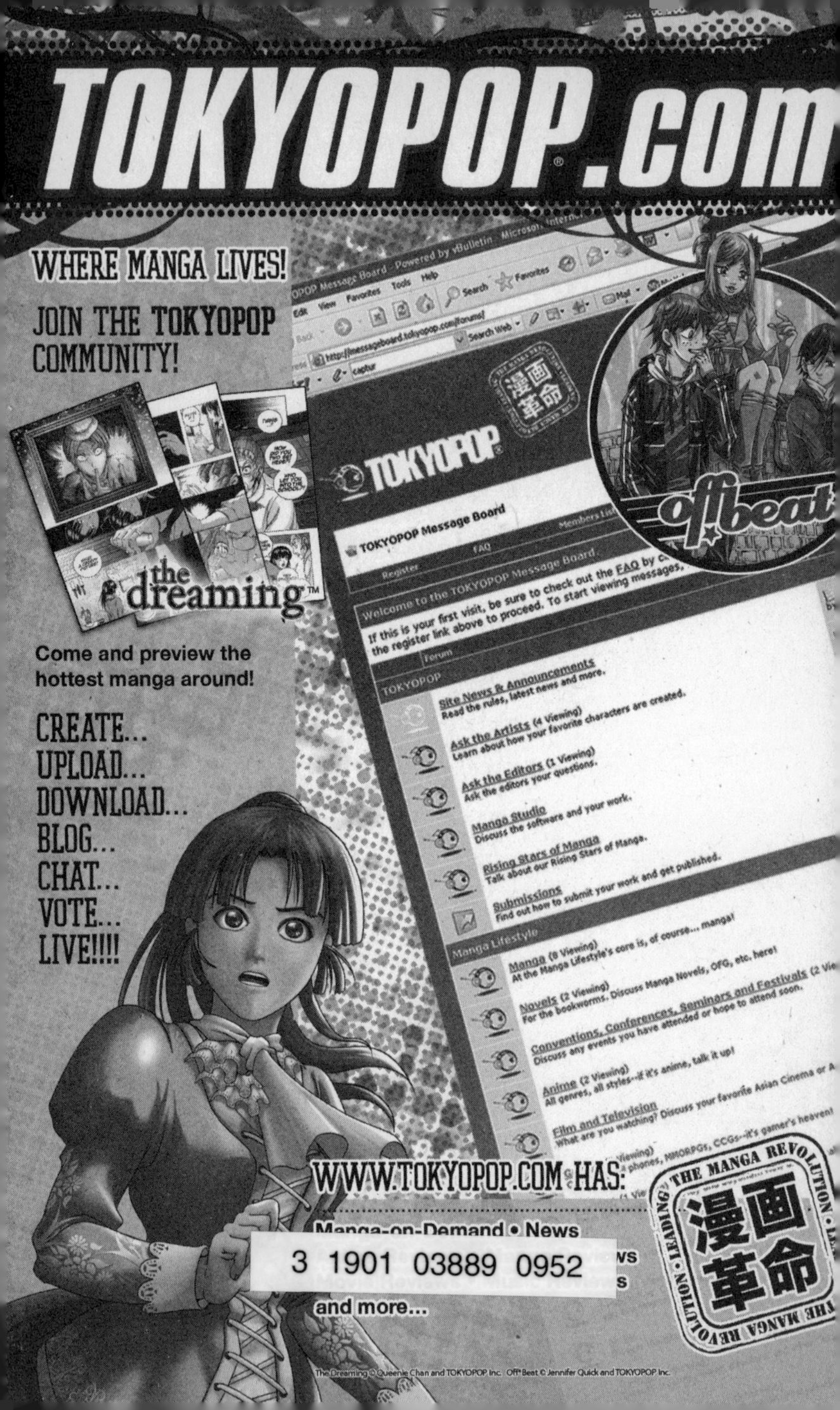
TOKYOPOP.com
WHERE MANGA LIVES!
JOIN THE TOKYOPOP COMMUNITY!
the dreaming™
Come and preview the hottest manga around!
CREATE...
UPLOAD...
DOWNLOAD...
BLOG...
CHAT...
VOTE...
LIVE!!!!
TOKYOPOP
TOKYOPOP Message Board
Welcome to the TOKYOPOP Message Board.
Site News & Announcements
Read the rules, latest news and more.
Ask the Artists (4 Viewing)
Learn about how your favorite characters are created.
Ask the Editors (1 Viewing)
Ask the editors your questions.
Manga Studio
Discuss the software and your work.
Rising Stars of Manga
Talk about our Rising Stars of Manga.
Submissions
Find out how to submit your work and get published.
Manga Lifestyle
Manga (8 Viewing)
At the Manga Lifestyle's core is, of course... manga!
Novels (2 Viewing)
For the bookworms. Discuss Manga Novels, OFG, etc. here!
Conventions, Conferences, Seminars and Festivals
Discuss any events you have attended or hope to attend soon.
Anime (2 Viewing)
All genres, all styles--if it's anime, talk it up!
Film and Television
offbeat
WWW.TOKYOPOP.COM HAS:
Manga-on-Demand • News
and more...
THE MANGA REVOLUTION • LEADING THE MANGA REVOLUTION
漫画革命
The Dreaming © Queenie Chan and TOKYOPOP Inc. Off*Beat © Jennifer Quick and TOKYOPOP Inc.